The Internet Legal Guide

The Internet Legal Guide

*Everything You Need to Know
When Doing Business Online*

Dennis M. Powers, Esq.

JOHN WILEY & SONS, INC.

Published by John Wiley & Sons, Inc., New York.
Published simultaneously in Canada.

This publication is designed to provide accurate and authoritative information in regard to the subject matter covered. It is sold with the understanding that the publisher is not engaged in rendering professional services. If professional advice or other expert assistance is required, the services of a competent professional person should be sought.

Designations used by companies to distinguish their products are often claimed by trademarks. In all instances where the author or publisher is aware of a claim, the product names appear in Initial Capital letters. Readers however, should contact the appropriate companies for more complete information regarding trademarks and registration.

Library of Congress Cataloging-in-Publication Data:

Powers, Dennis M.
   The Internet legal guide : everything you need to know when doing business online / Dennis M. Powers.
     p. cm.
   Includes bibliographical references and index.
   ISBN 0-471-16423-2 (pbk. : alk. paper)
   1. Internet—Law and legislation—United States. 2. Electronic commerce—Law and legislation—United States. I. Title.
KF390.5.C6 P69 2001
343.7309′944—dc21

                2001045394

To Scott, Denny, Kim, and Judy,
You're the best. . . . And to the Powers
and Debler clans, over all these years.

Preface

My interest in technology, especially the Internet, dates back more than 15 years. Using my first computer, I created sets of computerized legal software forms (the *Power of Attorney* series). Since then, I've been surprised—and at times awed—by how "the Net" has grown, its many applications, and its dramatic effects on our daily lives.

As the Net and broadening technology swept into our world, I waited for a time when cyberlaw, or the law of the Net, would become sufficiently certain to allow my writing down the major "rules of the Internet road." It was natural for me to explore these rules. I had created my own business Web site, consulted with cyberclients, and researched and wrote about this new phenomenon. As I waited and researched, I wrote legally oriented books (and practiced law for over 20 years). The books that I authored were designed to help nonlawyers understand and deal cost-effectively with the law and lawyers. In their order of appearance, they were: *Legal Street Smarts* (1994—on individuals and the law); *Beating the Tough Times* (1995—on finance and the law); *Legal Expense Defense* (1995—on businesses and the law); *The Office Romance* (1998—on sexual harassment versus romance in the office).

Meanwhile, the total number of Net surfers worldwide grew from next to nothing seven years ago to 400 million in 2001; users in the United States then comprised 150 million, or over one-third of this total. By the year 2003, the number of global users is expected to be well in excess of 500 million (with 200 million in the United States), and by 2005, that number will climb to 1 billion worldwide.

Countries around the globe have been readying their populations for the Internet and its demands. Aside from the United States, the countries with substantial Internet populations in 2001 were: Japan (40 million), China (40 million), Germany (25 million), England (20 million), Korea (20 million), and France (15 million). Although all countries are experiencing unprecedented growth, the greatest growth in Net users will be in these countries, especially in China. And all nations of the world share the legal concerns experienced by U.S. users—whether they are dealing in cyberspace with U.S. residents, people in other countries, or their own citizens.

As I explored cyberspace and the law, I recognized that the fundamental laws and concepts used in years past were being applied to this new technology, just as they had been during the then-startling introductions of the telephone, telegraph, Xerox, TV, and cassette recorder. The underlying legal concepts of the United States and other countries again proved to be a strong foundation in establishing what is basically okay or what is illegal—this time, in cyberspace.

When I researched the book lists to see what was available in this area, I didn't find what I would have bought for myself: a book with commonsense, easy-to-read information on what's legal and practical when using the Net. I wanted one that was "hands on" and would help consumers, small businesses, entrepreneurs, managers, and even those in the nonprofit sector (including government and education), who, like me, thought they were somewhat "technologically challenged" (but maybe weren't) but wanted to enjoy all of the Web's benefits. Thus, *The Internet Legal Guide* was born.

From past legal books I had written, I knew that this book would:

- Be written with "easy words" and understandable concepts—no confusing use of "legalese" or treatment earmarked for attorneys.
- Cover business and personal concepts that an average user would find interesting or would need to know.
- Explain computer terms simply in the text to make it easier, even for the uninitiated, to understand cyberlaw concepts.
- Contain easy-to-use forms that complement the text and discuss how they are useful for the reader.
- Treat areas from an international perspective, so as to highlight the Net's worldwide impact and illustrate how the U.S. and other countries' laws differ or approximate one another.

This book is designed so that the most important person—you, the reader—will know:

- Ways to avoid the common (and not so common) Net legal pitfalls, so that you can keep your cyberlaw costs down—or change them to your advantage.
- Factors to help you avoid becoming a victim of cyberscams, lemon purchases, and bad deals.
- The law of the Internet and what it means for your business and personal planning.
- Cybersense with tips for creating and operating your own Web site.
- Less costly ways to solve your Internet disputes.

Whether you're operating your own Web site now—or never intend to—the areas covered will make you more informed. You'll see how the Internet has created a global conflict of laws, and how the world's courts and governments are dealing with this conflict, along with encouraging the rise of "Netiquette." Owners and surfers alike will learn just when and how they can legally (and practically) copy or "borrow" interesting images or audios. Did you know that a potent U.S. law allows copyright owners (including yourself) to force an Internet Service Provider (ISP) to "pull the plug" on an offending site that has ripped off one of your copyrighted works? Or that attorneys can easily pierce a "Net name" to locate someone's actual home or office address and telephone numbers, even through the "anonymity" of cyberspace? Whether you're purchasing for business or personal reasons, selling products or services, or creating a subscription site, you will discover the rules of e-commerce (and the right "wording" to give you that needed edge). I reviewed the important areas so that you would know, for example, how to:

- Minimize the problems of returns and sub-par purchases.
- Avoid flying to faraway states or countries to defend yourself in an expensive lawsuit.
- Use lower-cost ways and more hassle-free alternatives—such as cybermediation, arbitration, and other cyber-techniques—that are appropriate to solve disputes outside the courtroom.
- Protect your domain name and/or trademark, secure someone else's who doesn't know the law, and force a cyberpirate to give up his or her domain name.
- Know what Terms of Use provisions are important and what information, including privacy policies, you should have on a site.
- Craft a Web Site Development Agreement, so you don't lose the rights to those well-paid-for images on your site and aren't surprised by later problems.

Beginning with when you need permission to link to the tips you must know when you're operating your own Web site, *The Internet Legal Guide* is designed for both new Internet afficionados and those who are more experienced. There are tips on how to design and create your own site—and fulfill important legal requirements. If your site is already in operation, read the sections that deal with how to protect your site's trademarks, service marks, domain names, copyrights, linking, and security, as well as how to insulate yourself from lawyers and lawsuits—whether your Web site is a commercial business/service, a hobby, or a non-profit venture.

The book concludes with a look at some of the areas where legal "shape-shifting" will continue, given that the Internet has brought such immense changes to our lives, and more are already on their way. The book ends with this statement: "The legal system has met the challenge, but the world will never again be the same." This is so true—and you'll be so much the wiser for knowing the rules of cyberspace.

Thank you. It's my true pleasure to be of service.

DENNIS POWERS

Be aware that later Internet court decisions and new statutes may change what is legal or not, and that laws differ from state to state (and country to country). Therefore, any particular recommendation made here may not be wholly appropriate for any set of specific facts, given all of the circumstances. Thus, this book isn't intended to give legal or other advice for specific problems, and you are advised in that instance to consult an attorney, accountant, or specialist in the particular Internet problem area that you're facing. When you have a cyber-question, the law is uncertain, or you're facing a complex problem, be sure to confer with an attorney who specializes in that area.

Acknowledgments

I wish to thank my editor, Matt Holt, at John Wiley & Sons, Inc. for his support of this project from the start—it has made a difference, so thanks, Matt. I would like to thank Tamara Hummel at Wiley for her fine support, as well.

I thank my friends at the School of Business and other disciplines at Southern Oregon University, who were understanding when I was preoccupied with writing this book, and who gave needed advice during this process: John Laughlin, Jan and Val Swanson, Curt Bacon, Terry Gaston, Judee and Neil Kunze, Chuck Jaeger, Rene Ordonez, Dan Rubenson, and so many others—you know who you are. James Munn provided valuable factual verification and assistance.

As usual, my literary agent, Jeanne Fredericks, and her husband, Wes, were invaluable with their help—Jeanne, with her unstinting persistence and suggestions to get this book published, and Wes, an ever accomplished lawyer and partner at a major New York City law firm, with his thoughts and advice.

I want to thank my wife, Judy, for her patience, love, and support—I love you.

D.M.P.

Contents

CHAPTER
1

The World's at Your Fingertips

The Internet and ongoing digital revolution have completely changed life as we know it in so many extraordinary ways. From the ease of instant business communications and personal "chatting" with people around the globe to the purchase of office supplies, cars, books, or computers—all without leaving our business or home, wherever that's located.

In scant years, the Web has become a giant information-based "Yellow Pages" directory without geographical limits or control. Surfers can visit Web sites hosted from Japan to Canada, then leap back into the United States, all in a matter of seconds. Sites advise digital audiences on their strategic business, medical, and even genealogical needs while selling their services, and other locations captivate people with on-line forums, live auctions, and educational seminars. With the click of a mouse, users download music, watch videos, or even listen to radio Web sites playing audiotapes from stations heard around the world.

We can track down hard-to-find people through Internet Web sites, whether they're customer deadbeats or long-lost friends. "Virtual" banks lend monies to borrowers at interest rates lower than those quoted by local banks, and airlines sell discounted E-tickets in cyberspace. People gamble on the Internet at cybercasinos without leaving their living room, and the only requirement is owning a credit card. Anyone can buy a gift certificate, redeemable at someone's favorite restaurant even when it's located thousands of miles away from the purchaser. From stamp collecting and comic books to bonsai trees and ragdoll cats, hobby enthusiasts, sellers, and small businesses can now all connect virtually.

From publishing to retailing, every industry today is grappling with an Internet that puts its manufacturers, providers, and competitors directly in contact with the same customers, no matter where anyone travels or does business. Thanks to the broad array of suppliers that can be tied up in one virtual place, Web sites from Walmart.com to the smallest of companies can exhibit a breadth of inventory that was never before imaginable. Business and personal shopping is one mouse-click away—and at decent savings for those who take the time to surf around, comparison shop, and then buy.

Despite the consolidations that have taken place in the dot.com world (primarily in the direct-to-consumer area), the simple truth is that this new medium connects more people to information faster and cheaper than anything experienced before. Business-to-business usage ("B2B" in Net lingo) is booming, not just in selling goods and services, but in its ability to link distribution channels and customers—regardless of a company's size. For example, trucking companies rely on the Web and its global satellite tracking abilities to keep their customers informed precisely as to shipments' locations and can make destination changes almost instantaneously. Businesses have discovered that large Internet savings can be found in the smallest of places by researching suppliers and handling routine paper transactions digitally. Although the Internet world no longer views business-to-consumer ("B2C") Web sites as completely replacing the way consumers buy goods and services (although a few B2C sites may have this potential down the road), they already are seen as highly complementary sales channels for retailers with physical store locations (the "click and mortar" retailers).

People buy and sell anything these days on Web sites located all over the globe. The transactions range from stocks and bonds to raw materials and machinery, and companies move daily to fill vacuums present since time began, but now through a Web presence. Businesses can bid on patents and even on cargo damaged in maritime accidents, no matter where the event occurred; farmers now bid directly with their suppliers of insecticides, seeds, and livestock antibiotics. Car manufacturers such as General Motors, Ford, and Nissan, representing one-half of the total worldwide automobile production, have formed Covisint—a virtual joint venture in product design, supply chain management, and parts purchases, with links to the two dozen largest suppliers of spark plugs, tires, and car accessories. Using the same principles, small companies, entrepreneurs, school systems, and government entities have created buying groups to purchase what they need at volume discount rates.

Entire industries are in transition, and let's look at sports as just one example. Web sites abound from NCAA soccer and professional canasta to skeet shooting and sumo wrestling. Media networks, sports associations, universities, and even Little Leagues picked up on the advantages of the Internet for capturing markets and fans in very competitive industries. Fans are able to locate up-to-date statistics on their favorite players or participants. Baseball buffs can locate statistics on any active

Major League ballplayer, including the most recent game, any season he was active, and complete career statistics. Inning by inning, play-by-play baseball Web broadcasts are a mouse-click away, and when that interest wanes, the fan can whisk away to England for the latest rugby matches. Information on sports Web sites—whether it's NFL football, NBA basketball, or ML baseball results—is available faster than radio and TV stations can announce them. And with much more detail.

From sports to travel agents, the Internet creates fundamental competitive pressures and thrusts. Travelers, for example, can completely bypass travel agents and gain from the Web all the information they want or need about places, costs, and schedules. Whether it's how to travel cheaper, or where the bearded men in checked shirts live, the Net has opened the world to people who want all of the facts. Information is available from the prime locations for big-game hunting and helicopter skiing to the best vegetarian restaurants, no matter what country, season, or locality. Service providers and the hospitality industry have swarmed onto the Internet to compete directly for their customers.

The Net similarly has transformed the airline industry. Web sites allow easy availability of trip planning, flight scheduling, and ticket purchasing direct from the airlines. Many of us, being savvy consumers, shop around at online airline "bucket shops" for the best air fare and the poor middleman travel agent is being squeezed out. Priceline.com with its "name your price" service now ranks among the U.S.'s 10 largest travel agencies, and airlines like Continental sell more than 10 percent of their airline tickets online, helping to cut the costs of travel-agent commissions. United, Delta, Northwest, and Continental Airlines have created a joint airline, hotel, car rental, and tourist-service Web site, betting that they can get a piece of the Internet travel pie by cutting into the online discounters' market share. In effect, they are competing against the initial sources that the Net created in the first place. All of these developments have resulted in lawsuits, as one party or another has attempted to "even out" the new competition through their attorneys and the courts.

Small businesses and professionals recognize the cost-efficient Net as a way to get their "word" out. A competing real estate broker, insurance agent, or title company is just as likely to be located across the street from a similar business, and each has its own Web "informational" site up and running. Legal sites abound, as well. People can access laws and information ranging from dog law to child custody and wills, along with public relation facts on the strengths of the particular lawyer or law firm. From greeting card companies and antique shops to interior designers and swimsuit manufacturers, having a Net presence today is a competitive reality.

All industries recognize the benefits—and experience the Internet's competitive pressures. As we shall see throughout this book, conflict comes along with these opportunities. Lawsuits, lawyers, and threatening letters routinely crop up from an entity's Internet operations, and all users need to know what is or isn't legal before they conduct business on the Net. From domain name disputes and copyright conflicts to buying "lemons" and dealing with dissatisfied customers, businesspeople have discovered that proper management—whether of a small business or global operation—involves understanding the Internet's important legal "rules of the road."

Educators, Egovernment, and "Hampsterdancers"

The nonprofit sectors gyrate in change, as their business counterparts do, and the education "industry" is in a transformation never seen before. Virtual online campuses now are a reality. Students are able to earn an undergraduate degree, or even a master's or a doctorate, without spending any time in a university classroom. Academic Web sites compete for students and sell college services. The subject may range from business administration and the law to poetry and botany; nearly all of America's 2,300 colleges and universities have education courses available off-site through the Internet. This is an international development as countries from Japan to Thailand and Germany to Brazil have educational courses and information posted online.

Students on campuses download lectures and take exams that are graded on the Net. They access Web locations that have links to sites geared entirely to their needs, whether it's the Encyclopedia Britannica or "homework help" sites. College students can analyze past exams posted on the Internet, or even download papers for a fee on nearly any subject (a controversial practice).

University administrators use the Web to post online course catalogs, admission information, application forms, instant news releases, public relations and marketing releases, payments of tuition and fees, scholarship and loan information, and other newly discovered functions. However, as the educational Net develops further, the legal conflicts over copyright infringement, trademark violations, defamation, and privacy claims have also escalated.

Governments didn't hesitate either to enter the world of virtual reality. Local, state, and federal governments, recognizing the advantages of egovernment, created sites that offer low-cost ways of collecting parking tickets, utility payments, and taxes, as well as allowing constituents to "chat" with their representatives. The cost savings by posting virtual minutes, notices of community and agency meetings, and regulations—from dog ordinances to building codes—versus the cost of mailing paper was too much to ignore. Government purchases are funneled through Web sites into direct bidding with suppliers at savings to the taxpayers; various entities have launched their own procurement sites. Local, state, and federal governments can now showcase "how they're on the job" and spotlight projects that they desperately want to sell to their voters, whether it's expanding airport facilities or building light-rail commuter-transport systems.

Politicians of every party affiliation own and operate Web sites, searching for both contributors and volunteers. The money raised often reaches seven figures (or more), and all politicians have tapped a new market of volunteers that wasn't possible before. Some states and localities use the much cheaper Web for online election balloting, which eventually may replace traditional paper balloting.

The Web is an international development, as one would expect. Australian local and state governments have launched their own procurement sites, joining the United States and other governments around the world. The government of Singapore has been operating eCitizen (ecitizen.gov.sg) for two years; its citizens can download application forms for utilities and parking permits, among other uses. England launched its UKOnline (UKonline.com) to offer advice and change-of-address services, and more services are on the way. [See also contractscanada.gc.ca

(Canada) and mineti.gouv.fr (France).] To reach overseas, simply use your search engine, type in a country designation, and surf the sites that you find.

The Web has a silly side as well; "Elf Bowling," dancing amoebas, prancing babies, and celebrating fish are a few of the laughers. In an instant, people and their Web sites can become spur-of-the-moment cult celebrities. The homepage of Turkish lover and journalist Mahir Cagris received international attention just days after he posted his famous "I Kiss You" page. (Enter his name in any search engine and check out the Web sites.)

Within four days, www.hampsterdance.com (now, www.hampsterdance2.com)—featuring 392 animated hamsters dancing in a repetitive fashion (and, yes, the misspelling of "hamster" is intentional)—received 60,000 hits. It had received only 800 visitors over the previous seven months; now, armed with advertising from international companies, it sells hamster-themed bumper stickers, pens, key rings, and other products. The overall hits to this site are numbered in the tens of millions, and some estimates place the hits, at their height, at 250,000 a day. As we shall see later, fame has its price, and the cute virtual hamsters eventually needed to hire legal counsel.

Even the homeless are taking advantage of the Net phenomenon. Free e-mail, online job searches, Web anonymity, and accessibility at libraries and homeless shelters have proven advantageous. For example, the Los Angeles Union Rescue Mission, a five-story, 225,000-square-foot facility, is one of the largest homeless shelters in the world. It operates medical, dental, and legal clinics, plus a computer center with 35 personal computers, requiring each homeless person to spend two hours a day in its computer learning center as a requirement for admission to its year-long rehabilitation program.

The examples would fill a book by themselves. What is striking is that these uses are just the start—along with the business disputes that become legal problems and conflicts. As we shall see, the legal concepts involved in all of these areas are basically the same—whether you are in business, government, or education—and are equally important.

Global Web Growth

The growth in Internet access and usage has continued to increase in unprecedented numbers. From next to nothing five years before, by the end of 1998, there were 200 million Internet users worldwide, and roughly one-half were in the United States. By the start of 2001, over 150 million Americans had access to the Internet at home. Over one-half of all U.S. teenagers are using a computer now, and experts believe that this percentage will increase to three-fourths within the next three years.

This Web explosion is also an international phenomenon—and all businesses and organizations must keep this in mind. The total number of worldwide users in 2001 was 400 million, of which the United States comprised only 150 million, or about one-third. Aside from the United States, the countries with larger Internet populations at that time were Japan (40 million), China (40 million), Germany (25 million), England (20 million), Korea (20 million), and France (15 million). The language spoken is a key determinant of the sites that a user tracks: Spanish is spoken in a number of countries (i.e., Mexico, Spain, Central and South American countries, as well as the United States), and the aggregate of Spanish-speaking Internet users (not including those in the United States) was 20 million. It is expected that the numbers of Spanish-speaking users will increase dramatically over the years.

Although over 80 percent of European-based corporate sites are multilingual, most of those in the United States at this time are not. There's no question that U.S. Web sites, over time, will become more multilingual for competitive reasons alone.

The greatest growth is expected to be in non-English-speaking countries. For example, the growth of Chinese, Japanese, German, and Spanish language users has been in excess of 25 percent per year, and this increase will continue. Given China's population base, it is no surprise that this country is expected by experts to show the greatest increase in Internet users over the next several years. Although generally looking toward the United States as a leader in Internet technology and cyberlaw, developed and underdeveloped countries alike have the same general legal and business concerns on a global basis—whether dealing with U.S. citizens, those of other countries, or their own.

By the year 2003, the number of worldwide users is expected to be well in excess of 500 million (over 175 million in the U.S.). Various studies estimate that these worldwide users will reach over 1 billion by 2005. This is indeed a growth of global proportions. (An excellent Web site to keep up with the growth of Net users by country, language, and region from year to year is Global Reach at www.glreach.com. This site updates its statistics on a continuing basis with links to support its conclusions.)

How the Net Works

To understand business and law on the Internet, we need to understand the system itself. The Internet consists of computer networks that are connected to each other by cables, telephone lines, and satellite links. The Department of Defense (DOD) originally created it for the U.S. military in the 1960s. It was then a DOD-sponsored interconnection among defense contractors, universities with defense research contracts, and the military. The system was designed so that these military interests could communicate, even if a nuclear war destroyed various sections of their computer connections.

The Defense Department's requirements gradually were relaxed as other federal government agencies, large corporations, and graduate students recognized the benefits of these computer interconnections. Among researchers, "the Net" quickly became popular for sharing information, avoiding the performance of identical studies, communicating new discoveries more quickly, and absorbing and utilizing, within moments of transmission and receipt, the new knowledge being generated throughout the world. Gradually, the Internet's uses became known to the general public.

The Web combines high-speed transmission for sending and receiving massive files in a way that requires a user to do little more than point and click with a computer mouse. Thus, the Internet is a global network that exchanges digitized data in such a way that any computer connected to a fiber-optics cable or equipped with a modem (or a connecting device that allows a computer to send and receive data through telephone wires) can participate as part of that network.

Users need to only turn on their computer, click on the Internet icon, connect with their modem and dial up the telephone line to their Internet Service Provider (ISP)—or connect through their ISP's or company's local network—and start pointing and clicking with their mouse (the device that allows users to connect with the Web site that they want). The connection may also be made with a handheld, wireless device.

Each Web site has a unique address known as the uniform resource locator (URL), which is its address for locating purposes (the http://www.DOMAINNAME .COM address that all of us are familiar with). When a user types in a name (depending on that name), the computer can automatically add the "www" and ".com" (or other locator, such as ".edu" or ".net") at the beginning and the end. Thus, navigating (or "surfing") the Web is straightforward enough. A user can either type in a known address (the URL or domain name) or enter key words into a commercial "search engine." The Internet, computer, and mouse do the rest.

The stock-in-trade of the Internet is global information—and lots of it. The Internet is a vast library containing millions of readily available, indexed publications, along with a sprawling mall of Web sites offering goods and services. It is a vast platform where buyers, sellers, e-mailers, and surfers can link up with information on everything. A computer user in the United States can connect to a Web site owned by a French company that has hired a Web site operator in Singapore, Malaysia. A German citizen can access a New Zealand Web site that's operated in the United States. And it's not uncommon to come across Web sites that offer two, three, or even four or more language options for a particular user.

Small businesses and entrepreneurs have discovered the ability to reach virtually beyond their geographical limits. From bridal shops and tuxedo rentals to retailers of World War II memorabilia, small businesspeople are developing new customer bases using the Web. An operator of a bed-and-breakfast now draws in customers from countries as far away as Mexico, Canada, and England. A businessman in Beatrice, Nebraska, who recharges cartridges for laser printers, now receives empty cartridges from as far away as Korea. People around the world are comparing the prices of antique furniture, tuxedos, and bonsai trees; at the same time, they're selling or purchasing computers, railroad shipments, and office supplies.

The Web is an international phenomenon, and its growth has required reasonable laws and regulations to guide its use within this global context. We shall see throughout this book that this is now taking place.

Surfing Planet Earth and the Clash of Laws

Before the Internet revolution, the globalization of information and commerce was just a concept. This is now a reality with extraordinary growth and continuing potential. However, the global strength of the Net's ability to zip information across continents by the flick of a finger can be its very weakness.

Prior to the coming of cyberspace, the place of origin and place of destination were usually the same: information and products were shared within the same country and regions. When a dispute occurred, the states and localities easily dealt with the problem of whose laws controlled. Unless a shipment of goods was exported from one country to another, the laws of only one country applied. The Net has changed all of this. Every country in the world now has access to the places of origin of products, services, or data, no matter where the order is made or where the product is destined to be shipped.

If someone from Santa Barbara, California, drives to Los Angeles to shop or sell for a business, State of California and possibly U.S. federal law would apply. However, if that person clicks onto the Internet to do that same transaction, then the laws of every state and country involving that product could possibly apply.

For example, if you manufactured candies in your hometown, you might have placed an advertisement in the local newspaper to sell your products. You might have even placed ads up and down your state or locality. If anything went wrong and a customer had a dispute, you knew which laws applied—those of your state, along with a possible conflict if two states or localities were involved.

However, you decide it's cheaper to create a Web site and market this wonderful candy to the entire world. Now, someone in Kyoto, Japan, or Chicago, Illinois, can see your product and buy it. That's good, because sales increase. But what happens if the buyer doesn't like the candy and wants to get his money back? Even worse, what happens if the buyer eats bad candy and suffers a severe case of food poisoning? What happens legally and whose laws apply?

If you manufacture your candy, let's say, in Guanajuato, Mexico, and a customer in Montreal, Canada, buys it and becomes ill (and your Web site is being hosted by a computer operator in San Diego, California), then whose laws apply? We could easily change the facts to where the product is manufactured in the United States with a Canadian ISP operator and a Mexican purchaser—the same questions still apply.

There is a clash of laws not only between the states and territories (if only one country is involved), but also between countries, given the ease with which the Internet shreds geographical and territorial boundaries. When a dispute or problem occurs on the Net, no one can assume that his or her country's laws will govern. There can even be legal fights over which country's laws are to control the *selection of* the laws that are to be applied to this case.

The Differences in the Laws of Nations

The laws among the various countries are quite different. Although these laws can be conceptually the same (i.e., providing remedies if someone is injured or defrauded), the specifics differ from country to country because each nation has its own unique history and legal development.

There are two basic legal systems in the world. One is the *common law*—the legal system of the United States, England, Canada, Israel, Malaysia, New Zealand, and others—which consists of the laws and rules set by court decisions and case precedent. The laws of common-law countries consist of statutes, constitutional provisions and case interpretations, and the case precedents from court decisions. Generally, the common-law countries are those that were once colonies of Great Britain and that retained the English system of law and case precedent.

A second distinct body of law is found in the *civil law*—the legal system of countries such as Argentina, China, Egypt, Germany, Italy, Japan, France, Mexico, and others. This legal system dates back to Roman civil code law. In a civil-law system, the primary sources of the law are the statutory codes. The court or case precedents are not as binding as they are under common-law countries. This system is followed in most continental European countries and Latin American, African, and Asian countries that were once colonies of those European nations.

Another separate body of law is found in countries with strong religious ties. For example, the Islamic courts in Muslim countries apply the provisions of the Koran and its teachings to their resolution of disputes. Although the Islamic system also has a civil-law side, its thrust is in the application of its religious teachings and tenets.

The upshot is that widely varying results will occur simply because of these differences in a particular country's legal system. If the laws and legal understandings vary greatly from country to country, what is prohibited in one nation may be entirely permissible in another.

As an example, a court in Japan or Germany might decide that a copyright infringement has taken place, whereas a court in the United States (which has a "fair use" doctrine) would come to a completely different conclusion. (See Chapter 4, "Copying in Cyberspace.") The laws in Europe on basic rights of privacy are quite different from those in the United States, and the respective courts will reach differing verdicts on what are basically the same facts. (We will look into this further in Chapter 6, "'Junk Dog' Statements and Privacy Concerns.") Whereas a Japanese court might not find product liability for a particular manufacturer, based on its conclusion that the user was at fault, a U.S. court would balance the respective faults of the two parties and allocate a proportionate share of the damages to the manufacturer.

International law is the global attempt of countries to address these legal differences and uniformly govern the legal relations among the various nations. National laws, customs, treaties, and international conferences are sources of international law. The realm of international law does apply at times to cyberspace, and where appropriate this is noted throughout this book. However, as a general rule international law does not govern Internet use and the changes that are taking place. Over time, and as treaties are agreed to, international law will have a greater role in this process.

Unlike an individual country's domestic laws with its citizens, international law generally is not enforceable between two countries unless they have agreed to it by treaty or some other understanding as to enforceability. Consequently, international courts do not have compulsory jurisdiction. They generally have only the ability to adjudicate a dispute that both parties agree to having a judgment being so made. Today, global business and information exchanges are clashing with local and national laws in this borderless new world of the Internet.

The basic *rule of origin* concept provides that the seller's local law applies to any transaction, regardless of where the consumer resides. This approach is being discarded in the multi-national e-commerce world, for example, when a purchaser receives a "lemon." There could possibly even be *no* recovery for such a "bad" deal, depending on the laws of a particular country (with no international supreme court to rule that those laws are unconstitutional). A series of approaches that view the parties' intent, what they agreed to in their contract, the extent of the contacts with the seller's Web site, and other considerations, has been put in place. However, different countries still come to different results, depending on their applicable laws and respective legal systems.

Does this mean that all is lost? Not by a long shot. The bodies of laws that have been nurtured over the years, in various countries, provide a foundation for the settling of disputes. (See Chapter 11, "But Can Your Court Hear the Case? What Law Is Applied?") However, keep in mind this international/global context and clashing of laws when you are viewing any potential large e-commerce or international transaction and looking for trouble spots.

Cyberlaw

The term *cyberlaw* is used to describe the emerging body of law that governs cyberspace transactions and disputes. It is evolving through the actions of the various new statutes that are being enacted, the case decisions, and the basic application of tradition legal concepts to the online activities of cyberspace.

As we shall see, the good news is that the United States through its case law and statutes has been laying a solid foundation for cyberlaw—ranging from establishing solid jurisdictional criteria for the conflict-of-laws question to enactment of the Digital Millennium Copyright Act (DMCA). The bad news is that the rest of the world has been lagging behind (although the European Union and other countries are working to fill this gap). Over time, this country-to-country disparity will be gradually eliminated to a substantial extent.

Some attorneys worry that there isn't enough Internet "law" to guide their clients in this "bizarre" new world. However, a historical perspective gives more assurances on this subject. President Harry S Truman once said, "The only history we don't know is what we haven't read." Basically, the same worries and fretting accompanied the advanced technologies at the time of the telephone and telegraph, and showed up again in the "new-age" media of radio and TV. The legal concepts used prior to each new technology gave a solid foundation that answered the new legal questions; over time, enacting statutes and case decisions finished off the uncertainty. This is what's happening with cyberlaw.

As we shall see in this book, although the development of specific laws on a country-to-country basis has not kept pace with the Internet's growth and changes, the vast structure of legal concepts and laws already in place (along with new Internet statutes and court cases already decided) is sufficient for many users to determine what they can or cannot safely do—and what will get them into expensive trouble or not. Further, the state and national legislatures have not been standing idly by. They have been busily legislating, at all levels, on issues ranging from Internet taxes, e-commerce laws, and restriction on certain Internet sales (i.e., gambling, alcohol, sexually oriented information, and so on) to encryption and security controls, online personal signatures, and false advertising—to name just a few. (See Chapter 17, "The Internet Faces More Legal Shape-Shifting Ahead," for more.)

Let's look at a few examples to understand some of the legal concepts that are in play.

A Few Examples

The fact that the Internet is involved does not transform the problem into legal uncertainty. It is clear that local laws prevail when there are sufficient connections, even if the Net is the involved medium (rather than radio, TV, or newspaper ads).

For example, one Staten Island, New York, entrepreneur sent virtually tons of unsolicited e-mail that advertised low-cost magazine subscriptions. Fifty unhappy customers from New York and around the world complained bitterly that they hadn't received their paid-for subscriptions, or they received fewer issues than were promised. The New York State Attorney General accused the Staten Island man and his companies of violating the state's consumer fraud and false-advertising laws. The accused countered that the New York State court could not possibly have jurisdiction over the geographically limitless domain of the Net. Although it helped that the man was a New York resident, the New York court held back in 1997 that it *could* apply its laws—including adjudicating the claims of those who lived outside New York and the United States. The court reasoned:

> There is no compelling reason to find that local legal officials must take a "hands off" approach just because a crook or a con artist is technologically sophisticated enough to sell on the Internet. Invocation of "the Internet" is not the equivalent of a cry of "sanctuary" upon a criminal's entry into a medieval church.

Nice ringing words. However, the problem is seen when the facts are slightly changed. Let's say the man set up his Web site in Indonesia, and only New York residents bought the products and felt that they had been defrauded. Or only non-Indonesian citizens were the ones defrauded. In that case, there would be little reason for Indonesia to become involved. If the person and the Web site are located outside the purchaser's country, then the enforcement mechanism under that set of circumstances could be virtually nonexistent (but depending on the country). The moral of the story: When you're looking at a "too good to be true" situation, be careful. It just might be. And deal only with reputable Web sites that have stated return policies and/or stores located in your area (i.e., some physical presence in your state or territory) over which authorities can find jurisdiction.

The fact that something is legal in your country doesn't mean that it will be legal elsewhere. For example, Amazon.com sold a copy of Adolph Hitler's treatise "Mein Kampf" to a researcher in Germany. The sale of Nazi literature is prohibited under German law, although it is quite legal under U.S. law. Serious legal threats were made by German government officials against Amazon personnel until an agreement was reached to put controls on those sales.

A few years later, a French judge under a similar law ordered Yahoo! to block French visitors from viewing any Nazi items on its American Web site. The judge gave Yahoo! three months to find a way to prevent French residents from accessing those pages. After the U.S. company changed its policies and banned the sale of any Nazi war pieces (followed in turn by eBay), Yahoo! in 2001 then brought a lawsuit in a California Federal District Court. Yahoo! challenged the French decision on the ground, among other arguments, that France had no jurisdiction to tell it what to do in its own country. (See also Chapter 11, "But Can Your Court Hear the Case? What Law Is Applied?")

Basically, the French officials in the Yahoo! case didn't care what the state law was in the locality where a Web site was operating. They felt that upholding their country's laws was more important than any argument that courts did not have the power to reach across borders and impose their law on Web sites in other nations. If illegal content under these laws was being shipped to their citizens, then retailers were liable under those laws, and the courts didn't care if it only took one mouse click to move among the sites of the world. The bottom line from these cases: Be aware that you might need to modify your Net operations for a particular locality, depending on how serious and committed the officials are in restraining what you are doing, no matter what your local laws permit. In such a case, you will be faced with a business decision: Fight those demands in court, rely on technology such as filters to be in compliance, or ignore sales from that country (including, with legal advice, ignoring the demands). These are not easy decisions, as you can see.

In another case, a United States court granted Playboy Enterprises an injunction against an English magazine entitled *Playmen,* prohibiting it from publishing or distributing that magazine in the U.S. Playboy later discovered that *Playmen* had created an Internet site housed in Italy through which the magazine could be viewed, including pictures and the ability to order products. However, the U.S. injunction did not include Italy. Although the injunction had not envisioned distribution through the Internet, the U.S. court subsequently held that the very existence of the site constituted a publication that could be prohibited in the United States. The court held that the injunction (which initially only applied to the United States) had been infringed by a site on a server thousands of miles away, because computers within the United States could access that site. Although the court held that the company could continue to operate its Internet site (the U.S. court really didn't have the right to order the Web site's discontinuance in Italy), the site had to stop accepting any subscriptions from customers residing in the United States.

Let's say that a Canadian company, Ace Supplies, uses a domain name (the Web site "word" address, like BestBuy.com) that doesn't infringe on any trademarks or trade names inside Canada. However, let's assume that this name is the same as or is confusingly similar to a trade name used in Mexico, or the United States, or some other country. If the Canadian company sold goods into or owned facilities in that other country, then these facts could confer "jurisdiction" (the ability of a foreign court to exercise judgment over a nonresident entity) over Ace. Given that the Mexican or U.S. court would be willing to exercise jurisdiction over that company, then there is a very real risk that Ace would be liable for its trademark being illegal under another country's laws—and if there was that physical presence by Ace in that country, then those assets could be seized to satisfy any damage award.

The question isn't just a clash between differing laws. It also involves whether a court has the ability to assume jurisdiction over an Internet Web site that's located outside its borders. *If the court has this jurisdiction, and if the case is important enough, the Web site owner must travel all the way to that foreign country and defend itself under those different laws. This is an expensive proposition, not to mention the jet lag, strange food, and living from a suitcase.*

Now, what if a person posts a statement on a U.S. Web site chatroom that's defamatory of a citizen of another country—let's say, Japan? Japanese law is clear that if the defamer is a resident of that country, then he or she can be sued there. But will Japanese law apply so that if the defamer is a nonresident (i.e., lives in the United States), that he can then be sued in Japan? Can an act done on a computer in the United States bind that defendant to the jurisdiction of another court? Maybe not. This doesn't mean that the plaintiff (the one who's suing) is out of luck. The Japanese citizen can travel to the United States and sue in U.S. Federal Court—and win. The question is: Can he or she get the defendant (the one being sued) into his or her home court? (This is treated further in Chapter 11.)

Internet law is being savagely forged in court decisions and delicately crafted in different statutes by various countries. Although a cyber-common law is being created worldwide, there is still room for legal guidance. When people need more guidance than there are laws, it's time to look at Internet common sense and basic civility—or, as it is called in the following chapter, "Netiquette."

CHAPTER

3

The Developing Law of "Netiquette"

"Netiquette" is the set of guidelines that advises users not to "dump" (post unwanted materials on someone else's Web site, even if it's a competitor's site); avoid "spamming" (sending unsolicited e-mails, especially commercial e-solicitations); and follow codes of acceptable conduct in communications, among many other detailed areas. Basically, Netiquette is about being polite and showing respect to others in all situations on the Net, whether business or personal. This "code of civility" is an important development because cyberspace has left its "early American frontier" stage. Numbers of Web sites, not to mention countless users, now enforce commonsense guidelines on online behavior and what is or is not acceptable conduct, both mannerswise and legally.

The development of Netiquette is not recent. As with other social and legal norms, it has been debated and developing since the Internet's earliest days. Who gets the credit for this development is debatable. Authors such as Virginia Shea, corporations such as Intel and its posted memos, and various Web sites all give wide support to this concept. Just type in the word Netiquette in any Web search engine and surf the sites that come up. There are quite a few of them, all of which give information or some different slant.

Netiquette

The concept itself has centered, so far, in the writing, sending, and posting of e-mail, whether the user is negotiating a deal, "chatting" with someone else, establishing e-mail guidelines, or enforcing rules at its own Web site. Internet etiquette covers many topics. To give you an idea of their focus and coverage, a sampling of them follows:

- Don't "flame" (send insulting or rude e-mails). Respect the privacy of others (don't resend a confidential message).
- Don't be emotional in your responses. Avoid being too "gushy" or disagreeable, and don't "shout" (send an e-mail in ALL CAPS).
- Don't dump unwanted material on others' sites or spam with too much e-mail.
- Don't send unsolicited e-mails. (It would be great if some businesses and entrepreneurs would discover this fact of life.)
- Don't send anonymous messages unless there's a good reason. (If you're turning someone in for breaking the rules, let the site handle it from there.)
- Don't send large files unless requested. Especially, don't send large files or post them in chat groups. Post a link instead.
- Do be careful about what you say—your messages last a lifetime.
- Do your best to stop the sending of false, misleading, or junk mail.
- Do respect that there are cultural differences and diversity considerations in your communications.
- Do respect the rights and privacy of others. Do not ask for first names, addresses, ages, or telephone numbers until appropriate business or chat relationships have developed.
- Do try to be accurate with your postings.
- Do receive an author's permission before posting material on any Web site.
- Do not infringe on the copyrights of others.

These "do's and don'ts" could continue for pages, as books and Web sites on this subject abound.

A Galactic Nation of City-States

One important Net fiction is that there is unlimited freedom and an egalitarian completeness or ownership in this galactic universe. Sorry, but that is a contradiction in terms. First, the Internet is a huge community that already is in the "hundreds of millions of users" category. It is simply not possible to have the absolute freedom to do what you want—in fact, this is what gives rise to the conflicts, hostilities, and lawsuits on the Internet. As the Net grows in size, there is a need and a solid requirement for rules of reasonable conduct so that everyone can enjoy this worldwide community. Hence, the development of Netiquette has occurred, and this is no different than the development of appropriate norms for any other civilization or society.

Second, although this Web nation can be envisioned as a huge galactic space, in reality it is a collection of numbers and numbers of tiny societal Web sites, of which many have their own rules and versions of Netiquette. As this galactic nation continues to expand past its already incredible size, these individual societies seem to turn inward with their own peculiar mores and enforcement rules. It is as if the Net community has grown to where there are different religions and interests, all of which have, and in turn enforce, their own uniform but unique rules of conduct.

Some rules will be uniform to all Web sites because of their commonsense civil applicability. For example, not monopolizing discussions to enforce one's viewpoint and not degrading others in any comments are rules that would be (or at least should be) universally enforced. Netiquette and its mores have tightened into more and more specifics: it is impolite to stop talking without explanation; postings should be concise; less is more (i.e., in what you say or post); check your spelling; don't capitalize too much; don't "pop up" the same message more than once; be conservative in what you send, but be liberal in how you react to what you receive; fire others in person, not by e-mail (you might "flame" a person into a lawsuit); don't use e-mail when the correspondence should be personal (i.e., a personnel issue); and more.

There is a broader Netiquette effect in cyberlaw, aside from these considerations. Keep in mind the following: breaching the law online is still a crime (e.g., a seller who fraudulently misrepresents a product or service); a "flame" dispute can easily escalate into a defamation lawsuit with proof that lasts forever; "ripping off" another's copyright is still actionable under the law, whether others do this or not; and not respecting people's privacy can lead to even more lawsuits (i.e., selling off sensitive customer profiles without restraint).

Aside from threatening legal letters and potential litigation, the question becomes: What is the punishment when these rules are broken? Although "manners are manners," it is true that people in real-time Net chats—when statements are posted as if speaking in a conversation—can really take exception to breeches. Simply ask around what has happened when someone has unwittingly broken a Netiquette understanding or a more formalized Web site Terms of Use.

For example, a person who uses foul language on a chat site is turned in by the group; when he or she tries to connect later, they might discover that their service to the Web site has been disconnected. Another person continually trashes somebody else at a site, until everyone else turns around and scolds the offender. Someone who posts a defamatory statement receives a threatening letter or is sued by the reader's lawyer—"What goes around, *does* come around." The "Wild Wild Web" is definitely being tamed by the mores of this large community and its tendency to impose necessary order over what was thought at first to be absolute freedom. This need for restraint also allows businesses with Web sites to control that site use through reasonable Terms of Use policies.

Technology has given the Internet community and Web sites a strong ability to enforce these policies and rules. Rule breakers may be gagged, banned, or terminated. If a user posts prohibited rude or indecent language, then he or she might first be "gagged." The user continues to type away and sees the typed text in the chat room; however, no one else does, as the software erases these specific digitized comments from what everyone else can see. Let's say that the gag order is lifted and the user's comments are allowed to be seen again. If this person violates the rules again, after appropriate warnings, the Web site or provider can temporarily ban that user from using the site at all, and may even terminate any ability to access it. Other software in use screens every posting that's made, then blocks letters typed on the screen when they spell an offensive word. Web sites employ paid or volunteer monitors who read chatroom conversations and act as monitors. Sites and providers alike have complaint mechanisms in force to address and correct problems regarding how others use their site. The enforcement mechanism behind Netiquette is now definitely in place. (See Chapter 16, "Web Site Operating Considerations" for more.)

> The Internet Golden Rule is being enforced these days: e-mail and treat the Net world as you would want in return to be treated or e-mailed.

The Internet Golden Rule and Web sites with their own posted (and sometimes unposted) rules are becoming forceful codes by themselves. However, these mores can change in sometimes confusing ways. For example, the use of the smiley face ("):", "☺", and other variations) is encouraged at some sites, both commercial and otherwise, but absolutely frowned on at others. However, the strength of the Internet is still that introductions aren't a matter of who has the best smile, or the cutest face, or the firmest handshake. These days, showing "your best face" of proper spelling, symbols, and Netiquette is taking its place.

Another rule that often comes into play is: "If someone messes with you, you mess back." In other words, violators soon learn that there is a connection between their ethical breach and ensuing negative consequences to themselves. There is a karmic twist to the way that unethical conduct seems to beget more unfavorable responses. For example, some companies that "spam" by sending out lots of unsolicited bulk e-mail messages, discover that Techies have attacked them back with "mail bombs" (sending in large quantities of e-mail that overwhelm the spammer's system and cause it to crash). This in turn exposes the Techies to lawsuits for the damages created by their intentional acts, and both parties can eventually lose in this game of consequences.

Entrepreneurs also can lose valuable public relations by giving in to a "spur of the moment" impulse to reach a broader market. For example, one religious organization's fund-raising director sent a mass e-mail about an event to hundreds of the community's leaders. A recipient saw an opportunity and replied to the entire list, plugging his small business. He could never have dreamed what happened next. Flame e-mails swept back and forth until the director sent out an apology to everyone for the first message. The small business owner didn't get any new business, and it can be assumed that he didn't make any new friends either.

And More Business Netiquette

Web sites need to anticipate where problems can occur. Companies should frequently check their e-mail sites, respond quickly to inquiries, and ensure that their system is functioning properly. Businesses should confirm that any links from their sites are up-to-date, working, and with no postings that are objectionable or inappropriate. They should check out the links to their pages, just to be sure that nothing objectionable is there now (i.e., a disgruntled user might have linked them to a pornographic site).

All material posted on Web sites should be reviewed on a periodic basis so that the information is always current. Placing a "date sign" on a page, indicating when it was last revised, helps readers know how recent the information is. Operators need to place conspicuous notices as to what they do or don't warrant, including highlighting what their important Terms of Use provide. These reasonable rules should be based on Netiquette, brought to visitors' attention, and enforced. (See Chapter 16, "Web Site Operating Considerations," for further details.)

Following these commonsense procedures will minimize the numbers of complaints, disputes, and litigated problems. Adhering to Netiquette not only minimizes these problems, but these procedures and policies have been and will continue to be utilized by the courts in reaching their decisions.

Netiquette and the Developing Cyberspace Common Law

The development of Netiquette has been part of the response to fill the once void of sparse cyberspace rules of law. It was only a matter of time before these customs, manners, and ethics became formalized, not only in the Terms of Use provisions posted by Web sites, but also by courts when deciding legal battles. Let's look at one of the times when a court so applied the concepts of Netiquette.

BeaverHome.com operates a home-furnishings Web site in Canada and sell products direct to customers. Nexx Online, Inc., a Toronto-based Internet service provider, hosted its Web site. In its written ISP contract with Nexx (nexx.ca), Beaver-Home agreed to conform to Netiquette, the "unwritten Internet code of manners." However, because the written contract didn't specifically forbid spamming (most ISP contracts now do), BeaverHome began sending out self-promotional e-mail through the ISP at the rate of up to 200,000 per day. After receiving complaints from the recipients, Nexx terminated BeaverHome's service and shut down its Web site. Beaver-Home sued to require Nexx to reactivate its service. The Ontario Superior Court in Toronto ruled that BeaverHome had violated the terms of its ISP contract—specifically, its contractual agreement to conform to Netiquette.

Judge Janet M. Wilson observed that the contract was explicitly governed by Netiquette, which she defined as an unwritten and evolving code of conduct "based upon good-neighbor principles for the orderly development of the Internet, and to prevent potential Internet abuse." After reviewing U.S. cases involving spam situations, the judge concluded in her 1999 ruling that sending spam, or spamming, was contrary to the "emerging principles of 'Netiquette' and would not be permitted unless the parties specifically agreed to allow this use." She wrote in her decision:

> The use of the Internet is in its infancy. In the words of counsel, it is "an unruly beast." Or so it will certainly become without a foundation of good-neighbor commercial practices.

This Canadian case reflects commonsense principles that have been and will be followed by other courts. First, the case holds that Netiquette has a commonly accepted meaning. Second, that these guiding principles will be given the force of law when it is so stated in a contract. Moreover, conduct that doesn't meet the rules and concepts of Netiquette certainly will be subject to closer scrutiny by the courts than conduct that does.

Subsequent rulings in U.S. courts apply these concepts as part of their decisions as to what is or isn't appropriate Net behavior, whether the problem involves inappropriate e-mail or copyright disputes. Users are accepting these rules of conduct as the norm for governing their Web behavior. These concepts are being cemented into foundational law as Web sites enact their provisions into contractually binding Terms of Use provisions. States and countries alike are enacting certain provisions into codified statutes, given their commonsense basis and acceptability as rules governing Internet behavior.

Spamming, as a marketing tool, has reached epidemic proportions. In fact, estimates indicate that spam now makes up one third of all electronic mail (and it seems more to the rest of us). In response, the majority of states in the United States have either enacted or are debating whether to enact legislation that would ban or limit this practice. The U.S. Congress is doing the same with public hearings aimed at some sort of legislation, as are other countries. Several courts in the United States already have concluded that spamming is an illegal intrusion onto an ISP's computer systems. This strengthens further what Netiquette informally prohibits. Netiquette and its sense of custom, acceptable behavior, and manners has been evolving into Internet common law.

Because it's a basic concept of what's right or wrong, this concept of "Web manners" has been developing further in other legal areas, such as domain name, trademark, copyright, linking, and framing disputes. For example, if a Web site adopts a trademark that's identical to another in the same line of business, then a classic case of trademark infringement has occurred. It is common acceptable behavior not to rip off someone else's trademark. If you do, then you suffer the consequences. The United States legally incorporated this concept by enacting legislation that prohibits taking any action whose effect is to dilute a valid trademark, including establishing procedures to cancel or oppose a conflicting use that's being proposed for a domain name. (See Chapter 13, "Domain Names and Conflicts.") Further, copying any material on the Web is an exercise of common sense and ethics: If you copy too much, then you've violated these norms—as well as probably the law. (See the next chapter for more.)

As we will see later in Chapter 15, "Can You Link Freely?", it is illegal to link to a commercial site, frame that information as if it is your own, and then sell a subscription to your site based on the linked data. This will buy you a lawsuit, no matter where you live. The illegality is simply an extension of the laws of civility that are contained in Netiquette. Knowing what is or is not legal can be as simple as understanding what is commonsense "fair play" and etiquette.

What is common sense *not* to do can also be prohibited by statutes at that time in the United States and other countries. For example, there shouldn't be any need to think about whether you can pirate software, violate the software's copyrights and trademarks, or make any number of copies to sell for a profit. As expected, the industries that have been incurring losses owing to such copyright infringement and piracy have been taking very strong counterattacks. Not only have they sponsored protective legislation (see the next two chapters), but they have also been attempting to educate the public in these areas.

You'll need to apply a standard of reasonableness and the "Golden Rule" to your dealings in cyberspace, regardless of whether statutes at that time regulate such conduct. The courts will, for sure.

CHAPTER
4

Copying in Cyberspace

What an amazing world cyberspace is. The Internet has made it extraordinarily easy for information to be instantly copied, e-mailed, and printed out. The copies are so perfect that it is not possible to determine differences between originals and copies—and while on the Net, no physical copies exist. Digitized data is uploaded onto a Web site or electronic bulletin board from which countless users make copies and distribute them to others, as each copy arrives in the blink of an eye. Your computer is a worldwide copying machine.

Geographical boundaries now break down in cyberspace. It is standard practice to click a mouse and access information in different languages. For example, one Myanmar (Burmese) Web site provides four choices of language to access its tourist information: English, German, French, and Japanese. From Japanese sake distributors and French shippers to German antique dealers and U.S. hotels, users easily slip from one country's Web site to another, accessing and copying information in English or their native tongue. You can completely access the world from your office or home.

Existing copyright laws, with some "tweaks" added for the digital age, are proving to be ample in covering the problems presented by this easy access to the information and works created by others. Historically, the widespread copying of information wasn't first brought about by cyberspace. As technology developed in the past, Xerox machines allowed printed works to be freely copied; the cassette recorder made it easier to duplicate records; videocassettes copied movies; and floppy disks replicated computer software. In each case, as is now with the Internet, the world by treaties and individual countries by legislation and court decisions eventually adjusted to the new technology by modifying existing legal doctrines.

A Global View

The central concept behind copyrights is that the creators of works should be protected against others' ripping their creations off and should be able to enjoy the fruits of their efforts. The copyright laws of many countries (through the Berne Convention dating back to 1886) grant the copyright owners of an original work the exclusive right, and the right to authorize others, to make copies of the copyrighted work, modify or prepare derivative works, distribute copies or recordings, perform and display the work publicly, as well as prohibiting others from doing any of these activities without their permission. In other words, they have the ability to stop anybody who copies or modifies their work without their agreement. Nearly all countries, including the United States, provide that this copyright protection begins upon the work's creation and is not dependent on the author's meeting any registration formalities. This protection lasts a long time—in most countries it continues for the author's life plus an additional 50 years. (Note: The 1998 U.S. Sonny Bono Copyright Term Extension Act extends copyright protection for most works from 50 years after the author's death to 70 years. This Act is being legally challenged.)

Copyrights are considered to be intellectual property rights, along with intangibles such as trademarks and patents. Trademarks include those marks and symbols that are used by companies to identify their products (such as Coke, Exxon, or Nike). The conflict between two domain names—the word(s) preceding .com—is a trademark issue, not a copyright problem (and will be discussed in a later chapter). Copyrights cover the creations of authors, photographers, artists, and composers.

Authors of newspaper and magazine articles, books, and other treatises (subject to the publisher's rights) have a copyright interest in their works, regardless of who "borrows" portions of them or where they're eventually posted. The creations protected include anything that's reproduced into a "tangible medium," and this legal phrase includes text, photographs, graphics, art, sculptures, music (both compositions and recordings), and even computer software. The electronic equivalents of these works are similarly protected. Thus, paintings, pictures, movies, photographs, poems, sound recordings, and the like, whether posted on the Internet or elsewhere, are subject to copyright protection. (Chapter 5, "Posting Pictures, Music, and Videos" discusses these areas.)

Each Internet user owns the e-mail that he or she composes and sends into the Net, but this protection is lost if the intent is to make it "public"—for example, by posting it on a site. The "look and feel" of a unique Web site, including its general arrangement, descriptive words, text, and even its sound bites, is similarly protected. Images copied and placed on a Web site continue to receive the same protection as the original pictures, drawings, or paintings.

The question of copyright violation occurs when you, for example, download an article from a newspaper Web site, and then post that article on your Web site. However, the ideas or facts contained in the article are never copyrightable, even if it took an archaeologist or physicist 10 years to discover those facts or to prove those mathematical equations. For example, the white pages of a telephone directory (under a 1991 U.S. Supreme Court case) are not subject to copyright protection, even though the information is presented in a certain way. News agencies that have electronic databases cannot prohibit you from posting facts, provided you haven't taken their text word for word. (Note: It does make sense to check out those facts from another source before going ahead.)

The Berne Convention (which has been approved by nearly all countries) governs international copyright protection and is administered by the U.N.'s World Intellectual Property Organization (WIPO). The bottom line of the Convention is that each signatory country agreed to legislate minimum standards for copyright protection in turn, including a protecting period of at least the author's life plus 50 years, and to protect the foreign copyrights of citizens of other nations to the same degree that it protects those of its own citizens. Although a nation has the power to protect copyrights of works first published within its boundaries, it doesn't have the ability to protect its citizens and their works when created in other countries. This protection depends on the other country's laws, and any enforcement of the creator's rights will be based on that foreign country's provisions. Because of their particular history or specific legal system, all countries differ to some degree as to how and when they'll protect the rights of authors in their creations, even with these minimum standards in place.

For example, civil-law countries such as Germany and France recognize an author's "moral right" to prohibit later modifications, or even the destruction of a work, by a third party who purchases that work. The United States doesn't recognize these moral rights. Instead, an author has no further rights in a creation after selling it. Additionally, U.S. law provides for a "fair use" defense in copyright infringements (that's treated later in this chapter), but Japan, Germany, and European Union countries take a more narrow view and basically don't allow this defense.

Copyright Law, U.S. Style

The absence of a copyright notice (the traditional © copyright, date of first publication, and publisher's name) doesn't mean that it's okay to copy something. Copyright law in the United States, as in many other countries, provides that any original work fixed in a tangible medium is automatically protected, whether a copyright notice is present or not. The absence of a copyright notice, under the Berne Convention, also doesn't mean that a work isn't protected by copyright laws (which may or may not exist).

Under the "works for hire" doctrine, there are two exceptions where authors do not own the rights to what they create. First, if an employee prepares the work specifically within the scope of his or her employment, then the employer is held to be the owner. Second, work ordered by a client (i.e., you hire a Web designer for your Web site) is also a work for hire, *provided* that the parties expressly agree in writing that this is the case and that the client owns those creations. Otherwise, the Web designer owns all of the rights, even if well compensated for those services. (See Chapter 14, "Creating Your Own Web Site," for this important discussion.)

Under U.S. law, some kinds of copying are legally permissible, even though the copyright owner would not or does not permit it. This doctrine is entitled "fair use," but many countries don't accept this concept within their territorial boundaries. Thus, if a U.S. citizen downloads a picture from a Japanese sake Web site, it is entirely possible that the Japanese court under its laws would not permit "fair use" actions that would be entirely acceptable to a U.S. court. (See Chapter 11, "But Can Your Court Hear the Case? What Law Is Applied?" for this discussion.)

The U.S. Copyright Act states that the fair use of a copyrighted work for purposes such as criticism, comment, news reporting, teaching, scholarship, or research is not a copyright infringement. So just what is "fair use"? For those of you who are looking for a way to justify your copying, unfortunately it's not easy to conclude just what is or isn't an allowed fair use. There isn't a straightforward standard, and the determination will depend on the facts in each case.

In U.S. courts, four prime legal factors are weighed to determine whether fair use is present. These factors are:

1. *The use of the copying.* (If the copying is for profit rather than education or research, then it's more likely that fair use isn't present.)

2. *The type of work.* (Factual works receive less protection than creative ones.)

3. *How much you quote.* (Two paragraphs from a 250-page book receive more protection than two paragraphs from a 250-word article?)

4. *The effect of the copying on the market.* (If the copying makes people less likely to buy the work from the author, then this probably isn't fair use.)

For example, if you copy two paragraphs from a text and post them on your home Web site, fair use is likely to be present. It would make a difference, however, if you copied those two paragraphs and placed them, word for word, into a 200-word article that you wrote and sold. This would be infringement, and it wouldn't make any difference if you gave credit for the quote. The credit only means you didn't plagiarize the work, since the author still hasn't given permission. If you use that same text, picture, or a competing site's "look and feel" as part of your Web site, it's quite likely this defense doesn't exist. You would be liable for damages, attorney fees, and costs, in addition to being enjoined (stopped) against any further use. The test is the same, whether or not someone "rips off" your Web site (or your creation), or you copy theirs.

The concept of implied license is another common counter to copyright infringement claims. Let's say you post a response to a discussion site, and another person quotes your message in his or her response. Is there a copyright issue? Not likely, even though your message is copyrighted (remember, you created it) and the other person copied it. Your posting of the message to the discussion site certainly gives others an "implied license" to quote it. When it's reasonable to assume that someone is allowed to make copies of what's posted, the law interprets this as an implied license to do that copying.

The following are basic guidelines, online or off: copying of small excerpts for nonprofit purposes tend to be fair; any copying for profit or reselling is generally unfair; noncommercial copying is generally fair unless the text you're copying is available for purchase (or for free on a site that carries advertising). *The test for noncommercial copying is: If the work was widely distributed or subject to extensive "hits," would the copying displace potential sales or advertising?* If it would, then this is unfair use and a copyright infringement.

If you quote a few sentences from a news Web site that you surfed, and then post those sentences in a chat room, this is probably fair use. (There's no profit motive, and the extent of the download is small.) However, if you purchase an entire article from a publisher's Web site and post it to other sites, this use is unfair because your actions would dilute the profit potential for the article. Suppose you receive an e-mail from a friend and pass it along to others. This would probably be unfair use, unless the language in the text created an impression that you could send it along to others.

Another example of implied consent occurs when a browser displays a site to you, while determining whether your computer's memory contains a copy (or cache) of the requested site. If it does, then the Web browser displays that copy within seconds. If the computer's memory doesn't have a copy of this Web site, then it retrieves a copy, simultaneously storing that copy (or caching) of the site in the computer's Random Access Memory (RAM). This routine scanning of Web sites, which involves observing the contained text, linking to other sites, and surfing, is generally held to be within the implied consent exception.

The basic defenses to copyright infringement claims are: independent creation (you created it by yourself, preferably before the other person), first sale or purchase (you paid for those rights—but be careful: this might not include Internet postings), fair use, and implied consent. There are other defenses specific to your situation; however, keep in mind that these are legal defenses and you don't want to be in court using them.

So What Should You Do?

The easiest solution is to contact the owner—let's say, of that ad slogan or testimonial—and get permission before you use it. However, be sure that the person contacted is the one who has the authority to give the necessary permission. For example, if you check out a site and really like a quote or some work that's flashing there, it's quite possible that these operators didn't receive permission from the person who is the real author—that's how they got it in the first place. Accordingly, any permission given by them would not be valid.

A Text Licensing Agreement is attached at the end of this chapter, along with a discussion of its important provisions. This agreement is typically used when the anticipated use is extensive (doesn't involve any possible "fair use"), involves a celebrity, or has a commercial purpose. The use of these agreements by nonprofit or smaller commercial Web users isn't "standard operating procedure" yet; however, it should be and will become this way over time.

Obtaining this permission is much more difficult than you might first think. Locating the whereabouts of the real owners can be difficult; it may turn out that they want to be paid for their consent (which may be the real obstacle); you might not hear back for some time, if at all, after sending in your request; and the people you are asking for permission might not be the ones who can say "Yes." Then what do you do?

Some people decide to "let the chips fall where they may" and copy whatever they want. Do that and you're taking your chances. The authors or owners, upon discovering this unauthorized use of their work and becoming incensed, usually send first a "cease and desist" or "remove that now from your site" letter. Many users comply when they receive such a letter, especially if it is sent on legal letterhead. They simply replace the offending material with something new. Others may weigh whether their actions are a "big deal" or not (qualify as fair use). They might toss the letter away or decide to keep the text display until they receive an actual legal complaint (which may or may not happen). It is very expensive to bring a copyright infringement lawsuit, and complainants may be only bluffing when they threaten legal action. In fact, they may decide to take no further action because of the high legal costs involved.

It may make a difference whether the complaint letter comes from a celebrity or someone unknown. People tend to take complaints from larger gorillas more seriously (such as a demand letter from Microsoft). The decision that's made is not just a business or personal choice; it's also an ethical decision. Simply eliminating the offending material upon receiving a reasonable objection, or not posting it in the first place, is what Netiquette is all about. How the "shoe fits" can also make a difference: Are you the one posting someone else's text, or are you complaining because somebody else copied yours?

> The copyright owner can complain to the Web server, demanding that a subscriber's posting of copyright-infringing material be deleted. If the ISP (Internet Service Provider) is located in the United States, then the complaint is made under the U.S. Digital Millennium Copyright Act of 1998 (DMCA).

Basically, the DMCA sets down the procedures for copyright owners to contact ISPs with their complaints about a subscriber's improper use of copyrighted material. (You usually can find a particular Web site's ISP at any Internet domain name registration service. Simply type in the Web site's domain name and hit the "Who's is it?" or "More info" button.) The ISPs under this law are mandated to remove the improper materials, given that they reasonably determine there are copyright infringements as alleged. However, if the subscriber files a counterprotest, then the ISP must repost the material unless the complainant files a lawsuit against the user for copyright infringement over that offending material. This legislation, in effect, creates an administrative procedure for removing infringing images. Many copyright owners can follow the procedure without needing to resort to the courts—and this by itself is a great improvement.

For those wondering about the liability of the host for their users' copyright violations, the DMCA provides a "safe harbor" for U.S. online servers. Basically, a server must file with the U.S. Copyright Office a registration with certain information. This filing must identify it by name or title and disclose its address, telephone number, and who should be contacted when there's an alleged copyright violation. If the online server follows the law, makes it easy for copyright owners to contact it, and removes the objectionable material from the site when content owners make proper challenges (and abides by the rules that protect users from false challenges), then that server will be legally protected from any subsequent infringement lawsuits brought by the copyright owners.

The definition of who's covered is broad and includes not only ISPs, but also facility operators and providers of network access and online services. Most legal experts believe that businesses, universities, colleges, municipalities, agencies, and other institutions with these Internet systems are covered. In addition, data locators such as search engines aren't liable for providing links to a site with copyright violations. *Check out the U.S. Copyright Office Web site at www.loc.gov/copyright for more information on the DMCA, including the agents of registered online Web sites to whom to address your copyright complaints.*

This novel procedure for "pulling the plug" on offending material was taken to bring the U.S. into compliance with an international copyright treaty (the WIPO 1996 Copyright Treaty). The U.S. is the first country to do so, although some 51 countries (including the European Community) are signatories. The European Union, for example, adopted a directive in mid-2001 that updated its general copyright laws and would bring it and its members into compliance with the WIPO treaty. However, each of its 15 member states must individually incorporate its own version of the DCMA into national law over the next 18 months—and this means that these countries will probably not adopt the exact approach of the U.S. in total. Also, as other countries are hesitant to grant a "fair use" exception for the general public, they also are reluctant to adopt a U.S.-style DMCA in its entirety. Yet, as other nations adopt the general approach of the United States with their own versions, more and more owners and users alike will have the ability to cause infringing material to be removed without the need to expensively litigate the matter in court.

If a competitor complains loudly about your copying, then it may be indicating its intentions to take further legal action. However, why not create a link to that site instead of copying the potentially risky text? For example, if you really like that text, work, or "look," simply link to it. (See Chapter 15, "Can You Link Freely?") There's no need then to copy and post questionable material to your site.

However, if conspicuous © copyright notices are on the site (or security locks requiring payment or identification to access the data), then you know that this site takes its copyrights seriously. You should proceed carefully, remembering that notices do not have to be in place to ensure any copyright's validity. Business sites should particularly be careful about potential copyright infringement situations—there are more valuable places to invest your time and money. Further, once you have invested money in your site's "look and feel," the last thing you want is for your ownership rights to be challenged later.

The "copyright rules of the road" are straightforward enough:

- Don't copy great "gobs" for your use; post links instead of large files that have potential copyright infringement problems.
- When in doubt, ask for permission or be prepared to give the material up—especially if you receive a threatening letter.
- Use common sense, apply Netiquette, and consult an expert legal adviser if your proposed use will be large, involve commercial purposes, and/or involve a "bet your company" situation.

Although contrary to what you would first think, even if you pay for an outside artist's rendering or a designer's "look and feel" for your Web site, those creators still have rights to that work, unless you have a properly written agreement. (See Chapter 5, "Posting Pictures, Music, and Videos," and Chapter 14, "Creating Your Own Web Site.") A person also has rights of privacy and a right of publicity in a picture—even if that person didn't take the photo (covered at Chapter 5). Further, registering your own copyrights in the United States and other countries has benefits, especially when you're concerned over potential violations at your site, ant this is discussed in Chapter 16, "Web Site Operating Considerations."

If you want to acquire the licensing rights to post copyrighted text, check out the Copyright Clearance Center (copyright.com) or the National Writer's Union, Publication Rights Clearinghouse (nwu.org/prc) for those rights and their cost. You can also use a search engine to find the author or licensing representative directly, but this process can become very complicated when needing to surf through all of the sites that turn up. If acquiring these rights are too costly, then you'll need to think up an alternative—but, at least, you haven't sunk in any lost costs at this point.

An International Example

Let's consider the situation where a German author discovers that a Japanese Web site with a U.S. ISP reproduced a work without permission. (Note: the points are the same if a U.S. author is complaining about a Japanese Web site with a non-U.S. ISP. It also makes no difference whether the type of copyrighted work involves book chapters, an article, pictures, or just advertising slogans.) Three countries are connected now to the dispute in this situation: Germany (the creator's domicile), Japan (the copier's domicile), and the U.S. (the ISP site).

The first step would be to file a complaint with the U.S. ISP to remove the offending materials under the Digital Millennium Copyright Act—and this would be the best step, given that a demand letter to stop was ignored. However, a U.S. court might decide it doesn't have the jurisdiction (or power) to intervene in this case unless there were more U.S. connections; or, the U.S. ISP possibly might not react. If the ISP were in Spain or Australia, let's say, then the author could complain to the online server, but the mandated approach of the DMCA at this time hasn't yet been formally adopted in those countries.

If the online server isn't helpful and the author is still serious, then litigation is next (assuming that negotiations have not proven successful). If the case is filed in Germany, the German court would need to find some connection with the Japanese Web site before it could assume jurisdiction. If the site had the necessary factors (i.e., e-mail, an international toll-free number, local advertising, and/or sales to German residents), then Germany might conclude that it could decide the lawsuit. Yet, even if the German court came to a favorable decision, the author still might not recover anything. Unless the Japanese defendant had assets in Germany, the author would need to enforce his judgment in Japan's courts—which might not recognize the German decision if the underlying principles in the German lawsuit were completely different from those recognized by Japanese courts.

The author could bring a legal action or pursue administrative actions in Japan (which hasn't yet adopted the U.S. approach), assuming that its laws in this case are as favorable as Germany's. However, there is always the risk of losing, no matter how good a case seems to be. Keep in mind that any basic problems of enforcing copyrights in a global economy doesn't change just because they occur in cyberspace. And the same reasoning applies as to the differing states in the United States or territories of any other country.

A good alternative is to consult an ADR (alternative dispute resolution) firm to explore mediation or other noncourt solutions. (See Chapter 12, "Cyberlaw Dispute Resolution.") Or, the author could ignore the violation, especially if the costs of the lawsuit would be more than what one could receive in damages, after deducting the projected expenses and legal fees.

The moral of the story: Copyrights are territorially based but cyberspace is not.

A *Text Licensing Agreement* follows. This agreement is used to gain or grant permission for the digital applications of text. A discussion of the provisions, keyed to the form, follows the text of the agreement.

If the other party is more informal (or isn't interested in signing a separate agreement), simply incorporate the important provisions in an e-mail and send it, along with a request that the recipient's reply includes their changes. To cover all of the issues, it is best to use these types of agreements. However, having something in writing that indicates permission is better than having nothing at all.

This basic principle applies to all of the forms presented in this book. Please remember that these form agreements may not be appropriate to your specific situation, and you should secure the advice of an attorney when it's important enough.

Text Licensing Agreement

This Text Licensing Agreement is entered on [*Date of Agreement*] between [*Name of Owner Granting Rights*], as Licensor, and [*Name of Party Receiving Rights*], as Licensee. The parties, in consideration of the mutual promises made by each other and other valuable consideration, agree as follows:

1. **Licensed Work.** The subject matter that's being licensed under this Agreement is: [*Describe the Text and/or Subject Matter Being Licensed*]. This subject matter is referred to throughout this Agreement as the "Licensed Work."

2. **Allowed Use.** The Licensed Work may only be used as follows: [*State the Allowed Use for the Licensed Text*]. This authorized use is referred to throughout this Agreement as the "Allowed Use." No other use is permitted.

3. **Nonexclusive Rights.** Licensor grants to Licensee, upon the terms and conditions of this Agreement, a nonexclusive license to reproduce, modify (for editorial purposes only), and digitize, including publicly displaying and distributing the Licensed Work for only the Allowed Use, including reasonably required advertising and promotion. If the Allowed Use includes a Web site, then this license includes the right for users to download and print one copy of the Licensed Work for their personal, noncommercial use on one computer, and the Licensee shall state this condition on its Web site. Subject to this nonexclusive grant of rights, Licensor retains all other rights of ownership, including copyrights.

4. **Fee, Credit, Copyright Notice, and Reservation of Rights Notice.** Licensee has or will pay to licensor $[*State Amount Paid, Installments (If any), and Dates*] as consideration for the rights so granted. Licensee also [*"agrees" or "does not agree"*] to give Licensor the following credit as to the Allowed Use: [*State Language as Credit for Grant of License*]. Further, Licensee [*"agrees" or "does not agree"*] to affix the following notices respecting Licensor's copyright(s) and reservation of rights for the Allowed Use: [*State Language for Copyright Notice and Reservation of Rights Notice*].

5. **Term.** This License Agreement begins on [*Beginning Date of License Agreement*] and shall end on [*Ending Date of License Agreement*].

6. **Licensor's Warranties.** Licensor warrants that: (a) it has the full power and authority to enter into this Agreement; (b) the Licensed Work is not in the public domain; (c) it created and owns all right, title, and interest to the Licensed Work, including all tangible forms of the Licensed Work; and (d) Licensee's Allowed Use will not violate any rights of any third parties in the Licensed Work, including, but not limited to all copyrights in effect.

7. **Indemnification.** Each party agrees to indemnify, hold harmless, and defend the other from and against any claims or actions, including reasonable court costs and attorney fees, resulting from its negligence or breach of its warranties or obligations underneath this Agreement. Each party agrees to promptly notify the other of such claim or action and cooperate in that defense.

8. **Termination.** Should Licensee fail to make any owing payment after receiving a written [*State Notice in Days*] days notice to pay, then Licensor shall have the right to terminate this Agreement. Either party may cancel this Agreement upon [*State Notice in Days*] days written notice upon the breach of any material provision or representation of this Agreement.

9. **Other.** Any dispute arising in connection with this Agreement shall be first settled by mediation. If that's not successful, then the dispute shall be settled by arbitration to be held in [*Location of Arbitration*] in accordance with the rules of the American Arbitration Association. This agreement to arbitrate shall be specifically enforceable. Any award shall be final and binding on all parties, and a final judgment may be entered in the appropriate court of law. Notwithstanding this, should any litigation ensue between the parties, then the prevailing party shall be entitled to reasonable expenses and attorney fees as set by the Court.

Text Licensing Agreement *(Continued)*

This Agreement is the final understanding between the parties on this subject matter, superceding all other previous agreements, and may be amended only by the written consent of all the parties. Should any court or proceeding determine that any provision is illegal or in conflict, then all other remaining provisions shall be held severable, valid, and be given separate legal effect.

Neither party may assign this Agreement without the consent of the other, which consent shall not be unreasonably withheld. This Agreement shall bind all the parties, their respective estates, heirs, personal representatives, successors, and permitted assigns; its legality and interpretation shall be governed by the laws of the State of [*Name of State Whose Laws Govern*] and of the United States.

This Agreement is accepted, understood, and executed as of the date first above written, by and between:

_____

[*Name and Title of Party Signing for Licensor*]
[*Licensor's Name and Address*]

_____

[*Name and Title of Party Signing for Licensee*]
[*Licensee's Name and Address*]

Text Licensing Agreement

Discussion of Provisions

1. **Licensed Work:** For this agreement, the "Licensor" is the party granting the text licensing rights, or owner, and the "Licensee" is the party paying for and/or receiving those virtual rights (including any sale of that text in tangible form). It is important for both parties to be as specific as possible about what's being licensed, including whether the entire work, or only portions of it, is being licensed. If possible, attach a copy of the text or work, along with any copyright registration details.

2. **Allowed Use:** Again, be as specific as possible regarding how the licensee can use the licensed work. Is further distribution, modification, copying, public display, or performance allowed? If a Web site is involved, then identify the domain name.

3. **Nonexclusive Rights Grant:** This agreement is nonexclusive, allowing the licensor to grant other licenses on the same work. If the licensee believes that other grants would compete with its license, then the provisions should be changed to reflect what subsequent licensing would not be allowed. If the rights grant is exclusive (i.e., the licensor retains no ability to make similar licenses of the work), then this should be stated. If users will be allowed to do more than to "download one copy for personal, noncommercial use on one computer," then this wording would be accordingly changed.

4. **Fee, Credit, Copyright Notice, and Reservation of Rights Notice:** The amount of money to be paid, whether in installments or not, and credit/notices to be posted are usually a prime focus of any negotiation. The credit typically identifies the work and the author. This agreement provides for credit and copyright/reservation of rights notices to be attached (or none at all, if the parties so agree). A typical reservation of rights provision is: "All materials contained herein have been reproduced with the permission of the copyright owners. Any further reproduction, other than as permitted here, is strictly prohibited. All other rights reserved."

5. **Term:** The term can be perpetual or limited in duration. If renewal options are negotiated, then language as to these specifics would need to be added.

6. **Licensor's Warranties:** Licensees insist on these standard representations. A licensee should be on full alert when any potential licensor waffles when asked to give them.

7. **Indemnification:** This indemnification clause is a mutual one that protects both parties against the other's fault or breach. As with all of these clauses and provisions, this section can be changed depending upon the final agreement of the parties. For example, you could place the indemnification responsibility solely on one party or the other. A provision could be added as to any cost sharing between the parties should an action be brought against a third party for its infringement.

8. **Termination:** An important, but neglected, area is: What do you do when a contract doesn't work out? Ironing out these "dos and don'ts" when entering into a contract makes more sense than leaving them to a later time when a dispute occurs and you aren't talking to one another. This agreement only allows a party to end it for a reason or "for cause" (as well as at the expiration of its term).

9. **Other:** This "boilerplate" stipulates that the alternate dispute resolution techniques of mediation and arbitration are to be used. Should arbitration not be agreeable, then these provisions would have to be accordingly changed to reflect the parties' agreement. Additionally, this form provides that any assignment requires the written approval of the other (which may not be "unreasonably withheld"). If either party desires the ability to assign without this restraint, then the following could be substituted: "Either party may assign its rights and responsibilities under this Agreement as it so chooses." Or, the parties may agree to add that specific conditions must occur before any assignment is valid. This agreement provides that U.S. law applies, but the wording could change if one or both parties are not U.S. residents.

CHAPTER
5

Posting Pictures, Music, and Videos

Your legal right to copy and post nontext items is subject to the same considerations we discussed in Chapter 4—but with a few twists linked to today's technology. The continuing and evolving technological developments make it easy to "copy" copyrighted intellectual property, but you do so at the risk of infringing on the owner's rights (or, if you own such property, it's that simple to copy from your site).

The creators of pictures, music, videos, movies, and other nontext works have a similarly protected copyright interest in their creations. That protection applies regardless of who "borrows" those works or where they're eventually posted, and it includes the digital equivalents of those works, whether or not they have been created for a Web site. Keep in mind that most countries don't recognize the U.S. "fair use" exception, which provides that some copying is legally permissible, even when the copyright owner wouldn't permit it. The use (i.e., commercial or personal), how much is copied (i.e., one picture is posted but it may comprise the entire site), and the effect of the duplication (i.e., whether the creator suffers lost sales) are important factors again in determining the extent of this defense. The amount of "hits" that an infringing site receives, of course, can be another important factor as to whether a producer or creator goes after a particular Web site.

Most people are Netiquette-conscious and don't copy indiscriminately. They try to gain permission, or they copy for their own noncommercial (i.e., educational, governmental, or other nonprofit) personal use. The minority is comprised of those who aren't bothered "by the details." Again, these people are taking their chances. TV, video, and movie producers are taking unauthorized copying quite seriously these days, although they're more concerned when an entire Web site is keyed to their creation (i.e., *the Simpsons*). Record companies and recording artists are very sensitive to any copying of their music, to say the least—especially with regard to the newer technologies such as MP3, which we will discuss later.

It's recommended that you try to secure permission for any copying and posting of copyrighted material, but the odds are that posting one of an artist's pictures on your Web site isn't going to bring a lawsuit down on your head. If an artist's software search robot finds your site, identifies the picture, and you receive a letter (which might be a "form" letter), then it's your choice as to whether you act on that warning or ignore it. However, Netiquette would demand that you "pull the plug" on any material that the true owner finds reasonably offensive.

The Digital Millennium Copyright Act (DMCA) applies fully to both non-text and text copying. Copyright owners may complain to their ISP about a subscriber's improper use of copyrighted material, whether videos, records, pictures, or words are involved. ISPs have disconnected countless numbers of Web site owners for not removing objectionable material, after receiving a bona fide complaint under the DMCA. This works both ways, whether you are a copyright holder or the Web site owner. If you don't have permission to use a copyrighted image on your site, then come to some arrangement with the owner before you expend valuable money on promoting any particular "look and feel."

Another U.S. law is noteworthy in this area. The No Electronic Theft Act of 1997 (NET) addressed the problem as to whether copyright piracy, whether committed online or not, is actionable when there is no profit motivation. For example, has a Web operator committed piracy by allowing surfers free downloads of a copyrighted software program? The answer is a resounding YES. Under NET, criminal prosecution and heavy fines can be imposed on people who exchange or barter unauthorized copies of software, videos, clips, or music, whether or not they receive money for those copies. The only requirement is that the value of the pirated material must exceed $1,000 in any six-month period. Although NET's enforcement has been limited to high-profile cases so far, all users should be aware of its provisions.

Can You Post Pictures or TV Clips?

We head right to the $64,000 question: Can you post copyrighted, nontext works? The legal answer is basically NO, unless: (1) you have received verifiable permission to use the copyrighted material; or (2) your use is small (one picture or clip, let's say, and the site's not dedicated to that subject), you have no commercial purpose, and you give proper credit to the true owner—in other words, you claim that the "fair use" exception applies, keeping in mind that this exception can be narrowly construed. If the actual copyright owner has a site already dedicated to those creations, this may affect the decision to contact others. If the owner hasn't created a specific moneymaking Web site for those creations, then he or she impliedly might not be as concerned (again, depending on how much you've "borrowed"). However, these positions are always subject to change.

You also should pay attention to a frequently overlooked fact of practical copyright law: *Individuals have a right of privacy and publicity in a creation (such as a picture), even if they didn't create it.* For example, an actress owns the right to the commercial marketing of a picture taken of her (i.e., it's printed on calendars or posted on the Internet), even when she apparently gave consent to the picture being taken and was even paid for it. Even if a photographer gained her consent to the picture taking and owns the copyright to the photo, that permission does not necessarily convey the right to use this image other than for the purpose that was first agreed. For example, if you paid a photographer to take a picture of someone for your marketing brochure, that act does not include the right to post the image on your Web site, nor would a release from the person whose picture was taken—unless specifically agreed to and, hopefully, in writing. Again, this concept applies whether you're posting a video, an image, or text. You need to gain permission even when you've taken a picture of your mother-in-law and plan to post that on the Net. Be sure to get the virtual rights to *anything* you post. (See the "Rights of Privacy Release" form at the end of this chapter.)

Court cases have further held that publishers must gain permission from freelance writers before putting their work in electronic databases—even if they were well-paid for that pre-Internet work. Recently, the U.S. Court of Appeals ruled that the National Geographic Society made an unauthorized use of pictures taken by a freelance photographer back in 1961 when, much later, it included them in a CD-ROM of its back issues. National Geographic was ordered to pay license fees for that use. In June 2001, the U.S. Supreme Court ruled that media companies must obtain the consent of their freelance writers (employee writers are "work for hire" and the employer gains most of those rights) before any text or other physical creation is posted online. (See also the "Image Licensing Agreement" at the end of this chapter.)

At first blush, it does seem strange that TV or movie producers would take exception to their fans' showing interest in their creations. The anomaly is that these creations, not to mention the movies, books, or records, don't sell very well when people have no interest in them. Then, when fans are attracted to these works, in effect honoring them with a Web presence, some of the owners (or their attorneys) seem to charge infringement in response. However, they are within their rights to do so; in effect, they are making a business decision.

This is easier to understand if the producer owns a for-profit Web site that showcases a particular program or movie. The conflict then comes down to the still fashionable worry over the loss of potential dollars. The competing sites steal interest from the producer's Web site, and fewer monogrammed T-shirts, autographed pictures, or multicolored coffee mugs are sold. At times, however, the owners chase after their fans' sites simply because they received outside legal advice that their copyright and trademark interests were being diluted (which may be legally true, but isn't practically correct). The owners might be better off ignoring all but the most conspicuous of these "competing" sites, spending their hard-earned business dollars on more promotion rather than litigating lawyers.

The fans' receipt of "cease or desist" letters for their postings may depend simply on whether the owner wants further "distribution" of those works or not, as well as how extensive their sites are with their pictures, products, and "interference." It will also depend on how interesting a specific fan's Web site is and how many hits it's getting. If you post one picture, let's say, of Ricky Martin or Brad Pitt on your personal family Web site and it receives 15 contacts a year from surfers, it's seriously doubtful that Ricky or Brad is going to care one way or the other—provided you didn't doctor up the picture to show them in an embrace. However, if you create an entire Web site showcasing Heather Locklear, complete with pinup pictures and selling Heather's coffee cups or insurance, then it's a sure bet you'll receive a letter (and, more than likely, a lawsuit) from her lawyers. At the very least, your ISP will receive a letter from those attorneys demanding that your site be unplugged.

PARAMOUNT PICTURES AND THE TREKKIES

It is ironic that some of the bitterest battles have been between TV studios and their own online fans. For example, starting in 1996 and continuing into the New Millennium, Paramount Pictures and its parent company, Viacom, have tried to crack down on *Star Trek* Webmasters who, they felt, were violating their copyrights. Viacom's attorneys at first sent broad demand letters to selected Trekkie Web sites, demanding that they remove from those sites all copyrighted material from *Star Trek* and its characters, including video clips, book excerpts, script and episode summaries, and photographs. In response, *Star Trek* fans around the Web world organized into a global "Online Freedom Federation" to negotiate an agreement that would allow them the use of this copyrighted material. (See www.off-hq.org for more on this.)

Some Web sites complied and others didn't. Pressure, of course, was directed at the larger *Star Trek* sites with their greater "presence." The suspicion among the *Star Trek* Web sites was that Paramount was trying to drive those fans and potential customers to its official *Star Trek* site (startrek.com), their motivation being more commercial than simply protecting copyright interests. However, in fairness to Paramount and Viacom, it appears that various *Star Trek* "lookalikes" had an interest in preserving their status. Those sites increased in their valuation by their exposure and numbers of hits, whether or not they had a prime commercial interest. Further, some of the sites collect additional moneys by displaying banner ads and selling products such as toys and merchandise. Notwithstanding the legal threats and some lawsuits, the Trekkie Web sites have continued growing.

THE PRINCE, THE FOX, AND DISNEY WORLD

Prince was one of the first recording stars to push Internet access to music. As early as 1995, he proposed "freeing the music" by taking it directly to listeners by way of the Web. In response, his fans built numbers of online Web sites that copied his copyrighted music, lyrics, and records. In 1998, Prince decided that he had had enough of this good thing, and his attorneys sent cease-and-desist letters to various sites that had posted his copyrighted and trademarked material. His attorneys then brought lawsuits against nine Web sites, two publications, and GeoCities, a search engine and major network of personal Web pages—all alleging infringement, sale of bootleg albums, and use of unauthorized photos. When commercial interests become present, you can forget the conceptual philosophies of freedom of the Net.

Twentieth Century-Fox Studios has aggressively gone after what it considered to be competing online Web sites. For example, a 25-year-old college student created a laudatory Web site for *Millennium* and launched it prior to the TV show's premiere. Fox quickly sent an e-mail telling him to erase the images, then contacted the University of Texas and persuaded it to shut off his ISP account. When other Fox fans and technocrats heard about this treatment, they inundated Fox with so much hate e-mail that its ISP crashed. The protestors then launched numbers of other anti-Fox sites.

The Simpsons reflects how important Fox considers its copyrights to be. Fox lawyers wrote threatening letters to numbers of *The Simpsons* Web fan clubs. The letters threatened that if the Web sites weren't dismantled, Fox would sue for damages, and "such damages can include statutory penalties as much as $100,000 (the statutory damages for copyright damages are the actual damages, computed damages, or $20,000 per occurrence up to a maximum of $100,000)." These letters had their desired effect. Many of the early Web sites were dismantled, but not for long; hundreds of other Web sites then surfaced, all centered on *The Simpsons*.

In fairness to Fox, some of the Web sites now link to sites that disparage Fox, catalog other *Simpsons* sites, and even display and sell merchandise (primarily non-*Simpsons* products). Given the proliferation of these sites, it would seem that Fox might have been better off to ignore the problem at first and, instead, to use its legal dollars to make its Web place "the best one in town." The later enactment of the Digital Millennium Copyright Act gives effective, less expensive rights to owners such as Fox to enforce their rights in the United States. However, until these provisions have been enacted worldwide, other "fan clubs" and sites can just as quickly and easily spring up overseas.

The Disney folks, however, have seemed to take a different approach, as least with Disney World. For example, some fans created sites that promote Disney World-Orlando (for example, see "ourlaughingplace.com"), complete with news on opening attractions, rating sites, and travel information. These sites, like other "fan clubs," know and even link to one another. Although some of these locations have travel businesses that book tours to Disney World (which the tourist attraction also does), these sites are flourishing, all with the apparent implied consent of Disney. Although no formal documents have been executed, these Web sites have continued to grow. A risky policy, perhaps, but it does seem to make a difference that these fans are promoting Disney's commercial interests by traveling in groups to its parks, as well as encouraging others to do this.

It is always a business decision as to whom you'll target to "cease and desist," if you're working for the copyright owner. If you are into preserving these interests, then you'll need to establish a hefty legal budget to follow up on the threatening letters and legal contacts, as well as the occasional lawsuit to back up your threats. Most of the sites will be left running, as it is cost-prohibitive and public relations unwise to go after all of them. You might follow Disney's lead and make the business decision that some segments just promote your interests.

A basic problem is that there are legal "gray areas" as to what constitutes "fair use" when Web-based activity is present. It's clear that a site that only sells competitive merchandise for profit would not be such fair use; however, it doesn't follow that noncommercial purposes (i.e., true fan clubs or a nonprofit museum promoting nonlicensed copies of a particular artist's works) would necessarily qualify as well. The fact that such sites draw interest and hits away from the copyright owner's site could be enough to prove infringement.

This will always be a question of fact for juries to consider, but who wants to be in this position? The Digital Millennium Copyright Act does give a measure of protection to those copyright owners who wish to avoid expensive legal actions. Then again, this Act has not yet been enacted overseas, and copycat sites do quickly spring up there. Further, even under this Act, unresolved differences over digital copying can only be resolved by litigation. That recourse will ultimately depend on the owner's final decision, notwithstanding the legal advice that is received at the time.

Creators and Web fans alike should consider mediation in lieu of the lawyers' approach to either "cease and desist" or "let's rumble" in litigation. There is a mutuality of interest in that both sides enjoy those works, despite the conflicts in ownership and the competition for interest. It would appear that alternative dispute resolution would make more sense as a first try in resolving these conflicts. (See further Chapter 12, "Cyberlaw Dispute Resolution.")

But Strength Lies in Numbers

As we have seen, the concerted actions of other Webmasters can tip the scales against an aggressive copyright owner, no matter what the law provides—although these collective actions aren't that common. A French Web site brought an interesting twist on this when it posted nude pictures of a French model, Estelle Hallyday, without her permission. A French judge hit the offending company, AlternB (altern.org), with a $70,000 fine for doing this bad deed. AlternB retaliated by shutting down its server, which hosted 47,000 other Web sites, and threatened to convince other French Web sites to move their operations to more friendly countries. "Keep the Net Free" groups formed or came to the defense of AlternB, and various sites posted more images of Ms. Hallyday throughout cyberspace. The model finally accepted an out-of-court settlement of $7,000, which AlternB paid to her favorite charity.

A similar protest in late-July of 2001 forced Adobe Corporation to change its position against a Russian cryptographer/programmer, Dmitry Sklyarov. Dmitry's problem was that he figured out certain weaknesses in Adobe's eBook encryption software, wrote a program to decrypt e-books that used Adobe's program, and his company employer then sold this program over the Internet. Basically, his work in Russia allowed people to download e-books without paying for them. Mr. Sklyarov then came to the U.S. to discuss his work at a Las Vegas conference. Adobe made a criminal complaint under a statute prohibiting such "decryption," and the FBI arrested him. The furor of the Internet community over the arrest, its calling for a boycott of Adobe's products, holding of demonstrations (both offline and on the Net), and establishment of protest sites caused Adobe to change its position. Within a couple of weeks, Adobe issued a statement calling for Sklyarov's release and withdrew its support of the criminal complaint against him.

The experiences of Great Britain with a former British spy highlight the elusiveness of shutting down high-profile situations. The ex-spook published online a list of the identities of certain alleged secret agents, and the U.S. Web site posting the list was shut down after British officials appealed for help. However, the list soon appeared on numbers of mirror sites. Although the British Government sued to try to stop these sites, it soon discovered that this was difficult to do in the anonymity of the World Wide Web. These same factors apply in business situations, whether you are Ford Motor Company or a startup.

Although it did not deal with copyright infringement, another cyber-event took place with a 1999 Oregon case. Planned Parenthood tried to shut down a Web site page entitled "The Nuremberg Files," which had posted "wanted posters" of medical doctors who had performed abortions. Planned Parenthood charged the Web operators with threatening and intimidating abortion providers in violation of the Freedom of Access to Clinic Entrances Act. An Oregon jury awarded $109 million in damages against that Web site—a substantial award, to say the least. Given the verdict, the ISP shut down the site, so this appeared to be a complete victory. However, numbers of Web sites mirroring "The Nuremberg Files" sprang up all over the world with the same information. In 2001, a unanimous Ninth Circuit Court of Appeals reversed that judgment, citing First Amendment concerns, and this site was back up on the Internet.

Despite the law, it is clear that the enforcement of intellectual property rights is a challenge in cyberspace. *Any infringer shut down by one ISP can create another site or move to another ISP, and copycat or mirror sites can quickly pop up to replace the one that has been eliminated.* Although the law is clear, what actually happens can be entirely different—and sometimes looking the other way is the best decision, especially if you have a small business or are just starting one up.

Nothing would be lost if copyright owners and users tried mediation and other alternative dispute resolution in the beginning, rather than relying on scare tactics that seem to estrange all of the parties from ever reaching an acceptable solution. At least, mediated settlements would be more likely to stop copycat sites from appearing in defense of those whose plug had been pulled. This approach makes more sense when interests are more allied—for example, between companies and their customers (i.e., Ford with Explorer owners or TV producers with their fans).

The Music World, Digital Technology, and MP3

The U.S. music industry has been taking action on many fronts in its attempt to stem the copyright rip-offs of its recordings. In fact, no other industry, including the software industry (there was no trading in software by large Web sites), has been hit as hard by copyright infringement. Under different legislative acts, the music industry has received protection through requiring the registration of digital recording devices, including the payment of royalties based on sales (the 1994 U.S. Audio Home Recording Act); the establishment of copyright infringement liability, even for not-for-profit copying (the 1997 No Electronic Theft Act); and the extending of statutory licensing schemes to certain online transmissions of music recordings and performances (the 1998 Digital Millennium Copyright Act), to name a few. All of this went to naught with the evolution of MP3 technology and the Diamond Rio.

The advent of digital technology makes it possible to reduce most creations— whether they're motion pictures, music, books, or pictures—to a digital format that can be transmitted or reproduced numbers of times with little loss of appreciable quality. This means that entire works can be copied with a mouse click, transmitted around the world instantaneously, and played with quality. However, the technical geniuses have not yet come up with an equivalent way to enforce the copyright interests of the creators in these works that now can be so easily copied.

MP3 technology came along and soon became the bane of the music industry. This popular digital compression technology reduces a digital audio file to at least one-tenth its original size, so that it can be easily reproduced and transmitted on-line—all with fine sound reproduction. The technology basically allows large digital music files to be stored on computer disks and portable devices.

It also has no built-in restrictions presently to prevent widespread reproduction of copyrighted music. In fact, any one using MP3 can duplicate music from a CD to a home computer and then send that along to a friend or post it on a Web site for anyone to download. Countless numbers of users collect and trade MP3 music, and there are thousands of MP3-formatted songs on the Web for downloading. In fact, "MP3" replaced "sex" as the most imputed term for search engines.

Some musicians, including David Bowie and Limp Bizkit, have placed their records onto the Internet willingly in MP3 form. If a copyright owner freely posts a song on the Web, then downloading the song is legal; but if the owner did not freely post it, then downloading that music is usually a copyright violation. Many MP3 users download this music, knowing that these are illegal copies, and will continue to do so as long as there are available Web sites.

What kept this situation under control at first was that users had to sit very close to their computers to listen to their MP3 "recordings." However, making everything worse for the music industry, Diamond Multimedia introduced in 1998 the Rio PMP300. This handheld device is smaller than a Walkman cassette player and can hold 60 minutes of MP3 music on its built-in chip (and later models can hold much more). The inexpensive Rio can download the abounding MP3 music from a computer and, just like a cassette player, play that music almost anywhere.

The Recording Industry Association of America (RIAA) immediately sued to stop the sale of the Diamond Rio to the public. This wasn't the first time, historically, that the entertainment industry had gone to court to stop threatening new technology from being sold. In the early 1980s, motion picture studios, such as Universal and Walt Disney, went to court to stop the sale of video recorders, but the U.S. Supreme Court didn't agree and allowed their sale. A U.S. Court of Appeals in 1999 held similarly that the Diamond Rio was legal for sale to the public, and now MP3 technology could serve the mass market.

As if the Diamond Rio wasn't bad enough, along came Napster (www.napster .com). Once this software program is downloaded on a personal computer (there was even one for Macs at macster.com), the program searches the hard drive and lists all of the MP3 music fields on it so that other Napster users can copy them. The program can connect through the Net to a Napster computer server, search for specific songs and artists recorded on the hard drives of other computers, and link the two to download sought-after songs, back and forth and even simultaneously. Written in 1999 by Shawn Fanning, a 19-year-old student at Boston's Northeastern University, the program moved throughout the universities of the world like wildfire. It became so popular on college campuses that hundreds of universities either banned or put controls on the practice, because the students' downloads were clogging up the schools' computer networks with MP3 transfers. The recording industry (RIAA) and its members quickly brought lawsuits against MP3 and the Napster Web site, alleging copyright infringement and other violations.

MP3 allowed users to listen to its online music collection via any computer hooked to the Net, and the five major record companies (Bertelsmann's BMG, EMI Group, Sony Music, Warner Music, and Universal Records) sued. However, after the company signed licensing agreements in 2000 with these companies (at a reported total of $134 million plus future royalties), MP3 shut down its My.MP3.com music site, then soon relaunched it as a fee-based site. It is similarly working toward settling several lawsuits by smaller independent record companies. Ironically, music companies then sued Universal Records (which had won a large judgment and settlement against MP3) for infringement, citing the titles it allows subscribers to download from its music site.

The RIAA and its members brought large, complex lawsuits against Napster. The site argued that because it only maintained a free music file directory, it never handled the music and only allowed "friendly sharing" of MP3 formatted digital music between its members. A Federal District Court judge unfortunately didn't buy this argument and issued a temporary injunction to shut Napster down, holding that direct copyright infringement had occurred, due to the large amount of pirated music that was being traded over the site. This holding was appealed, but when the smoke cleared (on this issue), the judge changed her decision and ordered Napster to exclude individual audio file names of copyrighted artists from its site as a condition of staying in business. Napster was forced to change its policies. Filters were put in place to exclude thousands of specific recordings that the copyright holders wanted blocked, and a fee service was enacted for the downloading of music. Napster's hit count fell dramatically in the process, as other free sites sprang up to handle the excluded music, including fast-growing Napster clones located outside the U.S. and its protective legal environment. For more on this, see KaZaa (owned by and uses Fast-Track's software), Bearshare, Audiogalaxy, and IMesh with multi-media ability or potential. They also are attracting the attention of the RIAA, and the battles are occurring around the world.

Late in 2000, Napster and Bertelsmann BMG (one of the suing parties) had shocked the music world by announcing their deal: Bertelsmann dropped its lawsuit, licensed its music to Napster, and agreed to invest in Napster in return for the site's establishing a subscription-based fee service. Although it remains to be seen how Napster eventually turns out (i.e., sells majority control or some change of form), the definite trend is for similar licensing deals to be cut by these file-sharing sites with the music industry. "If you can't beat them, then join them, so to speak." As no surprise, the music industry is offering its own fee-based Web sites, and consumers are paying now for music downloads that, in the beginning, were once free.

Aside from its legal battles, the music industry is pursuing different strategies on various fronts to cope with what the industry regards as a frightening technology. Some record labels have authorized smaller Web sites under licensing agreements to sell their digital music. The RIAA is trying to develop a digital music format that would be superior to MP3 but would still allow copyright protection. It has used the No Electronic Theft Act in widely publicized efforts to stop the unauthorized copying of its music. One unlucky University of Oregon student was convicted under the Act and sentenced to two years' probation. The RIAA and its members now use search "robots" and "spiders" (search software) to locate their music, so that they can extract licenses and royalties from the unearthed Web sites. The music industry will be in a technological and public relations war for years to come, but fee-based subscription services will dominate, as the "free sites" appear and then disappear in response to the music and multi-media industry's legal and business muscle.

The Future

As the music world battled widespread MP3 technology, other entertainment industries had similar challenges. The same technology is adaptable to thick books and long-playing videos, and these can be similarly reproduced in a digital format. With digital videodisks, or DVDs, even more movies are made available in a digital format.

Additionally, there is another technological development that the music and movie/video industries have been trying not to publicize (which might change, after the litigators get into this fray). It was one thing for competing Web sites to develop after Napster's legal troubles; it was another for the development of new technology with alternative file-sharing systems. While Napster created a centralized directory for trading music files, these newer Web sites use primarily a technology that can be used to trade *directly* (without a central directory) multi-media data. These systems are: Gnutella (BearShare and LimeWire utilize this technology), OpenNap's WinMx, and MusicCity's Morpheus. Although aspects of this technology require broadband, or fiber-optic cable transmission, its development and growth should also be a PR and legal battleground—but including visual, multimedia applications as movies and videos.

One U.S. District Court decision held that a search engine, Ditto.com, didn't violate copyright laws by allowing computer users the ability to find copyrighted photographs and other images on the Web, and then to copy them for the users' own sites. If this approach stands, then search engines such as Yahoo, AltaVista, and Excite don't violate the law when they copy and index portions of copyrighted articles, illustrations, pictures, and other protected works. A different U.S. District Court held, in 2000, that a Toronto-based firm, iCraveTV.com, couldn't put on its Web site programs intercepted from TV stations in New York and Canada, if U.S. viewers could see them. I Crave TV shut down its Internet operations, and Record TV closed its virtual VCR Web site, after losing a similar court battle with the industry. Courts have also ruled that auction houses such as eBay cannot be held liable for the selling of bootleg copies of music or videos by some members. This struggle between owners' copyrights and easy data duplication will unquestionably continue on many fronts for the years to come.

With the creation of AOL Time Warner, AOL's Internet pipelines can now flow through not only the products of Warner Music, CNN television, and *Time* magazine, but also Warner Bros. films. In early 2001, Miramax and the online media site, Sight-Sound.com, offered the first legitimate full-length, studio-approved Hollywood movie download. They chose 1999's *Guinevere,* which cost $3.49 to rent for one day: The file was encrypted so that it was unplayable and uncopyable after 24 hours.

Although the technology still needs further development, it is clear that the movie industry is following RIAA's lead. The studios have sued to shut down Web sites that allow people to swap film files, and they are pushing legislation to deal with this technology. They also are forming their own fee-based sites to provide digitized videos and motion pictures over the Internet. The bottom line is that these industry steps will ultimately preserve the artists' and entertainment industry's copyright interests and change downloading to a near complete subscription, fee-based standard owned or controlled by that industry.

In Chapter 3, "The Developing Law of 'Netiquette,'" we looked into what people shouldn't be doing. Now, let's look into what they really are doing. Although the statistics show that the great majority of us are law-abiding folks, this doesn't hold true when it comes to duplicating software and music.

An October 1999 poll of 600 adults, conducted by Baldassare Associates for the Orange County Edition of the *Los Angeles Times,* revealed several interesting responses. One out of four of those polled said that it was acceptable to copy computer software without paying for it, and nearly one in three said that it was acceptable to trade copyrighted music or computer games. The younger the respondents were (ages 18–34), the more likely they were to trade copyrighted music—in fact, they were more than twice as likely to do this as was the "over 55" age group. To an extent, this isn't too surprising: younger people are more likely to be trading in music and computer games than older people are. There was a gender gap as well; whereas 30 percent of the men said that it was always or sometimes acceptable to misrepresent oneself on the Internet, only 19 percent of the women so agreed. Some people just have to learn by experience.

When we add in globalization, we can appreciate what these industries face. It is one thing to send "cease and desist" letters within the United States, along with threats of lawsuits or the Digital Millennium Copyright Act (DMCA); it is another to send those same letters to Italy, South Africa, or Japan. Not only have the provisions of the DMCA not yet been enacted substantially overseas, but foreign legal systems are different, and lawyers must be hired if suits to enforce copyrights are brought there. Even when the rest of the world enacts the U.S.'s protective laws, the major media players still will be fighting a hard battle to protect their royalty interests against future technological digital developments—notwithstanding Netiquette and that most of us aren't interested (or don't have the time) to post or trade counterfeit copies of digital music, movies, or videos.

What Should You Do?

The decision on copying music or images is at times more an ethical issue than a legal one (until practical encryption is developed), provided the user: (1) doesn't create a Web site dedicated to that image; and (2) the use isn't large, there's no commercial purpose, and a copyright credit is given when due. Otherwise, try to secure permission first by using e-mail or the form at this chapter's end. You can search ASCAP (American Society of Composers, Authors, and Publishers at ascap.com) and its list of licensing representatives for obtaining music rights, as well as the particular studio for TV and/or movie rights. If obtaining the legitimate rights are too expensive, then you'll need to rethink this area—and if approval isn't obtained, then don't use it. Remember that copyright protection is automatic; the absence of the © copyright symbol, doesn't mean that the work isn't protected.

The rules are still straightforward: (1) don't copy great "gobs" for your Web site; (2) when in doubt, ask for permission or be prepared to give the material up—especially if you receive a threatening (but reasonable) letter; (3) use common sense, apply Netiquette, and consult expert legal advice if your proposed use is large, involves strictly commercial purposes, and/or is a "bet your company" situation. Above all, don't invest money in your site's "look and feel" until you have fully resolved the question of copyright ownership—otherwise, you can build up value in your site and then lose that value overnight with the arrival of one letter. Some businesspeople still "go with the flow" and copy what they want, when they want, and how they want. They'll need to secure experienced defense attorneys.

A *Rights of Privacy Release* and an *Image Licensing Agreement* follow. Use the Privacy Release when you want to post a picture (whether you took it or not), but do not have specific permission to use the subject's image, digitally and/or offline. As discussed previously, the people in a picture have certain rights of privacy that need to be released. The Rights of Privacy Release form is used for this purpose.

The Image Licensing Agreement is used to gain (or grant) permission for the digital applications of nontextual works such as photographs or videos. This form is similar in concept to the Text Licensing Agreement at the end of Chapter 4. A discussion of the provisions follows each form.

Rights of Privacy Release

This Rights of Privacy Release is entered on [*Date of Agreement*] by [*Name of Person or Entity Granting the Rights*] ("Grantor") and [*Name of Person or Entity Receiving the Rights*] ("Grantee"), as indicated below:

1. **Grant of Release.** Grantor, [*Name of Person or Entity Granting the Rights*], in consideration of receiving [*Select Either "valuable consideration" or State "$[Amount of Money Received]"*], grants to [*Name of Person or Entity Receiving the Rights*] ("Grantee") the following nonexclusive publication and release rights to that certain [*Describe Specifically the Photographs, Video(s), Interviews, or Material that's the Subject*], otherwise called the "Subject Material," and all as pursuant to this Agreement.

2. **Rights to Subject Material.** Grantee may digitize, reproduce, modify, edit (provided it doesn't materially alter or change the composition of the Subject Material), and publish, along with reasonable advertising and public relations material, the Subject Material as it reasonably deems fit, PROVIDED that the publication is limited to the following use: [*Specify What Limitations Are Present—i.e., Only on Grantee's Web Site*]. This release of rights includes the right to use the name of [*State Name of Person Being Released*], as Grantee reasonably determines.

3. **Copyright.** The photograph, video, interview, or other Subject Material [*State "was" or "was not"*] made, created, or taken by someone else. Accordingly, Grantor [*State "does" or "does not"*] have any claim to the copyrights in the Subject Material. If Grantor does have a claim to the copyright in the Material, then it is subject to the provisions of Section 2 above, and this Rights of Privacy Release includes a release of those rights to Grantee, as well.

4. **Other.** Any dispute arising in connection with this Agreement shall be first settled by mediation. If that's not successful, then the dispute shall be settled by arbitration to be held in [*Location of Arbitration*] in accordance with the rules of the American Arbitration Association. This agreement to arbitrate shall be specifically enforceable, and any award shall be final and binding on all parties. However, should any litigation ensue between the parties, then the prevailing party shall be entitled to reasonable expenses and attorney fees as set by the Court.

This Agreement is the final understanding between the parties on this subject matter, superseding all other previous agreements, and may be amended only by the written consent of all parties. Neither party may assign this Agreement without the consent of the other, which consent shall not be unreasonably withheld. This Agreement shall bind all the parties, their respective estates, heirs, personal representatives, successors, and permitted assigns; its legality and interpretation shall be governed by the laws of the State of [*Name of State Whose Laws Govern*] and of the United States.

This Agreement is accepted, understood, and executed as of the date first above written, by and between:

_____

[*Name and Title of Party Signing for Grantor (Granting the Rights)*]
[*Grantor's Name and Address*]

_____

[*Name and Title of Party Signing for Grantee (Receiving the Rights)*]
[*Grantee's Name and Address*]

Rights of Privacy Release

Discussion of Provisions

1. **Grant of Release.** As previously discussed, individuals have rights-of-privacy considerations, aside from the copyright ownership rights of whoever takes the picture or video. This release operates as a release of those additional rights. In this case, the release can be made with or without receiving money in return. Care should be taken to specify precisely what material is the subject matter of the contract and what is being released.

   Further, something of value should be given for the release when appropriate—whether this is money (which can be a token $1 payment), a book, or even a magazine subscription. You will want to be sure, if the person signing this is a minor, that the parents or legal guardians also sign. As this form gives "nonexclusive" rights, the owner can make similar grants to other users and Web sites.

2. **Rights to Subject Material.** Because individuals at times aren't interested in giving blanket or general releases, the rights being granted to the subject material are limited (nonexclusive). If the release to be given is a blanket one, then the use conditions in this contract can be eliminated, along with other changes.

3. **Copyright.** If the person who's signing this contract also owns the copyright, then this release will operate as a transfer of those rights, as well. However, it is important to keep in mind that the subject of a photograph or video does not own the copyright at the time of its creation—it belongs to the photographer, cameraperson, or video operator. This agreement allows for this distinction to be made; if the subject didn't arrange to own the copyright, then he or she doesn't own it and can't transfer it. You'll need to contact the person who does, in order to receive the necessary copyright permission (i.e., from the photographer).

4. **Other.** This "boilerplate" stipulates that the alternate dispute resolution techniques of mediation and arbitration are to be used. Should arbitration not be agreeable, then these provisions would have to be accordingly changed to reflect the parties' agreement.

   This agreement provides that any assignment requires gaining the consent of the other party (which may not be "unreasonably withheld"), thus giving some control over the ability to transfer. If less control is desired, then you could replace that with: "Either party may sell, assign, or transfer its rights under this Agreement without restraint." Or other conditions may be added to the assignment language. This provision flexibility, as with all other sections, applies to any of the forms in this book.

Image Licensing Agreement

This Image Licensing Agreement is entered on [*Date of Agreement*] between [*Name of Owner Granting Rights*], as Licensor, and [*Name of Party Receiving Rights*], as Licensee. The parties, in consideration of the mutual promises made by each other and other valuable consideration, agree as follows:

1. **Licensed Work.** The Work that's being licensed and subject to this Agreement is: [*Describe the Photo or Video Being Licensed*]. This subject matter is referred to in this Agreement as the "Licensed Work."

2. **Allowed Use.** The Licensed Work may only be used as follows: [*State the Allowed Use for the Photo or Video*]. This authorized use is referred to throughout this Agreement as the "Allowed Use." No other use is permitted.

3. **Nonexclusive Rights.** Licensor grants to Licensee, upon the terms and conditions of this Agreement, a nonexclusive license to reproduce, modify, and digitize, including publicly displaying and distributing the Licensed Work for only the Allowed Use, including any reasonable advertising and promotion. No modification is allowed that would adversely compromise the original Work's integrity.

   If the Allowed Use includes a Web site, then this license includes the right for users to download and print one copy of the Licensed Work for their personal, noncommercial use on one computer, and Licensee shall state this condition on its Web site. Subject to this nonexclusive grant of rights, Licensor hereby retains all other rights of ownership, including copyrights.

4. **Fee, Credit, Copyright Notice, and Reservation of Rights Notice.** Licensee has or will pay to licensor $[*State Amount Paid, Installments (If any), and Dates*] as consideration for the rights so granted. Licensee also [*"agrees" or "does not agree"*] to give Licensor the following credit as to the Allowed Use: [*State Language for Credit*]. Further, Licensee [*"agrees" or "does not agree"*] to affix the following notices respecting Licensor's copyright(s) and reservation of rights for the Allowed Use: [*State Language for Copyright Notice and Reservation of Rights Notice*].

5. **Term.** This License Agreement begins on [*Beginning Date of License Agreement*] and shall end on [*Ending Date of License Agreement*].

6. **Licensor's Warranties.** Licensor warrants that: (a) it has the full power and authority to enter into this Agreement; (b) the Licensed Work is not in the public domain; (c) it created and owns all right, title, and interest to the Licensed Work, including all tangible forms of the Licensed Work; and (d) Licensee's Allowed Use will not violate any rights of any third parties in the Licensed Work, including, but not limited to all copyrights in effect.

7. **Indemnification.** Each party agrees to indemnify, hold harmless, and defend the other from and against any claims or actions, including reasonable court costs and attorney fees, resulting from its negligence or breach of its warranties or obligations under this Agreement. Each party agrees to promptly notify the other of such claim or action and cooperate in that defense.

8. **Termination.** Should Licensee fail to make any owing payment after receiving a written [*State Notice in Days*] days notice to pay, then Licensor shall have the right to terminate this Agreement before the end of its term. Either party may cancel this Agreement upon [*State Notice in Days*] days written notice upon the breach of any material provision or representation of this Agreement.

9. **Other.** Any dispute arising in connection with this Agreement shall be first settled by mediation. If that is not successful, then the dispute shall be settled by arbitration to be held in [*Location of Arbitration*] in accordance with the rules of the American Arbitration Association. This agreement to arbitrate shall be specifically enforceable. Any award shall be final and binding on all parties, and a final judgment may be entered in the appropriate court of law. Notwithstanding this, should any litigation ensue between the parties, then the prevailing party shall be entitled to reasonable expenses and attorney fees as set by the Court.

Image Licensing Agreement *(Continued)*

This Agreement is the final understanding between the parties on this subject matter, superceding all other previous agreements, and may be amended only by the written consent of all the parties. Should any court or proceeding determine that any provision is illegal or in conflict, then all other remaining provisions shall be held severable, valid, and be given separate legal effect.

Neither party may assign this Agreement without the consent of the other, which consent shall not be unreasonably withheld. This Agreement shall bind all the parties, their respective estates, heirs, personal representatives, successors, and permitted assigns; its legality and interpretation shall be governed by the laws of the State of [*Name of State Whose Laws Govern*] and of the United States.

This Agreement is accepted, understood, and executed as of the date first above written, by and between:

_____

[*Name and Title of Party Signing for Licensor*]
[*Licensor's Name and Address*]

_____

[*Name and Title of Party Signing for Licensee*]
[*Licensee's Name and Address*]

Image Licensing Agreement

Discussion of Provisions

1. **Licensed Work:** In this agreement, the "Licensor" is the one granting the rights; the "Licensee" is the one paying for and receiving the digital, online rights (including any sale of the work in tangible form). It is important for both parties to be as specific as possible over what's being licensed, including whether the entire work or only portions are being licensed. If possible, attach a digitized image or physical copy of the work and any copyright registration details.

2. **Allowed Use:** Again, be as specific as possible as to how the licensee can use the licensed work. Is further distribution, modification, copying, public display, or performance allowed? If a Web site is involved, then identify the domain name.

3. **Nonexclusive Rights:** This agreement is nonexclusive, allowing the licensor to grant other licenses on the same work. If the licensee believes that other grants would compete with its license, then the provisions should be changed to reflect what subsequent licensing would not be allowed. If the rights grant is exclusive (i.e., licensor retains no ability to make similar licenses of the work), then this should be stated. If users will be allowed to do more than to "download one copy for personal, noncommercial use on one computer," then this wording also would be accordingly changed.

4. **Fee, Credit, Copyright Notice, and Reservation of Rights Notice:** The amount of money paid, credit, and notices to be posted are usually a prime focus of any negotiation. The credit typically identifies the work and the author. This agreement provides for credit and copyright/reservation of rights notices to be attached (or none at all, if the parties so agree). A typical reservation of rights provision is: "All materials contained herein have been reproduced with the permission of the copyright owners. Any further reproduction, other than as permitted here, is strictly prohibited. All other rights reserved."

5. **Term:** The term can be perpetual or limited in duration. If renewal options are negotiated, then language as to these specifics would need to be added.

6. **Licensor's Warranties:** Licensees insist on these standard representations. A licensee should be on full alert when any potential licensor waffles as to giving them.

7. **Indemnification:** This indemnification clause is a mutual one that protects both parties against the other's fault or breach. As with all of these clauses and provisions, this section can be changed depending upon the final agreement of the parties. For example, you could place the indemnification responsibility solely on one party or the other. A provision could be added as to any cost sharing between the parties, should an action be brought against a third party for its infringement.

8. **Termination:** An important, but neglected area, is what you should do when a contract doesn't work out. Ironing out these "do's and don'ts" when entering into a contract makes more sense than leaving them to a later time when a dispute occurs and you aren't talking to one another. This agreement only allows a party to end it for a reason or "for cause" (as well as at the expiration of its term).

9. **Other:** This "boilerplate" stipulates that the alternate dispute resolution techniques of mediation and arbitration are to be used. Should arbitration not be agreeable, then these provisions would have to be accordingly changed to reflect the parties' agreement. Additionally, this form provides that any assignment requires the written approval of the other (which may not be "unreasonably withheld"). If either party desires the ability to assign without this restraint, then the following could be substituted: "Either party may assign its rights and responsibilities under this Agreement as it so chooses." Or the parties may agree to add that specific conditions must occur before an assignment can be valid. This agreement provides that U.S. law applies, which could also change if one or both parties aren't U.S. residents.

CHAPTER
6

"Junk Dog" Statements and Privacy Concerns

One of the great misconceptions about the Web is that it's the "Wild Wild West" and that anyone on the Net can say what they want to, when they want to, and with perfect anonymity. That is simply NOT true. Let's say you use the "moniker" of FXSX. You enter a chatroom, post your comments under FXSX, then leave. Your posting reads: "Ace Drug's President [a competitor] is a convicted felon" or a fellow trade association member was "not only an imbecile, but FXSX knows his dirty little secret . . . He's a member of a terrorist group trying to overthrow this country." None of this is true.

Hiding behind your pseudonym of FXSX won't protect you. As we shall see, there are electronic trails that can be followed. In many cases, it's only a matter of time before your actual name and address are found. A certified letter or process server can eventually arrive at your home, if Ace Drug's President or that trade association member decides to pursue this fully. And if you are the person who has been defamed, you wouldn't want this any other way—whether it's over your business or not.

At the same time, every time you access a Web site, that site has the ability to see where you've been before, what purchases you've made, your preferences, buying habits (business or otherwise), and personal information. Web sites sell that information to marketing firms, which then can hit you with e-mails on buying their selected products. Hiding on the Web is becoming more difficult as both technology and the law advance.

Let's take a look first at some basic concepts on defamation and how they are applied to the Internet. We'll then follow that up with a discussion on privacy and what you or customers can do to retain some privacy in today's highly complex Net world.

Defamation Basics

Defamation is present when a material falsehood about somebody which harms that person's reputation is communicated to a third party. Invasion of privacy is present when such a comment is truthful but is unreasonably published or becomes an unwarranted intrusion into that person's private affairs. For example, let's say you post that Ace Drug's president has herpes. This is defamatory if you're wrong, and an invasion of privacy if you're right—both are legally actionable.

For a comment, whether written or not, to be defamatory, it must meet several minimum requirements: (1) it must damage someone else's reputation, whether that is a person or a business; (2) it must be the type that generally would adversely affect that reputation; and (3) it must be communicated to another person. Without going into a detailed discussion of defamation, the defenses to this action are: (1) the statement was true; (2) the communicator had a privilege, such as it was "fair criticism"; or (3) the statement was just your opinion (but be careful with this one).

Let's look at a few examples. If you sent an e-mail only to one person, calling that same person a "crook" and claiming he had cheated people out of money (but this one didn't), then there wouldn't be any defamation. Since you didn't send that statement to anyone else, there was no publication of it. However, if you posted that comment on a Web site or in a chatroom, then you have published an untrue statement about someone else to others and would become liable.

Let's say that you sent an e-mail to a friend of Connie's, writing that "Connie has put on a couple of pounds." If she *has* "put on a couple of pounds," then there's no defamation because the statement is true. However, even if she hasn't put on weight, this type of comment wouldn't be defamatory because it doesn't affect her reputation. What's a couple of pounds, anyway? However, if Connie was a paper-thin model and this statement caused her to lose a modeling assignment, then we would have a different situation.

If you post a message that "Kenmark's greeting cards use bad English," but no one believes this because Kenmark is an excellent writer, then there is no defamation. People must reasonably believe that what you say is true, before there can be actionable defamation. Keep in mind also that most defamation occurring on the Net is libel (written) and not slander (spoken). Further, even if you weren't trying to intentionally hurt someone and had checked the facts, but it turns out that you were wrong, you could still be liable if you were found careless (or negligent) in your fact checking and that this caused the other person to be damaged.

The arguments of "fair criticism" and "opinion" are present as defenses to defamation actions. For example, if you said or wrote that "Ace Drug is the worst company to work for," then that's your opinion and there's no libel. However, if you posted, "Ace Drug tests new drugs on cats and dogs where they eventually die, writhing in incredible pain"—but they don't—then this is defamation.

The distinction between fact and opinion can be difficult to draw at times. If you posted "Brad Pitt is the dumbest actor FXSX has ever seen," this is okay because it's your opinion—whether that's true or not. However, if you wrote "Brad Pitt is a drug dealer," then that is a wrong statement of fact, not an opinion, and legally actionable. And, there is a difference in whether you post a false comment about a coworker named George, or about President George Bush.

So far, we have been dealing in the area of free speech. Free speech is not unlimited; for example, society can't allow people to yell "Fire!" in a crowded, dark auditorium. Nor can we allow people to say untrue, ridiculing statements about others. However, a line is drawn to separate ordinary people from those who are called "public figures."

In the landmark case of *New York Times v. Sullivan,* the U.S. Supreme Court in 1964 held that "public figures" (or those who are continually in the "public's eye") could not win or recover damages for defamation unless they could show that a publisher: (1) knew that the fact was false; or (2) was "reckless" in not ascertaining the truth of the published statement.

In both cases, if FXSX knew that what was said about both George and President George was false, then there is potential liability. However, suppose FXSX said that both men lied on their federal income taxes. If FXSX had researched the two men's tax returns, but made an honest mistake in his interpretation of a tax law, then President George wouldn't have a case because FXSX wasn't being "reckless." However, individual George could still sue because FXSX was being at least "careless" and this George isn't a public figure who's subject to a higher test. This exception has been legally made because it is assumed that public figures have the ability to protect themselves via their access to the media, but private figures and nonpublic individuals have no such ability.

Let's say that FXSX, who's now on a roll, enters an online chat discussion that's dealing with weight loss. Dr. Real is hosting this discussion, but soon FXSX has spat out: "Dr. Real is a fraud. She's not a real doctor; in fact, she's a quack. She dropped out of law school, didn't attend medical school, and has been on welfare for the last two years." FXSX then heads off to do more mischief in another chatroom. Dr. Real's attorney contacts the ISP and tracks down FXSX's real name and address. Even if the ISP isn't cooperative, the attorney can file a lawsuit against FXSX, then subpoena (deliver a written demand to) the ISP to release the necessary identification data about FXSX. But suppose FXSX is nowhere to be found.

If FXSX has disappeared (he insulted one too many people and is now running for his life), then can the ISP, which also was the "publisher" of the defamation, be found liable? No, in nearly all the cases. The Communications Decency Act of 1996 provides that service providers, whether they are AOL or Microsoft, are not considered to be "publishers" of materials that they did not write. Further, courts have held that even absent such a protective statute, the First Amendment by itself protects an ISP against liability for defamatory material posted by others with whom the provider has no connection. Although the provisions of the Digital Millennium Copyright Act weren't strictly written to encompass defamatory statements, quick removal of offending material will mollify in any event how a defamed person views that ISP.

Freedom of speech does not mean that users like FXSX can freely e-mail others with degrading comments, even if the contents aren't legally defamatory. If someone harasses someone else or uses "offensive" language that isn't defamatory, an ISP can still discipline the sender under its Terms of Use policy, whether it issues a warning, suspension, or termination of service (sequential steps of warnings are usually coupled with increasing punishment, along with erasing the statement). (See Chapter 9, "Web Site Disclaimers and Protections.")

If a user continually posts "That was the dumbest statement I've ever heard" or "You're the biggest jerk ever placed on earth," then these actions can bring about suspension or a termination of service, even if the comments by themselves wouldn't incur legal liability. And if other subscribers complain that they don't want to hear from FXSX again, whether they're legally right or not, then that ISP just might pull the plug on FXSX anyway. This by itself might not deter FXSX—there are always other ISPs he could sign up with—but this action does push him away from those he had been harassing.

Suppose the tables are turned on FXSX when someone who has been upset with him posts in retaliation: "FXSX is certifiably nuts. In fact, he was chained in a mental institution for three years before he could break out." Although most people would think that this would be "just deserts," the legal world doesn't look at it this way. First, everyone whom he had defamed could still sue him for his past defamatory statements. Second, if someone defamed him back in response, even if the reply is addressed to his Internet pseudonym, then FXSX has a valid claim for damages to both his pseudonym and real name against this vigilante. Although a pseudonym deserves the same legal protection as does a real name, the extent of the damages would need to be proved, especially given the anonymity of a pseudonym and how easily one can be changed (as opposed to ones real name).

Trade Libel

As we have seen, the law against defamation protects businesses, just as it does individuals. People can be held liable when they post statements about any company or organization that falsely ascribe conduct or facts indicating improper conduct. This action is called "trade libel," and its use is increasing on the Internet—owing to the ease with which false statements can be made, published, and sent to such a wide audience, as well as the firms' ability to watch the Net carefully for what's posted about them. The legal test is basically whether someone has written material that (1) is false; (2) erodes commercial confidence in that company or individual who's doing business (whether under an assumed name or not); and (3) is published. An example of both personal and trade libel is the previously discussed case of Dr. Real.

Let's say that FXSX is back in business. He apologized profusely to the retaliator who was after him and gave some money in settlement, but he's still in and out of court due to his incredibly false comments. Other examples of trade libel that FXSX could be liable for (whether posted, written, or spoken) would include his statements that: (1) attorney Tom Mix bribed a judge to get that last legal judgment; (2) famed author Martha Stark plagiarized all of her material (she didn't); (3) his last online service provider sold its account lists to a spammer (it didn't); and (4) Ace Computer sells all of its customers' financial information to the IRS (it doesn't).

Keep in mind the big difference between wrong facts (i.e., "My ISP sold its account lists to a spammer") and opinion (i.e., "Ace is a lousy company to work for"), especially since a negative opinion can be protected but bad facts won't be. The strongest defense, of course, is that the statement is true. For example, attorney Tom Mix *in fact* bribed a judge to get that last legal judgment against FXSX.

Businesses, Pseudonyms (FXSX), and Lawsuits

Businesses are now more sophisticated when the Net's involved. Public relations companies and law firms scour the Internet for any derogatory information against their clients, including whether postings are libelous or not. They search for any possible clandestine ties between their client's Web site and controversial places, such as pornography sites. These agents or company employees use search "robots" or "spiders" (software programs) to crawl through bulletin boards, Web sites, chat groups, and any other places where their business could be mentioned. They'll utilize sites (for example, see "ewatch.com") to check out discussion groups and Web sites for misuse of slogans and brand names, and will enlist similar services to track copyright infringement, piracy, and online sales of counterfeit goods.

Depending on the severity of the offensive material (as determined by the company), the "critic" receives no contact, a "cease and desist" letter, or a lawsuit. In numerous cases, businesses "let sleeping dogs lie"—an acknowledgement of the quick ability of surreptitious Web sites to multiply unexpectedly in mirror ways. The response depends on the facts of each case, who the CEO or attorney is, and just plain life. Given the massiveness of cyberspace with all its tiny towns and city-states, attorneys and their clients make daily policy decisions as to which sites they'll go after and which ones they'll leave alone.

Unhappy customers and employees are prime forces behind these critical postings. Given the tens of thousands of Internet discussion groups and the hundreds of millions of Web pages, it isn't too hard to see the enormity of the problem from a business and corporate viewpoint. And to this extent, unrestrained "free" speech does exist on the Net simply because of the enormity of policing all of it.

A distinction needs to be made, however, in our precious freedom of speech between when we are criticizing someone extensively and outright defamation. It is not defamatory for anyone to criticize others, provided these statements are true or a protected expression of opinion. Even if a business feels that a critical posting or Web site is unfair or even wildly inaccurate, courts tend to uphold the statement or site if what was posted has some basis in fact.

As just one example, type in the search word "suck.com," head to the Web site "sucks.com," or type your favorite name (such as Microsoft or IBM) with a "suck.com" after it, and watch the numbers of complaint Web sites that pop up. The best of companies—ranging from AOL and Wells Fargo to Verizon, Allstate, and even Harvard—have had their problems with these consumer complaint sites. Most of these "suck.com" Web sites are still in business, because courts typically consider their expressions to be protected by the First Amendment, provided the allegations are basically true or represent protectable opinion rather than false facts.

These sites belong to a variety of entities and people—from disgruntled customers and ex-workers to competitors, current employees (believing they have anonymity), and cybersquatters. As a protective measure, businesses have taken the preemptive move to secure and reserve "suck.com" or anti-domain names. For example, Bell Atlantic reserved "bellatlanticsucks.com" to keep anyone else from using it in a derogatory way; similarly, UPS signed up for UPSstinks.com, IHateUPS .com, and UPSBites.com. In total, Johnson & Johnson locked up 43 anti-J&J names, Stamps.com took six, and Wal-Mart locked up more than 200 anti-domain names. In our example, Ace Drugs might register "Acesucks.com," "Ace'swild.com," "Aceyjerky.com," and so on.

Businesses faced with an operating "suck.com" complaint site take several tacks: ignore it, send threatening letters (which are usually ignored in turn), take legal action to force it out of existence (most aren't successful on free-speech grounds), or fight for the domain name. Most companies ignore these sites, believing that any other moves would just bring about more unwanted attention. The preferred mode of attack now is to challenge the "suck.com" domain name (if you are the registered or sole trademark holder of that name) under ICANN's policies. (See Chapter 13 further in this regard.) The odds of winning in this forum are higher and the legal expenses lower than with any other alternative.

FINDING FXSX'S TRUE IDENTITY

Let's say a search hound finds FXSX's postings and his graphic examples that "Ace Drug experiments cruelly on live cats and dogs." It doesn't. FXSX hates this company and found another ISP to continue his tirades after the first one ended his access. Your first thought might be: FXSX would be protected from lawsuits, given the basic anonymity that's the norm on the Net. Rarely does anyone ever use a real name there, and this is quite different from shareholder meetings in "the old days," when you could see people and learn their identity. You couldn't wear a mask then; now, someone simply adopts a pseudonym on the Web.

Ace isn't amused and decides to sue FXSX. The legal procedure begins with the filing of the lawsuit complaint (or cause of action) with the court. These lawsuits are typically filed in the city where the ISP (or the chatroom provider) is located. We discovered previously that the AOLs, Yahoos, and other ISPs of this world are not liable for the defamatory content posted on their online forums, provided they're not guilty of any complicity in those postings. However, although numbers of ISPs try to police their boards for accuracy and content, many others don't. They don't want to offend their subscribers. These ISPs choose to let the policing be done by the individual companies.

The filed lawsuit names numbers of "John Does." This is legal jargon for naming unknown parties to the lawsuit. Their real names are added later, after their true identities are found. The company next files a subpoena (demands for the desired information to be released) against the ISP or chat provider, to get the identity of the "John Doe" who posted the inflammatory remarks.

In this case, Ace serves a subpoena against the chat provider and demands the real name and address of the person who uses "FXSX." Although providers and ISPs have defenses against complying with such a subpoena, many routinely comply with such a demand—otherwise, they incur unnecessary legal expenses fighting on behalf of a user like FXSX (and they'll terminate his service anyway). If it turns out that the provider doesn't have on file the actual names of the anonymous poster(s), it does have their e-mail addresses. Ace Drug's lawyers, given the e-mail address of FXSX, can track back to his actual ISP or Internet provider. They'll make a similar demand, via another subpoena, for all the information about FXSX that his ISP has. Once Ace knows FXSX's identity, it's easy to hire a service processor or marshal who, in turn, will knock on FXSX's door and hand him the lawsuit papers.

This happens every day in the real world. Lawyers serve subpoenas daily on CompuServe, AOL, Yahoo!, Microsoft, and others, to retrieve some poster's identity. If the ISP doesn't cough it up, then the attorney heads into court to ask a judge to force the ISP to divulge this information. The judge balances the right to protect someone's anonymity versus the company's right to be protected from harm. The plaintiff, or company, usually must show that it cannot get relief without obtaining this information.

And don't think that virtual evidence for some reason isn't real or admissible—quite to the contrary. It's obvious that the e-mail text of FXSX's virtual correspondence (or anyone else's, for that matter) is sitting on his hard drive in the saved folder. *Erasing or deleting that data doesn't destroy them;* it's entirely possible that a tech expert can recreate them along with previous drafts. Keep in mind that deleting a file is more akin to removing where you can find that file, rather than erasing all of the bytes of information that comprise it. Additionally, think about all of the other places where this electronic evidence can be found or is hiding: the "sent" box of the e-mail sender, network back-up tapes, the sender's ISP records and backups, those of the systems that switched that e-mail on its way, the recipient's ISP and backups, and the recipient. *There are multiple places where virtual or electronic e-mail evidence shows up.*

A FEW CASES

A former doctor at Emory University School of Medicine came across a posting on a Yahoo! message board. It suggested that he had taken kickbacks from a urology company after giving his department's pathology business to the company and had been forced to resign over this. The message was from "FBIinformant," who later was discovered to be a former employee at that company and who disliked the doctor. In late 2000, a U.S. District Court judge awarded $675,000 to the doctor, all on account of that one anonymous Internet message.

One Oregon mortgage company filed a lawsuit alleging that several false postings on message boards operated by Yahoo! undermined the public's confidence in its stock. The posted information alleged that the company's executives had been "aiding and abetting" embezzlement of company funds. Other alleged defamatory comments were made about the company by posters using different screen names. After filing a "John Doe" lawsuit, the firm's next action was to subpoena Yahoo! to acquire the real names of the individuals who were behind the allegations. Once the attorneys knew who their "John Does" were, the rest would be easy.

American Eco and a former executive were awarded $8.3 million in compensatory and punitive damages against another online poster. This user wrote false statements about the company's chief financial officer that resulted in his suspension. The lawyers tracked down the real name behind the pseudonym that was used, filed a lawsuit, prosecuted it, and won this substantial verdict.

Internationally, an English court ordered a sandwich seller to pay "substantial" compensation for posting "personal details" about how to contact a business rival on a Web site that advertised the services of prostitutes. After receiving more than 100 telephone calls in two days, the plaintiff sued and won.

A Fort Worth, Texas, company sued a doctor's secretary who lived in Naples, Florida, over her posting of allegedly defamatory comments on Yahoo!'s Web site (headquartered in California's Silicon Valley). The secretary's access to the Internet was through an ISP located in Falls Church, Virginia. Her comments were about a lawsuit pending in Miami, Florida. The Texas-based company sued the secretary in Orange County, California, where the "messages resided or passed through," although Yahoo!'s headquarters were located 300 miles farther north, in Santa Clara, California, or Silicon Valley. These facts, which were confusing to even the involved parties, show how complex Internet lawsuits can become.

To Sue or Not to Sue

As you can tell from the above examples, these are very expensive legal actions. The average posting, of course, is not going to bring down this type of Armageddon. However, keep in mind that as the impact on the company goes up, the likelihood of litigation also increases. For example, rather than only giving his opinion that a firm is "poorly managed," a poster might tack on some false facts on a bulletin board and drive down the firm's stock.

The decision by any business (or individual) over what to do with a defamatory statement can be a difficult one. Companies have to balance the high costs of lawyers and courtrooms, not to mention the negative public relations and executive downtime, versus what they can achieve in return. For example, a lawsuit makes limited sense if the defendant has no money or the action would just give the "cybersmearer" more recognition. When the company is larger, suing an individual or smaller business might put that entity into an even worse light—in effect, saying that it can't take "a little criticism." *It might make more sense to take those budgeted legal dollars and invest them in more positive returns, such as public-relation efforts and community-awareness strategies.* For example, rather than earmarking lots of money for the lawyers, take that amount and donate one-half for a newsworthy community project, and the rest for a mass mailing of sharp-looking brochures about your business.

However, if someone does go too far with bad comments, then at least make a complaint to the ISP, pursuant to its policies. Don't take matters into your own hands and be equally defamatory in response. It's always better to get even by having the poster's access terminated. Or, if you must, hire an attorney when you've been truly damaged. The speed, breadth, and accessibility of the Net can bring higher damages than in non-online situations. But be sure to read Chapter 12, "Cyberlaw Dispute Resolution," before you head into an expensive court battle.

If someone, let's say, in France posts a "junk dog" comment about you then you might have to turn the other cheek—legally speaking, that is. It's very expensive to sue over defamation in different countries especially given the conflict of laws and jurisdictional questions. Try to limit your revenge by making termination demands on the ISP and pushing for a retraction with a demand letter. Leave the litigation to the most despicable of cases; otherwise, you'll be looking at the justice system the same way.

It's a good idea to keep in mind what Nancy Kerrigan, the world-class figure skater and Olympic medalist, discovered. When surfers entered her name into a search engine, they were directed also to a Web site in which her name appeared 32 times. The page contained 22 lines of obscenities, as well as numerous mentions of the words "free" and "video" to maximize the site's exposure to the search engines. The Web site also linked to a series of subscriber-based pornography sites. After Kerrigan's attorneys filed a lawsuit against the site, that site and its links disappeared from the Net. The good news is that she forced the operator to disappear; the bad news is that she won't be able to be compensated for any of the damages she had sustained.

As a practical matter, it is difficult to track down defamers who are sued but then disappear, only to reappear under a new and untraceable name. Along with First Amendment concerns, this is another reason why companies are reluctant to sue those who set up "suck.com" Web sites. Trying to shut down a critical Web site through a lawsuit is not only difficult legal-wise, but the outcome can even boomerang on you.

For example, Kmart once took exception to a critical Web site posted by a Brandeis University student. The company threatened the school with legal action, and Brandeis pressured the student into dropping the trademarked "K" from his site. He replaced it with an "X." Up to then, his site had received minimal "hits," probably no more than 200 (as the student estimated). When Kmart's PR firm talked about this particular case on CNN, the Web site became a focus of national attention, receiving over 10,000 hits in a six-month period.

THE RULES WHEN POSTING

The rules are easy. Don't "just post it like it is." It's easy for personal vendettas to become ugly on the Web—and defamatory comments last a lifetime there. It is better to be liberal in disregarding what someone says about you, and conservative in responding to them. And it does make a big difference whether you're posting "great gossip" about somebody else or reading it about yourself.

There is absolutely no need to back off from expressing your First Amendment rights as to your opinions on what does or doesn't make sense. Just limit your remarks and postings to facts, opinions, and reasonable statements. There's no need to "flame," be overemotional in your responses, or forge into an attack mode just because another person disagrees with you. That just buys you more headaches and downtime.

Basics on Rights of Privacy

The use of the word "privacy" doesn't mean the Constitutional "right of privacy" that courts oversee, such as the right of privacy sustaining the right to the use of contraceptives. Nor by this do we mean the Fourth Amendment and its Constitutional requirements, such as when a search warrant is required for police search and seizures in criminal investigations.

For this discussion, we are interested in the rights of people to keep private those facts and information that are important to them. There are two aspects to this right: (1) facts that you reveal about yourself to the public; and (2) facts about yourself that you want to keep to yourself. An example of the first is when you print your address on a check or reveal that you like wine when you buy a bottle and charge that on your credit card. Examples of the second aspect are how much money you make, whether you've declared bankruptcy, and your medical history.

The second aspect of privacy, or what you want to keep to yourself, is typically protected by the law. The first one is not. The law generally views what you choose to make public as being released from the privacy of your home and therefore not subject to legal protection. However, the Internet has put extraordinary demands on these distinctions, blurring what can or can't be protected in today's credit and technologically oriented era.

For example, people buy medicine for sleeplessness or depression and use their credit card, but they might want to keep this purchase information confidential and from others. Although what you read and watch on TV at home are private matters, these interests become part of the data compilation being collected on you when you purchase them by credit card, whether they're books (e.g., on serial killers) or videos (e.g., weight control or Zen Buddhism). These also are examples of what's typically referred to as "informational" privacy concerns.

Whether you own your own business or work for someone else, online or not, all of us are consumers. When your friendly retail chain offers a discount card that reduces the cost of your purchases, the information you put down on that application—your name, sex, income, employment, and other data—is given in return for the card. From food and liquor to medications and toiletries, what you buy with this card is registered to your account. Additionally, your credit card company has gained data on you that you've provided, ranging from the financial information and disclosures needed to get that credit card, to the purchases you make with it. Whether you purchase your products online, at a "brick and mortar" store, or both, all of this information is registered and stored somewhere.

Along with other consumers, let's say now that this personal data is sold (which shouldn't be a surprise). Supermarket chains, bookstores, discount stores, credit card companies, and other retailers sell to marketers and list brokers the information they have about your spending habits, your income, and what you can afford. At this time, there's no law in the United States (although there is in the European Union) that these entities must disclose to you how they'll use your information, nor are they required to gain your consent to this practice. In fact, you should know that credit card companies even have an agreement with the IRS to report to them any dramatic changes in a person's spending habits.

Is this entirely legal? Yes, in the United States. No, in many European countries. American law doesn't give much protection to individuals over what others can do with the information that's collected about them. This is why you receive all of that junk, snail, and spam e-mail. About the only privacy protection Americans have now is in their purchases or renting of videos. Under the Video Privacy Protection Act of 1988 (passed when people became outraged over the political disclosures about Judge Robert Bork's video rental habits when he was nominated for the U.S. Supreme Court), it is a crime to release the details as to what videos any person buys or rents. *However, there's no question but that this will change in the future. Various privacy bills are being considered on federal, state, and other-country levels. Stay tuned for further developments.*

Cyberspace and Cookies

Although it wasn't as technologically advanced then, this informational privacy concern existed before the Internet came into being. Prior to the coming of the "Age of Net," it was difficult to aggregate all of the data that retailers compiled. Once upon a time (and not too long ago), checkers manually rang up your purchases, checks were used more than credit cards, and no one had figured out how to put all of your purchases (business or personal) together into one envelope.

All of this has changed. The discount card you use at the supermarket automatically segregates all of your purchases into one account showing what you do or don't like. Credit cards and automatic debit cards (where your checking account is electronically debited) are used more and more each year, to the detriment of checks—all allowing massive accounts of what you spend, how much, and where. Automated Teller Machines (ATMs) sprang up to where you electronically get the cash you want without ever needing to talk with a human being. At the same time, all of this information about you is being sold to marketers who aggregate the data and decide whether you are a ripe candidate for one of their promotional programs. And they, in turn, can sell the same data to others.

Now add in the Internet and "cookies." A user leaves footprints every time he or she surfs the Web. It's no different than if you brought a supermarket "discount" card along with you every time you shopped on the Net, including the stores you visited when you didn't buy a thing. You don't have to identify yourself in a traditional retail store or carry a tag that identifies which departments you've already visited, but you do when you hit the Web. For this, you can thank "cookies."

Cookies have changed the face of the marketing world. When a user visits a Web site, the site can transfer a "cookie," or a piece of identifying information, on that user's hard drive, for "record-keeping" purposes.

Whenever a user visits a site again, that Web site recognizes the particular cookie that tells who the user is, what purchases were made before, what promotions he or she bought previously, plus interests, passwords, and amounts of other identifying information. The Web site can recognize what other sites were visited before (i.e., competitors) by searching to see what other cookies have been inserted. This cookie file is read every time you visit that Web site—and many other sites—because most Web locations are transferring and receiving cookie information when you surf other places. There is a wealth of information that Web sites have on you and many of your habits.

For the first time, this private information is being read, accumulated, and reread every time someone enters a particular Web site. Advertisers on that site receive an instant idea as to who's interested in what and when. With all of this information being accumulated, e-marketers can't wait to get their hands on it. And when the same marketers buy information not only from that Web site but from others that you've visited, they're able to compile a very accurate record of just who you are, your income, what you've purchased, and what you'll buy in the future, along with your prime interests, habits, and preferences.

So the problem is that everywhere you go on the Web, you're leaving footprints. Your ISP knows the moment you log on, as does the backbone service provider, not to mention all of those sites you visit. Everything you've said in a chat room is saved for posterity. At the same time, people can dig back through e-mail headers and cross-correlate with other online resources to put together more on your personal life. There are scant legal checks now on what your bank, security firm, or insurer can do with (or to whom they can sell) your personal and financial data. This includes the relative balances in your accounts, stocks you own, where you use your credit cards, and to whom checks are written.

Some Web browsers permit users to disable these cookie features. However, many Web sites deny access unless their cookies are accepted. If a site employs cookies to gain information on you, wouldn't you think it fair that the site operator includes a reasonable explanation of its collection and use of such data in an understandable privacy statement, and then precisely follows that statement? The great majority of customers give an emphatic YES.

All of us have privacy concerns, whether purchasing for business or personal reasons. *If you own or operate a user-oriented site, then you already know that customers won't patronize your site well until they feel secure that your operations safeguard their privacy and data security concerns. In this case, you will want to have in place—and follow—reasonable online privacy policies.* (See Chapter 9, "Web Site Disclaimers and Protections," for more on this important point.)

Poll after poll finds that the issue of privacy is paramount in the minds of all Net users. For example, the Boston Consulting Group's 1998 poll of 15,000 users (an excellent sample size) found that two-thirds of the respondents would abandon a Web site if there were no policies for safeguarding the personal information that was accumulated at that location. Later studies came up with the same conclusion: two-thirds of consumers worry about the online misuse of their personal data. And Internet firms have lost billions of dollars in sales, owing to just those fears.

The Public's Concern

Time and time again, dot.com companies and Web sites seem to misjudge the American public when it comes to privacy concerns. For example, Mattel officials apologized for adding a data-gathering program to aspects of its Learning Company unit's educational programs for children. It promptly ended the practice. Companies from Intuit to Netscape have been under public scrutiny because they used their products in gathering information, and some users complained. To date, the two companies that stand out are RealNetworks and DoubleClick—and there are more.

REALNETWORKS

In late 1999, the media reported that RealJukebox software, which can record and play CDs as well as download digital music (including MP3) from the Internet, continually transmitted personal information over the Internet about its users to its owner, RealNetworks. This data included the user's music preferences, the music files stored on the computer, the type of portable player in the hard drive, the quality level of the recordings, and other information—all tagged with a unique number. Because software users were required to disclose their e-mail address and ZIP code during the registration process, this personalized data would be sent to Real-Networks in instant transmissions and could be used for marketing campaigns, as well as potentially reporting copyright violations.

RealNetworks first announced that they had released a patch on their Web site that would prevent the program from relaying personal information about users to the company or to third parties. Two weeks later, two class-action lawsuits were filed in different states, accusing RealNetworks of violating its users' privacy by tracking their music listening and downloading habits without telling them. Later, RealNetworks stopped this practice and apologized to the public. The company is currently recognized for having developed the latest in software for transmitting digital audio and video programs over the Internet, all in competition with Microsoft.

DOUBLECLICK

If this wasn't bad enough at the time, DoubleClick then came along. The media reported, in early 2000, that the Internet's largest advertising company had quietly begun tracking consumers' online activities by name and address (the company's main business has been the selling and delivering of banner ads). DoubleClick's program also inserts cookie files on every computer used to visit its ads, allowing it to accumulate a large base of information on these visitors. This cookie data is tagged to the computers, but not to individual names and addresses.

The company later acquired Abacus, a large offline database. Abacus had accumulated records on nearly 90 million individuals and households from magazine subscriptions and catalog purchases—and that effort neatly complemented what DoubleClick was doing. The Abacus database and the new program would allow DoubleClick to merge its database of anonymous consumer information with a database that identified consumers by name—in short, DoubleClick gained the ability to identify its online and offline database by individual name and address.

A firestorm from consumers' advocates and ad customers ensued when these disclosures were made. Lawsuits were filed, and the FTC announced that it was investigating the proposed practices. Later in 2001, the FTC announced that it was dropping its investigation, although DoubleClick still had to contend with the class-action lawsuits and the investigations by states' attorney generals. However, it is working on a more acceptable way to match the cookie number with the person's offline data, but not have this data associated with a specific person's online activities (which sounds like a contradiction in terms).

Congress, the Industry, and Europe

The Federal Trade Commission (FTC) has had a "self-policing" policy, and it generally promotes industry self-regulation in the fields of data collection and customer profiling. Although the FTC promotes self-regulation, it has been pushing businesses to voluntarily formulate reasonable privacy policies to allay their customers' fears. Its hope was that this positive publicity would prompt more businesses to formulate reasonable privacy policies and forestall legislation regulating the privacy of customers. In response, more than 100 companies came together to form the Online Privacy Alliance (this business-oriented Web site is located at privacyalliance.org). The Direct Marketing Association, Microsoft, IBM, America Online, and others joined to help push other companies into establishing what they deem to be appropriate privacy policies.

Currently, dozens of Congressional leaders have offered (or are planning to offer) privacy-related bills. Even as they debate and enact their own legislative forays into the privacy area, some states have joined together to recommend to Congress broad federal protections that would also allow states some leeway in adopting even stronger rules. *It is only a question of time before federal legislation is passed to mandate privacy protection in some way for Internet users* and preempt the differing state laws. It appears that "opt-out" (the user must take the step to say "no") legislation would be first approved, as it is less marketing-restrictive, followed later by "opt-in" (the company must gain the user's okay before collecting any private data).

Congress already passed legislation dealing with the online privacy protection of children when it enacted the Children's Online Privacy Protection Act (COPPA) in 1998. This requires Web sites that are earmarked to children or that knowingly collect data on kids under age 13: (1) to obtain verifiable parental consent for this use (i.e., "no consent, no collection"); and (2) upon request, to provide the parent with the opportunity to review the personal information that has been so collected. The FTC has issued administrative rules on COPPA to guide these "kiddie" Web sites in the details of complying with this statute.

As Congress continues to review various privacy provisions, what will eventually survive these deliberations—and the inevitable court challenges—remains to be seen. It is anticipated that Congress will eventually enact (including follow-up legislation) bills regulating the use of unsolicited e-mail (spam), the sharing of personal information, and the use of encryption technology (a way to balance users' confidential needs versus those of the police to combat crime). The banking, finance, and insurance industries already have been subject to federal legislation, requiring them to disclose their information-sharing practices, privacy policies, and an "opt-out" provision. However, the response of numerous institutions in supplying confusing statements and burying the "opt-out" right was subject to widespread criticism. It is likely that these industries will be subject to further, more consumer-sensitive privacy restrictions; and these privacy protections will eventually be expanded to most major commercial areas. However, nothing is clear-cut, and the battle between the powerful commercial interests and consumer lobbyists is and will be a continuing strong one.

The differences between the United States and the European Union (E.U.) couldn't be more pronounced today than in the rights-of-privacy area. The U.S. basically believes in an unregulated "laissez-faire" approach to the issue of protecting the average consumer's privacy rights. The E.U.'s Data Protection Act, which came into force back in 1998, utilizes a completely different approach. Citizens gained enhanced rights to access their personal information, including rights to prevent the processing of their information in defined situations and even to ban "junk" mail. Further, pursuant to the E.U.'s Directive on Data Protection, which took effect in October 1998, E.U. countries may block the transfer of personal data regarding its citizens to countries that do not guarantee adequate privacy protections.

The United States and the European Union negotiated guidelines that serve as a "safe harbor" for U.S. companies that want to receive personal information from their subsidiaries and operations in the E.U. Effective since November 2000, this agreement requires U.S. companies operating in the E.U. to disclose how they use personal information, give European consumers a chance to stop their data from being released, and offer an impartial dispute-resolution service, among other strong privacy requirements. In return, U.S. businesses that elect to apply these privacy rules won't be prosecuted under the E.U.'s tough privacy laws. These laws require that all companies gain the consumers' prior approval ("opt-in") before their personal data can be sold or shared—which puts pressures on these businesses to put "opt-in" measures throughout their operations.

A U.S. company can elect to comply with this safe harbor by self-certifying to the Department of Commerce that it agrees to be bound by these privacy principles. (See www.export.gov/safeharbor/ for the details.) To date, only a small number of U.S. companies have so elected; most are waiting to see what happens with those who do. However, the program received a strong boost when Microsoft, in mid-2001, announced that it would sign and abide by the "safe harbor" agreement to allow the transfer of personal data to it across the Atlantic. The company strongly endorsed the concept of businesses taking these types of actions to counter the growing consumer anxiety over online privacy.

These transcontinental data movements and other nations' legislation are ensuring that the United States will join the E.U., eventually, in an "opt-in" system. The only question is: By when? For example, Canada's *Personal Information Protection and Electronic Documents Act* began to take effect on January 1, 2001, in three stages: (1) its federally regulated private sector and international exchanges where transmitting data is the transaction, in 2001, such as marketing lists or credit reporting; (2) health care in 2002; (3) by 2004, all commercial transactions involving personal information must allow Canadians the right of an "opt-in" system, including obtaining their consent to use data collected before the Act's effective date. All companies that receive or disclose any personal data about a Canadian citizen must comply with this legislation, and the Act applies to all Canadian citizens, no matter where they reside.

Add to this, Amazon.com.uk (in England) came under fire in 2001 with accusations that it transferred data about its British customers to the United States. Although it offered its British customers an e-mail link allowing them to stop the transfer of any of their private data to third parties, Amazon denied the charges that it was violating English law by collecting and "repatriating" this information back to the less stringent laws of the United States. The United States, in time, will come to where the rest of the world appears to be heading in regulating the virtual collection and transference of private information.

Rights-of-Privacy Responsibilities

It is taking the combined efforts of Web operators and users to settle this privacy issue, along with the efforts of the courts and legislators. For Web sites to attract customers, whose major concern is protecting their privacy and security, locations must responsibly ensure their visitors that their private information won't be misused. Whether purchasing for business or personal purposes, customers must also take full responsibility to watch out for themselves.

WEB PRIVACY STATEMENTS

Responsible Web businesses are doing what they can to gain the public's trust in their safeguarding privacy. They know that this makes a difference in their sales—and the surveys, as we have seen, bear this out. Whether you are operating a Web site or buying products from another, take the time to compare the privacy policies of your site, or other sites, with those of competitors. Other customers already are doing this.

It makes sense that users should limit their purchasing to sites with proven privacy policies. Given that employee training in the use of these procedures is also present, operators with reasonable policies have better safeguards in place than an unfamiliar Web site with none. In fact, IBM announced that it would limit its

All privacy policies should: (1) be clearly and prominently displayed; (2) tell users in understandable language what data is being collected and for what purpose; (3) disclose to whom the information will be transferred and why; and (4) indicate how consumers can gain access to and remove themselves from this data acquisition. The policy should contain a clear explanation of the company's particular use of cookies and other technology.

advertising in the United States and Asia–Pacific Rim countries to only those Web sites that have posted a privacy statement and follow it.

However, because there's a difference between what people say and what they actually do, this is still a "caveat emptor—buyer beware" Net world. And customers realize this. To help meet this reality, organizations like the Better Business Bureau (the "BBBOnLine" seal; see "bbbonline.com"), Truste ("truste.org"), and WebTrust ("webtrust.org") offer Web-site privacy seals for online businesses that wish to so assure their customers. These seals of "good housekeeping" approval are awarded after the Web site meets certain privacy criteria and pays an annual fee. The criteria depend on the seal company, but most listings involve the seal-bearer disclosing privacy practices, allowing outside audits by third parties, and providing consumer "opt-outs" on data sharing, dispute-resolution services, and access to their data. By adding a privacy seal from a recognized company, a Web site gains another way to assure its customers that their privacy concerns are being addressed.

Although these seal companies are a good start, they aren't the complete solution to this problem—users shouldn't just rely on the "look and feel" of a site's privacy policy and the presence of a seal. As just one example, Toysmart.com abandoned its privacy promise after the company experienced financial difficulties, and tried to sell, for cash, its customer list of 250,000 names, addresses, credit card information, and other important data. Truste, the privacy seal entity that issued the privacy promise for the company, took Toysmart.com to court to block that sale. Walt Disney (a majority shareholder of Toysmart) finally agreed in 2001 to buy the list for $50,000 and put an end to these privacy disclosure fears.

CYBERSPACE RESPONSIBILITY

Each of us has an obligation to watch out for our business and ourselves when we navigate through the expanse of cyberspace. Check out the nonprofit, volunteer Web sites on privacy (see, for example "epic.org") and review the data they have on the latest developments, as well as any sites that have been flagged for privacy violations. Consumers should try to know beforehand which locations are in trouble with the FTC, other agencies, and consumer privacy groups.

There are sites that provide, for a fee, commercial blocking software that will work to hide your identity when surfing the Net. See the Web sites of Anonymizer.com, Zero-Knowledge (zeroknowledge.com), Freedom Site (freedom.net), SafeWeb (safeweb.com), and PrivaSeek (persona.com), among others, for this software and services. Amazon.com has a program where users may surf anonymously for free with delayed responses in their interaction with sites; if an annual fee is paid, then users receive a much faster result. You can buy "firewall" software that can specify, for example, that names, credit card numbers, and other sensitive information are to be blocked from leaving your computer. The problem is that programmers can electronically mask that data, so sensitive information can still pass through. However, taking reasonable steps will minimize unwanted data disclosures.

TAKING PROPER PRECAUTIONS

Don't join sites indiscriminately and use common sense. If you are careful about the locations you use or join, then you will receive less junk e-mail and have less exposure. You should review a site's privacy policies, as other customers do, and watch for the legal phrases that a truck could drive through. For example, one site promises profusely to safeguard your privacy, then states: "We may release account information, pursuant to a valid advertising agreement that meets all provisions of the law." When you find this phraseology, be careful.

Rather than purchasing from many sites, you're better off to patronize the best of a lesser number. By doing this, you can cut down on some of that worthless junk e-mail (or worse) that you receive later. Be efficient and selective when purchasing. *Additionally, make requests that you or your business can "opt-out" of having any personal data released outside that site. If you have a good-sized commercial account, the odds are that the requests will be honored.*

Guard your password closely and do not give it out freely. If anyone asks for your password or other sensitive data—even if the request is from your ISP—ask for proper identification and ascertain that this is a valid request before giving anything out. You could set up a throwaway mail account at a free Web service (i.e., Yahoo or Hotmail) and use it—along with an assumed name—whenever you're required to fill in a survey to gain access to a site (admittedly, there can be an ethical argument on this tactic). This caution applies, of course, to giving out any data that is important to you or your business. You should analyze a Web site's stated policy on its safeguarding or encryption of your credit card information, both from the outside world and its employees. (Note: A good source of consumer tips is the nonprofit Privacy Rights Clearinghouse at www.privacyrights.org.)

You can use different passwords for different needs. For example, use one when you're searching for information, and then use an entirely different one when you're purchasing. It makes sense to use a third one only in important financial situations—for example, if you access your stock portfolio on the Web. You should create passwords with random characters, rather than common words. It's more difficult for a scammer to come up with "R2A7K9" than to fool around and type in "Love" or "Moon."

Sending e-mail is not an absolutely private matter, whether it's in transmission or held by the recipient (who's free to edit or resend from there). Consequently, don't put anything into an e-mail that you wouldn't want to see posted on a bulletin board. You'll also want to check your online server for ways to reduce junk e-mail, including the use of filters. ISPs are concerned with protecting their subscribers from junk mail, so talk to your ISP regarding the most effective ways to eliminate this headache. And remove yourself from the mailing lists of Web sites that you don't use often.

When you receive junk-mail messages, as all of us do despite the precautions, it makes sense to just delete them. Don't open them to see what's being offered; you can never tell what's inside. Hitting the "reply" button and typing in the message of "DELETE" or "REMOVE" just doesn't seem to work either, especially when the "REMOVE" e-mail returns to you for lacking a proper address. It's also good sense not to download or open any attachments from unknown sources; you're only increasing the odds of introducing a destructive virus into your system.

Are you really concerned over spam and security problems? Netscape Messenger and Outlook Express offer filters that will allow only users in your address book to send you mail. This is not usually a good solution—you also won't be unable to receive e-mail from anyone new. Aside from using common sense in what you download or register with, you can also: install the latest in virus protection, only open e-mail received in response to yours, and talk with your tech expert. There are technical weapons at your disposal, such as installing firewalls (see Chapter 16 further), and checking out your browser's preferences (i.e., to reject unwanted cookies), and clearing those cookies from your memory. Also, be sure to use encryption or secure transmission modes when sending sensitive data over the Net. The Junkbusters (junkbusters.com) and National Consumers League (nclnet.org) sites offer sensible advice on ways to avoid spam and privacy problems.

If you have children, then you should explore the Internet with your kids. It's the best way to see what they look for online. Explain why they should use the same caution that you do when surfing—and take an interest in what they're doing. Consider using a filter that allows you to place certain sites and subjects off limits (ask your ISP about these controls or where you can get them). You must set down reasonable rules with your children, such as: (1) you will look, with them, at all privacy policies and memberships, before your child joins anything; (2) the absolute one: no purchasing, unless you're around; and (3) your family will agree on the times when your children can be on the Net and when they should be doing homework or household chores.

The First Amendment

Although beyond the scope of this book, numbers of lawsuits are being fought to define the role that the First Amendment and its freedoms of speech and expression will have in shaping our Internet. For example, cases have been brought involving ISPs and databases that offer subscribers the ability to view information from public records (i.e., motor vehicle records). In one case, this information was used to track down and harass abortion clinic patients. The question involves the extent under the First Amendment to which database companies may disseminate public information that can be used in unanticipated or hurtful ways.

Other lawsuits have involved whether potential domain name operators have the right to register profanity-laced—the "seven dirty words" made famous by comedian George Carlin—names with domain-name registries. The name registrars have denied them that "right," and these decisions will carve out another part of Constitutional Net law. A federal judge ruled that an operator of a Web site could publish confidential Ford Motor Company documents regarding new car designs and other data, in what she described as a dispute between protection of trade secrets and freedom of speech.

Lawsuits over employers' Internet-use policies, provided the policies are reasonable, have been generally upheld in the employers' favor. The courts so far have not been receptive to employees' claims that work done on an employer's computer system is personal and entitled to Constitutional protection. Employers' use of Web-filtering software (where workers' e-mails are subject to scrutiny) is also under challenge; most legal scholars feel that these challenges won't be sustained.

Lawsuits dealing with pornographic Web sites and federal laws continue unabated every year. The litigation will go on and on, as lawyers and the courts carve out what the role of the First Amendment and U.S. Constitution will be in cyberspace. These legal conflicts will continue in defining when consumer profiles may be sold and the rights of Web users to keep their personal data secure, notwithstanding a slow-paced legislative environment.

CHAPTER
7

"Great Deals," "Easy Money," and Other Ads

The Web is based on selling products, services, and information. The problem is that the ease of entry into selling on the Net encourages fly-by-night firms to race in, skim off the money, and then disappear without a trace—leaving their customers holding the proverbial empty bag with no goods, empty promises, or half-filled orders. This happens regardless of where you live; the Web has indeed become global in when and how the unwary can be fleeced.

This chapter deals with fraud and scams, while Chapter 10 ("What If You Get a Lemon?") deals with product problems originating with apparent legitimate operators. The vast amount of advertising glitz that litters today's sites increases the risk of coming across misleading ads and facts, especially when you can't talk face-to-face with someone, or "kick the tires" of the products you want. Thus, everyone needs to be careful when dealing with potential online investments, suppliers, or manufacturers on the Net, especially paying close attention to those sites not heard of or dealt with before. This doesn't mean you shouldn't deal with small or unknown Web businesses, but just be sure to check them out before you do. Keep in mind that scammers target small-business owners and stock investors.

Buying products has always been an experience, whether you're shopping online or at a "brick and mortar" store. Every one of us has purchased something and then felt later that the item wasn't worth it or we had been "ripped off." When you buy a product from a retailer in your area and later discover it's a dud, you have an actual place to go to and demand the return of your money. However, it's a different matter when you're online and that digital office equipment supplier or furniture retailer is physically located thousands of miles away. For example, the FTC brought cases in 2000 against various defendants who operated Internet auction scams, including one where the defendants advertised computer software and electronic office equipment at various e-auction sites. These sites took cashier's checks in payment, but never delivered the products.

The "great deals" offered ranged from discounted Alaskan cruises and work-at-home schemes to nondelivered office supplies, computers, and even Beanie Babies. In that case, opportunists placed ads on AOL for the sale of discontinued Beanie Babies. Customers sent money orders or wired payments up to $5,000, but received nothing in return or, in some instances, damaged dolls. Although the people behind this were subsequently indicted on wire fraud, this wasn't much solace to those who had lost their money.

If the dollars spent are small when this has happened, then it's called a "learning experience." However, these problems can become real headaches when you've parted with a good sum of money. Although all fraud hits the pocketbook, really big dollars can be lost if you jump naively into an online investment or business opportunity.

Consider this example. One Charles Huttoe and 12 others secretly distributed to their friends and family nearly 42 million shares of Systems of Excellence, Inc., known by the ticker symbol "SEXI." In a classic "pump and dump" scheme, Huttoe drove up the price of the SEXI shares through false press releases claiming nonexistent, multimillion-dollar sales, a fictitious acquisition, and fraudulent revenue projections. He also bribed his codefendant, SGA Goldstar, with SEXI stock to tout SEXI to subscribers in its "Whisper Stocks" newsletter. Huttoe and Ted Melcher, the publisher of the online newsletter, were sentenced to federal prison and four others pled guilty to criminal charges. However, that didn't help the people who bought upwards of $100 million of the company's stock and lost everything.

The Law and Regulatory Agencies

No matter what state or country you live in, the law is quite clear: (1) any Web advertisement of illegal transactions under a particular country's or state's laws (i.e., gambling or usury) will be illegal there; (2) fraudulent, false, or misleading statements aren't enforceable, no matter where you live; and (3) the regulatory agencies in different states and countries vary widely in their ability to crack down on misleading advertising, even when customers have lost all of their money. These basic legal rules apply whether you're buying stocks, business opportunities, or chairs.

Whether they are buying for business or personal reasons, scammed consumers can complain to government agencies and bring lawsuits. Courts will not enforce illegal or fraudulent contracts entered into because of the misleading statements of another party. Let's say that you receive an online promotional e-mail in which Discount Office Retailers announces that it's selling inkjet cartridges for just $40.00 (plus $5.00 shipping). You place an order and give your credit card information. When the cartridges are delivered to you, the bill is for $50.00. It turns out that there was an undisclosed $5.00 handling charge. This is a classic case of fraud, and you don't have to go through with this transaction. If you were in business and bought 2000 of these cartridges, then you could sue in court to get your money back—and file a complaint with a governmental agency.

However, suing in court will force you to pay upfront for expensive attorneys' fees and court costs, and, in many cases, the scammer has already spent the money. If you do obtain a court judgment, then it's quite likely that you'll never be paid back. Governmental agencies will chase after scammers at no cost to you, and they'll try to force them to pay back what was defrauded. The problem again is that you can't "squeeze blood from a turnip"—if the con artists have already spent the money, any chance of payback is long past. *The moral of the story: It's better to spend your time in the beginning to review closely any proposed investment or "large ticket" purchase, than to spend it later trying to get your money back.*

In the United States, the Federal Trade Commission (FTC) is the federal agency that's charged with prohibiting unfair or deceptive commercial acts, including misleading advertising. (Fraudulent investments are handled by the SEC.) The FTC has dealt with countless numbers of fraud and misleading ad complaints in its effort to stop such unfair practices, both online and offline. (Note: The U.S. also created the National Infrastructure Protection Center, www.nipc.gov, to coordinate efforts against hackers, tech terrorists, and viruses.) Further, individual state laws and agencies concerned with consumer protection handle local problems that the FTC won't or doesn't get involved in; basically, the FTC covers widespread or multistate Internet frauds.

Individual states have enacted their own particular Internet regulatory statutes. For example, California enacted a statute that requires out-of-state sites that market on the Internet to conform to California's standard policies regarding refunds, returns, and disclosure of various consumer information. The penalty for noncompliance includes fines up to $1,000 and six months in a California county jail. Other states have also extended their commercial law requirements to the Internet, having applied their prohibitions against fraudulent offline sales practices to Net advertisements.

Nevada became the first U.S. state to prohibit the sending of unwanted advertising (or spam) on the Internet. This law became effective in mid-1998 and imposed a $10 fine *per consumer* on advertisers who failed to give the recipient a return address plus a way to tell the sender to stop sending future ads. Numbers of others states (such as California, Virginia, and Washington) have followed, and you should check out the provisions in yours. The problem, of course, is enforcing these statutes when a spammer can so easily erase one location, then start up at another.

Whether you operate a Web site or not, everyone should be familiar with the roles of their respective state and federal governmental consumer protection agencies. When a question or problem comes up, head to the applicable Web sites and find out what safeguards and laws apply. When you don't do your homework at first, many of the agencies (including the FTC) take online complaints.

The FTC

The FTC oversees numbers of U.S. laws and regulations. As well as overseeing unfair, deceptive, or misleading commercial advertising, this agency also regulates the selling and operation of business opportunities and franchises. The basic rule is that franchise and business opportunity sellers must give potential buyers of franchises a detailed disclosure document at least 10 days before the person pays any money or legally commits to a purchase. There can be exemptions to this rule if a state has similar requirements. If you've received a promotional e-mail to invest in some business opportunity without what seems to be a reasonable disclosure of the risks, or it's a "get rich" scheme, then contact the FTC—and fast! *Check out its Web site at www.ftc.gov.*

This agency also becomes involved in the investigation, regulation, and prohibition of varying multilevel marketing schemes. For example, pyramid schemes are a fast growing part of Net scams, especially when commissions are only paid to distributors for signing up new people who are "lower on the totem pole." Pyramid schemes are illegal in most states, so if you've received an e-mail touting one of these, then you should immediately contact your local state consumer protection agency and the FTC. To be legal, marketing schemes at a minimum must pay commissions for the selling of retail goods or services, not for only recruiting new distributors.

The FTC also is involved in enforcing truth-in-lending laws, such as the three-day right of recession when a lender is making a loan to finance a car or home purchase. The FTC also is responsible for monitoring the Fair Credit Reporting Act, which, among other provisions, requires credit bureaus and resellers of consumer reports to give consumers the ability to contest the accuracy and completeness of their credit report.

The activities this agency oversees are too numerous to list here. Review its Web site (ftc.gov) for further information, especially if you've received promotional material to invest in a business, or you feel you've purchased a real lemon. Given its general mission to prohibit unfair trade practices and protect consumers, the FTC has specifically earmarked the Internet as a prime target.

"TOO GOOD TO BE TRUE" ADVERTISING

The Internet is especially designed for rip-off schemes, given the ease with which scammers can spam so many of us at one time with "get rich" e-promotions. *In response, the FTC's rules and regulations against unfair or deceptive advertising specifically cover Internet transactions.* This agency has pursued pyramid schemes and fraudulent business opportunities that were hyped in cyberspace, and it has gone after bogus online claims for services and products. The FTC has pursued ISPs that crammed unwanted services to their users through purportedly free offers, and the agency has pursued the misleading practices of fly-by-night operators who "fleece today, then flee by tomorrow."

The FTC routinely scours the Web for evidence of scams and investigates complaints on misleading advertising. People can state their complaints directly on the FTC's Web site. Listed according to the amount lost, the first batch of the FTC's "Top 10" online scams are: identity theft, investments, business opportunities and work-at-home schemes, sweepstakes and lotteries, vacations and timeshares, pyramids and multilevel marketing, ISP and computer complaints, and Internet auctions. Small businesses and entrepreneurs are especially targeted, as 60 percent of all money lost during the year 2000 (by the FTC's own internal data) involved scammed investments, business opportunities, and work-at-home plans. The lost investments typically were from buying the promises of getting rich from day trading, oil and gas leases, gold, and gems that didn't pan out. The scam business opportunities sold by both spam e-mail and print ads ranged from medical billing and mobile car-wash operations to software and motivational tapes.

In 2001, the FTC opened up a Web site with statistics and information about Internet fraud and identity theft. The site is called "Consumer Sentinel" (see consumer.gov/sentinel), which started with a database of over 300,000 complaints lodged with the FTC over the past several years. The site had been previously restricted by password to law-enforcement officials around the globe, to provide one place for worldwide data sharing. Although part of this site is still password-restricted for law enforcement, it provides numbers of valuable tips, data, and the trends in the fraud area. It also allows for the online submission of complaints.

In one Internet cramming case, the defendants mailed $3.50 "rebate" checks to business and home consumers. When the recipients cashed the checks, they unwittingly agreed to allow the defendants to be their Internet Service Provider. The consumers found monthly charges placed on their telephone bills, and they learned that it was nearly impossible to cancel future bills or receive refunds. The FTC brought action and received a permanent injunction barring this practice.

A variation on cramming involves "Web cramming," or billing customers for a Web site page that they didn't even know they had. The "promoters" targeted small businesses and not-for-profit entities in their contacts to offer a "free" Web page. In place of this service, however, the customers found that their phone numbers were being billed monthly without authorization. One of the defendants was ordered to pay more than $3 million in damages and refunds.

One Web operator "page-jacked" 25 million Web pages and put the counterfeit versions on its Web site. Search engines then directed users to the counterfeit pages where "redirect" commands had been inserted. It made no difference whether the user clicked on a banner ad, kids' game, or some other icon, everyone was whisked away to the operator's sexually explicit Web site. Users were then "mouse-trapped" inside that location and couldn't escape easily, because the normal functions of their Web browser had then been disabled.

Another case involved visitors to an X-rated Web site where they were instructed to download a special program. Doing this instantly rerouted the unsuspecting victim's phone call from the local ISP to a phone number in Moldavia (a former Soviet republic). These phone charges were then billed to the caller at a much higher per-minute rate. According to the FTC, U.S. victims alone were billed for more than 800,000 minutes of calling time before the scam was finally shut down.

As seen in the Moldavia scam, fraud is sweeping around the world. From Asian and European countries to African and others, all nations are experiencing similar problems as seen in the U.S. The studies indicate that cybercrimes are the most feared of economic crimes for the near future by businesses, whether located in the U.S. or not.

Due to these concerns, the United States and 15 other countries agreed in mid-2001 to join forces to fight international consumer fraud. Countries already participating in this joint effort are: Australia, Canada, Denmark, Finland, France, Germany, Hungary, Japan, Mexico, New Zealand, Norway, South Korea, Sweden, Switzerland, and the UK. The U.S. Federal Trade Commission is leading the project, which has two thrusts: one is a multilingual Web site (www.econsumer.gov) where anyone may direct a consumer complaint involving these countries; the second is a database, password-protected Web site for law enforcement officials around the world with which to share their leads.

As the FTC is using its existing Consumer Sentinel Web site (www.consumer .gov/sentinel) and network to coordinate this effort (and is responsible for maintaining the econsumer site, as well), you can head to the Consumer Sentinel site to make a complaint for any country not covered by the other. *If you have any Internet fraud problems involving different countries, head to www.econsumer.gov (which has direct links to consumer fraud agencies in the listed countries) and www .consumer.gov/sentinel for others.*

The FTC also has created different "informational" Web sites on potential scam areas. For example, when surfers type in the words "arthritis cure," one of the Web sites they could be directed to is entitled "ArthritiCure." Its home page reads: "Be pain-free FOREVER! Read our testimonials! Only $19.95." When you click anywhere on ArthritiCure's home page, the message then reads "You could have been SCAMMED!" and gives advice on how to recognize fraudulent health claims. This Web-site product doesn't exist, but the FTC established the location as part of its consumer education on questionable marketing strategies.

Given the technological world we live in, some online operators actually programmed their sites to block out the snooping FTC or other agencies. In response, the FTC's Internet lab has worked on creating software to overcome those filters. Its staff members also are logging onto suspicious Web sites as potential customers, just to see what's going on.

The role of the FTC isn't limited to scam artists; it also includes quite respected businesses. In late 1995, Dell Computer Corporation advertised a bonus CD-ROM as part of its systems, but couldn't ship the CD-ROM with those systems due to production delays. In lieu of this product, Dell included coupons that could be redeemed for the CD-ROMs when they were ready to be shipped (which sounds fair enough). The FTC claimed that Dell should have offered buyers the option of either consenting to the delay in shipping or canceling their orders; Dell consented to the FTC's order and offered the option. In April 1998, Dell agreed to pay an $800,000 fine to the FTC, based on the agency's charges that it failed to include software that it promised with other shipped systems.

Iomega agreed, in late 1998, to pay another large fine ($900,000) to settle FTC charges that it failed to fulfill an online promised rebate and free merchandise program linked to the purchase of its portable data storage products. Both Dell and Micron, in 1999, reached settlements with the FTC regarding its allegations that the two companies used misleading print and online ads with computer leases that failed to include certain cost information in conspicuous places.

A few years ago, AOL came in front of a FTC inquiry. The agency alleged that AOL offered a "free" trial period with no charge if the services were used within 30 days of signing on and the user didn't exceed 10 hours of use. However, if the user exceeded the 10-hour time limit or failed to cancel the membership, then the user was charged the requisite fees. The FTC charged that a monthly membership fee was added to certain hourly fees and that AOL billed another 15 seconds to each session without adequate disclosure. It further claimed that AOL charged user credit card accounts before it received the written authorization to do so. Among other provisions, AOL's consent agreement with the FTC provided that AOL could use the word "free" or its equivalent only when AOL clearly and prominently disclosed a user's ability to cancel or take other action to avoid the use fees. AOL further had to provide at least one way to cancel by a certain date to avoid the future charges. The FTC undertook similar measures with Prodigy and Compu-Serve at the same time.

Gateway, the second-largest (behind Dell) U.S. direct seller of personal computers, also became subject to FTC scrutiny and joined this large and powerful elite group. In 2001, Gateway agreed to settle charges that it had misled consumers with promises of free Internet service, according to the FTC complaint. The FTC charged that Gateway had failed to prominently disclose in its advertising that personal-computer buyers could incur long-distance charges if they accepted a "free" one-year subscription to Gateway.net. Juno Online also reached a settlement with the FTC on similar charges of undisclosed extra toll-call charges for Internet connecting services, as well as for telling consumers that they could cancel free trials of a premium Internet service at any time without incurring extra charges (which were assessed).

These companies more than likely weren't trying to intentionally mislead their customers. However, it only takes a few out-of-control marketing people to make the claims that get everyone in trouble. Only when customers felt that they didn't receive the full story and complained to the FTC (which then investigated and forced a settlement) were these companies called on the carpet. *If you operate a Web site, pay close attention to your virtual and off-line advertisements (and salespeople). Close any loopholes that customers could later drive through.*

THE STATES AND FRAUD

There is definitely more than enough business to go around, and the states have been equally busy with consumer protection on the Net. An Internet retailer firm called Onsale agreed to pay $160,000 in civil penalties, costs, and restitution for allegedly violating California's unfair business practices act. The Santa Clara County District Attorney's office and the State of California Attorney General's office investigated Onsale for apparently telling its customers that they could purchase their products at cost—or at the same price that Onsale paid distributors for those products—plus the transaction costs of processing the payments, shipping, and taxes. Their Web site claimed that there were no product "markups" and that the company made its profit only through the transaction fees. The authorities claimed that Onsale kept part of the consumers' shipping fees since the distributors paid for the products to be shipped to the customer. Onsale also agreed to better define its Web site's sales terms.

The Arizona Attorney General's office gained a consent agreement with Fry's Electronics. Although headquartered in California (which didn't have the same restrictions as Arizona), Fry agreed not to use the word "sale" unless there was a price drop of at least 5 percent on any item costing more than $100, and at least 10 percent off less expensive items.

The New York State Attorney General's office sued a business called the Woodside Literary Agency for posting messages in Internet newsgroups to solicit manuscripts from promising writers and charging various "reading, market research, and contract" fees. Woodside only promoted its business in cyberspace and ended up with numbers of dissatisfied customers who paid fees (but weren't published). A New York judge ordered the Queens-based company to reimburse those dissatisfied clients and post a $100,000 bond to cover future complaints.

As the Internet and opportunities grow, the likelihood that you'll come across a misleading situation also increases. It pays to be watchful.

The SEC

The primary mission of the U.S. Securities and Exchange Commission (SEC) is to protect investors and maintain the integrity of the securities markets. With records showing that first-time investors still turn to the equity markets for retirement, down payments for homes, and children's college funds, the stakes become higher.

The basic premise of the SEC is simple: Institutions and private individuals should have access to certain basic truthful facts about an investment, prior to making it. To achieve this access, the agency requires public companies to disclose meaningful financial information to the public, and it oversees the practices of stock exchanges, stockbrokers, and mutual fund industries. The SEC brings 400–500 civil enforcement actions each year against individuals and companies that break the securities laws. Typical infractions include insider trading, accounting fraud, and providing false or misleading information about securities. For further information, check out its Web site at www.sec.gov.

Additionally, states have enacted their own version of securities laws, called "Blue Sky Laws." They're called this because stock manipulators seem to promise investors everything, including "blue skies." State "Blue Sky" regulations apply to intrastate transactions (or deals within that state's borders), whereas the SEC is interested in interstate transactions, or those deals that cross state borders.

The Internet is an excellent tool for investors. It allows them to easily and inexpensively research investment opportunities. The Net is also an excellent tool for shysters, hipsters, and con men. Cyberspace allows people to communicate instantly with a huge audience, without needing to spend a lot of time, effort, or money to create these communication channels. Anyone with a computer and a modem can reach tens of thousands of potential investors simply by creating an attractive Web site, establishing a chatroom, and sending mass e-mails. It's easy for people who want your money to look quite real and credible, and it's nearly impossible for investors to tell the difference between what's true and what isn't.

As online investment newsletters proliferate, it becomes harder to tell which ones are best. Investment chatrooms become new "buyer beware" sites because it's too easy for people who claim to be innocent investors (and who made "a mint" on certain stocks) to pump up worthless stock. This doesn't mean that most of these chatrooms or Web sites are dens of thieves—you just need to exercise caution when you're in one. With the advent of bulk e-mail programs, spammers can reach millions of Net users at one time with messages that appear personalized and just for you.

In response to the new Internet environment, the SEC established a national cyberforce of attorneys, accountants, and analysts who have been specifically trained in online transactions. Its premise is that although it's easier to raise money from unsuspecting investors, it's also easier for the SEC to watch over and monitor what's going on. In fact, when the SEC announced recently that it would conduct a massive sweep of people who used investment newsletters, message boards, and Web sites to pump up stocks and give misleading information, investors sent in 900 more complaints to it.

It's important to remember that the SEC is not able to intercept most scams *before* investors lose money. As with the FTC, by the time the SEC has completed its investigation stage, many investors have already parted with their hard-earned cash—and they rarely get it back. Later, when these promoters are in jail and huge civil fines and judgments are levied, the investors' money has already been spent—typically, on lavish living and expensive criminal-defense attorneys. However, these complaints and actions do put those operations out of business.

Investors must take responsibility for watching over their money and investments. The rules for investing online are straightforward: (1) verify independently every claim made by a stock promoter by calling the company's major suppliers, customers, and bankers, being sure to check out management and analyze all financial statements (or get an accountant to do this); (2) check to see if the company has made any regulatory filings with the SEC or is subject to complaints; (3) check with your state security regulatory agency for the same filings or complaints; (4) contact the National Association of Securities Dealers (NASD, at www.nasdr.com) to see if it has any information on that promoter and the company; (5) talk with experienced pros in the investment business to see what they have to say about this potential deal; and (6) if the claims seem to be too good to be true, then be careful—they probably are.

Be especially wary if you receive solicitations from firms located outside the United States (or your country). In this case, you will have limited ability to check data, and it will be difficult to use any government agency effectively if your investment turns sour. Additionally, be careful with any online auctions or sales of stock. Be sure that the stock being sold is registered stock (approved by the SEC, or with an appropriate exemption) and can be legally sold by that seller.

The cases of online investment fraud continue and continue. For example, the SEC issued cease-and-desist orders against three individuals for illegally offering their securities over the Internet when they placed them for sale on an eBay auction site. The SEC charged two Southern California residents with securities fraud after they had raised $8.8 million by selling stock online; a U.S. District Court froze the assets of the men, who had wired $3.2 million of these funds to Hong Kong and diverted money for their own personal use.

One "entrepreneur" recruited investors for his company, Interactive Products and Services, in a public offering conducted completely over the Net. He raised $190,000 from 150 investors; however, instead of using the money to build the company, the promoter pocketed the money and bought groceries and stereo equipment. The SEC sued him civilly, and the Santa Cruz, California, DA's office prosecuted the man criminally. He was convicted of 54 felony counts and was sentenced to 10 years in jail—but the investors had lost all of their money.

And new scams are created every day. Two men offered "prime bank" securities. Sounds nice, doesn't it—but these type of securities don't even exist. They collected over $3.5 million by promising to double the investors' money in four months (it does sound too good to be true). The SEC went to court, froze their assets, and stopped them from continuing their scheme.

These fleeces can occur in minutes. Another "entrepreneur" created a bogus online news release that caused the shares of one company to fall 60 percent in a matter of minutes. The man then covered his short position (he sold at the high price and bought back at the low), netting nearly $250,000. The SEC brought civil and criminal securities-fraud charges.

A second-year law student at Georgetown University set up a free Web site promising investors hot tips on penny stocks. According to the SEC, the student, his mother, and two other law students, bought the stocks in advance of the tips, then sold them as soon as their Web followers bid up the touted stock prices. The stock values then plummeted back to earth, causing substantial losses for the unwary investors in what the SEC called another classic "pump and dump" scheme. The promoters netted nearly $350,000 in a matter of months. In settling the charges the SEC brought, the five people entered into a consent order not to violate any securities laws in the future. Visit the SEC Web site to see what areas you should avoid, including tips on spotting these classic schemes; this experience will be more pleasant than heading there later to e-mail a complaint.

Later, three California college students agreed to pay a total of $229,000 to settle SEC charges that they used the Net to manipulate the stock of a commercial printing company. Using school computers, they posted false messages under 50 aliases about a fictitious corporate takeover on 500 Internet bulletin boards. One of the students was sentenced to 10 months in prison. Another recent college graduate in this group manipulated 11 other stocks, and the SEC searched his assets to try to reclaim nearly $500,000 in profits that had been illegally gained. These cases show that the Net is so open that young college students with limited experience can manipulate stocks in large amounts.

Then there was the 15-year-old computer whiz in New Jersey who, in 2000, became the first minor to be sued by the SEC. By "pumping" up his stocks in investor chat rooms, then "dumping" them when others scrambled to buy the shares, the SEC charged that he had created an illegal stock manipulation scheme on the Net. Starting when he was 14, the kid earned nearly $275,000. Although neither admitting nor denying guilt, the minor agreed to give up the money he made, plus interest. The media reported that his father was proud of his child's accomplishments.

A mid-2001 FTC case involved a company that used spam e-mail to announce an initial public offering (nearly all of us have received one), stating that it had been approved by the SEC and would realize at least $1 billion in eyewear sales. In fact, the company had never been approved by the SEC and didn't even have offices or inventory. The owner of the company used the "invested" money in restaurants, casinos, and adult entertainment clubs. In another case, a company included hyperlinks on its Web site to reports by a supposedly independent analyst who praised the firm's operations and outlook. The reports were false and, in fact, the analyst had been paid 12,500 shares of the company's stock in undisclosed compensation for issuing those reports.

You must be wary in any investment. Check out all claims with reliable investment research sources before making any investment, whether it's on the Net or not. Keep in mind: What one person makes in these schemes is always other people's loss—and you don't want to be one of them.

Technological Illegality or Netiquette Violation?

Some Web sites employ this procedure: If users desire data about a nonadvertising company, they instead are immediately transported to the Web site of a competing company that has bought advertising on that site. For example, a prospective employee types in the name of a company he or she is interested in working for, but is immediately transported to the Web site of a competitor who paid advertising dollars for that right. Although legislatures haven't addressed this problem, this does smack of at least a Netiquette violation. And in response to a complaint by Commercial Alert, a consumer activist group, the FTC is investigating currently the allegations that some Internet search engines ensure, for a paid fee, that specific Web sites will appear prominently in any search results. The complaint argues that these practices are deceptive for not disclosing that payments are made for the results.

Excite and AOL's Netscape (the entity that licenses the Excite search technology) were the subject of a lawsuit brought by *Playboy* over Excite's display of a non-*Playboy* X-rated advertisement. Internet surfers seeking *Playboy*'s Web site would also use Excite as their search engine. When the user typed in the word "playboy" in the Excite search box, a banner ad (the strip of commercials at the bottom or top of a Web page) for an explicit pornographic Web site appeared at the top of the list of page sites generated. This ad site, however, had no connection with *Playboy*.

Playboy sued, claiming that this was an illegal misrepresentation and infringement for Excite to display a non-*Playboy* advertisement to a user who entered the trademarked words "Playboy" or "Playmate" in their search. The U.S. District Court judge agreed with Excite that there was no violation of *Playboy*'s rights in this matter, holding that *Playboy* did not have a monopoly on the generic use of the word "playboy" in English. The experts believe that eventually firms will be required to disclose when payments are being received for online preferential rights.

Sometimes, "dirty tricks" are played, such as when programmers trap a user inside a Web site without an exit after he or she hits a misleading link. For example, a banner ad appears at the top of a screen, and this looks quite like a system alert box. It conveys the meaning that something "bad" is about to happen with your connection, maybe even with your computer. You click the designated "OK" icon. An advertising company's home page suddenly appears. Finally understanding what's going on, you decide to click on the "Back" button to return to the previous page. However, instead of returning back, you find yourself at another popup box from that same advertiser. Your choice is to either look at the advertisement or disconnect your Net connection and redial (or other alternatives). This type of programming doesn't create friends—and this experience has happened to many of us.

Other classics include those nonrelevant sites that constantly spring up when we type in our selected keywords on major search engines. This waste of time, of course, is due to the friendly software programmers and their clients, who create metatags (HTML code words that attract search engines to that site) with search words that have nothing to do with that site. For example, a Web site on cooking recipes programs in metatags such as "sex" or "MP3." Some companies have gone so far as to put in the names of their competitors as metatags on their own home page, so that users wanting—let's say, IBM—also find *their* business, AcmeFree Software (that well-known giant of the industry).

Another trick is to keep surfers connected to a site, even after they have left it to try and go to another. The HTML code writer tells the browser to treat the desired link as a new window, which opens on top of the first one. This is what happens when you disconnect your Internet or ISP connection and find ads and other open windows still on your screen. Sometimes, Web sites will "page-jack" a competitor's page and create a duplicate of it on theirs, then trap the user inside their Web site. Competitors set up Web sites using a ".net" or ".org" to trap unwary customers. For example, the competitor of "AceDrug's.com" creates a Web site of "AceDrug's.org"—just to catch people like us.

Ads sometimes intentionally mislead you or display more information when you're trying to leave. For example, the banner ad is designed to look like a place you might want to see. When you click on that icon, you're staring at another ad of that same advertiser. We see ads disguised as a trivia question, a poll to fill out, or a form for a "free" something. All of us get caught in this.

Have you ever noticed how difficult it can be on some sites to find the necessary product disclosures and information (the industry term is that they are "avoidable"). Potential buyers must hunt for their location, and when they don't find them, they just might order that product anyway.

> Good sites make it easy for potential customers to get right to the heart of wanted product warranties, disclosures, and information—and their customers don't have to hunt and peck for this. They build good customer loyalty by not using programming tricks to capture users. Instead, they rely on their site's "look and feel," creative but truthful ads, quality products or services, and a good reputation.

A Few Rules of the Road

It is a "buyer beware" Net world out there. The commonsense rules to avoid being caught by fraud are: (1) be aware of where your order is being shipped from; it makes a difference if this is an unknown site located in the Bahamas or BestBuy.com's; (2) be always watchful for those "It's too good to be true" claims—they usually are; (3) use your credit card when at all possible (the credit card company will reverse the charges when fraud or poor quality is present), avoiding money orders, wire transfers, or debit cards like the plague; (4) check the FTC (or the applicable country's equivalent), your state consumer protection agency, and/or the Better Business Bureau to see whether the Web site has a checkered past or is under investigation—before you order; and (5) always check out a Web site's policies and practices before ordering (see the next chapter, "Purchasing on the Net," for the details).

The key is to use common sense to avoid becoming a victim. For example, you should be extra careful if the seller operates from a post office box or an e-mail address of "hotmail.com." It makes a difference if the seller is an individual selling an item in an online auction or a company with a physical presence in your state. Save all e-mail correspondence, warranties, and written promises, so you can send that along to the FTC if the seller doesn't deliver as promised.

Be especially cautious with large-ticket items, as you have more to lose. It makes sense to use an escrow agent with expensive items; this neutral third party receives the item from the seller, holds it for the buyer's inspection, then wires the money to the seller upon the buyer's approval. If the buyer doesn't approve of the product, then the escrow holder ships the item back to the seller and the buyer gets the money back from the escrow. (See the next chapter for more on this.)

When ordering from sites in other countries, remember that there are differences in laws and how fraud is handled. Given the distance and foreign jurisdictional problems alone, you're going to have a real hard time getting your money back if you've bought a real lemon—unless you're dealing with a reputable seller. *Check out your sellers or buyers before you deal, not afterwards.*

CHAPTER

8

Purchasing on the Net

Most individuals, small businesses, and entrepreneurs purchase over the Internet, rather than sell goods over it—not to mention what they do when they're home and buying for their own personal use. And whether you are an insurance agent, contractor, doctor, or real estate agent, you will use the Net more for information (or to provide this about yourself), than you'll sell or receive as clients from it. Accordingly, this chapter focuses on the considerations when you are purchasing goods and services over the Internet. *The considerations when you're buying products are the same as those you need to meet when the roles are reversed—your customers have the same concerns, and these need to be answered if you are to be successful.* These factors are covered more fully in Chapter 14, "Creating Your Own Web Site," and Chapter 16, "Web Site Operating Considerations."

When buying products or services, it's no secret that Internet purchasing can be the most seductive and impulsive buying opportunity ever created. Its simplicity and "laziness" when doing comparison shopping, plus the ability to purchase without leaving your chair and buy by typing in your credit card number with a simple "click," are all without parallel. In minutes, you can race around the world and rack up transactions. However, whether you're buying for business or personal reasons, you must use common sense on the Net, even more so than when you purchase items at a "brick and mortar" store.

Look Before You Leap

- *Surf more, spend less.* It makes sense not to impulse shop, at least on large-ticket items. You should do your comparison shopping *before* you head to a Web site to buy. There are numerous comparison sites, such as DealTime, mySimon, eBay, Priceline (of "name your own price" fame), and others. Try out consumerreports.com (the favorite for years) and productopia.com, which offer product ratings and information on volumes of business and consumer items. Various Web sites compare products on nearly any item that you want, so simply hit your search engines with the product word. It's easy to do your research first.

- *Products look different in person.* "Kick the tires" of potential purchases at a "brick and mortar" store and decide before ordering whether the product you're choosing is the exact one you want. Keep in mind how and where you'll return it, if it doesn't meet your specifications. At times, Net shopping at local, more traditional stores is a definite advantage. It is easier to return a computer or desk, for example, to the local Sears or Wal-Mart in your area (and they might have matched your best Net price), rather than repacking the item, hauling it to the post office, and shipping it back. You will also be spared the return shipping expense. Shopping at an Internet site that has a store in your area can be advantageous, not only in saving the cost of sales taxes (but check this out first) and being able to see the product before purchasing it, but also if you need later to return a lemon. Some of these considerations, of course, don't apply to generic goods—reams of paper or large bags of standard fertilizer—but you should check to see where and how you can return bad products for credit or repair.

- *Look carefully when buying from an unknown Web site.* Sites like officedepot.com, costco.com, walmart.com, officemart.com, and Amazon.com, to name a few, have had to be very consumer-sensitive, but this approach may not be the same at unknown locations. Look closely at all posted policies and think about what their promises are. What are their procedures if you need to get your money back? If the site hasn't posted its return, refund, and shipping policies, e-mail it to find out why they're missing and what they are. Look closely at the address. Is it in your country or not (if not, then you won't get help as from your local consumer agency), and is it a post office box or some weird address (which doesn't breed a lot of confidence)? This doesn't mean you shouldn't use unknown sites, just that you should be careful.

- *Check out the Web site's Terms of Use policies.* You want to have a good feeling about any new site, and this starts with understanding that location's policies. Missing, confusing, and too long or complex polices are equally suspect. You'll want to call up the Better Business Bureau (or head to its Web site at www.bbb.org) to ask for any information on a particular retailer or service provider—especially whether the location has a "Good Housekeeping Seal of Approval," such as BBBOnLine's Reliability Seal Program, for its policies. (See Chapter 10, "What If You Get a Lemon?" for these details.)

- *Understand the Web site's security and privacy policies.* See how this site protects your credit card information, including the use of encrypted data. Is a closed-lock or unbroken-key icon in the frame of your browser window, indicating that this site uses SSL (secure sockets layer) encryption technology to safeguard this information? You need to carefully understand what data the seller collects on its buyers, how the data is used, and how you can block any further transmission of your personal information. Check out the privacy policy, keeping in mind that some sites automatically store data without asking. Carefully determine how the site not only safeguards the transmission of your data but protects against employees' misuse. The presence of a privacy seal, such as the Better Business Bureau's BBBOnLine Privacy Program or Truste's, indicate the site's interest in a customer's privacy concerns. This is covered more at Chapter 16, "Web Site Operating Considerations."

If hiding your true identity from online merchants is important, consider contacting companies such as PrivaSeek, Anonymizer.com, Zero-Knowledge, SafeWeb, Freedom Site, and others that offer downloadable software that you can work with to mask your true identity from online merchants and marketers.

- *Always pay with your credit card, never with a debit card, wire transfer, or check.* Consider obtaining a different credit card that you only use for Web purchases. In case that number is pirated, this tactic can safeguard your other credit cards. You will want to acquire one that has no fees and offers low interest rates, so shop around. Federal law limits a U.S. resident's liability now to $50 if a credit card number is stolen and used for fraudulent purchases. Many times, the credit card company will even waive this amount.
- *USE CAUTION when releasing any of your personal information.* Don't give out any personal data, especially your social security and credit card information, unless you are entirely satisfied that a Web site is honest *and* has adequate safeguards in place to protect sensitive information from even its employees. The stories are endless in this regard. One person bought discount insurance online; within a week, his credit card number was being used in a state thousands of miles away. Another bought a sweater on a Web site and, days later, his credit card number was out being used on the streets of Manhattan. Use common sense. In both cases, the sites didn't safeguard the data from their employees.
- *Online auctions are fine, but there are additional precautions.* Be wary of online rating services; they may not always be reliable, and favorable conditions can change quickly. If at all possible, arrange to have pictures sent to you before the bidding begins. Also, know your valuations. You won't be able to get out of a deal just because you substantially overbid an item's value. Find out what it costs to use an escrow account; in this way, you can

ensure that you'll get what you paid for—before money is handed over to the seller. Otherwise, you can have your money in the hands of some stranger located thousands of miles away, and you will still be looking through a small pair of old opera glasses instead of those powerful field binoculars you thought you had purchased. Check out whether the site provides fraud insurance, just in case you stumble onto a real scam artist.

Be educated in what you are bidding for—and keep an ever watchful eye. For example, even venerable eBay experienced shill bidding, otherwise known as self-bidding, which it strictly forbids. Three men created more than 40 different aliases to inflate bids on the paintings they were auctioning. One auction was so rigged that a Dutchman bid $135,000 for a fake Richard Diebenkorn painting. Upon discovery of the shill bidding, the men were federally prosecuted on wire and mail fraud. However, this didn't help their victims, who lost nearly $500,000.

- *Build a purchase file.* Keep every bit of documentation that's received, including all e-mails, warranties, and written promises. Don't throw these away, even when you receive the product in apparent good order. If it breaks down sooner than you thought, all of this information will be useful to your local and/or national consumer fraud agency, or when in a small claims court.

- *Watch for special promotions or Net coupons.* When shopping at your favorite retailer, keep an eye open for coupons or special premiums if you buy on the Internet. Major retailers run coupon specials to boost their Net sales, and these certificates are only redeemable for Web purchases. At times, these retailers will run offers at a particular location where you'll receive a coupon that's worth, let's say, $25, but is redeemable only toward another purchase at their Web site.

- *Be careful when purchasing unique items,* whether they are CDs or Grateful Dead T-shirts. These days, lawyers and their staff monitor Internet and online auctions closely, to be sure that pirated materials aren't being auctioned off. Question the authenticity of these materials *before* you buy, not afterwards. For example, a 1961 Kentucky Derby trophy attracted 41 bids and was auctioned off for the winning bid amount of $4,200. The auction unfortunately also attracted the attention of the police, because this particular trophy had been stolen from the jockey, John Sellers, 20 years ago. The deal was canceled when the police seized the trophy and returned it to Mr. Sellers. Know what the auction house's policies are in this regard, before you bid.

- *Be an aware purchaser.* Even when you're purchasing from your "tried and true" site, pay attention to these factors and any changes from usual procedures. And check out these Web sites' great tips: (1) the FTC's site on avoiding rip-offs (ftc.gov); and (2) the National Consumer's League Web site (www.nclnet.org, which offers information on how to avoid cyberscams at fraud.org). Plus, there are others.

- *Pay particular attention to your children.* While you are working or running your business, keep enough free time to pay attention to your children's interests and their use of the Net. You'll want to watch out for what they surf and see on the Internet, just as you do with TV. Keep in mind the story of the 12-year-old son of an eBay user who used his father's password to successfully bid $3.2 million for a Monet picture, a condominium, and a medical practice. Although these purchases were later canceled, there are real legal actions that can be taken against parents for not properly supervising their child—not to mention the uproar.

Contract Basics

The backbone of doing any transactions or business is that agreements between people and companies should be honored. If they aren't, then the aggrieved party can receive damages, as set by a court, to make up for that loss. Typically, there are no extra or punitive damages meant to punish those who break contracts, even if the breaking of the deal was done intentionally.

A legal contract requires three essential factors: (1) a meeting of the minds (i.e., a valid offer and acceptance); (2) valid consideration (i.e., each party basically gives up and receives something in return); (3) no legal defenses (i.e., the parties have the capacity to contract, the deal's purpose is legal, and it covers the essential terms, among other aspects).

When you buy or sell a calculator at a store, there is a meeting of the minds (i.e., a calculator is being sold for money); consideration (the buyer is giving up cash for the product; the store is selling the product for the money); and there are no legal defenses (at least, at this time). If the calculator turns out to be a lousy one (i.e., it gives a death rattle, then never works again), then the purchaser brings it back.

All three elements are needed for a valid contract, whether it is bought at a physical location or cyberstore. For example, if the buyer opens the box and finds a different calculator, then there is no meeting of the minds, no contract, and the buyer can get his money back. If the buyer buys on credit, but then determines that the interest rate being charged is higher than the law allows (or usury), then this contract is bad (a valid legal defense). *If a transaction is especially important to you, then talk to an attorney about your questions and get seasoned advice before completing the deal.*

Let's say that you're buying several expensive computers for your business. You and the computer manufacturer negotiate a written contract with the essential terms of the quantity, price, delivery date, who pays for shipping and from where, and various "boilerplate" provisions. You should be sure that these important terms are in every contract that you accept or sign. Should you leave these terms to be determined at a later date, it is possible that a court may determine what a "reasonable price" or the "acceptable delivery date" is.

The boilerplate typically concerns what you'll do if there is a dispute, which laws apply, whether there are "liquidated" damages if one party or the other doesn't perform, and so on. These terms have become even more important with Net transactions, given the ability to come to a "meeting of the minds" when the parties are thousands of miles apart. We'll take a detailed look at this boilerplate when we discuss electronic contracts ("e-contracts").

Cyberspace Offers and Acceptances

Offers and acceptances in cyberspace leave clear tracks that can last forever, so it's important to understand these contract basics. Let's say that a business acquaintance e-mails you: "I'll sell my XT7 computer to you for $4,000 in cash, payable one week from today. Do you want it on these terms?" You e-mail back, "I accept." You now have an enforceable contract with the consideration being the respective mutual promises of each to buy and sell that computer. If you change your mind later, you become responsible for your friend's damages. For example, if he sold it finally for $3,500 to someone else, then he could legally hold you responsible for the $500 that he didn't get when you breached your end of the deal.

If you didn't respond to his e-mail, then the offer would eventually die by your not accepting it. Or, if you e-mailed back, "I'll pay you $3,750 in cash," then that counteroffer kills the first offer. If you changed your mind the next day and e-mailed, "Okay, I've changed my mind, I'll pay you the $4,000," you're still out of luck. Your first e-mail was a counteroffer. When it wasn't accepted, then it legally erased the first offer. Your friend would have to agree to your last counteroffer for any deal; if he doesn't, then there is no contract. Again, these considerations apply whether you're the buyer or seller.

Let's say you open up your e-mail box and find the following: "We at Ace Investment Publications appreciated your visit to our Web site. We, accordingly, have entered you as a subscriber to our newsletter at a fantastic savings of $40 a month—ONLY $50 per month for the first nine months, then our regular price of $90 per month is due. We will send you an invoice every month. You may cancel your subscription at any time." You do nothing. Are you bound?

The commonsense and legal answer is "No." Your silence cannot constitute acceptance in this case. You would have to say "I agree" or some other reasonable indication of your intent. If Ace sends you its first electronic copy anyway, then the facts change somewhat. You should return it with the message of "Cancel" so that there will be no further misunderstandings.

e-Contracts

Let's say that you visited Ace Investment's Web site and then discovered their offer. However, underneath the Net solicitation was the following: "If you want our newsletter at this great introductory price, then click the 'SUBSCRIBE' button. By subscribing, you agree to all of the terms as set forth in our Contract. To read the contract provisions, click on 'Contract Terms' below." You fill in the details of your name, address, e-mail address, and the necessary credit card information, then hit the SUBSCRIBE button—but you're not interested in reading all of that legalese. You then click the Contract Terms icon, but, like the rest of us, you don't read all of what you consider to be "confusing, legal jargon."

Have you formed a valid contract? The answer is "Yes." Will the details in the Contract Terms section bind you, even if they were presented to you on a "take it or leave it" basis? Even though you can't change those terms, courts lean to upholding them (but that's not always the case).

The general rule is: As long as the terms of the contract were available to you before your accepted the offer (you could have hit the Contract Terms button first), and as long as they aren't unconscionable, then you can be bound by those terms—even if, in the event of a dispute, it provided that all lawsuits would be heard in Miami, Florida, and you live in Los Angeles, California, or Montreal, Canada (although this won't always be enforced). The reasoning of the courts is: If you didn't like those provisions, then you could have headed over to a competitor's site and purchased the desired items there.

Clickwrap Agreements and Electronic Signatures

The above example illustrates the typical "clickwrap" agreement. You can't sign an e-contract with your real name, as you could if you were in a face-to-face meeting with a sales representative. In place of this, the law provides that you agreed to the terms and conditions of the agreement when you "clicked" the SUBSCRIBE button. Regardless of what's bought, when you click that "I agree" or "I'll buy" button, you have entered into a binding agreement. This "clickwrap" concept is a takeoff on the "shrinkwrap" software license agreements. These agreements provide that removing an outer sticker or tearing off the plastic shrink-wrap covering indicates the purchaser's approval of the conditions and terms of use that are printed inside the software product package.

Similarly, the click of the mouse on the agreement button sets the approval to the conditions on the purchase of a Web site's services or products. The courts have upheld this as being as valid as if a written contract was signed on the dotted line. Any on-screen click, no matter where it's located (but provided it's identified as the "clickwrap" agreement button), will do. Whether you're agreeing to download files or software from a Web site, buying merchandise, or using an informational or service site, your click at the appropriate place (or your use of that Web site by itself) is enough to grant your assent to that contract or the terms and conditions of that Web site's use—all as if you had signed your name. The premise of the law is that the medium in which a record, signature, or contract is created shouldn't affect its validity, and the transaction is enforceable whether the medium is paper or electronic.

Moreover, Web sites are posting their "Legal Notices" and "Terms of Use" provisions, separate from these purchasing decisions. These sites condition a user's acceptance of their terms by the simple use of that Web site—and not by or through any purchase. The original clickwrap agreement and the assent to the site's policies are then narrowed to the user's surfing of the site. This is done to meet the consideration, or value, criteria for having a valid contract. Both sides are gaining something from this: the user, by seeing the site (or buying the product), and the provider, by the user's presence (or selling the product). However, this doesn't mean that all of the Web site's provisions will be upheld to be legally valid. The courts like to see affirmative steps that users need to do in giving this assent—and the more, the better. There are other considerations, and the next chapter goes into this discussion.

Nearly all of the U.S. states, and the federal government, have enacted some form of an electronic signatures statute. In fact, the federal Electronic Signatures in Global and National Commerce Act took effect on October 1, 2000. This U.S. legislation basically mandates that an e-signature will be enforceable if both parties agree to the technological format. It legally validates electronic records, signatures, and contracts, thereby validating commerce that occurs online. The signature verification can be based on fingerprint scanners, a SmartCard, PGP (encryption software), a pad-based signature, eye lasers, voice recognition, face scans, or whatever the parties agree to use in their contract. It is an enabling statute that sets down standards to be followed and allows states to enact their own but consistent legislation within this umbrella.

An electronic or digital signature is usually not a digital form of a handwritten signature; it's generally an encrypted message or recognition that's included with the text. This recognition uniquely identifies the sender. As with a written signature, the purpose of a digital signature is to guarantee that the individual who's sending the message is really who he or she claims to be—on both ends of the transaction. For an electronic signature to be effective, the digital signature identification needs to be nonforgeable, which means that this I.D. must be encrypted (or protected, and special to the identified person). This allows for digital documents eventually to be recorded (e.g., deeds and mortgages); it ensures that a signature is valid and that the "signing" person is authorized to order the goods or services being purchased.

Way back in 1995 (quite distant in Internet time standards), Utah was the first state to pass a comprehensive law regulating the use of digital signatures in e-commerce. Nearly every state has now joined Utah in passing some form of enabling legislation. However, the states differ widely in their authorizations; some are applicable to all electronic transactions, and others are much more limited in their applications. Some laws create governmental entities that issue required digital certificates; others simply provide that digitally or electronically signed e-communications satisfy the signature and writing requirements of their state law. Although there can be a risk that one state may recognize one type of signature and another won't, the U.S. federal legislation allowing uses as agreed between the parties should control in most situations—provided each locality is silent, doesn't exclude that e-signature technology, or does cover that particular conflict. For important and large deals, you should check these specifics out with an experienced cyberlawyer.

This is, however, an important legalization. Typically, customers and businesses wait days, or even weeks, for documents to work their way through being mailed, signed, and delivered to one another. There are transactions, such as buying and selling real estate, that require tens of documents, and some must be notarized to be legally valid. Some experts maintain that electronic and digital signature acceptance will lead to most financial transactions being completely automated this way in five years. Signed into law by President Clinton in July 1999, the Y2K liability bill (which turned out not to be really needed) marked the first time e-signatures and electronic signature technology was used to enact national legislation.

Internationally, many countries around the world have or are in the process of legitimizing electronic signatures and, in turn, e-commerce. The thrust of all these legislative acts, although specific provisions can be dissimilar, is to give digital signatures and virtual agreements the same legal status as paper contracts and ink signatures. From Brazil and Asia to Taiwan and the European Union (12 of its 15 member states already have passed e-signature laws with the others expected at any time), numbers of nations already have enacted e-signature laws. As it is in every country's interest to support international e-commerce, supporting this aspect of cyber-commerce will not have the hesitation as seen, for example, with international copyrights (see Chapter 4). However, if you anticipate doing e-contracts abroad (whether in the U.S. or any other country), be aware that the specific laws of the various nations will differ. You'll need to look at what a particular country has specifically provided for in this regard (use your search engine), or hire an experienced cyberattorney if the transaction is important enough.

Web Site Purchase Considerations

Many Web sites separate the necessary purchasing information from their legal terms of use and privacy statements. Depending on how skilled the Web designer or programmer is, this can be an easy ride (or a tough one) to get the necessary information before deciding to purchase. Customers need to know: (1) the site's return policy, including where, how, and under what conditions it controls (you'll usually be paying for the return delivery costs, unless it was the site's mistake); (2) what the costs of delivery are, which depends on how soon you want that item delivered; (3) the site's refund policy; (4) how to order or change an order; and (5) the various ways that items can be paid for, among other information.

Typically, you're not going to find much in the way of warranties or guarantees for any product that you buy or download (other than a refund of the purchase price). Product Web sites are generally retailers, not manufacturers. If a problem arises with respect to a product that you've purchased, Net sites direct you to the manufacturer to answer your questions and make good on products not returned to the retailer. However, this doesn't mean that a Web site can get off the hook if a defective product injures you, regardless of its warranty and liability disclaimers in place. We will treat this later in this chapter and the next.

THE TERMS AND CONDITIONS

As you can imagine, there haven't been substantial numbers of cyberspace court cases deciding the validity of these Terms of Use provisions. Over time, courts will decide what can or can't be done under certain sets of facts, but this process will be measured in years, and no one expects total uniformity in these decisions.

Provided the terms and conditions are reasonable, the experts believe that these provisions will be generally upheld—even if they aren't really read until after the money has been paid, and even if the user wouldn't have agreed to those terms in the first place, had he or she then really understood them. Be sure to familiarize yourself with the standard "Terms and Conditions" or "Legal Notices" posted on the Web sites that you like to use and patronize.

Although the general areas treated are quite similar, each site's written Terms and Conditions will be different. This can also depend on whether the location is strictly an informational site, sells products, provides services, conducts chatrooms, or engages in some combination. However, the general concepts covered are basically the same, although the specific wording varies greatly from site to site and often depends on what lawyer drafts the language.

Given that the basic terms (i.e., quantity, price, time for delivery, and delivery modes) are present, what was once "just legal boilerplate" has now become much more important: the risk of loss, disclaimers of liability, indemnity, handling of disputes, applicable law, dispute resolution, assessment of sales taxes, and others. This is especially true when distant localities are involved. Keep in mind that the purchase details (i.e., return, refund, and delivery cost policies) are more business-oriented, and this information is typically kept apart from the legal factors. Other legal concepts are also covered in the Terms of Use, such as rules as to copyright use, trademark infringement, online conduct, linking, chatroom rules, use by children under 13, and the like. These areas will be discussed in the next chapter.

The following "boilerplate" provisions are typically found in the Legal Provisions or Terms of Use policies:

- *More than legal provisions.* (This is covered in greater detail in Chapters 9 and 16.) Some sites do place real business information into their Legal Provisions text. For example, a site might insert that "all sales are final and sold 'as is,'" or even put in its return, refund, and delivery policies. An apparently innocent prohibition against "any commercial use of information on this site" can turn out to be very protective of an owner's interests. For example, one case held that eBay could prohibit a competitor from deep linking into its banks of information, because its legal terms prohibited "commercial use." Another case held that a similar prohibition, along with other facts, allowed a Web site that was selling tickets to prohibit another competitor from copying its information for commercial purposes. As to Web sites that sell services and/or goods, the differing legal provisions in their use policies are described below.

- *Risk of loss.* This provision usually states that the buyer bears the risk of loss once the product has been delivered to the transportation carrier. Different sites can have different provisions on this, depending on the product (i.e., expensive, heavy equipment versus cheap books). Some provide that if the buyer never receives the product, the seller may wait a reasonable time period and then grant a refund, given that the transaction is a small one. If a larger transaction is involved, the buyer definitely should ensure that adequate insurance coverage is in effect to cover any loss.

- *Disclaimers of liability.* These provisions typically limit the liability of the seller for injury, or for loss by the buyer, to exchanging the product or receiving a refund of the purchase price, all at the seller's option. This refund policy is usually included with a standard disclaimer of liability as follows:

    Seller disclaims all warranties, express or implied, including the warranties of merchantability and fitness for a particular purpose, and the company shall not be liable for any consequential or incidental losses or liabilities, whether they are loss of business, files, work stoppage, profit, revenue, or any other loss.

    The intent of these provisions is for the seller to "duck away" from liability, leaving the manufacturer or the customer on the hook. Although not unanimously, the courts tend to uphold these limitations on consequential damages in commercial transactions. However, they generally won't be upheld if there's a personal injury—for example, if a customer is injured when using that product. This and other liability considerations are discussed further in Chapter 9, "Web Site Disclaimers and Protections."

- *Indemnity.* Like the others, these provisions are in favor of the seller and/or manufacturer, as they are the ones that draft them. The buyer agrees to indemnify (be responsible for) any damages or losses that occur to the seller by reason of the buyer's negligence or how the buyer receives, uses, stores, or resells the product. A balanced approach would provide that the Web site would indemnify the buyer similarly for any losses owing to the negligence of the seller. However, such a provision would be rare.

- *Handling of disputes.* This section usually is headed by the words "Dispute Resolution," "Conflicts," or even "Legal Fees." A growing trend is for Web sites to establish arbitration (a less expensive, quicker, and less formal legal procedure than litigation) and mediation (informal conflict resolution through the services of a third-party mediator) as the agreed methods to handle disputes arising between the parties. (Consult Chapter 12, "Cyberlaw Dispute Resolution," for further information.) Should litigation flare up, then the typical provision usually authorizes the payment of attorneys' fees and court costs to the "prevailing party"—the one that wins in court.

- *Applicable law and location.* This is a very important section; it covers where disputes are to be heard and what law is to be applied. At times, this provision may be found in the "Handling of Disputes" section. Whatever the wording or wherever it's located, Web sites always choose their hometown and their hometown's law. If the state or country of the seller isn't particularly generous in its support of that entity in a typical dispute, then the seller will always designate the place that is.

   Let's say the seller designates that United States and New York State laws apply, and the proper venue (where you try the lawsuit) is New York City. This means that if you, the buyer, live in Dallas, Texas (or England, for that matter), and the seller is located in New York City, then you must fly to New York City and argue the merits of your case there, under U.S. and New York law. Jet lag, large hotel bills, strange attorneys, weird laws, and weirder hotels can be daunting if you need to travel that far to be heard. See Chapter 11, "But Can Your Court Hear the Case? What Law Is Applied?" for the details.

- *Other.* The "miscellaneous" boilerplate usually will provide a "severability" clause, or one that holds: Should a court find that one provision is illegal, the entire agreement still stands, except for that one bad section. An "entire agreement" clause also will be present. It states that this contract is the entire agreement between the parties and reflects their final understanding. Other sections could include the address for notices, how notification is to be made, provisions on assignments, later parties who are bound by the deal, and even the use of mediation and arbitration.

Whether you are selling or purchasing on the Web, you will need to center on at least these provisions. Should the transaction be large or important enough, then you should hire an experienced cyberlawyer to work with you on that deal.

Web Taxation

With its Internet Tax Freedom Act, the United States took the lead in capping taxes on online sales. A three-year moratorium on any special, multiple, or discriminatory tax on the Net was enacted on October 21, 1998, but then expired on October 20, 2001. However, as this book goes to press, the experts believe that the basic concept of protecting the Internet from excessive taxation will be embodied, although the moratorium may be modified in its effect. This federal legislation barred all state, local, and federal governments, including Congress, from enacting new Net taxes until the expiration of the time period. The basic premise was that to give this medium a fighting chance, it was better to declare the Net a "no-tax zone." However, keep in mind that all governments keep a watchful eye on the Net as a source of desired revenues.

It is a common misconception that the Internet and its sales are free from taxation. Numerous states even now impose taxes on Internet access, telephone services, and other digital or telecommunication activities. A "grandfather's" clause in the Tax Freedom Act permitted a variety of states that were already taxing the Net to continue those taxing activities, provided they could demonstrate that their taxes had been "generally imposed and actually enforced." Further, Web sites already collect sales and excise taxes on the online sales of goods when they have "brick and mortar" retail stores in those states, some other physical presence (i.e., they own a warehouse or regional office there), or would rather "voluntarily" collect these taxes in disputed situations rather than be held responsible for such taxes later.

Customers who use a company's Web site to order goods online, but later accept delivery of those orders from facilities located within their state, are liable to pay a sales tax. This creates interesting differences. Amazon.com, with its pure online operations, presently collects sales taxes only in the state of Washington (its headquarters); Eddie Bauer collects sales taxes in 23 states on its online sales (it operates retail locations in those states, among other factors). *At a minimum, a Web site will be liable for sales taxes (like Eddie Bauer) where it maintains a "brick and mortar" presence, such as offices, warehouses, or other facilities, in addition to any later legislative changes.*

The World Trade Organization (WTO) approach has been to basically support the U.S.'s general approach. As explained further in Chapter 16, "Web Site Operating Considerations," there are pressures on both the U.S. and the rest of the world to open up this revenue stream. When making an online purchase, be sure to review that site's disclosures on sales and use taxes on your transaction before ordering (or talk "live" with someone), including how you can appeal that assessment, should you disagree with it.

An *E-Commerce Agreement* is discussed next. This form illustrates the provisions that could be included in an agreement that is negotiated by two parties concerning the e-sale of services or products. It can be signed by electronic signature or printed out, then signed and faxed by the parties. If a formal agreement isn't desired, then e-mail the essential terms to the other party and request a response. It's important that you have some documentation indicating there's a "meeting of the minds" as to the essential terms of any agreement. Please be advised that this form is presented for informational purposes only and may not be suitable for your specific situation.

E-Commerce Agreement

This E-Commerce Agreement is entered on [*Date of Agreement*] between [*Seller's Name*], called "Seller," and [*Buyer's Name*], called "Buyer." The parties, in consideration of the mutual promises made by each other and other valuable consideration, agree as follows:

1. **Agreement.** Seller agrees to sell and Buyer agrees to buy the following described products and/or services: [*State Generally (Service or Sale of Products) and Specifically the Agreement's Subject Matter*].

2. **Purchase Price.** Buyer agrees to pay Seller the following for these products and/or services: [*State Number of Units, Unit Price, Total Purchase Price, Down Payment, Installment Payments (if at all), and Other Details*].

3. **Seller Warranties.** Seller makes the following express warranties with respect to this transaction: [*State Express Warranties Made by Seller*]. Seller further warrants that it has full legal title, has the power to enter into this Agreement, that its sale will not violate any other contract or understanding, and that the property/services will be sold free and clear of any liens or encumbrances.
   However, SELLER DISCLAIMS ALL IMPLIED WARRANTIES, INCLUDING BUT NOT LIMITED TO, THE WARRANTIES OF MERCHANTABILITY AND FITNESS FOR A PARTICULAR PURPOSE.

4. **Risk of Loss.** The parties agree that title to any products will pass upon Seller's delivery of same to its carrier for purposes of transportation to Buyer. At this time, Buyer shall be responsible for the costs of delivery on and risk of loss.

5. **Return.** The parties agree that Buyer shall be able to return any products to Seller at Seller's cost, if within 10 days Buyer decides, for any reason, that the products don't meet Buyer's expectations. Seller shall promptly refund Buyer's purchase price to Buyer upon Seller's receipt of the returned products.

6. **Export.** Current United States export control laws regulate the export and reexport of technology and other information/products originating in the United States. Buyer warrants that it is not a foreign national nor has a foreign destination that would be subject to the regulation of these laws.

7. **Not a Minor.** Buyer warrants that he/she is not a minor, has full power to enter into this Agreement, and does not need to have a parental or guardian's signature to accomplish same.

8. **Indemnity.** Each party agrees to defend, indemnify, and hold harmless the other, its officers, directors, employees, agents, and providers, from and against all claims, actions, or demands, including reasonable attorney fees and court costs, resulting from the indemnifying party's fault, negligence, or breach of any warranties/representations.

9. **Disputes.** Any dispute arising in connection with this Agreement shall be first settled by mediation. If that's not successful, then the dispute shall be settled by arbitration to be held in [*Location of Arbitration*] in accordance with the rules of the American Arbitration Association. This agreement to arbitrate shall be specifically enforceable. Any award shall be final and binding on all the parties, and a final judgment may be entered in the appropriate court of law. Notwithstanding this, should any litigation ensue between the parties, then the prevailing party shall be entitled to reasonable expenses and attorney fees as set by the Court.

10. **Jurisdiction and Venue.** The laws of the State of [*State Whose Laws Control in a Dispute*] and of the United States will govern this Agreement, its interpretation, and all rights and duties of the parties. Each party consents to submit to the exclusive jurisdiction of the courts of the State of [*State Whose Laws Control in a Dispute*] and of the United States for any litigation arising from this Agreement, waive any objection to this State on improper jurisdiction and/or venue, and agree not to argue that any such litigation brought there has been brought in an inconvenient forum.

E-Commerce Agreement *(Continued)*

11. **Other.** If any provision(s) of this Agreement are deemed unlawful, void, or for any reason unenforceable by any proceeding or a court of competent jurisdiction, then that provision(s) shall be deemed severed from the rest and shall not affect the validity or enforceability of any of the remaining provisions. Any notices, correspondence, or communications to be given under this Agreement shall be delivered personally or mailed to the party designated at the last address given in writing to the other party. This Agreement constitutes the entire understanding between the parties with respect to the matters contained therein. This Agreement shall not be modified in any respect except by a subsequent writing executed by both parties.

This Agreement is accepted, understood, and executed as of the date first above written, by and between:

_____

[*Name and Address of Seller*]

_____

[*Name and Address of Buyer*]

E-Commerce Agreement

Discussion of Provisions

1. **Agreement.** The parties should be sure to describe all of the business details of the contract. As this is a form agreement, this and all of the provisions may need to be changed to reflect any particular transaction of goods or services.

2. **Purchase Price.** If the purchase price is to be paid in installments, then the parties should consider the questions of security to ensure that full payment is made, a service and interest (%) charge for late payments, and default provisions.

3. **Seller Warranties.** In this case, there is a disclaimer by seller of implied warranties. Should that not be the case, then this language would need to be changed. It should be noted that warranty waivers are limited by law in various countries and may not be upheld by a court of law in any particular state, jurisdiction, or country.

4. **Risk of Loss.** This provision, as with the others, is negotiable between the parties and can be changed.

5. **Return.** Seller's standard return policy usually is inserted in this section, unless this is a large transaction and the return provisions are specifically negotiated by the parties.

6. **Export.** If the sale is between United States citizens who have no export/import ties, then this language may be eliminated.

7. **Not a Minor.** In important enough transactions, the seller should make reasonable inquiries to ensure that this warranty can be made.

8. **Indemnity.** This provision states that each party will indemnify, or insure, the other against any loss owing to that party's negligence, fault, or breach of warranties.

9. **Disputes.** This "boilerplate" stipulates that the alternate dispute resolution techniques of mediation and arbitration are to be used. Should arbitration not be agreeable, then these provisions would have to be accordingly changed to reflect the parties' agreement.

10. **Jurisdiction and Venue.** A heavily litigated area involves where lawsuits can be tried and under what applicable law. If a user or customer lives in California, or even Paris, France, then does this mean that person has to travel to New York City to try a lawsuit (given that's where the Web site's operations are located)? Although sites try to limit lawsuits to being tried on their "home turf," this doesn't mean that another state court, or even a foreign court, would honor that provision. These provisions may be upheld, but this will depend on the facts of each particular case. This contract also provides that U.S. law applies, which would change if one or both parties aren't U.S. residents and agree otherwise.

11. **Other.** Severability clauses should be present in these contracts. If a provision is subsequently declared void (i.e., the choice of law or waiver of jurisdiction provision is usually attacked first), then the entire contract could be at risk unless the ability to separate the "good from the bad" is present. If the parties desire, other provisions such as an assignment clause could be added.

    Additionally, the parties may well agree to use an e-signature technology to assure each other that all "signatures" are genuine. This approach is mandated if a document is to be recorded (i.e., a mortgage or trust deed); however, it may not be necessary in different non-recording situations between private parties, although, over time, the trend is in this verification direction.

Web Site Disclaimers and Protections

Whether representing commercial businesses, educational interests, or nonprofit entities or lawyers for Web sites recommend uniformly that their clients post restrictive Terms of Use and Privacy policies that are in their clients' favor—and that's what all sites are or should be doing. These policies include the major legal disclaimers discussed in this chapter, along with those we discussed previously. Your personal viewpoint of this approach will differ, depending on whether you see these policies from the viewpoint of the user/purchaser or the Web-site operator.

When purchasing products or services, you need to take the time to read the important provisions. The great majority of us scan or scroll through quickly, simply to get to their end, not realizing that these provisions are of binding legal significance. If your purchase is large or important enough, then take the time to read all of that Web site's Terms of Use and Privacy policies before you decide. If your company or purchase is that important, you or your attorney should negotiate specific changes in those provisions when purchasing, just as the largest companies always do when they purchase in volume.

If you aren't sure of what the wording for one provides, then e-mail that site for clarification (and keep that e-mail with the reply). Otherwise, start patronizing locations that post provisions that are more understandable, simpler, and apparently fairer—and purchasers already are doing this.

When you're operating a Web site, you'll want to be sure that your policies are at least more understandable, simpler, and somewhat balanced, because the law is heading in that direction. Your customers will appreciate this. The rules for designing your own site's Terms of Use provisions are set forth in Chapter 16, "Web Site Operating Considerations." However, because these are based entirely on the discussions in this chapter, you'll want to read this first for the background as to what's happening and what users are looking for. Keep in mind that these issues and considerations apply, whether your Web site is based in the United States, the European Union, or in Asia. And note that terms of use policies can be called "Terms of Service" (Yahoo!), "User's Agreement" (eBay), "Conditions of Use" (Amazon.com), and other approaches.

Terms of Use Agreements and the Legalities

The courts so far have given limited review on whether (1) these "take it or leave it" agreements are enforceable; (2) the limitations on liability and damages are valid; and (3) other provisions, such as the forum selection clause (i.e., if there's a dispute, you fly to the site's home court to duke it out), are legally enforceable. We'll examine each of these in turn.

Most courts will uphold the legality of the "take it or leave it" type of e-agreement, provided: (1) the terms are written in understandable English with readable print and not hidden from the user's view; (2) the user has the opportunity to read and understand these terms, all before having to make a purchase or use decision; (3) the provisions are reasonable; and (4) the user has to take some affirmative action to agree (such as clicking an "I agree" button). As courts tend to enforce software shrinkwrap agreements, it appears they'll do the same with Web site Terms of Use provisions—at least if all of these elements are present.

Courts have been accepting the argument that the consumer can always travel to a competing Web site and buy the same product or service there, assuming also that the Terms of Use at that site aren't any more onerous. However, the flaw in this argument is that many other Web sites are doing the same thing: disclaiming liabilities, contracting for the most favorable law forum, and designating their faraway location as the best place to argue differences. So, unless a site just happens to be in your state, the possibility is that you'll have that out-of-state's forum law applied—and everything else. This forum is advantageous if you're the Web site, but not if you are the customer or consumer.

Basically, courts tend to agree that the mere posting of terms and conditions at the bottom of a site's home page is not enough to establish an enforceable agreement. There must be some knowledge (the terms are easily found, identified, and understandable), prior decision making (you can decide before ordering), and facts showing at least an implied agreement (i.e., clicking on an icon). Clearly unreasonable terms probably won't be enforced, such as, "You agree to litigate all complaints in Paris, France," and you've just purchased an executive fountain pen from that South Dakota Web site.

However, if the language used is hidden or not conspicuous, in small print, or wholly unreasonable in effect (i.e., "This Web site is not responsible for any of your damages, regardless of how much we are at fault"), then the courts will probably not uphold it. It is clear that, in most situations, the courts will uphold these agreements on a general, conceptual basis.

Some sites provide that the contract doesn't come into existence until 30 days after the customer's receipt of the product or software download. The argument is that the user then has 30 days within which to see whether the products work, and, presumably, to read the Terms of Use and agree with them—or disagree, in which case the items can then be returned. This takes the sting away from the "take it or leave it" approach. Courts that have reviewed this approach (i.e., "If you don't return the product in 30 days, then you've agreed to our terms and conditions"), have generally upheld these provisions.

LIMITATIONS ON LIABILITY AND DAMAGES

The enforceability questions with liability and damage limitations have been nearly hidden by the legal community's focus on the overall enforceability of Web site use agreements. However, they may NOT be enforceable, depending on the circumstances. Let's say that you bought a high-intensity lamp for your home office or business from Ered-Web.com, and this product was manufactured by Ace. The boilerplate on the Web site and enclosed product brochure (which you had no way to change) simply read: "The manufacturer, retailer, and/or Web site assume no liability for this product's malfunction, regardless of negligence or claim; buyer assumes all risks of operation, damages, and loss."

One week after the item was delivered, you turned it on and the lamp shorted into showers of sparks and flames. Nearby drapes caught fire, and your $300,000 office interior (or home) burned to the ground. Or worse, you were severely injured in the fire that was caused by the shorted lamp. (Note: It makes little difference whether the item was a lamp, chip fabrication device, or hair dryer.)

Your attorney looks closely into the facts. Ace obviously manufactured a defective product, and this defect caused your damages. This is a classic example of strict product liability, and every entity in the distribution chain has a joint and several liability (i.e., depending on who has the money, all, some, or just one pays up), from Ace to Ered-Web. Your attorney would sue everyone in this chain of distribution and let the jury decide who was most responsible. If Ace was bankrupt, then Ered-Web could pay for everything. In any event, Web sites are liability players in these actions (and we're not even using the argument that Ered-Web had knowledge of the defects or the last chance of inspection).

Ered-Web's lawyer argues that the limitation of damages and liability insulates the company from liability. Wrong! As a basic legal concept, no one can contract against the effects of strict product liability or his or her own negligence. If that was the case, there could never be any product liability, because every manufacturer and retailer in the world would be contractually announcing: "Sorry, if there's a problem with our product, even if it's all our fault, we don't accept that liability—you do."

Depending on the circumstances, Web sites can be held completely responsible for a customer's damages, notwithstanding these one-sided contract provisions. For example, if a pharmacy Web site erroneously fills a prescription for a high blood pressure medication (your job has had some really bad moments lately), that Net retailer will have to compensate you for your damages from those bad pills, regardless of any Terms of Use limitations in effect. Similarly, if a Web site e-mails that this chemical will do the trick (but it causes a fire instead), that site will have similar liability, regardless of its posted limitations.

The moral of the story: If you have an unfortunate damage or liability situation, let your attorney determine whether those limitations are valid. Don't assume that they will be upheld just because a Web site says so. Similarly, Net providers must understand that their liability limitations aren't foolproof and are subject to legal attack.

INDEMNITY PROVISIONS

Standard Terms of Use agreements also provide "tight" indemnity provisions. These terms basically state that the buyer or user indemnifies, or is responsible for, any damages that occur to the Web site by reason of how the buyer acts or uses that product. These statements imply or state outright that the Web site has no reciprocal obligations for its users or customers. If you have a difficulty with a Web site (and the dispute is worth it), don't unilaterally accept this assumption. Instead, consult with an attorney. Courts tend to look at how "fair" provisions are, and this one could be thrown out. However, the outcome will still depend on the facts and applicable state or national law.

"MY LAW, MY HOME" CLAUSES

These conflicts-of-law provisions are called "forum selection" clauses in the legal community. As we discussed, simply your use of that Web site can indicate your approval to these clauses; if a dispute surfaces, then you're faced with flying to, let's say, New York City, from your home in Hawaii. Or worse, you live in Tokyo, Japan. It is true that this clause's presence can make it more difficult for you to stay in Hawaii (or Japan) to litigate your differences, regardless of the type or size of your claim.

Although courts can defer to these standard provisions, as the business connections of your situation grow with your location, your state's (or country's) courts are more inclined to apply their law and forum to those proceedings—regardless of what a Net retailer says are the proper courts or law to use. For example, Ered-Web e-mails you back and forth as to which products are the best for you to purchase. Through its Net location, the site regularly sells, accepts returns, and answers questions from you and from other residents in your state. Then the lamp or equipment explodes. Because the injury and damage also occurred in your state, there are substantial connections by which your state court could not only hear that case but also apply its law—despite Ered-Web's provisions on this matter. You'll sue in your court, because it's not only easier and less expensive, but your attorney knows those laws. And you just might win.

Further, these basically "seller's choice" clauses can run smack into what another state or country just isn't willing to accept. For example, the German Parliament passed a sweeping law providing that all Web sites accessible from that country (which amounts to the world) are subject to German law. Ered-Web's standard conditions provide that the law to be used is that of New York State and the United States, with all lawsuits being brought there. If the hairdryer explodes in Hamburg, Germany, with the lawsuit being brought there, does anyone want to guess which law is more likely to be applied by the German court and where?

The same issue is raised if an injured consumer's state law provides that its law and venue (place to be sued) govern. It's important to remember that these Terms of Use provisions are not chiseled in concrete. In an important enough or "bet-your-company" situation, hire an attorney who can advise you on the likelihood of your beating such a clause. (See Chapter 11, "But Can Your Court Hear the Case? What Law Is Applied?")

OTHER PROVISIONS

Terms of Use agreements contain numerous other provisions. For example, they will have proprietary rights notices on copyrights and trademarks; rules for chat room conduct; "No professional advice's being given" notices; prohibitions on posting defamatory comments, linking conditions, or disclaimers (i.e., "You link with us at your own risk" or "Get our permission before you link"), or framing prohibitions (i.e., "Don't create links that bypass our home page, avoid our advertising, or make our site look like yours"); rights to any comments that you post at their location; the rules for games or sweepstakes; and on and on. If you are thinking about setting up your own Web site, take a look at what is covered on competing sites. *In "bet your company or house" purchases or informational reliance, it's advisable to consult expert legal opinion on the applicability of any of these provisions to your specific case—before you agree to that transaction.*

COPYRIGHTS AND TRADEMARKS. Web operators typically place a copyright notice on their sites (for notice purposes, even though it's not legally required) and limit what can or can't be done when copying from their site. If software programs, information, or other data are allowed to be downloaded, the typical copyright restriction limits that download to "one copy on any single computer for personal, noncommercial home use only, provided all copyright notices are kept intact." If you have a commercial reason for purchasing, then any infringement will depend on the extent of the use, whether you are a competitor, and any "fair use" arguments. Of course, if this is a B2B site, you won't find the commercial restriction, but there is usually a statement that the purchase can't be resold to others.

Whether listed under the heading of "Copyrights," "Restrictions on Use of Materials," or "Proprietary Rights Notices," these restrictions on use always will be overbroad. If you are the Net operator, then this will be standard practice because you'll want the additional legal protection. For example, another typical provision warns: "You may not reproduce, post, transmit, or distribute in any way whatsoever any Materials from our Web site without the prior written permission of the Company."

Sorry, nice try on this one. Regardless of what statements are posted, Web sites cannot limit what the law already allows. We have seen previously that the United States observes a "fair use" exception for copyrights. As we discussed in Chapter 4, "Copying in Cyberspace," the U.S. Copyright Act provides that copying copyrighted work in fair amounts for purposes such as "criticism, comment, news reporting, teaching, scholarship, or research" is considered to be fair use and is not a copyright infringement—no matter what a Net site (or any other source, for that matter) provides to the contrary. Courts will not allow these limiting statements to erode the doctrine of "fair use." Web operators should keep this in mind when they are deciding whether to send a threatening letter regarding a user's copying. However, most sites make the business decision to keep the stronger wording; it might deter some users who don't know their rights.

Lawyers who draft these provisions do seem to be working, at times, under the assumption that the more "dreary" this language is, the more likely that users won't care and will pass on it. Well, that wasn't the case when Yahoo! GeoCities's Web hosting service (http://geocities.yahoo.com) decided to change its Terms of Service. The change to now item "number seven" in its Terms of Service appeared to make Yahoo! GeoCities the legal copyright owner of all content stored on GeoCities Web pages. Even when material was clearly owned by the individual Web-site creators (businesses and individuals alike), this provision seemed to hold that every picture, word, or media file on a GeoCities page was considered to be Yahoo!'s property. To say the least, the users hit the ceiling.

GeoCities users quickly organized an effective boycott. Some moved their sites to other free Web hosting sites, and others replaced their Web page content with gray protest pages. Yahoo! was forced to revise its Terms of Service to make it clear that all users owned what was really theirs. Despite GeoCities' technical licensing of digital space to its users, the new section provides that the people keep their ownership of content. It is better to be fairer in the beginning, than to be scrambling later on.

ONLINE CONDUCT. A major area where users and Web sites enjoy commonality is in their mutual prohibitions against offensive, threatening, or other objectionable conduct by other users—whether the conduct involves a chatroom, a bulletin board, or simply a swap of e-mail. The typical Terms of Service or Terms of Use statement goes into detail on a site's rights in this regard. Most locations don't monitor their location on a 24/7 basis as to postings or messages; instead, sites typically react to any complaints that are made. Depending on the action complained about, the Net site will investigate, make a finding, and then send a warning to an infringing user. Site operators will move from a warning to suspension and then to the ultimate punishment of terminating use. However, sites will, at times, look the other way, so that they don't offend their users. The "Web Site Terms of Use" form, later in this chapter, provides a typical "Online Conduct" provision, as well as sections dealing with linking, use by children under 13, and other "boilerplate" that's usually included.

FORUM RULES. Some Web sites are primarily informational providers, and they use discussion groups as part of this function. These locations typically don't rely on selling products or subscriptions (i.e., Vault.com versus the *New York Times* [nytimes.com] with its different subscription and archive services). The definition of "Forum" is broad and can mean any discussion group, chatroom, bulletin board, or e-mail posting that's offered by the site as part of its services. Forum agreements contain several of the typical sections we have discussed so far: ownership of posted content, copyrights, links, disclaimers, and other similar boilerplate. However, their disclaimer and liability language are usually different, owing to the type of service that's provided, and their Terms of Use provisions go into more detail as to what conduct of their users is okay and what isn't. If you are considering creating a forum as part of your provided services, then check out the rules posted by competitive sites already on the Net.

Privacy Policies

We discussed the needs, requirements, and concepts of privacy policies in Chapter 6, "'Junk Dog' Statements and Privacy Concerns." All of the surveys and experts agree that a Web site must provide reasonable, detailed, and understandable statements on how it protects a user's privacy and then must follow these without fail. Also, displaying a privacy seal with its independent verification of procedures is another important step to take (and see Chapter 16 further). Net customers *are* skittish on this subject—and they should be, given the pace at which technological advancements are eroding what once were basic rights or comfort zones.

Privacy policies don't have to be necessarily long-winded, detailed, or complex—and they shouldn't be. Take a look at HealthyPlace.com, Priceline, and Amazon as examples, and see how readable their privacy policies are. Privacy policies should address at least the following basic questions:

- What information do we collect?
- Why do we need it?
- How do we use that data?
- How do we protect your data, including credit card information?
- What are "cookies" and how do we use them?
- Do we disclose any of this information to outside parties?
- How do we allow our customers to change or update their information?
- How can further data collection be terminated?

Examples of two privacy policies are reproduced at the end of this chapter. The first is simple and very short; the other is more typical. See Chapter 16, "Web Site Operating Considerations," for the guidelines on creating your own policy.

Read the Fine Print

You need to read the boilerplate, and if the language is nearly impossible to decipher due to its high-content legalese, then move to a Web site that uses more understandable words. Do not take anything for granted, nor trust that any particular Web site looks out for your specific business or personal interests. When developing or operating a Web site, keep in mind that your customers and users will be wary about privacy and these issues. Develop policies that address all of these concerns.

> If you are the purchaser, read the fine print and understand what a site states to be your business (or consumer) personal rights. If you are the Web operator, understand that fairly addressing privacy, service, and legitimate complaint concerns is always your best legal protection.

Keep in mind that Terms of Use and Privacy policies can vary extensively, depending on the type of site, its objectives, and its business. For example, is the location an informational site, nonprofit or educational, or are its operations more complex? Is it selling a variety of products, operating numerous bulletin boards, and running numbers of promotional activities? Some Web sites appear to be more consumer-sensitive than others. For example, look at how understandably Amazon.com with its widespread operations expresses its "Conditions of Use" and "Privacy Notice." They are simple and to the point. Its return, payment, shipping rates and policies, and more business-oriented policies are stated in detail by themselves—just as they should be.

A "Web Site Terms of Use Agreement" and two Privacy Policies (one short-form and one long-form) are provided here, as examples only. Although the concepts are generally the same, there are nearly as many different ways of wording these policies as there are Web sites. Each Web site has its own varying business, product, and service requirements—hopefully, based on decisions regarding the provisions best suited for it and its users. The legal provisions may also be different, owing to the differing operational policies that have been established: for example, how the site handles orders, payments, delivery, returns, and complaints, along with different product and service requirements. *Although you should consult an experienced lawyer for specific or complex questions, your Web site should strive to enact understandable, simple, and "consumer-oriented" policies. In fact, the simpler, the better.*

Web Site Terms of Use

Welcome to [*Company's Domain.Com Name*]. [*Company's Domain.Com Name*]'s goal is to provide the best services and products to you. To ensure that we can provide a safe and friendly environment for all of our users, we have established these TERMS OF USE. It spells out just what you can expect from us and what we can expect from you.

PLEASE READ THESE TERMS OF USE CAREFULLY BEFORE USING THIS WEB SITE OR ANY OTHER [*COMPANY'S DOMAIN.COM NAME*] WEB SITE. THEY ARE LEGALLY BINDING ON YOU.

By using this Web site, you signify your assent to these Terms of Use. (Note: The use of the word "Terms" also includes the term and concept of "Conditions.") We reserve the right, at our discretion, to modify, add, or remove portions of these terms at any time. Please check these terms periodically for changes. Your continued use of this site now or following the posting of changes to these terms will signify that you accept these Terms and/or changes. Your violation of these Terms, at a minimum, will result in your loss of the right to use our Web site, as we may decide in our absolute discretion.

1. RESTRICTIONS ON USE OF MATERIALS.

All materials on this site, including but not limited to text, images, designs, audio, graphics, logos, software, and the like (collectively called the "Materials"), are owned or licensed by [*Company's Domain.Com Name*] (called also the "Company") or its content suppliers and protected by U.S. and international laws. All trademarks, service marks, and trade names are proprietary to Company. You may not copy, transmit, post, create derivative works from, or republish in any way whatsoever any Materials from our Web site without the prior written permission of the Company. However, you may download or make one copy of the Materials and other downloadable items for personal, noncommercial home use only, provided all copyright and other notices on the Materials are left intact. Any modification or use of the Materials for any other purpose is an infringement of the Company's copyrights and other proprietary rights. Use of these Materials on any other Web site or other networked computer environment is prohibited without the prior written permission of Company.

2. DISCLAIMER.

THIS SITE IS PROVIDED BY [*COMPANY'S DOMAIN.COM NAME*] ON AN "AS IS" BASIS. WE MAKE NO REPRESENTATIONS OR WARRANTIES OF ANY KIND, EXPRESS OR IMPLIED, AS TO THE OPERATION OF OUR SITE, ITS INFORMATION, CONTENT, MATERIALS, OR PRODUCTS. TO THE FULL EXTENT PERMISSIBLE BY LAW, WE DISCLAIM ALL WARRANTIES, EXPRESS OR IMPLIED, INCLUDING BUT NOT LIMITED TO, THE IMPLIED WARRANTIES OF MERCHANTABILITY AND FITNESS FOR A PARTICULAR PURPOSE.

WE DO NOT WARRANT THAT ANY FUNCTIONS OF OUR SITE WILL BE UNINTERRUPTED OR ERROR-FREE, THAT DEFECTS WILL BE CORRECTED, OR THAT THIS SITE OR OUR SERVER(S) ARE FREE OF VIRUSES.

WE DO NOT WARRANT OR MAKE ANY REPRESENTATIONS REGARDING THE USE OF THE MATERIALS ON THIS WEB SITE AS TO THEIR ACCURACY OR RELIABILITY. YOU (AND NOT US) ASSUME THE COST OF ALL NECESSARY CORRECTIONS OR REPAIR. FURTHER, APPLICABLE LAW MAY NOT ALLOW THE EXCLUSION OF ANY IMPLIED WARRANTIES, SO THE ABOVE EXCLUSIONS MAY NOT APPLY TO YOU.

3. LIMITATION OF LIABILITY.

UNDER NO CIRCUMSTANCES SHALL [*COMPANY'S DOMAIN.COM NAME*] BE LIABLE FOR ANY CLAIMS OF NEGLIGENCE OR BREACH, INCLUDING BEING LIABLE FOR ANY SPECIAL OR CONSEQUENTIAL DAMAGES FROM THE USE OR INABILITY TO USE THE MATERIALS ON THIS WEB SITE, EVEN IF WE HAVE BEEN ADVISED OF THESE POSSIBILITIES. APPLICABLE LAW MAY NOT ALLOW THESE LIMITATIONS ON LIABILITY OR DAMAGES, SO THE ABOVE MAY NOT APPLY TO YOU.

IN NO EVENT SHALL OUR TOTAL LIABILITY TO YOU FOR ALL DAMAGES, LOSSES, AND CAUSES OF ACTION (WHETHER IN CONTRACT, TORT, NEGLIGENCE, OR OTHERWISE) EXCEED THE AMOUNT PAID BY YOU, IF ANY, FOR ACCESSING THIS SITE.

Web Site Terms of Use *(Continued)*

4. **ONLINE CONDUCT.**

Any communication which you post to our Web site is nonconfidential, and user agrees to use [*Company's Domain.Com Name*] only for lawful purposes. You shall not post or publish on our Web site any content which is defamatory, obscene, threatening, illegal, infringes on copyrights or trademarks, or is otherwise objectionable, including but not limited to any material encouraging conduct that would constitute a criminal offense, civil liability, or otherwise violate any applicable law.

If we are notified of any alleged content violation, we may investigate this and decide in our sole discretion whether to remove that content from our Web site. We may disclose any content or electronic communication of any kind (i) to satisfy any law, regulation, or government request; (ii) if such disclosure is necessary or appropriate to operate our Company; and (iii) to protect the rights or property of our Company, its users, or providers.

[*Company's Domain.Com Name*] reserves the right to prohibit conduct, communication, or content that we deem in our sole discretion to violate any law or be harmful to the rights of any user, our Company, or any third party. Provided, however, neither we nor our provider(s) can ensure the prompt removal of questionable content after online posting. Accordingly, neither our Company nor any of its officers, employees, or representatives shall assume liability for any action or inaction taken with respect to removing such material from our Web site.

Our Web site shall be used only for personal uses consistent with our site's operations. You shall not distribute or otherwise publish any commercial material soliciting or promoting any goods or services. You specifically acknowledge that soliciting any users of this Web site to become members of any commercial online service or other organization is expressly prohibited.

By uploading or submitting any materials to us, you automatically grant and warrant that the content owner has expressly granted us a royalty-free, irrevocable, nonexclusive right and license to use, publish, modify, and distribute the content worldwide, including the right to use it in other works in any form, media, or technology for the copyright term of this content. Subject to this grant, the content owner retains any and all rights which may exist in that content.

Any advice, services, or offers that are expressed by you, or made available by third parties, are those of the respective authors—and not of [*Company's Domain.Com Name*] or any of our officers, employees, or representatives. Neither Company nor any of its representatives guarantee the accuracy, completeness, or appropriateness of any content, opinion, or advice, nor its merchantability or fitness for any particular purpose. Under no circumstances shall we be liable for any loss, damage, or harm caused by a user's reliance on any information obtained through this Web site. It is the responsibility of each user to independently evaluate the information, advice, or other content found at this Web site.

5. **THIRD-PARTY SUBMISSIONS.**

User may upload to or distribute on our Web site only content that is not subject to any copyright or other proprietary rights protection, or content in which the author has given express authorization for Internet distribution. Any content distributed with the consent of a copyright owner should contain a phrase such as "Copyright, date, owned by [name of owner]; used by permission." The unauthorized submission or distribution of copyrighted or other proprietary content is illegal.

In compliance with the Digital Millennium Copyright Act, users and other persons can report any potential infringements and recommended corrections to us, in care of [*State E-mail Address for Complaints about Copyright Infringements*]. We will address those concerns in accordance with that Act. Neither our Company, it officers, or representatives will be liable for any damage resulting from any infringement of copyrights or proprietary rights, or from any other harm that arises from user submissions.

6. **PRIVACY POLICY.**

It is [*Company's Domain.Com Name*]'s policy to respect the privacy of our users. Our Privacy Policy is set forth at [*Indicate Where Privacy Policy Is Located*].

Web Site Terms of Use *(Continued)*

7. **LINKING FROM AND TO THIS WEB SITE.**

To the extent that this Web site has links from and to other Web sites, we cannot endorse nor control their content, accuracy, compliance with laws, or accessibility. If you decide to access these linked sites, you do so at your own risk. Any concerns regarding such outside Internet sites, or any link thereto, should be directed to that particular Web site.

Any link to our Web site is subject to our approval, conditions, and agreement, as we may decide in our sole discretion. Additionally, any linking, whether it is a hyperlink, use of spiders or robots, or whatever applicable technology, of a commercial, competitive, or offensive nature is strictly prohibited.

8. **TERMINATION OF USE.**

[*Company's Domain.Com Name*] reserves the right to refuse service, terminate accounts, suspend activity, and/or cancel orders in its sole discretion, including, without limitation, if we believe that any customer's conduct violates applicable law, is harmful to another user's interest, or is harmful to the Company's, a third-party's, or a service provider's interests.

9. **USE BY CHILDREN UNDER 13.**

[*Company's Domain.Com Name*] cannot prohibit minors from visiting our Web site. We must rely on the supervision of the responsible parents, guardians, and those responsible for supervising children under 13 to decide which materials are appropriate for children to view and/or purchase.

We require that all purchases be made either: (i) by individuals 13 years of age or older; or (ii) by minors under 13 whose parents or other guardians will pay for the minor's purchases, give verifiable permission for those purchases, and give verifiable permission to us for the collection of certain information in accordance with our privacy policy terms. Every time you purchase a product or service from our Web site, you are representing to us that you meet these criteria.

10. **INDEMNITY.**

You agree to indemnify, hold harmless, and defend [*Company's Domain.Com Name*], our employees, officers, directors, agents, and providers from and against all claims, actions, or demands, including reasonable legal fees and court costs, resulting from any breach by you of these Terms of Use or other liability.

11. **OTHER.**

Any legal dispute arising in connection with these Terms of Use shall be first attempted to be settled by mediation. If that is not successful, then the dispute shall be settled by arbitration to be held in [*Location of Arbitration*] in accordance with the rules of the American Arbitration Association, and this agreement to arbitrate shall be specifically enforceable. Any award shall be final and binding on all parties, and a final judgment may be entered in the appropriate court of law. Notwithstanding this, should any litigation ensue between the parties, then the prevailing party shall be entitled to reasonable expenses and attorney fees as set by the Court.

This site is created and controlled by [*Company's Domain.Com Name*] in the State of [*State of Operation and Whose Laws Control in a Dispute*], whose laws will govern these Terms of Use and any legal controversy. You consent to submit to the exclusive jurisdiction of the courts of the State of [*State Whose Laws Control in a Dispute*] and of the United States for any litigation arising out of our Web site's use and operation, waive any objection to this state on improper jurisdiction and/or venue grounds, and agree not to argue that any such litigation brought there has been brought in an inconvenient forum.

If any provision of these Terms of Use shall be deemed unlawful, void, or for any reason unenforceable by any court of competent jurisdiction, then that provision shall be deemed severable from the rest of the provisions and shall not affect the validity or enforceability of any of the remaining ones.

YOU AGREE TO BE BOUND BY THESE TERMS OF USE by your accessing, viewing, and/or using our Web site.

WEB SITE TERMS OF USE

Discussion of Provisions

Web sites need to have rules of conduct that protect their rights and outline what is or is not acceptable conduct. Further, sites need to have in place certain terms or conditions of use to spell out what their policies are. Otherwise, they may be waiving those rights when a legal controversy occurs.

Through this Terms of Use form, users signify their acceptance of those conditions by their use of that site. As we discussed previously, courts favor procedures whereby users can affirmatively indicate their acceptance of these provisions, such as by including the insertion of an "I Agree" button—and preferably before making any purchase decision as to products or services.

1. **Restrictions on Use of Materials.**
   This section advises a user that the text, design, graphics, and the like are the property of the Company, cannot be freely copied and transmitted around the world, and are protected by the law. This section limits the use again to downloading one copy for personal, noncommercial home use. If a Web site allows a broader use, then that should be substituted for this wording.

2. **Disclaimer.**
   Another standard provision is the section on disclaimer of warranties. This basically states that users assume the risk of use, that there is no warranty that operations will be error-free, as well as that certain implied warranties are waived. It should be noted that these warranty waivers are fairly limited by law and may not be upheld by a court of law in any particular jurisdiction or country—basically, entities are not allowed to contract against their own negligence. However, this disclaimer language is present because it will be upheld in different jurisdictions, and some users might rely on it as being legally binding.

3. **Limitation of Liability.**
   Similarly, it is standard practice for Web sites to include more limitations of liability and damages to accompany their disclaimers of warranties. These limitations are attempts to limit the damages a Web site could be held responsible for, in case a user experiences problems. These limitations are also not generally favored by courts and countries—however, they do give a degree of protection to a Web site, depending on the facts of each case and the particular court that's involved. This section's approach limits the dollar exposure to what the user paid for accessing the site. The terms of use at other Web sites set a dollar limit, such as $100 (or less), limit it to a refund of the purchase price or exchange of products, among other damage limitations.

4. **Online Conduct.**
   Web sites definitely need to set standards as to what conduct they consider to be unacceptable. This puts any user on notice as to what isn't permissible conduct, and gives the site the authority to "pull the plug" on someone who violates these rules. These provisions are commonsense ones, such as providing that defamatory, obscene, or threatening conduct won't be tolerated—and they shouldn't be. Web sites lose customers when their users become the target of such tantrums.

   You will want to read these provisions thoroughly, as with all other ones in this agreement and book, to be sure that they are entirely applicable to your operations. Similarly, users should know the differing use provisions of the Web sites they visit and buy on. Please keep in mind that these conditions of use are not made of steel and concrete—depending on any particular situation, if a Web site is responsible for creating a problem, that site may very well be held responsible for remedying it.

   A quite standard provision is that the sender of e-mail to a Web site gives a license to that site to use that communication. In other words, there is a loss of copyright protection by sending it and impliedly giving permission to the host site to post or even republish it. Further, if a Web site hosts chat rooms or uses guest moderators, it will usually disclaim any posted statements as not being representative of the company's views and opinions.

Web Site Terms of Use *(Continued)*

5. **Third-Party Submissions.**

   Some Web sites encounter a difficult area when users post material that they have no copyright ownership in—in other words, they've ripped the material from somebody else's site and posted it on their own. This section states a typical Web site approach in dealing with this risk of virtual operations.

   Web sites pay particular attention to the provisions of the Digital Millennium Copyright Act (see Chapter 4, "Copying in Cyberspace," for the details). In return for reasonably following up on copyright complaints, most Web site operators receive legal protection under this Act's provisions. It is important to designate someone who will receive these complaints (as well as other types).

6. **Privacy Policy.**

   Most Web sites separate their privacy policy from their long terms-of-use policies so that their privacy statements stand out on their own.

7. **Linking from and to This Web Site.**

   This standard provision basically states that users assume the risk when they use links from this Web site to others. Whether this in fact will be legally upheld, given a close working relationship between that site and the linked one, will depend on the facts and what the host site actually knows. This provision also states that links cannot be made to it for commercial purposes and that this site can control any links that are made.

8. **Termination of Use.**

   Web sites retain the right to terminate any user whose use violates its rules of conduct. This section states that right.

9. **Use by Children under 13.**

   Web sites experience a particular problem in that they generally can't tell the age of someone who is using their site or purchasing one of their products. Auction houses have experienced high-profile problems when underage bidders have entered the bidding process and used parents' credit cards with no authorization. Simply including the statement that users warrant they are of the right age (or a parent will "co-sign" their purchase) may not be enough. For large transactions, sites should require further verification and will need to adopt business practices to narrow down these risks, including parental contact and verifying birth information.

10. **Indemnity.**

    This section typically is present in Web site Terms of Use. It states that the user will indemnify, or insure, the Web site against the illegal consequences of that user's conduct or a breach of these provisions. As discussed in Chapter 9, the typical site indemnity provision tries to only protect the Web site.

11. **Other.**

    A heavily litigated area involves where lawsuits can be tried and under what applicable law. See the particular discussion under previously reviewed forms, including the chapter discussions, for these and the other provisions in this section.

Privacy Policies

Privacy Policy I

[*Company's Domain.Com Name*] does not acquire nor share personal identifying information with any third party without the express permission of the User. Such consent is usually requested in the following situations: [*State When Company Requests Consent for Information to be Released*]. We don't share personal information about individual Registered Users to any outside third parties for commercial purposes.

[*Company's Domain.Com Name*] aggregates statistics of Registered Users for statistical analysis and shares such information with third parties only in an aggregated form. We don't sell information to outside third parties, nor do we release individual information in any way to outside third parties.

We will not monitor, edit, or disclose the contents of e-mail, correspondence, orders, or any other electronic communications received from you, unless required in the course of the normal maintenance of this Web site or as we're required to do by law or in the good-faith belief that such an action is necessary to: (1) comply with the law or legal process served on us; (2) protect and defend our rights or property; or (3) act in an emergency to protect the personal safety of our users or the public.

Privacy Policy II

At [*Company's Domain.Com Name*] we are committed to respecting your privacy. While we collect some information from you, it is our committed policy to ensure that all of your personal information remains private and secure. As part of our privacy policy, we: (1) provide a privacy notice and/or a link to this Privacy Policy statement on all pages that ask for personal information; (2) will not sell or release personal identifying information about you to any other party without first obtaining your consent; and (3) will not knowingly collect or use personal identifying information from children younger than 13 without obtaining verified parental or guardianship consent.

1. **What Information We Collect.**

    When you visit our Web site, [*Company's Domain.Com Name*] collects basic information that does not identify individual users. This includes which pages are visited, the types of products purchased, and any feedback from our visitors. We then aggregate this information with volumes of other pieces of information to improve our site for you.

    We may assign your computer browser a unique random number, called a "cookie." These provide a secure way for us to verify your identity, personalize your experience on our Web site, speed navigation, keep track of items, and make your visit to our site more convenient. Your privacy and security are not compromised when you accept a cookie from our Web site, and we don't use cookies to collect specific personal information.

    We also use cookies to remember information you gave us so you don't have to reenter that data every time you visit our site. By showing us how and when users use our Web site, cookies also help us see which areas are popular and which are not. Many improvements and updates to our site are based on data such as the total number of visitors and pages viewed. Most browsers are initially set to accept cookies. If you would prefer, you can set yours to refuse cookies, but that also can disrupt some of the functions when you use our site.

    When you create an account with us, you provide to us such personal information as: first and last name, billing address, shipping address, e-mail address, telephone number, credit card account number, and the names of items you purchase from us. We collect this information on the pages where you create your account and at other pages where you sign up for our services.

Privacy Policies *(Continued)*

2. **How We Use It.**

   Based on this information given on your account, [*Company's Domain.Com Name*] fills, ships, and provides you with information about your order (i.e., whether your order has been received, processed, or shipped). We ask for your phone number (but this is not required) in the event that our service representatives can't reach you by e-mail. We use your mailing address not only to ship your orders, but also to tell you about special offers, products, or events we think will interest you (as we do by e-mail). Credit card information is used to bill you for products you have ordered and to track sales.

3. **Whom We Share that Information With.**

   - **Credit Card Processing and Security**

     You don't have to worry about credit-card safety when you shop at our Web site. [*Company's Domain.Com Name*] guarantees that each purchase you make is protected and safe. If fraudulent charges are ever made, you will not have to pay for them. We use the latest encryption technology to keep your personal information safeguarded.

     All your order information (i.e., your name, address, and credit card number) is encrypted using a secure server for maximum security. Your credit card and billing information cannot be read as it travels to our ordering system. To ensure that your information is even more secure, once we receive your credit card information, we store it on a server that isn't accessible from the Internet. We train all of our employees in how to best safeguard your confidential information.

     Credit card transactions are handled by a third-party financial institution, which receives the credit card number and other personal identifying information only to verify the credit card numbers and process transactions. If you feel more comfortable doing so, you are welcome to call in your credit card information and complete your purchase by phone. Or you can pay by check, and the product will be shipped once your check has cleared.

   - **Advertiser Links**

     [*Company's Domain.Com Name*] does work with certain advertisers who require that we disclose information about their customers who visit their Web site through the linkage from our Web site. This information is not disclosed in an individual capacity, but only in an aggregate way. Information such as numbers of "hits," average income, and average contacts per user are disclosed. In return, these advertisers share similar aggregate information with us, as to what happens on their Web site from these contacts.

   - **Special Promotional Offers**

     From time to time, [*Company's Domain.Com Name*] likes to share with you special promotional offers, which have been specially screened by us and can provide valuable savings to you. All of our customers are given the opportunity to not receive these offers, if they so choose, either by responding to the unsubscribe directions in any of these e-mails or by going to your account page and changing your general preferences.

4. **How You Can Change the Information.**

   If at any time you would like to change any information in your account, just go to the [*State How Users of Your Site Get to their Account Information*]. Once here, you can change or update your e-mail address and password, billing address, payment options, shipping options, and other information. You can save your changes then by: [*State How Changes Are Saved*].

5. **How to Stop Us from Gathering Information about You.**

   To unsubscribe from any e-mail messages, simply hit Reply to any message you receive and type the words "UNSUBSCRIBE" and the particular subject in the subject field. Please reply to the e-mail using the e-mail address at which you have received mailings from us, and we will remove you from our list. If you have more than one e-mail address, please include those others in your e-mail.

Privacy Policies *(Continued)*

You will be given periodically an opportunity to notify us of your preferences for receiving notifications and special offers. You can choose to receive news of these special opportunities in addition to updates on site features and new services, or you can choose not to receive them. Simply follow the instructions that are given to you at the time, and we will update our records accordingly.

6. **Protecting the Privacy of Children Under 13.**

[*Company's Domain.Com Name*] does not knowingly collect any personal information from a child without the consent of the child's parent(s) or guardian(s). Before signing up for a service that requests disclosure of personal information, children under 13 are advised to obtain parental consent. By participating in such a service, the user is representing that he or she is in compliance with this paragraph. We suggest that parents become involved with their children's access to the Internet and our site, to ensure that their child's privacy is always well protected.

7. **Other.**

By using our Web site, you consent to the collection and use of your information by us, as described in this policy. We will not monitor, edit, or disclose the contents of e-mail, correspondence, orders, or any other electronic communications received from you, unless required in the course of normal maintenance of this Web site or we're required to do so by law or in the good-faith belief that such an action is necessary to: (1) comply with the law or legal process served on us; (2) protect and defend our rights or property; or (3) act in an emergency to protect the personal safety of our users or the public.

[*Company's Domain.Com Name*] fully cooperates with law enforcement agencies in identifying those who use our services for illegal activities. We reserve the right to release information about members who we believe are in violation of our content guidelines. We also reserve the right to report to law enforcement agencies any activities that we reasonably believe to be unlawful.

We want you to be aware that when you click on links and/or ad banners that take you to third-party Web sites, you will be subject to those third parties' privacy policies. While we support the protection of privacy on the Internet, we cannot be responsible for the actions of third parties. We encourage you to read the posted privacy statement whenever you're interacting with any Web site.

[*Company's Domain.Com Name*] may update this policy from time to time; please check this page periodically for changes. By using this site, you signify your acceptance of agreement to [*Company's Domain.Com Name*] Privacy Policy.

We welcome comments and questions. Please contact us at [*State e-mail Address for Correspondence*].

Privacy Policies

Discussion of Provisions

Privacy policies are very important in this age of electronic commerce. Users and customers are reluctant to part with their personal information to "strangers," and Web sites must assure people that their personal information is required, that this is in their best interests, and that none of this data will be misused.

When one has been posted, the privacy policies of Web sites and businesses vary quite extensively and widely, depending entirely on what the site's objectives are, the overall services it provides, its business operations, and its philosophy. As distinct from a Web site's "Terms of Use"—which can become somewhat standardized in concept and practice—the same cannot be said about privacy policies, owing to the widely diversified operations and information-collection practices.

Two policies are attached that indicate the extremes within which these policies can differ. Privacy Policy I is for a Web site that only receives e-mail messages, sells no products or services online, and is basically an informational site. This form is a "short-form" policy—and additional provisions can easily be added, depending on each individual site..

Privacy Policy II is more typical for a site that sells products. However, this policy does not reflect any promotional venturing with other businesses, partner arrangements with other Web sites, different categories of users (which bring about different privacy policy disclosure requirements), and other Web site arrangements. This policy does give a simplified privacy disclosure as to its selling of products, including the use of credit card information.

Privacy Policy II breaks down its policies into simple components: what information is collected; how it is used; with whom the data is shared (i.e., credit card processing, security, advertiser links, and special promotional offers); how users can change any supplied information; and how users can stop data gathering (other than not buying any more products).

Web sites also experience a particular problem in that they can't tell the age of who's using their site or purchasing their products. The irony is that minors can easily decide what to do on their end, whether it's legal or not, but the Web site can be faulted for taking the personal information of that "innocent" minor. Regardless of this fact of life, Web sites should establish policies to weed out underage users, as well as minimizing the times they innocently acquire this personal information. When minors under 13 are part of a Web site's market, then it should gain, by e-mail, the written consent of the parents prior to collecting any data. Check the sites in your field and review the specific methods that are being used.

Last but not least, it is obvious that users do not have an absolute privilege for privacy. We have seen this elsewhere; for example, if anyone wants to purchase a product, he or she will have to supply the necessary information just to fill in the order and pay by credit card. Moreover, there is no privacy protection for a user who is engaging in illegal activities, disruptive conduct, or antisocial behavior.

When you are designing a privacy policy, review what other sites in your subject field are doing in this regard, and then decide what makes the best sense. Research the area online, including BBBOnLine, Truste, and other privacy-seal companies. (Truste also has a build-your-own privacy policy model.) If you're purchasing on the Net, then compare Web sites to see which ones make you feel most comfortable with their policies—then patronize those locations, all else being equal.

As with all other form agreements and policies included in this book, please understand that the above policies contain provisions that may not be appropriate for a particular Web site, its users, or customers. The policies presented here are for your general information and knowledge, and they should be modified to reflect your site's particular conditions and operations.

What If You Get a Lemon?

The problem of not getting what you want is so important that we are treating this subject in a separate chapter. Whether you just don't like the performance to specifications, the "darn thing" doesn't work, or you've been scammed, the question of dealing with "lemons" is a prime issue with Net purchases—and it makes no difference whether these are business or personal purchases.

Although you can "kick the tires" at brick-and-mortar stores, you're now making purchasing decisions from behind a computer in your office or study. The Internet's easy access and its ability to put on a smiling Web face allow the flimflam experts widespread maneuvering room. Although it's true that the great majority of Net operators are honest and have good intentions, it only takes one to ruin your business day. Even simple returns can take time and aggravation, given the necessary crediting to your credit card and the time spent ironing out the difficulties—even with the biggest and best of Web site players. Here are some considerations for you to think about so you can minimize these problems.

It Starts in the Beginning

The Internet is the most appealing sales opportunity yet created for business and individual consumers. You name the operation: whether it's Office Mart, Office Depot, Costco, or Sears, all of the largest retailers have linked e-commerce operations with their store networks and joined the legions of smaller sellers with an Internet presence. You can buy today whatever you want on the Net. The attractiveness of Web sites, the convenience of "click" shopping, and that Christmas feeling when you open the package are almost irresistible. That is, until you discover that the purchased item isn't what you thought it was.

Online shoppers need to use common sense when making their purchases. It makes sense to review the return policies of all Web sites before buying, whether the seller is a recognized company or not. And the better approach—or the one preferred by businesspeople—is to deal primarily with established companies or Web sites with stated, consistent return policies. As the cost of an item increases, users for good reason avoid locations they have never heard of or don't have the necessary policies conspicuously posted. (See Chapter 8, "Purchasing on the Net," for more on this.)

You can purchase your requirements in a variety of ways: by online classified advertisements, chat groups, unsolicited e-mails, online auctions, larger office/business Web sites, and even sites that specialize in what your business needs (i.e., from agricultural and medical equipment to chemicals and office supplies). Use your search engines with the descriptive words and watch the sites that pop up.

However, when dealing on the Net, be careful with any individual that you don't know (or can't verify). This doesn't mean that you'll have fewer problems with established companies, but it is easier to handle lemons with someone you can find than with someone you don't know or who isn't as interested in repeat customers. It also seems to be easier to deal with companies that you know are concerned with customer goodwill, or at least have stores close by to handle returns.

If the Web site is one that you aren't familiar with, check it out with the Better Business Bureau (see www.bbbonline.org, or ask your local BBB for suggestions). Additionally, the Better Business Bureau has a BBBOnLine Reliability Seal Program (at bbbonline.org) where merchants can sign up for a fee. Entrance into this system doesn't guarantee that you'll receive what you want from a site with this seal, but participants in this program have agreed to meet BBBOnLine's standards, including resolving customer disputes in agreed ways. Complaints made about a BBB member to the Better Business Bureau will obviously carry more weight than one about a site that no one has heard about.

The Internet Fraud Watch at www.fraud.org also provides helpful tips. Chapter 8 discusses the fraud area in greater detail. Prior to any purchase, think about the problems you might find and ask your friends what their experiences have been. You'll have fewer problems by taking the time to get your questions answered in the beginning, than e-mailing strong messages to that Web site afterwards.

CHECK OUT THE POLICIES FIRST

When you purchase an item from a brick-and-mortar store and discover you've bought a lemon, you simply head back there or to its service center with your purchase. If you're buying large machinery or quantities of office furniture, you've hopefully negotiated specifically what will be done with repairs, returns, and refunds. However, you don't know where a tiny dot.com's actual physical location is. For all you know, it's located in the bedroom or garage of a house—and if this is the site of your startup, you know that your company will have to convey a larger, more responsible image.

When purchasing on the Net, you should ask various questions before making your initial decision. These considerations will make a noticeable difference later, should you then find yourself with a lemon. Ask yourself:

- Does their policy state: "Satisfaction guaranteed or your money back?" Or are "all sales final," as they are at many bid and online auction centers?

- Are there "restocking" charges if you do return an item? Is there a "service and handling fee"?

- Is there no charge with shipping costs reimbursed if the return is due to the fault of the seller (i.e., it shipped the wrong item)? Many sites provide for this, but their policy should clearly state it.

- How long does it take before your account or credit card is given the proper credit for a return? It might be worth sending an e-mail query about this to the company, if this policy isn't prominently displayed. *Some firms take up to two billing cycles before you receive a credit, and you're assessed the interest on that fictitious credit during this time period.*

- Does the company allow returns to be taken to a local store, or must they be repackaged, hauled to the post office, and mailed back by you? Depending on the site, you should know first whether returns are to be mailed back (if not prohibited by size), at whose cost, and what happens in that event.

- Does the company's local stores in your area accept returns? Most large business and consumer retailers indicate on their Web site where you can find this out. However, you should call that store just to be sure it does accept potential returns involving your purchases, what the procedures are, and its location—especially before you buy large, bulky items such as heavy office equipment, quantities of supplies, or other goods. At times, what the local store does and what the Web site provides can be two different things.

- What are the postage or delivery costs, should you return your order by mail? These expenses can vary for the same product offered for sale by competing Web sites.

- How convenient is it for you to return a product? For example, does the retailer include a preprinted label? If so, how simple or expensive is that process? Some sites include a preaddressed U.S. Post Office return label in the package. If you need to return an item, you use that label, and the company charges your credit card a flat but small charge when it receives your package. Others include the label but it's up to you to take it to the post office, weigh it, and get the right postage.

- Is this a product you can't return? For example, online sellers typically don't allow the return of videos, CDs, or cassettes when the package has been unwrapped. If the purchased item is a collectible or one-of-a-kind, it is quite likely that all sales are final.

- Is a customer service center available where you can talk to an actual human being about your problems? This can make a real difference; you will avoid trading escalating e-mail insults when you get even more frustrated over this inability to solve the problem.

- Does the Web site allow you to track your orders? For example, it can be a benefit to know how long it takes before the order is filled, when it's ready to be sent, the date it was mailed, and the expected delivery date. This can be essential if your business needs the item promptly.

- Can you cancel an order without incurring a penalty? And by when? People do change their minds when buying something, and some Web sites say flatly that all sales are final.

- If installation is needed (i.e., you're buying equipment for your manufacturing plant due to that great price), then does the site tell you all that you need to know about the best ways (and costs) to do this?

- What if the purchase needs to be repaired later? Are any warranties in place—or can you purchase an extended warranty program (if you really want to)?

BIDDING OR ONLINE AUCTIONS

Among consumers and businesses, a major area for complaints involves bidding sites or online auctions. The advantage of virtual auctions, of course, is that you can get great values through the bidding process, whether you're buying tons of chemicals, office supplies, or Amani suits. These are real-world auctions where you submit cyberbids. If you're the highest bidder, then you've bought that item. A reputable auction house or Web site typically doesn't own or sell that product; instead, an individual seller who might be living thousands of miles away is the intended seller. *The problem is that you can't usually inspect the merchandise ahead of time, determine its authenticity, or receive a refund if you decide to return it, unless that online auction seller is honest and ethical.*

The statistics support being careful with online bidding. Whether it's the number of complaints received by the Better Business Bureau, Internet Fraud Bureau, or state consumer agencies, bidding and online auctions are a major source of all complaints received from virtual buyers.

The courts have consistently held that Internet auction or bidding Web sites are not required to ensure the authenticity or quality of what outside sellers put up for sale. Of course, if the Web site has knowledge of or some connection with those sellers, then they would have a shared liability with the sellers of "lemons." However, the great numbers of these locations have no such knowledge or connection.

Reputable online auction houses, such as eBay, have taken these matters seriously and have enacted various policies. Before jumping in and bidding for office supplies, equipment, or collectibles, you need to acquaint yourself with all of these policies. For example, just what do you do if the seller has disappeared with your money? For example, eBay currently offers free insurance up to $200 (with a $25 deductible) for its users, if they run into an unreturnable lemon. To qualify for this insurance, the user must buy an item listed on eBay and comply with the site's guidelines. However, as these policies change from time to time, you'll need stay current with what eBay or other sites provide at the time.

You form an enforceable contract to buy when your bid is selected as the highest or best one. If you try to back out later, then you can be sued over that breach. Accordingly, it's important to know what you're bidding on and what are the best values. This also means you had better be able to pay the price, if your bid is accepted. If you have children, then keep a rein on their "bidding" activities. We still remember the poor parents of the kid who bid millions of dollars for an office building, paintings, and other items (the transactions were rescinded but the parents found themselves in very hot legal waters).

An important rule of thumb is: NEVER pay in cash, use a debit card, or send a check for any online purchase. ALWAYS use your credit card. Credit card companies allow you to rescind a fraudulent deal or reverse the charges when you have a legitimate complaint, and your losses are limited to $50 under current law. This "chargeback system" is an excellent, cheap method of dispute resolution, so never use cash or its equivalents to pay for your Web purchases.

One problem occurs infrequently but can become nasty. Some sellers aren't able to handle credit cards; they haven't worked out the necessary arrangement with their local bank. Or worse, they have such an arrangement, but they don't want credit cards used—they want a check or money order. The absence of a credit-card processing ability says something, by itself, about that business, so be careful if you run across this situation. As we discussed before, an alternative way to handle this and other problems is to use an independent escrow service.

Escrowing purchases has advantages in numbers of situations. Let's say that you submit the winning bid in an online auction of heavy equipment and machinery, but contingent on resolving a few issues. You've seen pictures of the bid items beforehand, perhaps even inspected them, but you have questions about title and delivery. An escrow company would be a practical answer to these concerns. The escrow could hold your money until the questions about title and delivery are answered. Until you approve these conditions (or any other ones), the escrow company holds onto your money. Once you approve all of the contingencies, it authorizes the seller to ship off the equipment and machinery. At the agreed time when the seller is entitled to your money, the third party delivers those proceeds. This approach can be used for everything, ranging from real estate and cars to one-of-a-kind baseball cards.

These services are not free—as one example, check out Tradenable and its subsidiary, i-Escrow (www.tradenable.com) for services and costs. eBay currently links to Tradenable as its recommended escrow holder. The costs range from 4 percent to 1 percent, depending on the transaction amount and how the fee is paid (cash or credit). Keep in mind that any reputable escrow company can be used; it need not be an online one. You can check out these companies for your or the seller's area in the Yellow Pages.

The usual rules apply. Check out all sellers through the Better Business Bureau or research the auction site's "feedback" section before submitting your bid; get the seller's return and refund policies, including any warranties and representations, in writing before bidding; determine when the item can be delivered and what to do in case repairs are needed; only deal with someone who answers a telephone and has a verifiable street address (i.e., to be sure that no mail will be returned for a wrong address, send paper copies of e-mails to that address, asking for verification); and document everything, just in case later problems develop. Never pay by check, of course, and use an escrow service whenever possible.

When Buying a Business or Stock

So far, we've been discussing the problem of buying a "lemon." *However, be especially wary of fraud if you're looking at buying a business, or stock, offered by individuals on the Net. There are good reasons why investment advisers warn their clients not to do this.*

It is simply too easy for promoters to show a glitzy, fabulous-looking site that's only operated out of a garage in, let's say, Tahiti or the Bahamas. These sites will e-mail tons of information to you, even talk with you at great length in soothing and assuring tones about the merits of their stock or business investment. They will send impressive-looking brochures that promise a doubling or tripling of your money in very short time periods. As soon as they have your money, it only takes a few minutes to trash that Web site and they're gone forever.

A major problem when buying stock offered on the Net is gaining the necessary assurances that this stock not only can be sold to you (i.e., it's been properly registered with the right state and federal authorities, or there's an exemption from this requirement), but that you have the legal right to resell this stock later on.

This concern is not applicable to e-transactions in which you're placing orders through a recognized cyberbroker to buy stock on a recognized stock exchange. However, the danger when you're buying promoted stock over the Net is just as high as when you're looking at buying business opportunities. Be especially wary of promoters who are trying to sell work-at-home, multimarketing, pyramid (you get others involved and then they pay you), or business-opportunity "get rich" schemes. These "be careful" areas also include advance fee loans (you pay a large fee up front for a promised loan), credit repair (payments are made first, before they'll "fix" your credit problems), and credit card issuing (arranging credit when you have especially bad credit).

The Internet Fraud Watch (at www.fraud.org) provides excellent information on avoiding online scams, as well as tips on how to keep your credit card number safe. For example, don't immediately buy on the sales pitch. Take the time to get all the answers to your questions—and check out unknown companies before you buy (or use an escrow service). Be careful when you're giving out financial information, your credit card number, or any information that is of a private nature.

Dealing with a Lemon

If you are dealing with a reputable company and know its policies, then you have an easier situation than if either of these conditions is missing. There are several areas to keep in mind—all of which deal with the general concept of "Escalate the pressure until you finally get the results."

DOCUMENT, DOCUMENT, AND DOCUMENT

When you order online, you should acquire the habit of setting up a file that contains all of the information used to make your decision. Print out all offers and purchase forms, keep copies of all e-mails, and file away all correspondence. If you have questions, don't rely on what you're told over the telephone. Confirm it by e-mail and put that response into your file.

If you're buying only supplies or raw materials—let's say, under $250 (or whatever your threshold is)—then you wouldn't worry about this as much. However, if the purchase is important to you, then immediately download and print out everything from the Web site that bears on your decision, from pictures and representations to telephone numbers and addresses. Information changes quickly and regularly on the Net, so what's needed to prove who's at fault could otherwise disappear too quickly. These files will prove your case, if you must later make a complaint to the Web site, the Better Business Bureau, or even the FTC or a state consumer fraud agency. The files also are helpful in negotiating with an inflexible seller.

BE SURE IT'S NOT YOUR FAULT

You've ordered a TXC computer with standard memory. If you really needed a DNT computer with expanded memory, then you have to be honest with yourself and your online seller. If the Web site's records show that the TXC computer was shipped as ordered, then you will have problems convincing anyone that the wrong equipment was selected by the seller. If the site's return policy is one that "guarantees full satisfaction, otherwise your money's returned," then you don't have a problem. However, most firms require that you assume the return delivery costs, unless it was "their fault" (i.e., you ordered a DNT and they really shipped a TXC). As discussed before, it makes more sense to know the policies and procedures *before* there's a problem, rather than afterwards.

BE NICE, AT LEAST AT FIRST

A friend of mine who worked in a company's complaint center said, "If someone wasn't nice to me, then I wasn't that interested in going out of my way for them either." This is a commonsense point. Even if you have problems down the road, it is better not to flare, soar into a tirade, or use four-letter words. What amazes me is that if attorneys who are constantly battling with other lawyers in court can keep their "cool," then everyone else can surely do the same. True, this can be a very difficult thing to do, but people will work more with those who show courtesy, than those who don't.

Try to follow the complaint steps that the Web site provides. If it has a customer service center and a real person you can talk to, then so much the better. If you send e-mails to the Net site and receive nothing back, then print out a copy (with your supporting documentation) and send that by snail mail. Try to be polite, of course, with all of your complaint correspondence. Don't defame the other side—but be firm.

FOLLOW THE PROCEDURES AND BE PERSISTENT

Before you complain to any agency, Better Business Bureau (BBB), or other entity, you need to complete that Web site's procedures, including its stated appeal policies. Let's say that you jumped the gun and complained to someone before the Net company finished its process. If an agency makes an inquiry on your case, the firm could answer simply, "Gosh, we're still working on it." And you're back to square one again, waiting for that site to complete its investigations and the complained-to agency again filing away your complaint.

If the firm is slow in getting around to your problems, then call and prod it into action. Again, don't flame or become too upset; keep a "cool" mind and demeanor. Life is too short, otherwise.

The winner in these situations is always the one who keeps plugging along, and persistence is definitely a virtue in these cases. Whether you're able to settle everything directly with the site or must enlist the aid of outside and agencies, you just keep going. The tortoise wins this race, not the hare.

There's No Response or Help

If you receive some response, then determine whether you should keep going. For example, if you bought a lousy cellular telephone for $100 and the seller sends you a credit for $80 (less a handling charge), is it really worth continuing the fight over the $20? The real problem comes when you get a lousy response or none at all. Then, it's time to escalate your response.

DO YOUR RESEARCH

An initial step is to find out what law applies to your case, whether it's the "lemon laws" dealing with problems on automobiles under warranty, or regulations on veterinary drugs and supplies. Using your trusty search engine with keywords involving your product and disputes is a start. Or try the Academic Legal Information site (academicinfo.net), which provides links to various legal research sites. Two good ones are: FindLaw (findlaw.com) and Hieros Gamos (www.hg.org). You would look under your particular state or country and see what laws apply to the particulars of your case. For example, if you bought a computer at an auction and it was a lemon, try key words such as "auction disputes," "online auction problems," "computers and refunds," "defective computers," and the like.

Another way is to use a search engine and surf for your state's or country's consumer fraud or misrepresentation laws, whether it's a business or a consumer purchase. For example, if you live in California, try "California consumer laws," "California consumer protection," "fraud," or other variations. If your problem is much bigger and you hire an attorney, your lawyer will take a look at which defective product, return, and refund laws apply to your case. Keep an eye out for clash-of-laws problems, especially if your purchase was from an out-of-state seller. (See further Chapter 11, "But Can Your Court Hear the Case? What Law Is Applied?")

For those of us who aren't used to this type of research, telephone your local Better Business Bureau or state consumer fraud unit and ask what laws apply to your particular case. Given their global exposure, Web sites should explicitly detail their refund and return rights. If they don't, however, they may be violating a local disclosure law—and this can be used in your negotiations or complaint to a governmental agency.

States, provinces, and some countries have passed laws that set the time period within which Net companies must issue a refund, mandate the disclosure of the site's return and refund policy, and require other Net-retailer legal compliance. For example, California's refund law affecting online sellers became effective way back in that ancient time of 1997. This law requires all out-of-state companies that use the Internet in advertising or selling products or services to state their refund policies. Before any seller could be paid, that entity had to inform the customer about its: (1) product return and refund policy; (2) assumed business name, if different from that of the real owner; and (3) complete street address where the seller conducted its business. The seller could disclose this information in writing, by e-mail, or in an on-screen notice; under the law and among other requirements, vendors must ship ordered products within 30 days of receiving payment. Violators face up to six-months in jail and a $1,000 fine.

If you lived in California, bought from a Web site, had problems with the item, and the site didn't have the required disclosures, these laws would give you a much stronger bargaining position. With such a violation, you also could get the attention of the California authorities that much quicker. Check to see whether your locality has such a provision, or one that's similar, and whether your Web site violated those requirements. It makes no difference whether that site operates in your locality or thousands of miles away. It is still subject to those local laws, conditioned only on their reasonableness and the extent of their contacts with your state.

WHEN YOU'RE THE WEB SITE

Every Internet company must look at its operations from the viewpoint of its customers and clients. As more countries and states enact consumer-friendly legislation, being consumer-friendly simply makes good business sense. Net operators already are generally providing reasonable privacy, refund and return, and other use policies, because various countries, localities, and governmental agencies require them. With millions of new Internet users coming online every month, the overseeing legislatures and regulatory agencies are being hit with increasing numbers of complaints and requests for help. The business environment these days requires being proactive, consumer-sensitive, and skilled in avoiding unnecessary consumer complaints. (See Chapter 14, "Creating Your Own Web Site," and Chapter 16, "Web Site Operating Considerations," for more.)

A STRONGLY WORDED COMPLAINT

If your first letter doesn't bring results or isn't answered, send a second strongly worded complaint, stating that if the site doesn't refund your money, you will take this situation to the authorities. Include copies of your supporting data and indicate on the letter that you're sending a copy of it to your local consumer protection agency, the Better Business Bureau, and perhaps even the Federal Trade Commission. It is your choice as to whether you actually do so at this point in time.

Additionally, try posting your complaint on that bidding or online auction site and see what develops. One man posted such a notice on an auction site and asked anyone who felt ripped off by one particular seller to contact the police in their state. The police received numerous complaints and issued an arrest warrant against that seller for fraud. Although apparently what was paid was never recovered, the seller's rip-off tactics were stopped—at least for that time.

CONTACT THE FTC (OR OTHER AGENCIES)

When all else has failed, you should work with the outside agencies, as well as your local and state ones. First, contact the National Consumer Fraud League (www.fraud.org). This site is helpful for customers who have received a raw deal. You may also call the Internet Fraud Watch at their hotline telephone number (1-800-876-7060). This nonprofit consumer group will take your complaint, whether offline or online (it has an online incident report form), and enter it into its computer program.

After you send in your report, your complaint will be sent to the FTC and will be transmitted to any of 160-plus law enforcement agencies whose responsibility could include your situation. You should also review the Internet Fraud Watch's "links" page, which provides links and addresses to U.S. federal consumer law agencies, all state Attorneys General, and numbers of different-country consumer protection agencies.

If you want, you can go directly to the FTC (www.ftc.gov), the SEC (www.sec.gov) on stock swindles, various states' Attorneys General, and other jurisdictions. OK. Don't forget to make a telephone call to your local consumer protection agency and ask what they advise. Check out also the Better Business Bureau (www.bbbonline.org) and see Chapter 7, "'Great Deals,' 'Easy Money,' and Other Ads," for more ideas.

International Considerations

The problems of poor quality, no shipment, undisclosed charges, and invoices for unordered services or products are universal. Should you be unfortunate enough to end up with a B2B/B2C lemon from a Web site in a foreign country (or a consumer overseas has one from you), there are existing consumer protection agencies in countries located across the globe. These entities vary in their regulation and enforcement powers—although outside of the European Union, many won't be as "consumer-oriented" as the U.S. FTC and its state counterparts. However, these agencies are in existence to protect consumers, and they range from ones in the UK (see the Office of Fair Trading, www.oft.gov.uk) and Canada to Brunei and Korea. Surf a particular country's Web site or use your search engine for it with the words "consumer protection," or similar phraseology.

We discussed the FTC-run, international Web site at econsumer.gov (see Chapter 7, " 'Great Deals,' 'Easy Money,' and Other Ads") that provides links to numbers of consumer-protection/enforcement agencies in different countries, should you purchase or sell a lemon involving another country's resident. Next, there is the FTC's existing Consumer Sentinel Web site at consumer.gov/sentinel, to address international complaints that are outside the e-consumer Web site.

Another development is in international tie-ins between various regional and country entities. For example, BBBOnLine (the Internet arm of the Better Business Bureau, www.bbbonline.org), FEDMA (Federation of European Direct Marketing, www.fedma.org), and Eurochambres (Association of European Chambers of Commerce and Industry, www.eurochambres.be) joined forces in 2001 to develop a new international seal or "trustmark" program for e-business. Businesses that adhere to the initiative's business practice standards will be entitled to use a single, internationally recognized "trustmark" to indicate its good standing in building consumer confidence. Over time, it is expected that these associations, seal programs, and cooperation between countries will ever increase—to increase international e-commerce consumer confidence and to dampen fraudulent practices.

Complaint Web Sites

Some frustrated consumers have felt that because the Internet caused their problems, they would use the Net to solve them. The nightmare among legitimate Web companies is that unhappy customers will take to the Net with their criticisms—whether these comments are founded or not. As you would expect, there has been a proliferation of sites totally critical of specific companies and their practices. Use any search engine to see if one exists for the business you feel has "done you wrong." For example, if Ace.com hasn't been fair with you, then enter "Ace," "Ace sucks," "Acebeware.com," or other similarly descriptive words with search engines. Then contact the complaint site with your story and see what reply you get.

Numbers of "suck.com" sites have been established with Microsoft the apparent leader (which is the target of over 20 protest sites). These locations have become so popular that companies like Bell Atlantic (now part of Verizon), Chase Manhattan, and PaineWebber have registered their own "dot.suck" or other protest domain names to keep these unavailable. In fact, various businesses now routinely check domain name registrars and the Net for derogatory names, then take steps to acquire them. From United Airlines, Allstate, and U-Haul to Bally Total Fitness Centers, Delta Airlines, and Ford, every major company it seems has had its share of being the target of this practice (or problem, depending upon your viewpoint). (See Chapter 6, " 'Junk Dog' Statements and Privacy Concerns," for more.)

BE CREATIVE

If you are mad enough and have the time, set up your own suck.com or complaint site. For example, one couple endured a bad experience with a moving company. When they arrived at their new home, some of their furniture and property had been damaged and other articles were missing in the process. The movers rejected their complaint, even though they had suffered nearly $2,000 of damages. Feeling helpless, they decided to create their own critical Web site.

On that site, they detailed their experiences accurately. As other users accessed it, their Web site became more popular. About one month later, they were negotiating with a claims adjuster for the moving company, who offered only a few hundred dollars in settlement. The couple then told the adjuster to punch in the name of their Web site. Ten minutes later, they received a telephone call from the adjuster, who told them that the company would settle all their claims as they wanted, provided they dismantled their site. They agreed, received their money, and took the site down. Although numbers of people probably wouldn't spend this much time, it was a creative way to solve the lemon problem. As discussed previously, another creative approach is to post your complaint on the Internet, either at the site where you purchased the problem or at a "complaint site," and see what happens. Be sure, however, that your complaint is factual and legitimate.

On the other hand, businesses can be confronted with complaint sites used as technological-complaint weapons by irritated customers who have time on their hands. One customer launched an anti-Dunkin' Donuts site, alleging that he'd been served skim milk in his coffee. The doughnut maker eventually bought the site from him for an undisclosed sum. Some busy "entrepreneurs" try this in an attempt to sell that site name back to the target company for a tidy sum of money. Given the legal developments in the United States against "cybersquatters" and ICANN's domain-name arbitration procedures (see Chapter 13, "Domain Names and Conflicts," for more), businesses have more weapons on hand to combat overzealous complainants.

However, legitimate "gripe" sites have been consistently upheld by U.S. courts as protected by the First Amendment of the U.S. Constitution. In fact, a U.S. Court of Appeals case upholds the right to create a Web site with a protected trademark and trade name that includes the word "sucks," if this is used to legitimately criticize a specific company's product or service.

Small Claims Court

Suing in small claims court can be a problem, unless you have a way to obtain lawful service of process (serving lawsuit papers properly to require their defense in your court) on an Internet company. For example, if you live in Canada and the Web site is in the United States, or vice versa, small claims court will not usually be an alternative. Further, if you live in Illinois and the Web site is located in Colorado, then you still can have a real problem with jurisdiction and conflicts of laws.

In these cases, checking out the product, the site, and its return policies should be done in the beginning.

Aside from these considerations, suing in these courts can be a viable alternative. Small claims is just that: these courts are limited to claims that have a small dollar value. Most states have enacted limits of $5,000 or less (although a few go as high as $10,000 or more), and you can't win more than that dollar limit. However, the services of an expensive lawyer aren't necessary or allowed in small claims courts, and the cases are resolved within 30 to 60 days of filing your legal complaint. Check with your local small claims court on the current rules and whether you can sue an out-of-state Web company in your state (this will be the major problem). On the other hand, this procedure can be especially useful if the Web operator owns stores in your area or has some physical presence that may allow you to legally sue the company.

ADRs versus Lawsuits

If the matter is important enough, you will consider legal action. As we've pointed out before, the problem is trying to find and sue an out-of-state (or different-country) Web operator. This can be an especially daunting and expensive proposition, although that doesn't mean this can't be done.

You might consult with a lawyer—but try to keep any initial meeting on a free consultative basis. If anything, you could threaten the firm with a lawsuit. One attorney, who bid on an expensive Chanel three-piece suit (but was sent a size 4 instead of the advertised size 10), threatened a lawsuit over that purchase. The seller finally agreed to give a credit toward additional purchases, but still wouldn't grant a full refund. If a lawyer, whose time in court is free, has difficulties in gaining a full refund, then you should always weigh how much an attorney will cost versus what you can force in return.

Before deciding on the litigation alternative, you should definitely consider using alternative dispute resolution (ADR) techniques. Litigation is generally a poor way to solve disputes, unless you have a bet-your-house or bet-your-company problem and there's no other alternative. Lawsuits are expensive, time-consuming, become public knowledge, and are quite negative.

In place of litigation, look at using ADRs such as mediation, arbitration, private judging, and other concepts. In fact, online firms are now providing mediation services over the Net (see Chapter 12, "Cyberlaw Dispute Resolution," for the details).

What Did You Learn?

Even if you had a difficult time dealing with your lemon, you probably won't give up purchasing on the Net, but you won't be doing business with that particular Web site again. Hopefully, you've learned to do your homework in the beginning, not after you've discovered there's a problem.

CHAPTER 11

But Can Your Court Hear the Case? What Law Is Applied?

Cyberspace knows no boundaries. It envelops the world as a giant network of interconnecting small groups, laced with smaller ones, down to its smallest component—you—the one person sitting behind a computer, who then interfaces with everyone else. This network of networks links businesses, institutions, governments, and people around the globe. A company in Malaysia can purchase electronic equipment from a Canadian business whose sales rep, Web site, and Internet server reside in the United States. A Michigan commercial real estate broker can download needed software from a firm in Dallas, Texas, that utilizes a Web server in New York City, and then, in the next minute, be "chatting" with clients in different countries on its own Web server located in Ohio.

The story sounds as fantastic as it is—until the problems occur. The Malaysian discovers that the equipment is defective, and the question becomes whose law controls and where can the lawsuit start. In Malaysia, Canada, or the United States? The Michigan broker's software crashes, losing all of its important business data. Whose law controls and where does the broker sue: Michigan? Texas? Or New York, where the defendant's ISP is located? As people who are connected to a dispute become more scattered around the globe, the question of which court can hear a case or make any binding decision becomes more complicated.

The key issue in any Internet legal action becomes whether your court can hear and decide the case. For example, what if your business is in the United States and you buy needed photographic and printing supplies (at a great price) over the Internet from a manufacturer who's headquartered in Japan, but when the crates of the ordered product arrive, they turn out to be waterlogged? Or, vice versa, what if you're the manufacturer and you're located in the United States? If your court can hear the case (exercise jurisdiction over it), then you can sue in your country and not travel a long distance to sue in some foreign court. Your adversary then has to travel to your court and contend with the hotel and travel expenses, different language, strange customs, and stranger laws.

The crux of these cases is simply that if the problem is big enough, you want *your* laws to apply (or those of a place that has more favorable statutes). But you also want to be able to eat and sleep in your own home, work at your office while you're not in court, and not have to hire an expensive attorney in a foreign state. If you live in one country, you want to be able to sue there and not come down with jet lag, bad food, and weeks of separation from your family. Similarly, if you work in Seattle, Washington, you don't want to fight your court battles in Miami, Florida, where the plaintiff works and lives. These are very simple, basic reasons why this complex subject is battled so hard.

U.S. Jurisdictional and Conflicts Law

It's clear that if you live in Colorado and buy a forklift from a business in Colorado, then Colorado law applies. If a Colorado resident crosses the border into Kansas, buys that same forklift in Kansas, and the Kansas dealer services the equipment there, it's clear that Kansas law should apply. The question becomes, however, if you buy equipment on a Kansas Web site but you stay in Colorado, which state law then applies? Before we answer that problem, let's look at bottom-line law, whether you're dealing with the Internet or not.

Let's say that you are a resident of New Jersey and driving on a long vacation to visit relatives in California. However, as you travel through Chicago, your car is hit by one driven by an Illinois resident. Your car and vacation are wrecked, and you must spend one week in a Chicago hospital before you can fly back to your New Jersey home. Let's say that it's hard to prove who was really at fault in this accident. The Chicago driver sues you first, using an Illinois long-arm statute which provides that out-of-state drivers, who are involved in Illinois accidents, must accept its courts' ability to hear those cases. In other words, the Illinois courts have jurisdiction (i.e., those courts can hear the case and make a binding decision in the matter).

All U.S. states have enacted some form of a long-arm statute that allows residents of one state to sue a nonresident for injuries caused by the nonresident in that state; nonresident drivers, in essence, consent to being sued in the state in which the accidents occur, because they are also protected by that state's laws. Unless you find a way to successfully beat the jurisdictional question, you will have to travel to Chicago for the trial. The Illinois court will apply Illinois law, not New Jersey law, because the law that governs car and personal injury accidents is the law of the state where the accident occurs.

If the lawsuit could be brought in a federal court (and if the attorneys consented), then the question would be: In which district—Illinois or New Jersey—would the lawsuit be tried? What law would be applied? Although this can be a very complicated question, basically the plaintiff (the one bringing the lawsuit) could bring the lawsuit in the Illinois district, and the Federal District Court would apply Illinois law on the question of accident liability and damages.

For the most part, when a U.S. court is allowed to assert jurisdiction over any particular transaction, it also can apply its laws to that situation. Thus, the big question typically is: Which state (or country) has the ability to assume the jurisdiction, or the control of a lawsuit, and make that binding determination?

In its landmark 1945 *International Shoe* decision, the U.S. Supreme Court's established U.S. law in this area. To have proper jurisdiction, a defendant must have purposely availed itself of the privilege of doing business (i.e., traveling, selling, advertising, and so on) in a state, and these "connections" to that state must meet minimum levels of due process so as not to offend "traditional concepts of fair play."

Let's say that a Wyoming rancher died and left all of his land and ranching operations to his son, a resident of Wyoming. It would offend our sense of "fair play" if a second son, who happened to live in Alabama, could sue his Wyoming brother and haul him into an Alabama court. There are no connections with Alabama in this case, so the only court with jurisdiction should be in Wyoming—and that court would apply Wyoming law (the property is there, the decedent and his heir lived in the state, the will was executed there, and so on). It wouldn't be fair if a Wyoming resident could be dragged into an Alabama court just because the Alabama gentleman didn't want to travel to Wyoming.

Now, let's apply this concept to an actual international case. An American receives a mail-order catalog from England. It lists various computers, including one for $1,000, a very low price for this particular model. He sends in a deposit on an order to buy 1,000 of those computers at $1,000 each—a $1 million contract—and the English firm cashes the check. However, he soon receives a fax that says there was a mistake in the catalog. The actual price for each computer, which the firm says he should have known about, was really $1,500, so there was a $500,000 mistake. The English firm sends back his deposit. U.S. law would generally hold that there was an enforceable contract because the check was cashed; however, under English law, there was no contract. British courts would generally hold under these facts that the catalog was simply an invitation to make an order. Which law governs and who wins?

First, whether this transaction involved brochures and "snail mail" or took place entirely over the Internet does not change the basic international and conflict-of-laws doctrine. The Net is simply a medium that allows parties to communicate with one another. In pre-Net days, businesspeople relied on telephone, fax, overnight delivery, telegrams, and the like, all to transfer information and make their deals. Now, they rely on the Internet. Although the basic concepts don't change when the Net is concerned, the numbers of interstate and multicountry disputes these days do escalate.

If the parties negotiate which law is to apply and where the lawsuit is to be heard, then that usually settles the matter: their agreement controls, and this has been the law since before the Net arrived. However, if no understanding can be reached, then the question depends on which court believes it has the greatest "connections," or the greatest interest in protecting its citizens in a particular case. The result also can depend on any international treaties in existence, but it's still quite possible that the courts in two countries could reach completely opposite results. In fact, this has happened numbers of times. In our British computer case, the lawsuit was brought in England and that court held that there was no contract (and no breach of one could occur).

U.S. Cyberspace—Jurisdictional and Conflicts Law

The problems created by conflicting local laws and the Internet's ability to leapfrog territorial boundaries increase daily. A business that displays a Web site for its customers is now suddenly pulled out of its usual geographical and distribution area. Let's say that a New Jersey company sells its jams only to local restaurants, but decides to create a Web site. Its site only displays pictures of the jams, tells how they're made, and shows an address and telephone number. There is no further interconnectivity, and this is a true informational site.

A Florida wholesaler comes across the site, calls up the company, gives a large order for different jams, and sends in a check. However, the New Jersey company quickly e-mails back a response, saying that it is sorry, but the temporary person who said that it could do this didn't have the authority to cut the deal. In fact, the company has discovered that the Florida wholesaler is supplying restaurants in New Jersey. If the Florida firm sues in Florida for breach of contract and the New Jersey company argues that Florida has no jurisdiction, then what happens? Under the developing U.S. cyberlaw, the New Jersey company would be right. There weren't enough connections with Florida for that state to have an interest in this lawsuit. The lawsuit would have to be brought in New Jersey, and the Florida wholesaler would need to hire lawyers there and fly to New Jersey to litigate the matter.

Let's say that a mother in Texas buys baby food from a California manufacturer via a California Web site. The firm sends numerous promotional e-mails from this location across the country, including into Texas. The firm receives 15 percent of its orders over this site and, each month, ships thousands of jars of its baby food to Texans. It has an "800" number that Texans use. A jar of the food turns out to be bad, and the mother's baby gets food poisoning from eating it. When she bought the baby food, the mother scrolled through the site's Terms of Use, but the mother didn't really understand any of that "foreign language."

The Web operator used a Terms of Use clause that provided all lawsuits would have to be brought in Los Angeles, California, and that California law applied. (See Chapter 9, "Web Site Disclaimers and Protections.") The mother had no idea of this when she bought the product. Under current U.S. law, a Texas court could hear (assume jurisdiction) of this case for product liability damages over the child's sickness (there's also Federal Court jurisdiction). A Texas court would probably uphold the application of Texas law in a lawsuit brought there, especially if this would bring about a different result.

Let's look at why these results take place. As we can see in these examples, the prime arguments today are between the place of origin and the place of destination. Prior to the Internet's formation, these two places were usually the same place: the New Jersey maker of jams sold them only in New Jersey. The question now is: Who will have the say when lawsuits can be brought nearly anywhere? Will it be the Web operators who are selling products, or the consumers who are buying them? Although U.S. law on this issue develops more each year, the cases already have crafted a fairly clear picture of just when a user can bring a lawsuit successfully in his or her own state.

In one landmark case, a domain-name dispute flared up over the use of the term "Zippo." Zippo Manufacturing is a Pennsylvania company that manufactures "Zippo" cigarette lighters; Zippo.com is a California corporation that operated an Internet news service through a Web site called and located at "zippo.com." The California Web site contained an online application that allowed visitors to subscribe to it. Subscribers could use their credit card to purchase subscriptions over the Internet, by telephone, or by fax. Once subscribed, the user could access the premium news services by using a password. At the time, the defendant Web site had sold passwords to over 3,000 Pennsylvanians, who constituted about 2 percent of its subscriber base. The Pennsylvania court agreed that it had jurisdiction over the California corporation, holding that this business had freely chosen to sell its services into Pennsylvania. As there were sufficient contacts to support this jurisdiction, the California business had to travel to Pennsylvania and defend itself there, under Pennsylvania law. To find out who finally won these battles, see "zippo.com" (it was the Pennsylvania company).

In another leading case, Bensusan Restaurant is a New York corporation that owned the New York City jazz club known as "The Blue Note." A Missouri man, Richard King, owned a small nightclub that he also called "The Blue Note." King's Web site could be accessed by anyone and contained general information about the club and what was being shown there. It provided the addresses of ticket outlets in Missouri, but while it gave a telephone number for ticket orders, the tickets could only be picked up on the night of the performance; no tickets were ever mailed to anyone. The New York federal district court (affirmed on appeal) held that it had *no* jurisdiction over this Missouri defendant, concluding that King had only put up an "informational" Web site on the Internet. Because nobody could buy tickets through that site, the court held that it wouldn't be fair (under the U.S. Supreme Court's *International Shoe* decision) to hold that anyone in any state in the United States could force the Missouri man to appear in another state's court. It would have to be the other way around, and disgruntled plaintiffs or customers would need to fly to his state and sue there, hiring attorneys in that state and staying in its motels.

In general, U.S. courts look at a Web site's level of Internet activity and draw distinctions between passive and active locations, when they review this jurisdictional question. This distinction will probably be made in foreign courts, as well. At one end of the spectrum, businesses that enter into contracts with out-of-state residents over their Web sites involving repeated contacts, e-mails or other correspondence, and selling noticeable amounts of products or services into that state are held to be "active" Web sites. These "active" sites can be sued in the state of their customers or out-of-state residents, as the *Zippo* case held. Given the existence of such sufficient contacts, a local court could (depending on the facts) disregard a Terms of Use condition of the Web site that provided it could only be sued in its home state.

On the other side of the equation, companies that merely advertise or only post information about their business on the Internet—without taking any orders or conducting business through that Net site—are held to have "passive" Web sites. These Internet "informational" sites generally cannot be sued out-of-state and dragged from their home base into foreign courts, simply because they maintain a virtual presence. "The Blue Note" litigation is an example of a passive Web site.

In between are sites providing more connections between users in one state and Net operations with a host computer in another. The question then becomes whether the facts of the case indicate that sufficient contacts with an out-of-state resident are present to enable a customer's foreign court to hear that case. If specific order information isn't given nor filled over the Internet, then simply having an "interactive" ability (i.e., e-mail) usually doesn't grant a foreign court sufficient contacts to assume jurisdiction over that Web operator.

Simply advertising over the Internet by itself doesn't normally meet this test; it usually takes more than just having an e-mail capability and a toll-free number. E-mailing questions about a potential purchase (without interactive sales or more connections) doesn't generally meet the test either, although some courts view this as getting close. Basically, you can't drag a Web site into a foreign court just because it has an Internet presence. To hold differently would be to subject that Internet operator to being sued in every state and territory of every country of the world that could access that site from someone's computer.

Let's say that a defendant Web site displays a downloadable mail-in order form, a toll-free telephone number, and an e-mail address, but people don't actually make orders over its Net site (they talk with the phone operators). This normally isn't good enough, and most cases have held that such a site would still be a "passive" site; it could not be sued by an out-of-state resident in a foreign state. However, several courts have held that having an interactive Web site, a toll-free number, and local advertising (i.e., placing advertisements in that state) *by itself* is enough to secure jurisdiction by a customer in that state's court over a nonresident Web site owner. A factual decision is made in each Internet case as to whether these minimum connections for due process reason are present. And different courts can reach opposite conclusions on the same set of facts.

In our example of the Kansas Web site and the Colorado purchaser, it's clear that a purchase of a forklift through that Web site would be enough for a Colorado court to hear the lawsuit against the Kansas site—given that its interactive Net site solicited those sales in Colorado and took orders through that site. Unless the sales are clearly incidental and not part of the Web site's design to do business in a particular state, conducting sales through that site would meet the "minimum contact" test.

One U.S. court, however, did hold that all it took was a Web site's presence, an e-mail capability, and a toll-free number on the Net—nothing more—to give a disgruntled customer the ability to sue in his own state. This court reasoned that the *potential* that states' residents could receive "hits," not the actual use, was important (and this court didn't even consider the low hit count in that state at that time).

A recent libel decision gives a good idea as to how this extends into other areas. An Oregon resident posted allegedly defamatory messages on her Web site, and on e-mail discussion groups, about a doctor. The doctor, a resident of Pennsylvania, filed a defamation lawsuit against the Oregon woman in a U.S. District Court in Pennsylvania. The Court ruled that there was no basis to exercise personal jurisdiction over the Oregonian. It held that the messages posted on those Web sites were not targeted toward Pennsylvania; hence, this was akin to a "passive" Web site, and the court could not hear that case. The doctor would have to travel to Oregon and sue her there.

Keep in mind that the U.S. Supreme Court hasn't yet ruled in this area, nor has a body of law developed as to the extent a Web site's contrary Terms of Use provision (i.e., "Any claim will be litigated at this site's city and state location, including choice of applicable law") can supersede this concept. The tendency of the courts has been to uphold a Web site's stated Terms and Conditions, given that they are easily seen, understandable, demonstrably agreed to (by a "click"), and fair.

However, these courts can and do give "wild" judgments. For example, one Texas AOL subscriber was in a defamatory debate with another subscriber who happened to live in Virginia. The judge held that the Texan could be sued in a Virginia court (and forced to travel there to defend himself), based entirely on the fact that the message must have been temporarily stored in AOL's UseNet server in Virginia before it was sent to other UseNet servers. Under the state's long-arm statute, this gave jurisdiction over the out-of-state defendant. Legal experts are not sure about this case.

International Jurisdiction and Conflicts of Law

If an American slips and falls in an Italian hotel, can she sue in her state, New Jersey, because the hotel advertises globally over the Internet? And when a Christmas tree catches fire in an American home and causes a death, can the Arkansas store where the tree was purchased then sue the Hong Kong manufacturer in a U.S. court, just because the Hong Kong company advertises on the Internet?

Two United States courts have said "No." Their reasoning was that simple advertising on the Internet was not sufficient enough to confer jurisdiction in the United States, even if it was foreseeable that sales would be made to Americans who contacted the Web site operator. In both cases, these Web sites were basically "informational" or passive sites, where any contract arrangements were made outside the Internet site. Both cases referred to the *Zippo* sliding scale of interaction and sales. Thus, courts in the United States are applying their domestic cyberlaw holdings consistently in international lawsuits.

In the United States, the test of constitutional minimum contacts and the *Zippo* factor analysis will be the foundation for legal jurisdictional decisions. However, because all of the decisions to date have been by lower courts, legal experts await the day when the U.S. Supreme Court makes a final determination, setting down the major concepts as it did in its famous *International Shoe* case. However, legal experts at this time do not anticipate any major shifts from the fundamental due-process criteria used so far.

The good news is that U.S. courts have been developing a fairly uniform approach to the question of jurisdiction. The bad news is that the rest of the world hasn't seemed to adopt that yet.

International Legal Concepts

Unless an international treaty [such as the United Nations' Contracts for the International Sale of Goods (CISG)] binds countries to using the same criteria in their international law cases, all countries are free to apply their own quite differing laws and concepts to any situation. (See Chapter 2, "Surfing Planet Earth and the Clash of Laws," for more on this topic.)

However, most countries apply several standard concepts that have international legal significance. One is the concept of "comity," whereby one country will defer to the laws of another, primarily from a concern for respect, reciprocity, and the stability of the international community. Another is the concept of "territoriality": A state has the authority to claim jurisdiction and apply its own laws to uphold those laws and preserve the sanctity of its legal concepts. A third is the principle of "nationality," which grants independent nations the right to regulate the conduct of their own citizens. Note that these principles are applied by the individual high courts of a particular country, as they see fit, and that these concepts conflict with one another.

National courts may simply decide that they want to protect their own citizens—notwithstanding how the United States applies a balanced and consistent approach in this area. For example, one German court held that it had jurisdiction over a case when there was little more than a clash between two organizations over a domain name (the URL address). A U.S. company was conducting business in both Germany and the United States. It had registered its domain name and all ".com" sites in the United States. The German court held that it had jurisdiction over the dispute because the domain names were accessible from the plaintiff's location in Germany. In other words, this court assumed control over the case, applying its own laws, because the German competitor could see the Web site of that ".com" address—and this address was in conflict with its trade name. The German court held that the country within which the domain name had been registered (the U.S.) was not relevant to determine jurisdiction. The fact that the U.S. company also was doing business in Germany mitigates somewhat the "weirdness" of the decision. Legal experts aren't sure about this decision either.

THE AREAS RIPE FOR CONFLICT

Numerous legal areas reveal fundamentally different approaches between the United States and other nations of the world. We have seen one prime issue in the extent of an ISP's liability for copyright infringements by its subscribers. Until a substantial number of countries pass legislation similar to the Digital Millennium Copyright Act, ISPs will have a potential liability, throughout the world, for postings that aren't actionable in the United States. For example, an English court had affirmed that ISPs can be sued in England for libelous third-party postings, provided that the English court could hear the case. As we discussed in Chapter 4, "Copying in Cyberspace," England and other European Union countries currently are enacting legislation that would grant ISPs a similar level of protection (but there will be differences with the U.S. Act).

In 1998, a German court also held that an ISP in one country could be held liable under the laws of another. It ruled that the German manager of the U.S.'s CompuServe was liable for violating German antipornography laws (a third party posted the offensive material on its Web site). The manager received a two-year suspended jail sentence and a $56,000 fine, although there would have been no liability under U.S. law under our First Amendment. In response, the English-based Web server, fearing new violations of this law, moved its operations that year out of Germany.

We discussed, in Chapter 2, the decision of a French judge to order the U.S.-based portal Yahoo! to block Web surfers in France from an auction where Nazi memorabilia were sold. Although Yahoo!'s offering sales of Nazi items was legally protected in the United States under the U.S. Constitution, it voluntarily banned the sale of these items in response. Arguing that the French court had no jurisdiction over it, Yahoo! then countersued in California to overturn that decision's effect in the United States. As this case progresses with two legal systems, it is an excellent example of what happens when the legal principles in two different countries collide.

Another area involves the issue of privacy rights. European Union and other countries protect individual rights to informational privacy more than the more commercially oriented United States does. (See Chapter 6, " 'Junk Dog' Statements and Privacy Concerns," for more.) Although the United States and its First Amendment is much more protective of freedom-of-speech issues (e.g., the ability to buy and sell Nazi literature in the United States), other countries, such as Germany and France, flat out prohibit such sales in continuing these anomalies. Where countries under different legal systems pass laws against "public disorder and inciting violence against the country's administration" or "hateful speech," the U.S. First Amendment is instantly in conflict.

A recent case in Denmark emphasizes this difference. A Danish court held that an Internet user was guilty of violating that country's law prohibiting racist speech. The Danish computer user had originally been charged with posting slurs on the Internet via a U.S.-based ISP; however, those charges were dropped when the authorities discovered that they couldn't obtain an injunction against this type of speech in the United States—the U.S. Constitution prohibits injunctions (i.e., prior restraints) against potentially offensive or defamatory speech. However, the police charged the user over his comments made on the Danish UseNet group, which the user accessed through the U.S.-based ISP. Because the server for the UseNet group was located in Denmark, the Danish court held that it had sufficient contacts to assume jurisdiction.

What about a defamatory statement that is published in one country, then disseminated around the world? The United States and the European Union countries have adopted basically similar approaches. The decisions hold that the courts of countries where an Internet publication originated have the jurisdiction to award general damages over the publication of the libel. All other countries can award damages only for the specific harm that this libel caused specifically identified residents of those nations.

In England, a lecturer filed a lawsuit in a London court against Cornell University and one of its graduate students over alleged defamatory statements. The lecturer claimed that the student had defamed him in postings made on a UseNet newsgroup, and the university owned the computers on which the student posted those statements. United States law would have shielded Cornell, but, in the United Kingdom, an opposite result was found. The court entered a default judgment against the student, who failed to appear, and Cornell settled out of court with the lecturer.

If you have a particular controversy that involves international legal issues, be sure to consult an experienced cyberlawyer, especially if this is a "bet your company" or "bet your job" problem. These problems can be as much politically oriented as they are legally.

All countries have the problem of policing "wild" Web sites. For example, German authorities ordered the closing of a Web site operated by Dutch citizens when that site published materials on how to sabotage a train station. Before the injunction could be granted, however, free-speech advocates established numerous other duplicate sites throughout the Internet. This "cloning" of alternate sites also occurred with the AlternB nude pictures problem of French model Estelle Hallyday. Imitation sites also abounded after an adverse court decision (see further Chapter 5, "Posting Pictures, Music, and Videos").

Questions will always persist in this overall area of international jurisdiction. European consumer protection laws may apply when U.S. and other foreign businesses make sales to European consumers over the Internet. However, the European Union provides that the law governing consumer contracts is always the law of the consumer—or the purchaser's European country. Germany already has passed legislation mandating that all Web sites accessible from Germany are subject to abiding by German law.

Let's assume that a United States Web site provides in its Terms of Use that U.S. law applies and all lawsuits must be brought at its U.S. headquarters. A German consumer feels that he has received a "lemon," so he sues—in Germany, of course. Which law is Germany going to apply? You're right—German courts will apply German law. If the company sues in the United States, what law is that court going to apply? Probably U.S. law because this country has a material interest in those proceedings. There is no international Supreme Court for adjudicating private business matters, so there will be no real way to settle this problem unless the parties later agree to those procedures. The resolution of this problem would have been much easier had the parties agreed beforehand in their deal to the location, procedure, and applicable laws to be used in settling any later disputes.

Let's say that a Japanese Web site with a U.S. ISP defrauds a customer in France by shipping an inferior product ordered from its site and already paid for. Whose laws govern? Basically, the issue is between the consumer (France) and the Web operator (Japan). Given that the French citizen sues in her country, the question is whether the French court will assume jurisdiction. If it adopts the U.S. position of jurisdiction over an active Web site, then the French court will accept jurisdiction and apply its laws. However, there will be no way to enforce that judgment unless the Japanese company has assets in France, or there is a contractual agreement to arbitrate those differences. (Note: International treaty provides that an arbitration award is enforceable in most countries. There is the question of whether a Japanese court would even recognize the French court's judgment.)

Given that these fundamental areas are in such conflict (even if a jurisdictional and conflicts-of-law treaty is eventually agreed to and passed), the question becomes: What can a Web company do? It seems inconceivable that any multinational company could meet all of the varying requirements of nations ranging from Mexico and Japan, with their civil systems, to Moslem countries and their different approach. Businesses are forced to set up either separate Web sites to comply with all local laws, or one megasite that meets every nation's requirements—which seems to be a contradiction in terms—and both options are quite costly. Some companies establish provisions that are more likely to be upheld in most countries, knowing that it's impossible to be in compliance with everyone; this is done in conjunction with creating country-specific Web sites for the larger nations that they market to. (See Yahoo!, Lycos, Excite, and Amazon, as a few examples.) Others create separate Web sites for all the countries where they have operations. For example, IBM set up 167 different Web sites for the 167 countries it operates in (and the different sites, languages, and provisions are interesting to view).

A business strategy employed by smaller companies is to establish reasonable Terms of Use policies that are oriented to meeting applicable U.S. laws. If they have an identifiable foreign country Net presence (i.e., customers in Japan buy continuously through their site), then they hire counsel to advise them as to which of the U.S. use and privacy provisions need to be modified to be in compliance for their Japanese clients. This is accomplished by crafting a separate Japanese Terms of Use section—typically written in Japanese—that is identified as only applying to residents of Japan. They don't worry about countries where they have no *actual* or incidental presence. If an order comes in from a country not on their list, most companies will see how they can fill that request. If one country is known to create problems over another, they have the option not to take the order. They can marshal their efforts for those countries they service the best or for those with the highest sales potential.

Criminal Violations

Although it's difficult for countries to enforce their criminal laws when Internet acts occur outside their geographical boundaries, nations do have an easier ability to enforce their laws, of course, against those living within their borders. If an illegal act injures one of its residents, then that state or territory has an interest in arresting and convicting the perpetrator. For example, in Chapter 2, "Surfing Planet Earth and the Clash of Laws," we discussed the New York entrepreneur who sold low-cost magazine subscriptions over the Internet. The New York court upheld the use of consumer fraud laws against the man, including enforcing the claims of those who resided in other countries.

All nations enforce their criminal statutes within their boundaries, even when the illegal act includes cyberspace. We previously discussed the German court that convicted a CompuServe manager in Germany for indirect violations of its laws on acts that would have been entirely legal in the United States. Further, countries have the ability to prosecute people who use the Net to commit consumer fraud in their nation, just as the FTC has similar federal jurisdiction in the United States—and we have seen how this approach carries through.

With criminal statutes, states and countries look at jurisdiction from the point of view of their laws and their interest in protecting their citizens. For example, if gambling is illegal in State A but not State B, then a Web site in State B could be prosecuted for allowing the residents of State A to use that Internet gambling site. Similarly, if State A prohibits the online sale of wine but State B does not, then any online Web site selling wine to the residents of State A (regardless of where that site is located) could be prosecuted by State A for those online sales. The reasoning is that every Web operator has the ability to be in compliance with State A's laws by simply refusing to break those laws through not selling to any residents of State A.

Drawing the line between reasonable and unreasonable interference by a country or state in its enforcement of its criminal statutes on the Internet can be difficult. Enforcing a foreign court's decision that it had jurisdiction over another country's citizens, with the power to haul those citizens into that foreign court, is another question. We will discuss more of these issues, along with the questions of virtual gambling and online sales of wine, in Chapter 17, "The Internet Faces More Legal Shape-Shifting Ahead."

12

Cyberlaw Dispute Resolution

One cyberlaw fact of life stands out: Resolving disputes arising from the Internet's global reach through litigation is complex, expensive, and loaded with unclear results. Whether the controversies involve bad purchases, customer disputes, "junk dog" statements, domain name conflicts, or Web site disclaimers, solving Net problems by courtroom battling just leaves an unsettled feeling. What's amazing is that the burgeoning trend to settle non-Internet disputes by alternative dispute resolution (ADR) techniques has moved swiftly into cyberspace. Before we review this trend and some players, let's take a brief look at what ADRs are and why they've become such a legal force today.

Alternative Dispute Resolution (ADR)

One client who endured a courtroom battle observed: "Whether you win or not depends upon how good your attorney is, how good the other lawyer is, and how the judge feels that day. Then, the process is long, expensive, and never conforms to what's really important in your life." Another said, "What I learned about the judicial system was enough to last a lifetime. Most people don't have any experience with the system. It's like a disease: you don't know what it's like unless you get a big dose of it."

The vast majority of cases (90 percent by numerous surveys) settle *after* the major costs have been incurred, and these costs are high. The legal fees, court costs, costs of depositions (informal questioning of witnesses under oath), expert witness expenses, and travel costs add up to frightening proportions. Then add in the long delays before a decision is reached, potential bad results, negativism of this fighting (the name calling and "kill or be killed" attitude), stress, bad publicity, and the destruction of long-standing relationships. Think about the "win or lose" coin; there are no middle grounds in courtroom fights.

Decades ago, attorneys realized that there must be a better solution to the inevitable problems that incur between people, no matter where they live or what the fight is over. Rather than continuing this gladiator approach, it made more sense to use alternatives that would be less formal, faster, less time-consuming, cheaper, and would open up communications between the warring parties.

The American Arbitration Association (AAA) was organized in 1926 and took the lead in resolving disputes by nonlitigation methods such as arbitration. For years, this organization was the dominant force in the use of ADRs, and various dispute resolution alternatives grew, over time, to include mediation, arbitration, neutral evaluators, and "rent a judge" alternatives, among others. Today, the AAA has offices in most U.S. states and international cooperating agreements with ADR firms in over 50 countries.

In the 1970s and 1980s, other lawyers recognized the potential of these alternatives and formed more ADR firms specializing primarily in mediation and arbitration. Law firms joined the bandwagon and formed their own ADR departments that competed for their litigation business. In 1979, a former California state court judge founded JAMS (Judicial Arbitration and Mediation Services), which has become the largest private ADR firm at this time.

The most prevalent ADRs used are mediation and arbitration. Let's take a look at what these (and others) are all about.

MEDIATION

Mediation doesn't impose a solution, as does a court judgment or even arbitration. This process focuses on the parties' resolving their dispute through the use of a neutral third party that "mediates" their differences. The strength of this process is

Mediation is used today in nearly every conceivable situation, ranging from personal injury and child custody disputes to sexual harassment and trademark controversies. It is used domestically in settling labor disputes and internationally in trade problems between feuding countries. Given that two warring parties agree to settle their differences by mediation, study after study indicates that four out of five such cases ultimately settle their differences through this process.

that it's an informal proceeding that requires no one except the parties and the mediator to carve out a settlement. The mediator shuttles back and forth between the opposing camps, pointing out the strengths and weaknesses in each party's position in encouraging a final resolution. The people are able to craft their own flexible solution to complex problems without having to go before a judge who may not have the technical expertise needed in complex matters, and who can only rule inflexibly for one party or the other.

Mediation's strength is that it is fast and quite inexpensive (basically, only the shared costs for the mediator's fee). The parties can forge their own deal (i.e., the sharing of a trade name, rather than the "win/lose" decision of a judge), and the negativity of litigation is avoided. Its weakness is that mediation isn't particularly suitable when one party feels that it has "the winning hand." It is generally useful when facts aren't in dispute or one-sided. If one party is shouting, "You tried to screw me and you lost, you SOB!"—then the mediation probably won't be successful.

Mediation can be used whenever the parties agree to use it. The mediator doesn't even have to be a lawyer. It can be anyone whom the parties trust and who has experience in their matter. For example, two parties in a dispute over the quality of software downloads could select a mediator who understands the inner workings of such software. The process is nonbinding, so the parties can stop it at any time, continue with their litigation, and then pick up the mediation again when they're exhausted from the courtroom battling. The process is started when one party contacts a mediation service and consults about the procedure. The mediation service then contacts the other side and works with both parties in understanding the benefits of mediation.

In the Yellow Pages, look under "Mediation," either as a separate entry or under the heading of "Attorneys." In addition to the for-profit ADR groups, various nonprofit community associations run mediation centers as a public service in many cities. They handle and solve problems that range from neighbors' disputes to landlord-tenant controversies and creditor-debtor problems.

A good rule of thumb: Talk first with an ADR firm before you see a litigator.

ARBITRATION

This resolution process is very different from mediation. Arbitrators hand down binding decisions, reached only after a hearing on the merits of a case. This procedure is more like litigation, but the decision of the arbitrators may be appealed only on limited grounds (i.e., fraud or improper conduct by an arbitrator) and not on the facts or decision. However, arbitration is much less formal than using the courts, and an arbitrator isn't required to strictly follow the rules of evidence. Expensive multiple depositions and discovery practices aren't necessary, and these proceedings can take place in an office, with only the two parties, their attorneys (but they are not always required), the arbitrator, and a court reporter in attendance.

The parties typically select one arbitrator, or a panel of three, to hear the evidence and arguments of the attorneys and then render a judgment on the presented facts. The proceedings generally follow the rules of either a state arbitration act or those employed by the commonly-followed American Arbitration Association.

Arbitration is more cost-effective, faster, and more private than litigation, although it isn't as inexpensive, flexible, or fast as mediation. Litigators argue that there is limited appeal from an arbitrator's decision, there are no (or only limited) provisions for punitive damages (those "extra" punishment damages that don't go to pay out-of-pocket damages), and the process shouldn't be used if you can enforce your will in court. However, the push of the law is to encourage the use of these more effective solutions.

For example, the 1998 U.S. Alternative Dispute Resolution Act requires that all U.S. District Courts authorize the use of ADRs such as mediation and arbitration in all civil cases and promote their use. The great majority of states mandate that mediation is to be used in domestic relations cases. State laws require that arbitration be employed at certain times (for example, in civil actions up to a certain amount of damages), and most states require the use of nonbinding arbitration as a prerequisite before parties may litigate a matter in court.

Arbitration is used frequently by parties who agree to its use under a contract provision in their agreement. This is called "contractual" arbitration. The sweeping requirements of U.S. states, the federal court system, and other countries to mandate arbitration's use in the courts is called "judicial" arbitration. Many ADR firms offer both arbitration and mediation services. The parties then can quickly move to arbitration if they aren't able to reach a mediated agreement.

OTHER ADRS AND INTERNATIONAL USE

Other forms of ADRs include negotiation, neutral evaluators, private judging, and minitrials. A neutral evaluator is used so that parties can evaluate how good their positions are. The two sides present their arguments to this neutral third party, who tells them how he or she would have ruled on the case, had this been a binding decision. The evaluator informs the parties of the strengths and weaknesses of their case; the two parties then caucus together to see if they can reach an agreement. Given the neutral evaluator's comments, each knows the strengths and weaknesses of both sides, making it easier to reach an agreement.

Another ADR is "rent a judge" or private judging. A key problem of litigation is the long delays before a decision can be made. Typically, it will take two years or more before a judge has the opportunity to make a final decision. This ADR comes into play when the parties stipulate that a retired judge can hear the case, using normal trial procedures and rules of evidence, and then renders a binding judgment. The advantage of this ADR is the ability to obtain a quick decision with confidentiality (which can be advantageous in trade secret, patent, and Internet operating system disputes).

The most common ADR is a settlement that two parties hammer out and negotiate between themselves. This is the least expensive of these techniques because it involves only two persons. The problem is that it involves the cooperation of both sides. If the amount of money and the time at risk are small, then you can always use the time-honored ADR of simply "walking away from it." In retrospect, forgetting small hassles always seems to be the best alternative. The bigger hassles are the problem.

Internationally, ADRs have received widespread use. The World Intellectual Property Association (WIPO) established a Mediation and Arbitration Center where over 800 specialists focus exclusively on mediating and arbitrating intellectual property disputes concerning copyrights, trademarks, trade names, and patent problems. The

WIPO offers these dispute resolution mechanisms in 70 countries around the world, and it is one of the approved panels authorized to hear the arbitration procedures now being used to resolve international domain name disputes.

The National Association of Securities Dealers (NASD) mandates the use of arbitration in its disputes with customers; this use applies also to cyberspace and international transactions that have gone awry. Foreign countries employ ADRs in labor disputes and mandate their use in various situations; their approach is similar to that of the United States. Nations use mandated arbitration panels in trade disputes, and they employ mediation to resolve international political disputes. The United States does emphasize these techniques more in its legal system than other nations seem to do. Then again, other countries don't litigate as many matters as is done so frequently in the United States.

Before You Sue

First, you need to check whether there's an ADR provision in the disputed agreement, and whether there's a requirement in your locality that an ADR be used during the litigation process. If there is a provision or local law mandating the use of an ADR, then why not use this in the beginning and save yourself some money?

At times, trial lawyers use nonbinding arbitration to learn the other side's case, then go to trial with that information. However, because the process puts a premium on no surprises in litigation, you'll want to check with your attorney as to whether this is a real risk in your state or locality. Normally, it isn't.

It makes sense to check out the availability of ADR firms in your locality and see whether they are interested in taking on your case—before you incur heavy litigation costs. And consider small claims court if your damages aren't high. (See Chapter 10, "What If You Get a Lemon?" for more on this.)

Before you start a lawsuit, it's crucial that you have a strong idea as to what the range of costs will be, and then balance this against the value of what you're trying to achieve. For example, if your attorney estimates that the range of litigation costs (i.e., legal fees, court costs, witness fees, travel costs, and the like) will be $40,000 to $50,000—which is a "cheap" case when you consider that international disputes between multinational companies run into tens of millions of U.S. dollars—next decide what it is that you really want to achieve. Then balance this goal against the probable cost and make your decision.

Let's say that there's a conflict involving the use of the same domain name. One user is in France, running a hotel, and you're in the United States, operating a software company. Will you really lose a meaningful amount of profits over time to a hotel? Probably not. You might be better off to negotiate or mediate what each could do with that domain name (i.e., coshare it, with later transfers only to parties in the same line of business), than to fall into an expensive court battle that you might lose.

As part of this decision, you'll want to assess just how important winning this case is. For example, if your situation is a "bet your company" or "bet your home" problem, then you might look at courtroom battling as the only way to gain time and survive. Before you decide to battle with all swords drawn, just be sure you've tried your best to reach an acceptable deal with the other side.

However, we know that there are times when you must sue because there isn't any other alternative. For example, if you patented a "two-click" shopping procedure (Amazon has patented the "one-click" system), but another competitor is ripping you off, you might not have a choice. Let's say that you bought an expensive new car for the business from an Internet dealer, and the automobile suddenly veered out of control, ruining it and injuring others. This dealer has a product liability problem, just as the manufacturer does. Unfortunately, settlements aren't easy to come by in high-damage situations. If the risk or problem is high enough (i.e., your competitive advantage will be ripped away or your medical bills are extraordinary), you will have to litigate the matter when the other side "stonewalls" your demands.

If you made a mistake and sent money to a Web site that never answered you again, an ADR would not be workable. Whether you should sue or not is even another question. Scammers usually don't have much money left, especially after a judgment. They've already spent it on high living and defense costs. In that case, you might be better off complaining loudly and persistently to a government consumer fraud agency, and then walk away from the problem. It can, however, depend on how much money you lost.

ADRs in Cyberspace

Suing or being sued has always been expensive, not to mention the negative downtime and the fact that you might lose. These negatives are multiplied over, when you add in that the defendant resides in a different state or country, not to mention the jurisdictional and applicable law issues we've previously discussed. Long-distance Internet problems are especially oriented for ADR use.

The Net community is actively pursuing ADRs to solve cyberdisputes. Web sites and online operators actively promote them in their agreements and Terms of Use provisions. Consequently, ADRs have been used to settle arguments between Web partners, Web sites, domain-name holders, ISPs and their subscribers (i.e., termination of a subscriber's service), spamming, copyright infringement, and all other Net matters. JAMS created an online dispute resolution approach called "EJams," which is earmarked for business-to-business Internet disputes. Credit card companies use an alternative resolution form when they use "chargebacks" to end a customer's complaint with an online seller. Companies such as America Online, Microsoft, AT&T, IBM, Dell, Network Solutions, and others signed an "E-commerce protocol" (drafted by the American Arbitration Association), calling for ADRs to be incorporated in resolving online disputes between companies or suppliers and their customers.

We will discuss fully in the next chapter the ADR policy adopted by the Internet Corporation for Assigned Names and Numbers (ICANN), the nonprofit Internet regulatory body. ICANN established a worldwide arbitration procedure to resolve domain name "cybersquatting" disputes when one person violates another's trademark rights by sitting on a domain name. It adopted this ADR policy due to its much lower costs and quicker decision time, and this method has proved to be a highly effective technique in resolving these types of disputes without litigation. See Chapter 13, "Domain Names and Conflicts," for more on this development.

The U.S. Digital Millennium Copyright Act (DMCA) provides for an ISP administrative procedure, very similar to an ADR, to resolve copyright disputes. As we discussed in Chapter 4, "Copying in Cyberspace," the DMCA provides for an ISP to decide whether a copyright owner has a legitimate complaint against a posting made on that server's facilities. The matter can end there with the parties' acceptance of the ISP's administrative decision, after each side has sent in the arguments on its position.

In the beginning of the Net, attorneys at first were concerned over the potential for widespread Internet litigation from crude e-mail postings, defamatory comments, "flaming" responses, and the like. This hasn't occurred as initially expected because (1) the costs of litigating these types of matters are generally prohibitive; and (2) the moderator, Web site operator, or other members of the chat group generally intercede to settle problems in their own nonlegal ways. Targets of criticism make instant rebuttals (or issue statements), other users put peer and Netiquette pressure on the "outspoken" ones, and the ISPs typically punish "flamers" through suspension or termination of service.

For example, let's say someone posts "TRT Business [your company] lies, cheats, and steals from the public." First, you would complain to the Web operator or ISP and have that statement erased. Nothing upsets "flamers" more than being made invisible, and they usually vent their emotions at the ISP. If you're not publicly traded, with no fall-off in business or really negative PR, you could forget about it.

Cybermediation

One of the striking ADR advances has been the rise of online cybermediation Web sites that primarily work online. For example, one party contacts the cybermediator about a problem; the mediator then contacts the second. If both parties agree to use a mediated approach and accept the ground rules, then the online mediation begins. Typically, each party e-mails the mediator to state a position or the settlement amount that would be acceptable. The mediator then intercedes, shuttling back and forth electronically to reach a settlement.

In financial disputes, each party e-mails back and forth the amount it would settle the claim for. The rules of one process provides for three rounds of such settlement offers. Each party has also consented to lower its demands by an agreed-on percentage—let's say, 10 percent. By the third round, if the sides are close (let's say, within 20 percent), then that difference is halved by prior agreement and a deal is struck. We'll discuss later the approach of Cybersettle and others in this area.

A second approach is used in nonquantitative areas, such as a complaint between a Web owner and a developer. Let's say that the Web operator doesn't feel that a software developer met certain technological standards that the operator wanted. The two have tried to work out their difficulties by themselves, but haven't been able to do so. A third party would be a very appropriate intermediary to mediate these problems. Each party e-mails its initial position to the mediator or the cybermediation Web site.

The mediator has full discretion regarding whether to pass on any messages, in case one party or the other becomes too heated or personal in any communications. By e-mail, the mediator makes suggestions to each party on how the differences can be settled. The parties e-mail their replies to the mediator, who then posts them for each side to see. As the two sides work closer and closer, they may even begin to telephone one another—which is a win by itself.

The mediation can be done completely online, or involve face-to-face meetings with the mediator, or some combination. For example, the Better Business Bureau's BBBOnLine Reliability Seal Program (bbbonline.org) requires each participant to adopt its dispute resolution service for disgruntled customers; after receiving an online complaint, BBBOnLine contacts both parties to decide on the best way to solve the problem—by online or offline mediation, as well as arbitration. For situations requiring face-to-face meetings, online video systems also can at times be an effective alternative. Eventually, the odds are that the parties will work out a solution. For example, the Web operator agrees to pay more, because it had requested the changes that made the developer's work more complex; the developer, in turn, completes the job to bring the system to the agreed standards. An example of this approach is seen in the activities of the nonprofit Center for Information Technology and Dispute Resolution (CITDR).

CENTER FOR INFORMATION TECHNOLOGY AND DISPUTE RESOLUTION

Affiliated with the University of Massachusetts, CITDR (or "the Center") provides research to organizations and mediation to parties in conflict. Cases are presented by referral or Net application (see http://aaron.sbs.umass.edu/center/projects.html), and applications may be made to its Online Ombuds Office on that site. This group doesn't charge a fee for its work; its focus is primarily research and academic investigation. The Center also publishes the *ADRonline Monthly,* which is a good source for the latest developments and thoughts in this area.

The first mediation that CITDR conducted was between a Web site and a newspaper. A Web operator created a site that contained local news. He summarized some stories from the newspaper and placed links to other local sites of interest. The first contacts between the newspaper and the site operator weren't successful, to say the least. As the dispute inched closer to litigation, the Center, through its Online Ombuds Office, was contacted. With the guiding help of its online mediator and numerous e-mail messages sent later, the Ombuds Office helped the two parties finally reach an agreement. The newspaper developed its own Web site, and the developer's Net location stayed up and running. (You can visit the details of this fascinating mediation at http:www.ombuds.org/narrative1.html.)

This group has mediated problems ranging from domain name disputes (see Chapter 13, "Domain Names and Conflicts") to ISP problems with subscribers. As you can see, mediation is an ideal way to handle differences between entities and people who might just want to continue on with their business relationship and don't have or want to pay a lot of money for expensive attorneys.

One highly publicized effort by Online Ombuds involved its mediation with upset buyers who had used eBay's online auction site. In March 1999, eBay promoted the services of this group to see how online mediation would work in auction disputes. The Ombuds Office agreed to mediate these differences for free, as a pilot project for its research purposes. eBay, in turn, placed a link to the service on its customer service pages for two weeks.

Some 250 complaints poured onto the Online Ombuds site. Most of the disputes involved bought items that were not received, merchandise damaged in delivery, misunderstandings over an item's quality or appearance, or arguments over comments delivered into eBay's "feedback file." The procedure was straightforward: each side e-mailed its positions to the third party; the mediator sent back to each side, via e-mail, his observations and points, eventually nudging both parties into an eventual agreement.

Mediation didn't handle all of the complaints. Some were settled by the parties before the mediator contacted them, and others owing to fraud couldn't even be started. Of the 150 cases that entered mediation, the mediator estimated that 25 percent "didn't get off the ground" because one party or the other refused to mediate. Of the approximate 150 cases left for mediation, about one-half (50 percent) were settled in the mediation. The rest remained deadlocked.

If the mediations had been conducted in face-to-face meetings, with the mediator and the parties present, there's no question that the mediation success rate would have been higher. What's amazing is that the success rate of these mediations, conducted only online, was as high as they were. The Online Ombuds Office and most mediation experts agree that situations requiring both parties to mediate and work together would not include spamming, fraud, or criminal conduct situations. People who consciously disregard the rights of others typically don't cooperate—and they usually don't care about what happens to other people. Straightforward litigation, judicial arbitration, and criminal proceedings are more in order for these folks.

CYBERSETTLE.COM

Another online mediation service is cybersettle.com. Among its services, this Web site employs an online program to settle claims. Designed by two lawyers, the site compares numbers placed confidentially on the site by claimants and insurers, then electronically brokers a settlement. When an agreement occurs, only the amount is disclosed. If there is no agreement, then the parties—as in all mediation situations—are free to continue on their merry litigating way. It is a brilliantly simple approach.

The procedure is straightforward: (1) one party simply registers and e-mails a first, second, and third-round settlement offer; (2) the site sends an e-mail "alert" to the second party, simply stating that the case is online and available for settlement (now who wouldn't submit an offer in response?); (3) the second party responds with an e-mail of its three rounds of settlement offers; (4) each party's offer must change by 5 percent (downward by who's demanding money and upward by who must pay it). If the offer and demand meet on any round, or are within an agreed formula (i.e., typically, within 30 percent or no more than $5,000 of each other), then the case immediately settles for the mean amount (i.e., they split the difference).

If a settlement is reached, then Cybersettle contacts the parties and issues a written confirmation. Otherwise, they keep on going in the traditional, expensive litigated approach. Their fees presently are: $100 for claims under $5,000; $150 for claims from $5,000 to $10,000; $200 for claims from $10,000 to $20,000; and on in increments. (See the Web site at cybersettle.com for the complete and up-to-date details.) The fee slides gently upward as the amount in controversy increases, and there is no fee paid unless there is a settlement.

These approaches are certainly the wave of the future, if not the present, in handling at least small and medium-size controversies, as well as insurance claims. Cybersettle states that over 475 insurance companies use its services at this time, either directly or through their third-party administrators. The beauty of this service is the assumption that offers to pay increase (by defendants), offers to accept decrease (by plaintiffs), and settlement margins narrow—all over time, until an eventual settlement. And all do, whether expensive litigation is finally used.

The weakness of any mediation is evident when someone believes strongly in a case and won't materially change his or her position. A weakness of online mediations is seen when someone simply accepts an apology or non-money considerations from a face-to-face meeting, which might not come from a less-spontaneous virtual meeting. However, given its flexibility (24/7 availability), low cost (lower than offline mediation), and convenience (from your home), cybermediation is here to stay—and Cybersettle.com is one of the players.

CLICKNSETTLE, SQUARETRADE, WEBDISPUTE, AND OTHERS

As you would imagine, there are other strong virtual ADR providers in this field. For example, ClickNsettle.com uses an approach similar to Cybersettle.com. It allows users to make an unlimited number of e-mailed settlement "bids" over the 60-day life of the mediation "case." Each time a new bid is submitted by either party, it's compared electronically to the last bid received from the other party, and another settlement calculation is made, to determine whether the positions are within the agreed-on range. If they are, then there's a settlement. Each party is required to move at least 5 percent toward the other party's position with each new settlement bid. ClickNSettle also uses a "final bid" feature: a notice to one of the parties that its opponent has entered a "walk away" figure. The remaining party then can keep submitting new bids in an attempt to reach that figure. Again, all of this is accomplished electronically or by e-mail. Amazing, isn't it?

Other ADR sites include SquareTrade.com, an online mediation service that also has established a seal program (somewhat similar to BBBOnLine's certification program) for online retailers and other sites. The SquareTrade logo on a Web site indicates that the location meets certain reliability and creditability criteria, and that the site agrees to use the dispute resolution and mediation services of SquareTrade if a problem arises. eBay also utilizes SquareTrade's mediation services when there's a dispute between a buyer and seller on its auction site.

WEBdispute (webdispute.com) provides online arbitration of claims, as well as other services. InternetNeutral, SettleOnline, and SettlementNow also provide ADR services, both online and off (as with the others). This combination of both worlds is advantageous, giving the ability to tailor solutions to different situations. Please be advised that we aren't specifically recommending any of the ADR online services mentioned in this chapter, nor are we being negative about any ADR firms that aren't so mentioned. A potential user is advised to check out several sites before deciding to use one for a specific situation.

Internationally, ADR firms and organizations are also springing up in cyberspace. From Canada (eResolution and NovaForum, among others) to Singapore (www.e-adr.org.sg, with leads to ADR firms in Singapore) and Australia (see www.nadrac.gov.au), governments and lawyers have seen the global benefits of online ADRs. The American Arbitration Association (www.adr.org) is establishing a dispute-resolution procedure and policy for B2B e-commerce disputes. Check it and SPIDR (Society of Professionals in Dispute Resolution at www.spidr.org) for their international news and developments. For a localized ADR agency/firm in the United States or another country, other than what's already been discussed, search Hieros Gamos (an excellent legal international directory is located there, try hg.com), findlaw.org, the American Arbitration Association and SPIDR—as well as exploring a particular country's Web site, using a search engine with the words "alternative dispute resolution" and/or that country's name, and working through your lawyer for leads to legal specialists in that nation.

Using ADRs

The best way to bring ADRs into your Net life is to place them in your contracts and use them to solve your seemingly "unsolvable" problems. A good first step is for users and Web sites to start thinking "ADR." For example, if you're planning to contract with a Web site developer to build you a site, then be sure to put an ADR provision in your contract.

These approaches make sense in any business associations where an ongoing relationship could evolve or be continued. ISPs are adding ADR provisions to their contracts, as are Web sites—all after consulting with their attorneys. *The definite trend is for virtual operators and developers to add and use contractual ADRs.* Examples of ADR provisions are present in the forms that are discussed throughout this book. A fairly basic type of clause provides:

Any dispute arising in connection with this Agreement shall be first settled by mediation. If that's not successful, then the dispute shall be settled by arbitration to be held in [*Location of Arbitration*] in accordance with the rules of the American Arbitration Association. This agreement to arbitrate shall be specifically enforceable. Any award shall be final and binding on all of the parties, and a final judgment may be entered in the appropriate court of law. Notwithstanding this, should any litigation ensue between the parties, then the prevailing party shall be entitled to reasonable expenses and attorney fees as set by the Court.

These clauses can and should be added to most agreements, whether they concern online activities or not.

If you use a bidding or online auction service, see if that Web site is connected with a cybermediator. Whether you're the Web operator or an unhappy customer, if that site doesn't now provide for ADR usage, then suggest or use this approach with your dispute now. Regardless of the type of dispute, contact a local ADR firm for local problems and talk with them. If the dispute is online and the parties are separated distantly from one another, you can contact a cybermediator. Or contact mediators in the other party's home or city, and see what they advise you to do. You haven't lost anything; you can always settle for less, drop the matter, or still litigate it to the highest of courts.

Copyright disputes also are being settled through ADRs. For example, an ISP gave notice that part of a subscriber's Web content was to be deleted. Rather than file the required lawsuit to blunt the ISP's actions under the DMCA (see further Chapter 4, "Copying in Cyberspace"), the subscriber contacted an ADR firm in the copyright owner's city. It, in turn, contacted that owner. The parties negotiated a satisfactory licensing agreement, and the settlement saved much more in legal fees than was ever paid under the licensing payment provisions. This isn't to say that using an ADR is the cure-all for the litigation disease, but it does mean that you should seriously consider using these alternative approaches to solve your Internet disputes.

In the previous chapter, we discussed the problems of conflicts of laws and jurisdiction. Let's say that the French customer (in that chapter's example), who felt she had been wronged by a Japanese site, concluded that there would be real problems in enforcing a French court's judgment in Japan, and the Web site had no assets in France. Rather than spend considerable legal dollars for uncertain results, and lose the use of her money during this time period, the French customer could take a portion of those savings and decrease her demands. If she contacted a cybermediation Web site or used an ADR firm in Japan (i.e., the American Arbitration Association, or another one acceptable to the Japanese site), she might be able to avoid the entire morass of unclear, conflicting legal systems between different nations.

It might be worth settling for less than you want, rather than getting caught up in establishing very expensive legal precedents over just the issue of which law applies and where. Once past this, you still must fight the main legal case. Think ADRs.

CHAPTER
13

Domain Names and Conflicts

The domain name for a Web site is the electronic address that identifies its location on the Internet, such as www.pacificschooner.com or www.microsoft.com. Internet users who wish to access a particular Internet host computer to obtain a program or a specific Web site must enter that location's unique site address in order to make the connection. Domain names have a unique numeric address, such as 145.324.241.32, as well as the alphabetized name—and both comprise a domain name. When you type in a domain name, you don't see the underlying unique numeric designation, which specifies the exact computer target for your quest. Each Internet host has a conversion table that converts this name into its unique numerical equivalent, and your browser whisks away to that destination.

With the use and numbers of Internet users still increasing at an exceptional pace, the problem of domain-name conflicts multiplies, especially given the inaccurate attitude that "anything goes" on the Web. It doesn't. Domain names are unique; no one else can use them, because there's only one with that precise designation. It's like a human being—there's only one of you.

The current growth in domain names is as incredible as the past and projected growth in Internet users, both worldwide and in the United States. The annually registered domain names rocketed from 100,000 in 1995 to 5 million in 1999. Current estimates place this number at 30 million worldwide in 2001. Various analysts predict that these numbers will exceed 100 million registered domain names within the next three to five years (a conservative estimate, to some), and the great growth will be in countries other than the United States.

Domain names ending in three letters are designated as top-level domain names. At the beginning of the New Millennium, there were six endings to identify users that existed globally: (1) ".com" (for commercial entities); (2) ".org" (nonprofit—although it seems anyone can reserve this); (3) ".edu" (education); (4) ".gov" (government); (5) ".mil" (military); and (6) ".net" (miscellaneous groups).

In one way, domain names are also geographical in nature. Without any further designation, a mysite.com heads to the United States. However, other countries register domain names within that specific nation by adding a specific country designation: ".uk" (United Kingdom), ".mx" (Mexico), ".tw" (Taiwan), and so on. Thus, a commercial Web site in England would be mysite.com.uk (or mysite.co.uk); in Brazil, it would be mysite.com.br. These distinct geographical destinations can only be used after the appropriate country or regional licensing body has been approved to register those names by ICANN, the entity that oversees domain-name registrations (or Net addresses).

On November 16, 2000, ICANN approved seven new domain extensions: (1) ".aero" (air-transportation industry); (2) ".biz" (for commercial businesses); (3) ".coop" (nonprofit cooperatives); (4) ".info" (unrestricted use, or anyone can use these); (5) ".museum" (museums); (6) ".name" (for individuals); and (7) ".pro" (for accountants, lawyers, and physicians). These new extensions were the first approved by ICANN in over a decade, and the additions multiply the range of available domain names. The effective dates for these new extensions are toward the end of 2001 and on, and this expansion will spur more virtual domain-name gold rushes (although trademark holders were given a preferential "sign-up period). The new ".info" went online in September 2001 (see www.nic.info for the details), while ".biz" went online in October of 2001 (see www.nic.biz). The other new names are to be introduced after that; however, owing to the selective group that they encompass, three domain names won't be available to the public—".coop", ".museum", and ".aero".

The number of permutations for any one company then can be all of these countries that can register names, as well as these different top-level classifications. For example, Ace Drugs could register acedrugs.com or even acedrugs.biz (for the U.S.), and if Ace Drugs had an operation in England, then that site address could be acedrugs.com.uk or acedrugs.biz.uk. However, if FXSX was back in business and registered acedrugs.com first (the U.S. domain name address), Ace would make a complaint with FXSX's registrar and challenge this, given that it owned the trademark—and this is discussed later. However, if Ace wanted to put a Web site up before then, it could register (given the name availability) acedrugs.net or any of the discussed permutations.

This multiplicity of domain name variations and registrars creates the volumes of domain name/trademark conflicts, as well as the opportunities for cybersquatting (registering as many names as possible, then selling them back at a high profit to the legitimate user—who might settle at a lower expense than a fight would cost).

The Shared Registration System

In order to have any validity, domain names must be registered. Until 1999, Network Solutions (NSI) was the exclusive registrar for every generic ".com", ".org", and ".net", as well as being the leader in every other top-level domain name. It registered for every country in the world, as well as for these top-level domain names.

The problem was that NSI didn't worry about who owned the rights to these names and marks that it registered. This was a "first come, first serve" basis. After the problems of domain-name conflicts, pirating, and squatting spiraled nearly out of control, the system was changed to where domain-name applicants must now warrant that their use of that name won't interfere with any other legitimate user's rights. The domain-name holder now must agree to give up that address, if it violates the valid trademark or service-mark rights of another holder—provided that is proven in an administrative or legal proceeding, as we'll see later—and registrars are enacting dispute resolution procedures.

Registrars today still don't conduct any background checks as to the validity of an applicant's representations. They leave it up to the applicant (who may or may not be worried about this) to determine whether that domain name will infringe on the trademark of somebody else. Given the numbers of forms (by country and classification) that registered domain names can take, it's nearly impossible for any one person or business to garner worldwide rights in all countries to any particular trademark or service mark. The largest companies do come close.

After VeriSign acquired NSI, VeriSign became the name of this registrar. Although VeriSign is no longer the exclusive registry for domain names, it is still the dominant player in ".com", ".net", and ".org" registrations. However, now more than 150 firms, in numbers of countries, have registered and been accredited by the Internet Corporation for Assigned Names and Numbers (ICANN) to compete with NSI and register domain names. Any of these entities can register names and different domain extensions, with the provided services and charged fees varying widely (see www.icann.org).

ICANN is the global, nonprofit corporation set up by the U.S. Department of Commerce to oversee a wide range of Internet functions that were once wholly overseen by the U.S. Government, including the issuance of domain names and management of conflicts. The experts debate the extent to which the Commerce Department still exercises "policy" authority over ICANN, but this influence is expected to decline over the years.

A Shared Registration System (SRS) has been in place for some time. This is the domain name registration system for competing registrars in the ".com", ".net", and ".org" top-level domains (including the new extensions and top-level country codes). The Commerce Department created the SRS in 1999, under another agreement with NSI (see www.nsiregistry.com; although "nsi" is in the address, the site is VeriSign's). Under this domain name registration system, competing ICANN-accredited registrars can register domain names, regardless of country of origin, and share this central registration system now operated by VeriSign. Although there's no limit on the number of registrars that may ultimately register names using SRS, every entity desiring to become a registrar for any domain names must first be approved for this purpose by ICANN.

As we discussed, registrars don't assume responsibility for whether any proposed domain name infringes on some individual's or business's rights. In fact, the court cases have uniformly upheld that registrars don't need to check out anything that bears on whether a proposed domain name would infringe on another's trademark. ICANN, in response, enacted uniform procedures to arbitrate domain-name disputes that involve trademark infringement allegations. Under this policy, most types of trademark-based domain-name disputes must be resolved by agreement, court action, or arbitration before a registrar can cancel, suspend, or transfer a domain name.

Trademarks, Service Marks, and the Problem

For decades prior to the Net, trademark law had been relatively straightforward. A trademark is any combination of words, symbols, signs, or the like, that identifies specific goods or services and distinguishes them from *similar* goods and services. Thus, the logo/name (with its distinctive colors, type styles, and shapes) of Apple (its rainbow apple), Coca-Cola (even the shape of its bottle), Amazon.com, Netscape, Nike, McDonald's (the "golden arches"), Pepsi, and Porsche are widely accepted and registered trademarks. Trademarks simply arise from a company's use of marks identifying certain products or services as being theirs. Both trademarks and service marks (i.e., H&R Block for accounting and tax services) can be registered with the federal U.S. Patent and Trademark Office and/or individual U.S. states, not to mention foreign countries all around the globe.

The concept of trade and service marks came about to keep competitive businesses from "passing off" their products as being those of others that had worked hard to build up their brand and customer loyalty. The test is basically whether the use of the other trademarked product would create a likelihood of confusion in the minds of consumers. Let's say Pepsi brought out a Coca-Cola brand of soft drinks with the same logo. If Pepsi started marketing this new Coca-Cola image, then the real Coke could sue it for the next century on trademark infringement and win big-time.

However, the key is whether a consumer would become confused if someone else used that trademark for its products or services. If the consumer would not be so confused, then this is a permissible "fair use" and a defense in U.S. trademark infringement cases—just as it is in copyright actions. This trademark law provides that various entities could use the same mark, provided they were in different lines of business and there wasn't a likelihood of confusion in the minds of consumers. If a shoe company marketed a Nike High-Topper, there's no question that Nike could stop it from using the Nike logo on the basis of trademark infringement. However, if a person named William Nike wanted to manufacture saws under the name "Nike's Saws," then there wouldn't be such a conflict and he could do this. (Note: Although business names and DBAs can't, by themselves, be trademarked, a design of that name in a distinctive style, or within a logo, is trademarked—and this is done all the time.)

A second area of concern is that trademarks can become so distinctive that the mark can and should receive protection against any "dilution" of its value. This means that any use by someone else that diminishes that mark or "dilutes" its value can be stopped. If a tiny "Coca-Cola's Fine Beer and Wine" came into existence, the real Coke could stop it. In our example with William Nike, he wouldn't be allowed legally to call his business "Nike's Ladies of the Night," if he decided to add a night-club to his ventures.

When someone registers with the U.S. Patent and Trademark Office (PTO), that registration is prima facie evidence of the registrant's right to use the mark nation-wide—in all U.S. states. It is constructive notice of that entity's national right to that mark. Businesses also register their marks only in states and not federally, es-pecially if they are denied a federal registration. These registrations do not extin-guish the rights of an unregistered mark owner, if he or she was using that mark before the entity that registered it (the PTO checks only federal registrations, not states' or trade directories). These rights—referred to as common law rights—are valid, but only as to the actual territory of use. As you can see, there is an inherent conflict simply in the way common law and state/federal registrations can overlap.

The problem was that the Internet came along and caught large corporations asleep at the switch. More nimble Net entrepreneurs saw openings a truck could drive through, quickly taking advantage of them. They figured out that a business, large or small, would want to create its own Web site, using domain names that would identify that business in the minds of consumers—and get users straight to that Web site. Quickly, these "entrepreneurs" registered scores of the largest and leading com-panies' names with Network Solutions. Sites that could be worth something, such as "harvardyard.com," "business.com," "NFLtoday.com," and even "ameriascup.com," were also gobbled up.

A market soon developed for the buying and selling of these domain names, and numbers of them infringed directly on the trademarks of established larger com-panies. Using our Nike example, individuals would have tried to register domain names such as "Nike.com," "NikeHighRiders.com," "Nikeshoes.com," and so on. Depending on the circumstances, this could have been a trademark infringement, but no court at the time of these registrations had ruled on this issue. And, large corporations had not yet picked up on the true, explosive potential of the Internet, let alone preserve their domain names for use on the Net.

The other problem was that large companies such as Nike, the large athletic sneaker and apparel manufacturer, in Portland, Oregon, didn't care about "Nike's Saws" in San Francisco, California, when both were running such different types of businesses and one was so tiny. It made little difference, at that time, whether they were even in the same town. Neither one really knew or cared about the other. Then the Internet burst onto the scene and turned all of this around. Let's say that Billy Nike then registered "Nike.com" before the Nike of athletic shoes fame got around to it.

When Billy put up his Web site, it could be seen around the world—and in Port-land. Let's say that Billy just started up his saw company, and if there were any other rights in the trademark "Nike," the shoe company owned them. Now, was a domain name also a trademark? There were no legal answers at the time, and the question was set to be litigated in numerous situations. The large companies went totally into orbit when they saw people using their good corporate name on different Web sites, side by side with the cyberpirates who would only sell them back at exorbitant amounts.

Domain Names vs. Trademarks

These Internet cases began filtering through the legal systems of countries around the world. The courts applied standard trademark law to these situations. Basically, three thresholds were applied on domain name registrations, depending on the applicant's intent: (1) no intent to operate any business under that name ("cybersquatting"); (2) registration by a business already in operation; and (3) coming as close as one could to a validly registered name (i.e., registering "microsoft—.com" or "microseft.com"—also known as "cyberpirating").

The courts have clearly held that there is no right by itself to use a trademark as a domain name. For example, in *Hasbro v. Clue Computing,* the courts held that Hasbro, which owns the famous mark of the board game "Clue," wasn't entitled to use that mark as a domain name. Clue Computer had first registered the Clue name with a domain-name registrar, and Hasbro could not prove the likelihood of confusion (they were in different businesses) or that Clue Computing's use had diminished Hasbro's mark. This case squares entirely with another case holding that a company called Virtual Works could use the domain name "vw.net," over the strong objections of Volkswagen, because they were in different businesses and the likelihood of consumer confusion was not present.

In the *Clue* case, the judge specifically held that holders of a famous mark were not automatically entitled to use that mark as their domain name. This case also illustrated the situation in which two different companies with entirely different product markets can use the same trademark, but there can only be one domain name (the multiple legitimate user problem). Thus, given a legitimate business purpose and no likelihood of confusion in a consumer's mind, the larger company lost out. However, justice has its price. Clue Computing's legal fees were some $125,000 in battling for its principles. The company had three full-time and a few part-time employees before the litigation; afterward, it reportedly was down to the owner and a couple of part-timers. Please, keep in mind the disastrous effects that court battles can have on both your checkbook and your psyche.

Another well-known case was settled between Amazon.com, the huge Internet book retailer, and a tiny feminist bookstore called "Amazon," which operated in Minneapolis. The bookstore had been operating since 1970, and Amazon.com had not started its operations until long after that date. Prior to trial, the two parties settled. Under the terms of the settlement, both parties were allowed to keep using "Amazon" in their names. The bookstore agreed to refer to itself by its full name, Amazon Bookstore Cooperative. It assigned its rights in the Amazon name to Amazon.com, which licensed the name back to the small bookstore. This situation underscored another basic tenet: The registration of a domain name doesn't include any rights to a prior, valid trademark.

Then along came Joshua Quittner, a reporter for *Wired* magazine, who, for fun, registered the "www.mcdonalds.com" domain name for himself. He wrote a column asking readers for suggestions on how to dispose of this "asset." McDonald's, of course, didn't think this was so funny. Quittner settled with McDonald's by agreeing to assign "their" domain name back to the company, in return for its donating $3,500 to his favorite charity.

Large companies tried to muscle out smaller domain-name owners with threats of lawsuits and damages, but if the "little guys" didn't buckle under, then the larger companies had to decide what to do next. Sometimes, they forgot about that reserved domain name and used a different one. At other times, they sued these "cybersquatters"—with very inconsistent results at the time. For example, in *Avery Dennison v. Sumpton,* the court found that Mr. Sumpton's registration of "avery.net" and "dennison.net" did *not* constitute a trademark violation. The court emphasized that Sumpton had a ".net" address, and Avery Dennison hadn't proved that its name had any degree of recognition, at that time, with Internet users.

Actions swirled between virtual entities. eToys (when it was in operation) brought legal action against etoy, an avant-garde Swiss art site, to enjoin the site from using "their" name. There were plenty of legal problems with eToys's claim, starting with the fact that etoy was a nonprofit art group not operating under U.S. law and had registered its domain name in 1995, two years before eToys.com had started up. Originally, eToys approached Swiss etoy to buy the domain name. When that didn't work, it sued. A Los Angeles Superior Court judge granted a temporary injunction against the art group in December 1999. It was ordered to tear down its site or pay $10,000 a day in fines.

A sea of Net activists came to the support of the art group and put the word out over the Internet. An entire Web site, called "Toywar.com" and dedicated to the etoy fight came online. News groups pilloried eToys in the press, and others began to swamp the site with threatening and angry e-mails. Just before the New Millennium slipped in, the large Internet toy retailer announced that it was calling it quits and bowing to public opinion—the art of etoy and the e-commerce of eToys would be allowed to coexist. eToys.com dropped its suit against etoy and agreed to pay $40,000 to the tiny company for its legal bills and expenses.

In about half of the litigated cases before federal legislation was passed, the courts decided that the offending domain name did *not* infringe on the rights of the trademark holder. For example, in *Bally Total Fitness Holding Corp. v. Faber,* the court found in favor of the defendant's use of "Bally sucks" as the domain name for his complaint Web site. The court held that there was no likelihood of confusion in this, because no one would think that "Bally sucks" had anything to do with the real "Bally." The holdings held clearly that where there was an honest intent to use a name, and there was no likelihood of confusion, the duly registered owner of that domain name could use it. However, cyberpirates and cybersquatters were another matter.

Cybersquatters, Pirates, and Bad Faith

Just a few years ago, "entrepreneurs" saw an opportunity in domain names. In a style reminiscent of the old Gold Rush days, they raced to tie up as many of those good corporate names as they could. Later, they would send a demand letter to those companies and offer to sell back the names at a tidy profit. If they didn't get a deal, then these domain-name owners would sit on their names and wait—conjuring up the words "cybersquatting" and "cyberpirating."

Add to the equation that there are layers of the Web, depending on the classification (i.e., ".com" or ".biz") and countries. You can use the same domain name, but by changing the ".com" designation to ".org," or by registering that name with another country's registrar (i.e., France—".fr"), then you've tied up that good corporate name at another potential site.

These practices became a subject of real concern to businesses. Cyberpirates grabbed one pet logo name after another and tied them up, in different levels or countries and through different registrars. There are over 100 possible code extensions now (and they are increasing; most are different country designations), including ".ws" (Western Samoa) and ".tv" (Tuvalu). In return for money, Western Samoa leased its code to registrars, who are leasing this extension to Web customers. Tiny Tuvalu, a poor Polynesian island-nation of some 9,000 people, bettered its conditions through a similar agreement.

People began cashing in by selling their registered names to operators who either wanted them or owned the trademarks. The cyberpirates became emboldened and started registering whatever they could, whether it was "AT&T.com" or "burgerking.com." Since individuals also want a domain name that's their actual name, names like "John Smith" were registered—and there are quite a few John Smiths in the world. Even today, after various legal changes, there's a brisk market in the buying and selling of domain names; just hit the keyword "domain name" in your search engines and see what comes up.

However, the people who registered general or generic names, such as "business.com" or "altavista.com" made excellent business decisions. One Houston businessman paid $150,000 in 1997 for the rights to "business.com." He hit the proverbial jackpot when he sold that domain name to a California company for a cool $7.5 million two years later. The previous high price was the $3.3 million that Compaq Computer paid for the rights to "altavista.com," which became the name of its search engine. Another entrepreneur sold "wallstreet.com" for $1 million. Similar extraordinarily high payments are expected for names such as "loans.com," "cinema.com," and "taxes.com," given that "engineering.org" (a different level) sold for nearly $200,000.

A situation with *Esquire* magazine illustrates those times. The editors of *Esquire* printed an April Fool's joke purporting to chronicle a startup company that gave away free cars and made money by plastering advertising slogans over the vehicles. The article's writer didn't want to run into legal problems, so he registered the domain name of "FreeWheelz" as the name of that Web site, and paid $70 as the initial registration fee. Lo and behold, a group of entrepreneurs called up after the article was published and said they wanted to buy that URL for their startup site. The founders of the real company reportedly paid the reporter $25,000 for the rights to that address.

Head to any Internet name-auction site and you'll find literally thousands of catchy (and some not-so-bright) domain names that can be bought for anywhere from hundreds of dollars to millions (see greatdomains.com and afternic.com). One Internet statistic site, Dotcom.com, discovered in a survey that 41 percent of domain names registered for a year were still inactive (or "parked"), and cybersquatters appeared to be responsible for most. At some time, the FTC and other regulatory agencies will need to regulate the buying and selling of domain names, just as they have done with other business opportunities. As the Internet continues to increase in use and value, so do the valuations of these names.

The corporate world didn't take kindly to the cybersquatters and "typo pirates" (i.e., "billygate.com") that circled around their trademarks. One case granted Paine-Webber's (now, UBS PaineWebber) request for an injunction against a man who had registered the domain name of wwwpainewebber.com—which is one omitted period away from its address of www.painewebber.com (you don't feel sorry about these cases). Large corporate attorneys unleashed software "spiders" and "robots" that crawled through the millions of Web pages, looking for any mention of their clients and valued trademarks. Offenders were quickly sued if an agreement wasn't reached.

The majority of courts held that if consumers could be confused over whether a Web site registered in a protected trade name belonged to that company or to the cybersquatter, then this would dilute that trade name and was a violation. Most courts didn't hesitate to punish cyberpirates for trying to extort sizable "green-mail" payments in exchange for a sought-after domain name.

For example, Wendy's received a letter asking the company to buy back its domain name, "wendysrestaurant.com." Wendy's promptly sued for trademark infringement, and the claimant eventually backed down, agreeing to remove his claim to any of the Wendy's-related names that he had registered. Some corporations, like America Online, paid to keep their desired domain names. However, using settlements and lawsuits to cancel what were inexpensive registrations (about $35 per year) proved to be a cumbersome and expensive process—and they lost sometimes (i.e., the *Avery Dennison* case).

In response, the Anticybersquatting Consumer Protection Act (ACPA) was passed in late 1999. This Act allows civil lawsuits to be brought for trademark and service mark violations against anyone, who with a "bad faith" intent to profit from a mark, registers, uses, or attempts to sell a domain name that's identical or confusingly similar to that protected mark. Bad faith is a factual determination: did the person intend to divert the trademark owner's customers, offer the registered name for sale without having used it, and/or register multiple names, among other factors. *Under the Anticybersquatting Act, the courts can cancel a "pirated" domain name, assess attorneys' fees and costs, and levy penalties of up to $100,000 per domain name against an infringer (depending on the level of bad faith and the actual damages).*

This legislation also made it illegal to register the name of any living person without that person's consent, while intending to profit by that action. Actor Brad Pitt and singer Kenny Rogers immediately filed suit on this provision alone, Kenny Rogers being upset over the "kennyrogers.com" registered to a California wedding-service Web site. Lawyers already had brought a copyright infringement lawsuit against the owners of the "gwbush.com" site, which satirized the "Bush for President" campaign.

As soon as the Anticybersquatting Act became law, lawsuits were pressed by organizations against alleged cybersquatting infringements. For example, Harvard University filed a lawsuit arguing that two men had registered 65 domain names that infringed on its trademarks. The men had registered names such as "harvard-collegeonline.com," "harvardjobs.com," and "harvardyardsale.com," among others. The men had offered to resell them back to the university, which in turn rejected their offer. At the same time, Network Solutions confirmed that there was no way that it, or any other registrar, could check out any trademark claims prior to registration. Following Harvard's lead that week, the National Football League sued an individual over his Web sites of "NFLtoday.com," "NFLtoday.net," and "NFLtoday.org." Quokka Sports, the company managing the Web site for the New Zealand America's Cup yachting team sued two Australians for their domain name of "americascup.com." It was alleged that the domain-name owners had offered to sell them back at prices up to $50,000 in one case.

This legislation changed the map for cyberpirating and cybersquatting. Nearly all of these legal actions were settled or won in the trademark holder's favor. Wendy's International won its case; even Ireland-based Stanley Steamer sued and won under the U.S. federal cyberpiracy law against one person who registered "stanleysteemer.cc." A businessman agreed to turn back the domain name of the largest Columbus, Ohio, law firm in another federal lawsuit. And it should be no surprise that Brad Pitt, Kenny Rogers, Harvard, the NFL, and Quokka all wrested their domain names back (but the parody on President Bush is still up and running).

Generally, only large companies have the money to hire the expensive lawyers needed to win these actions, so the complaint is that legitimate small businesses and entrepreneurs are also losing under this act. However, this law put a strong crimp in the actions of U.S. cyberpirates—and more responses followed.

Late in 1999, ICANN and Network Solutions agreed that domain name registrations had to be prepaid. Before this change, cybersquatters could buy a name with the hopes of selling it later; if they didn't find a buyer, then they let the unsold names expire for nonpayment. The amount of statutory damages for copyright infringements was increased. And an amendment to existing trademark legislation was enacted; it permitted trademark dilution to be used as a cause of action in canceling domain-name registrations.

Early in the New Millennium, ICANN's president announced that more than 800 addresses of "dash dot" domain names had been revoked. In a "dash dot" name, "www.microsoft.com" would be registered as "www.microsoft-.com." A software glitch apparently had allowed these registrations to proceed—and the excesses of the past were now being corrected.

ICANN's Dispute-Resolution Procedures

ICANN then instituted a procedure for resolving domain-name disputes (see www.icann.org for the latest details). Under an agreement called the Uniform Domain-Name Dispute-Resolution Policy, companies and individuals with a dispute can file a complaint and trigger a low-cost arbitration proceeding. The arbitrator(s) make a ruling as to which party has the legitimate right to that name. If either party disputes the ruling that's made, the next step is to litigate this in court. A judge will review then all of the facts and isn't necessarily bound by the review board's determination. Once the determination is final, the registrar will transfer the domain name as the court or panel has decided.

Trademark and service mark holders, whether registered or not, can take their case to one of four arbitration and mediation centers. Under this process, 200 to 300 new cases are accepted each month. This is a good number of cases and an increasing trend. The United Nations World Intellectual Property Organization (WIPO) hears most of the cases (check www.icann.org for the complete list of dispute resolution providers).

Basically, the claimant must prove that (1) the domain name very closely resembles a trademark registered by that entity; (2) the party that registered the domain name has no rights or legitimate interest in that name; and (3) the domain name was registered and used for illicit purposes or in bad faith. This process is inexpensive: a one-person panel at this time costs the complainant $1,500 and a three-person panel costs $3,000. It is also fast (the arbitrator's decision is to be rendered within 45 days) and convenient (there is no hearing to attend; only a complaint and response is reviewed by the arbitrator). As anticipated, the decisions have favored the complainant (four-fifths have been won by the trademark owner).

The first complaint seeking international arbitration to resolve such a dispute was filed in late 1999. Over 100 cases, involving businesses from more than 30 countries, were filed during the first three months, and the filings have accelerated since then. The initial decisions on domain names reached favorable conclusions for companies with recognizable names, such as the World Wrestling Federation, Stella D'oro Biscuits (a Nabisco affiliate), and Telstra (the Australian telecom company), and the panels ordered that their domain names be transferred back to those trademark holders. A WIPO panel ruling also gave back to Julia Roberts the domain name of "juliaroberts.com" from the operator of a parody site about the actress. (The operator promptly brought a lawsuit over that decision.) WIPO arbitration panels have handed back the "Corinthians" name (owned by the Brazilian soccer team) and Yahoo! back to itself (a Phillipino entity had reserved it under that country's code), as well as Web addresses bearing the names of Dan Marino, Ally McBeal, ESPN, and Wal-Mart.

A WIPO panel granted Time Warner, which holds the marketing rights to British author J.K. Rowling's Harry Potter books, ownership of 107 Potter-related Internet domain names. Another panel awarded domain names incorporating authors' names back to the authors, who ranged from Louis Sachar (Newbury Award winner) to Thomas L. Friedman (Pulitzer Prize-winning journalist). Madonna won back her name (madonna.com) from the Madonna Rehabilitation Hospital in Lincoln, Nebraska, which had received it gratis from the entrepreneur who first bought it (he correctly figured out that he'd lose it anyway). However, the singer Sting, whose real name is Gordon Sumner, lost his battle for the address "sting.com." A panel ruled that the word "sting" is generic and not subject to a trademark.

As you would imagine, most disputes stop here. However, the complaint continues that these laws and domain-name processes favor the much larger companies (which can afford the lawyers for the ICANN complaints and litigation battles) over the much smaller ones and entrepreneurs. *The bottom line: Register a domain name that doesn't infringe on a larger company's turf. If in doubt, find another one.*

Internationally

At the same time that arbitration panels are deciding domain-name disputes, businesses will be busily registering their trademarks and service marks at the ".biz", ".info", and other levels. Interestingly, this should generate even more problems. As companies across the world grab ".biz" addresses that are in conflict with ".com" ones, there is the potential for even more confusion.

In the United States, the game of cybersquatting is over, at least against large corporations (which critics accuse of "cybersquishing"). The Anticybersquatting Act gives them strong weapons in their battles against what are usually small operators, and other countries are deliberating on whether to enact this legal concept. If these companies don't want to attack someone in court with high-cost legal weapons, they can head into a registrar with ICANN's dispute-resolution policy and use that process. Because these devices also protect smaller, legitimate businesses, you should be mindful of their provisions. However, you'll generally need an attorney who specializes in cyberlaw and trademarks to guide you through the process.

The rest of the world is not as restrictive, however, and the game is still being played in some fashion. Countries in Central and South America, Asia, and the old Russian Republic, among others, have not yet tightened their laws to the degree that the United States has. Over time, it is expected that they will. Small nations like Tuvalu and Moldavia (where doctors like the ".md") will be available for cybersquatters to purchase domain names that aren't already reserved, and the conflict-of-laws question will pop up again when lawsuits are brought to challenge such registrations.

As part of this, it's important to know that ICANN's mediation/arbitration Uniform Domain-Name Dispute-Resolution Policy only applies in its entirety to the TLDs, or top level domains, of ".com", ".org", ".Net", and the new extensions, such as ".biz" (the dispute-resolution policy for the new extensions will be "similar" to the present system, according to ICANN). However, it does *not* extend to the "ccTLD's" (country code, top level domains), such as those ending in the destinations of ".fr" for France, ".jp" for Japan, ".uk" for England, ".cn" for China, and the like. For example, at this time "yourfirm.com" would be subject to that policy, but "yourfirm.com.jp (Japan)" would not be. The ICANN-mandated dispute resolution applies *only* if a country-code registrar agrees to use them. Or if the parties to the dispute so agree.

However, there are only 18 countries presently (Antigua, Guatemala, Panama, Philippines, Romania, Western Samoa, etc.) who have agreed to use ICANN's mandated mediation/arbitration approach, and none of the major, industrialized countries have yet agreed. This does not mean that all's lost. These countries, ceded the responsibility for their country's domain names, have been establishing their own dispute-resolution centers, apart from who their registrar is. For example, the Japan Network Information Center (JPNIC) is in charge of the ".jp" suffix, while its Arbitration Center for Industrial Property (ACIP) is deciding its domain-name disputes. However, should a country not yet have an ADR firm in charge of this, you'll be duking it out in expensive court fights. *Should you have an international dispute over a domain name with a country destination-suffix, you'll need to determine if that nation has signed up with ICANN, or not (check out icann.org), and who provides its domain-name, dispute-resolution services.*

It will depend on the country, as each develops its own law. For example, England was the site of a controversy entitled the "One in a Million" case. A company with this name registered domain names in the trade names of several famous British companies, such as "virgin.com.uk" and "marksandspencer.com.uk," then tried to sell them back for a sizable fee. The English Court of Appeal held that the company was using the domain name as an "instrument of fraud" and enjoined it from using or selling these sites in that manner. The court ordered the company to transfer the names back to the true trademark holders.

Litigation over these issues are becoming more prevalent in Japan, as well. Toshiba and Kyocera Corporation won battles over their domain names, although Fuji Photo lost a case when the court held that the word "fuji" is generic and is widely used by the Japanese public. Japan Airlines also lost a legal battle with an American who had registered his name's initials, "J.A.L."

One "impoverished English academic" (by his own admission) registered the best-known British authors, including Martin Amis (www.martinamis.com), Julian Barnes (www.julianbarnes.com), and Iain Banks (www.iainbanks.com), among some 100 literary names that were registered or purchased by him. However, the authors complained to the registrars, and the administrative ICANN panels began ruling in the authors' favor, deciding in those proceedings that the concerned domain names were to be returned to the complaining authors.

A long-standing agreement called the Madrid Agreement covers international trademark law. Although the treaty has been signed by 68 countries to date, the United States has not yet agreed to it. (For more, see www.wipo.org, under "trademarks.") Accordingly, U.S. companies must file trademark registrations in all of the countries where they need protection. Agreeing to the Madrid Agreement would mean that a U.S. business would have to file only one application for international protection with the U.S. Patent and Trademark Office (PTO), because this treaty provides that such a filing is, in effect, an application to all of its signature countries at the same time.

For international protection, businesses at this time will need to register their trademark or service mark with the U.S. PTO and then file that registration (with other requested information) with the appropriate agency of the countries that they're doing business in.

When Reserving a Name

If you're interested in creating a Web site, research the availability of your name on a registrar's Web site (enter "domain name" and "domain name registration" on a search engine). This will tell you whether someone else has already reserved your proposed domain name. If the name has already been reserved, then you can find out from that registrar the details of who owns it and how to contact that owner. *Your options will be: (1) negotiate to buy it, (2) wait to see if the registration lapses, (3) change your marketing thrust, or (4) select a different domain name.*

It makes no sense to cybersquat these days—no matter where you live. If you're a gambling person, then you could surf over to a foreign country's registrar and see what you could tie up through that system. Some countries have enacted rules, however, that you must have an office or some physical presence in a nation before a registration will be issued—an obvious effort to cut down on cyberpirating and cybersquatting. If you find a country that doesn't have this requirement, then you could take the chance. However, be prepared to play poker when the inevitable demand comes from a big player to cough up the name. Or worse.

Before you buy or register any available domain name, however, you should conduct a trademark search of that name. At least, do this search before investing any moneys after registering a domain name. As we have already seen, if you pick a domain name that's in conflict with another firm's trade or service mark in the same line as your proposed business (being a startup, you won't have the defense of "fair use"), you will most likely lose that name. A sizable expenditure of time and money can be at risk in any Web address, so it is better to be safe, than sorry.

You can conduct your own trademark search for federal registrations at the U.S. Patent and Trademark Office Web site (www.uspto.gov). Keep in mind that trademarks superior to yours won't necessarily be picked up by the federal PTO search, as this search only covers federal registrations. If you want a more detailed search of state registrations and common law rights from nonregistered use, you'll need to cover Yellow Page directories, industrial directories, and the various states. You can hire someone else to do a complete search, either by looking in the Yellow Pages under "trademark search" or on the Web with your search engine. Outside searches can be relatively inexpensive; they range upward from $250, depending on the complexity and what you want.

Some of the acts we've discussed were downright foolish. Yes, some people made a bundle on their domain names—but they didn't violate someone else's trademarks. They were creative and inventive. For example, the person who first registered "business.com" and the businessman who resold it. The great majority of cybersquatters who violated an existing company's trademarks paid dearly for that activity; win, lose, or draw, they incurred sizeable legal fees.

This doesn't mean you shouldn't buy or sell domain names; it does mean that you need to do your homework first. Not only should the name be available, but also you shouldn't be infringing on somebody's mark at the time. Keep in mind that "fair use" (you're in very different businesses, operating in good faith) is a valid defense, depending on the circumstances. For example, if you like "AceZ.com" and there's an AceZ running a theater chain just in your state, just be sure you're not going to show any motion pictures in a theater.

It's okay to create a domain name that's close to another, because trade names and trademarks are distinct from domain names. However, you'll need to: (1) intend to set up a viable business that's not competitive (or likely to create confusion in a consumer's mind) with that domain-name holder; (2) be sure that your domain name isn't just a "knock off"; and (3) show no "bad faith" on your part (i.e., that you're actually using it in your business).

In our Nike example, if you're going to set up "Nike's Saws," then set up a saw business. However, it doesn't make sense to reach for "Nike.net" or "Nike.com.uk," even if your name is William Nike. If you want to use your name in the domain name, then try "williamnikesaws.com" and start your home page with the title of "Nike's Saws." Given the millions of domain names already registered, you'll be lucky to come up with one you fall in love with, let alone find one that precisely represents you and your business.

When you find a domain name you like, don't take risks to change it ever so slightly so that it sounds like a recognized name, especially if you're in the same business. Further, if the trademark search indicates that someone in the same industry has that name trademarked, then find and use another one. Remember, you don't have to use a domain name that's the same as your trademark or business name. For example, use "Nike's Saws" for your sign and logo, but register a domain name instead of "bestsaws.com," or another available name.

Keeping Your Domain Name

This is a "dog-eat-dog" world, so you need to take reasonable steps to safeguard your domain name. This begins with knowing the rules and procedures of your registrar—in case you need to challenge someone who's ripping off your name. *You should mark down the renewal date of your registration and when to pay the fee, so you don't lose it to a watchful competitor.* Be sure that your registrar always has your correct and updated business name, office address, and e-mail address. If your registrar charges maintenance fees, draw up a schedule of the due dates so that the fees are paid timely. There's no need to run into unnecessary problems with a lapsed registration.

Once you have acquired a proper domain name, take the necessary steps to trademark it. To register federally, a person must file an application with the U.S. Patent and Trademark Office (check out www.uspto.gov). Under current law, a mark can be registered: (1) if it is currently in commerce; or (2) if the applicant intends to put the mark into commerce within six months (and this period can be extended). You will need to attach logos and samples of this trademark or service mark, including how you're using or intending to use it. If there are no trademarks registered, it is possible for you to register directly your dot.com domain name as a trademark (or service mark).

It usually takes 1½ years or more to get an application approved. When the PTO examines a trademark for registration, it will search for any prior registered marks that are "confusingly similar" to yours. Keep in mind that a federal registration will not erase the prior common-law rights of an unregistered mark owner. However, this registration can make winning your case that much easier in an ICANN domain-name dispute proceeding, should someone try to rip off yours.

At the PTO's Web site, you can search for prior registrations, download forms, and even file online trademark and service mark applications. The cost is presently $325 for an application (per classification) and $400 for a renewal. Registrations are renewable between the fifth and sixth years after the initial registration and every 10 years thereafter.

If you can't register federally, then see if you can register in your state—provided that the federally registered mark owner isn't already doing business in your state. For information on this process, including arranging for the proper application, call up your state's Secretary of State's office or check your state's Web site. Then fill in your application pursuant to your state's procedures. If your domain name is the same as your trademark or service mark, then your application can be made without the ".com" or ".net" attached; however, if your business is the Web site (e.g., "Ace's Goods.com"), then it will be with the ".com." Trademarks are separate from domain-name registrations, and this distinction also prevents others from trying to "freeze" your trademark under the ICANN domain-name dispute policy.

In an Internet economy, the decisions to register can become more complicated. For example, if you enjoy a Web presence with good sales coming from both Mexico and the United States, then you should consider registering your trademarks in both countries (regardless of the country that you're domiciled in). You will need to decide whether you should register your domain name in both countries as marks, as well. As your business services more countries, you'll need to consider registering marks and domain names in those nations, as well.

You should conduct domain name/trademark searches at least annually, if possible (some lawyers recommend sooner, if you're in a technological, fast-moving business), to ensure that no one is violating your property rights. Any check of your "dot.com" address would need to include "dot.net" and "dot.org", as well as other levels and those countries within which you do business.

This would include a detailed search of all registered and common-law (but watch the cost) trademark equivalents to your domain name, in the relevant countries. Going international can be an expensive proposition; however, if you want to have this presence, then you'll have to deal with this cost. The problem comes when you learn that someone's using your domain name.

When Someone Infringes Upon You

Whether your domain name is the same as your trademark or not *isn't* that important for legal purposes. In fact, businesses at times are viewing this difference to be an advantage. For example, the owner of Ace Trust Deeds would be ecstatic if he could own the rights to "loan.com" (which he doesn't). Surfers throw in key words totally unrelated to a specific business when they use a search engine, and companies know this (which is why "wallstreet.com" went for such large bucks).

You will want to talk with the offender in the beginning, to see what he or she plans to do. A nice chat, arranged early, can sometimes do wonders in working out a deal. If this doesn't work, then you'll need to decide how important the matter really is. If your financial pocketbook isn't being hit, then you could walk away from it. However, if you're losing business because a competitor is picking off sales by using your mark/domain name, then you'll need to consider tougher action. Think ADRs first—and talk with mediators in both yours and the infringer's area to get their advice. Also, remember that ICANN's dispute resolution policy only involves filing a complaint and information (a hearing isn't needed), and the expenses and legal fees are quite low.

If your demand letter has been ignored (and ADRs are unworkable), then consider the tradeoffs on using the Anticybersquatting Act (the "ACPA"), an ICANN proceeding, or both. ICANN gives a fast resolution, but ACPA litigation can take one to two years (or more) for a decision. Although the federal lawsuit allows for a preliminary injunction, an opportunity to be awarded good damages, and transfer of the domain name (which is all that ICANN can do), this course is expensive, complex, carries a danger of never recovering your attorney fees, and takes up much more management time. The ACPA is a final determination, whereas the extent to which an ICANN decision can be litigated is currently being determined. The high majority of companies choose ICANN proceedings.

You'll need to discuss your problem with experienced legal counsel—at a consultative, no-charge initial meeting whenever possible. Once you have an idea as to what the legal costs could be, you can make a cost-benefit decision before you take it further. The decision also depends on the infringer's location and type of business.

For example, let's say you discover that someone else is using your trademark of XX3. If the infringer, XX3, operates a reputable travel agency in New York City and your company develops software in Carmel, California, then this might not be a great problem or worry—whether XX3 is using a similar domain name, service mark, or both. On the other hand, if XX3 also sells software, then you'll need to weigh how that competition is diluting your mark and product (if at all) versus the costs of getting that action to stop.

If you don't feel that it's worth the cost, then you could let this go for the time being. It might be worth continuing a dialogue with the other party to try and work out an eventual solution. If the negative sales effects increase over time, then there's more cost justification to take the expensive legal steps. Some attorneys understandably argue that you need to litigate quickly, not only to stop this dilution, but also to guard against waiving your legal rights. However, you might try to buy out an infringer, especially if that's less costly than the legal battles. Paying "greenmail" is a tough decision to make, but you should consider the overall net costs and benefits in any final decision. Of course, it's easier to do this when the other party is an innocent party like you: caught in a system that lets vast numbers of businesses use the same trademark and similar domain names.

If you have a deep legal pocket, then you might sue first and ask questions later. This approach can force a recalcitrant party to the bargaining table, but you'll need to be careful with this tactic. Legal expenses always seem to increase faster than as first budgeted, especially if the other party meets your aggressive approach head-on. If you are a small business, the best approach is to do your homework in the beginning and save yourself these later headaches.

In any event, think ADR, remember the problems of jurisdiction and applicable law, and weigh what you're losing versus the costs of stopping it. Or simply register a new domain name and go on from there.

A *Domain Name Transfer Agreement* is presented and discussed next. This form is used when you want to purchase or sell a domain name. As you read through the comments on what can be included in such an agreement, you see that the considerations involve more than just agreeing to a price. As with the other forms in this book, you'll need to modify this one for the specifics of your situation. It is, like the others, informational in nature.

Domain Name Transfer Agreement

This Domain Name Transfer Agreement is entered on [*Date of Agreement*] between [*Name of Person or Entity Selling the Domain Name*], the "Seller," and [*Name of Person or Entity Buying the Domain Name*], the "Buyer," all on the following terms and conditions:

1. **Agreement.** For valuable consideration, Seller sells, transfers, and assigns to Buyer all rights of ownership in the domain name of [*State the Domain Name Being Sold*], the "Domain Name," of which Seller registered that domain name on [*Date of Domain Name Registration*] with [*Domain Name Registrar*], the "Registrar."

2. **Consideration.** Buyer agrees to pay Seller the sum total of $[*Total Purchase Price to be Paid*], of which $[*Cash Deposited on Signing of this Agreement*] has been paid on the signing of this agreement and $[*Remainder of Purchase Price to be Paid in Cash*] shall be paid no later than by [*Date on Which Rest of Purchase Price is to be Paid*].

3. **Transfer.** Seller agrees to prepare at its own expense all necessary paperwork required to transfer the ownership of the domain name, [*State the Domain Name Being Sold*], to Buyer, including but not limited to that required by [*Domain Name Registrar*] to evidence such transfer, a bill of sale, and all other documentation that may be reasonably required by Buyer. This documentation shall be shown to Buyer prior to execution for Buyer's approval. All formal documentation shall be signed and executed to Buyer's satisfaction, then exchanged in return for the $[*Remainder of Purchase Price to be Paid in Cash*], all to take place prior to the date indicated in Section 2 above. If the Buyer is not satisfied with the documentation, then the cash deposit shall be returned to the Buyer, and neither party shall have any further responsibility to the other.

4. **Seller's Warranty.** Seller warrants that it: (a) owns all right, title, and interest in the Domain Name without offset, liens, or encumbrances; (b) properly registered the Domain Name with the above Registrar; (c) has maintained the registration in the Registrar properly and with full legal effect; (d) has the full power and authority to enter into this Agreement; (e) will not infringe upon the rights of any other entity by entering into this agreement; and (f) unequivocally warrants Buyer will have full and complete title to the Domain Name, without claim or controversy, upon its purchase of same (including no copyright, trademark, or service mark infringements or violations).

5. **Indemnification.** Seller agrees to defend, indemnify, and hold harmless Buyer, its officers, employees, and representatives, from and against all claims, actions, or demands, including court costs and reasonable legal fees, resulting from any breach of the warranties in Section 4 above. Buyer shall promptly provide notice to Seller of any such claim or proceeding, and shall assist Seller, at Seller's sole expense, in defending any such controversy. This provision shall survive past the closing and transfer of the Domain Name.

6. **No Assignment.** This Agreement and the rights thereunder may not be assigned without the written consent of the other party, which consent may be withheld for any reason.

7. **Other.** Any dispute arising in connection with this Agreement shall be first settled by mediation. If that's not successful, then the dispute shall be settled by arbitration to be held in [*Location of Arbitration*] in accordance with the rules of the American Arbitration Association. This agreement to arbitrate shall be specifically enforceable. Any award shall be final and binding on all parties, and a final judgment may be entered in the appropriate court of law. Notwithstanding this, should any litigation ensue between the parties, then the prevailing party shall be entitled to reasonable expenses and attorney fees as set by the Court.

This Agreement is the final understanding between the parties on this subject matter, superseding all other previous agreements, and may be amended only by the written consent of all the parties. Should any court or proceeding determine that any provision is illegal or in conflict, then all other remaining provisions shall be held severable, valid, and be given separate legal effect.

Domain Name Transfer Agreement *(Continued)*

This Agreement shall bind the parties, their successors, and permitted assigns; its legality and interpretation shall be governed by the laws of the State of [*Name of State Whose Laws Govern*] and of the United States.

This Agreement is accepted, understood, and executed as of the date first above written, by and between:

_____

[*Name and Title of Party Signing for Seller*]
[*Seller's Name and Address*]

_____

[*Name and Title of Party Signing for Buyer*]
[*Buyer's Name and Address*]

Domain Name Transfer Agreement

Discussion of Provisions

1. **Agreement.** Domain names don't exist unless they have been properly registered with an authorized registrar. Whenever possible, the requested documentation should be included as a separate exhibit.

2. **Consideration.** This Agreement provides for a cash payment upon the execution of the contract, the remainder being paid when the transfer and registration paperwork have been completed. However, the payment for such a purchase may take any number of forms, ranging from a trade of software and property to installment payments. If installment payments are agreed to, then the seller should take security, in case an owing installment is not paid. Depending on the security taken and terms of payment, this provision would be accordingly changed.

3. **Transfer.** This section allows for the buyer to inspect the transfer and bill of sale documentation prior to making the final payment. Once buyer is satisfied with the paperwork, the deal is then completed. Otherwise, the deposit is returned to the buyer and this transaction is at an end.

4. **Seller's Warranty.** Buyer should be sure seller has the full rights to enter into this sale and owns the domain name that it's selling. Additionally, copyright, trademark, and service mark searches should be completed to ensure full and complete title is being secured. Otherwise, the wording should be changed to reflect an "as is" purchase.

5. **Indemnification.** If it turns out seller doesn't own all of the rights, then it's only fair that the seller takes care of the problem—not the buyer. However, there may be times when this indemnification should be mutual, and this provision will be accordingly changed.

6. **No Assignment.** This contract provides that no assignment can be made of the agreement. At times, buyers may attempt to resell the domain name to another party, but at a higher price, and before they need to pay the final amounts. Sellers always take exception to this, especially if they learn about this later. If the buyer is preparing this contract, then the language can be changed to reflect that the agreement can be assigned, provided that consent is obtained from the other party but which won't "be unreasonably withheld"—or even that the agreement can be assigned "without limitation."

7. **Other.** This "boilerplate" stipulates that the alternate dispute resolution techniques of mediation and arbitration are to be used. Should arbitration not be agreeable, then these provisions would have to be accordingly changed to reflect the parties' agreement. This section provides that U.S. law applies, which could also change if one or both parties aren't U.S. residents. The other provisions included are as found in the forms presented throughout this book. If you have any additional questions, please see the discussion at this section for these other forms.

CHAPTER 14

Creating Your Own Web Site

It can be an emotional roller coaster when you create your own Web site. Whether you're leasing space from a large portal such as Yahoo! GeoCities, pursuant to its rules, or hiring your own Web designer, you learn a basic fact: If it's possible for something not to work, it probably won't. Obtaining and arranging text, pictures, and links isn't as easy as you first thought, and the technological "ease" initially taken for granted now seems to be more complex.

Regardless of your using a local server, a large portal, or a company network, the considerations discussed in this chapter are applicable to all. And getting the site set up starts first with deciding on what you want to accomplish.

Know What You Want to Do

If you're creating your own personal site, then there are fewer considerations. This location will be about you and your interests—whether it's showing your poetry, posting your latest adventure-travel pictures, or creating a family site for the relatives. Although the general factors apply to all sites, you'll need to take more time when creating a nonpersonal Web site, whether it's solely earmarked for e-commerce, an extension of your present commercial activities, or a nonprofit informational site. Understandably, there are more issues to decide.

It's difficult to mix personal and business-related activities on the same Web site. The advice of the experts is: "Don't." The market appears to be solidly segmented between personal and business uses. If part of your appeal is a "homespun" approach, then find some other sites that have a similar tone, and study how this was best accomplished. For example, if you want to create the Colonel Sanders type of approach that made Kentucky Fried Chicken famous, then do that, but don't spend your time talking about the Colonel (yourself). Try to go one way or the other. If you are creating a Web site that sells products, then do talk about how your life and background relate to your selling the best ones. The same suggestion applies if you are selling a service whether it's insurance, a bed and breakfast, or adventure tours. However, don't sell yourself so much that people lose sight of your service or products.

When creating a business Net presence, one initially important question to answer is whether your site will be an informational site or a sales-oriented one. We already learned, in Chapter 11, "But Can Your Court Hear the Case? What Law Is Applied?," that a pure advertising site without the ability to take orders or conduct business doesn't have the required contacts with other states. Thus, nonresident complainants don't have the ability to force you to travel to their state and defend yourself in court. However, taking orders on that site, selling items into the state, e-mail or other interactive features, and 800-number availability seem to do the trick.

An informational site advertises your "story," how products or services can be purchased, and your availability, so that a user knows how to contact you offline or online for business. A sales site orients itself to taking orders from clients and customers on that site. There is no question that an informational site is an easier Web presence to create: you don't have to worry about safeguarding credit card information, encryption technology, return and refund disclosures, and detailed delivery cost information. You'll handle that when an interested customer calls up your office and talks to you in person.

There are many other considerations, and numbers of books are already on the market detailing these "do's" and "don'ts," whether you're a profit or nonprofit entity. *The important point is to know first what you want, how you're going to do it, your audience, and the implications.* Regardless that you're creating an informational "passive" or sales-oriented "active" site, that Web site will need to have in place reasonable Terms of Use and Privacy Policies. And you'll need these notices whether you're a nonprofit, for profit, educational, or governmental institution.

KNOW YOUR MARKET

Another key assessment in the creation of a Web site is determining what is your specific market, who's going to visit you, and what do they want. For example, whether you sell big-ticket items (i.e., antiques, refrigerators, or expensive jewelry) or less costly ones (i.e., greeting cards, books, or office supplies) is a critical difference as to what you'll be displaying and how. A person who purchases expensive items is more deliberate, has more money to spend, and may want the feeling of a "luxury" page. A person with less money in hand may make instant purchasing decisions based on speed of delivery and product availability.

A service site will have different considerations, depending on how complicated, unique, or regulated that service is. For example, if you are a business consultant, then your message—and the regulations as to what you can or cannot say—will be different, let's say, from that of a lawyer or a doctor. Professionals, such as attorneys or accountants, are bound by strict rules that regulate the extent to which they can advertise, what can be said, and what testimonials are used, whether they create an Internet Web site or a TV ad.

Whether you are selling goods or services, creating an informational or sales site, or starting up or expanding, you will need to consult with the applicable regulatory body as to what laws applies to you and your site. For example, if you are planning to sell insurance, you had better meet your state's licensing requirements for insurance salespersons. If you are selling organic vitamin supplements, it is possible that you will need to be careful with your state's and the federal Food and Drug Administration (FDA) regulations in this area. You'll want to be sure that whatever you say is truthful, not fraudulent or misrepresenting the truth. (See Chapter 16, "Web Site Operating Considerations," for more on these important assessments.)

These factors also include the geographical area that you're selling into. Let's say that you're a real estate agent and want to establish an Internet presence. It would be nice if you could set up anything on the Web, and people from all over the world would call you right up after viewing it. Unfortunately, your business will be concentrated, more than likely, among people who are trading up to homes within your local area, or moving into your town from locations within your state. This type of site should emphasize local attractions, developments, and history. To a great extent and unless you own a large firm, most service Web sites will be serving local or regional markets, and their marketing message will be usually more localized than if products were sold.

On the other hand, if you want to sell one-of-a-kind artifacts on the Internet (i.e., sculptures, paintings, or even weavings), then you'll want to think about a much broader marketing area and approach. You should consider a broader appeal, emphasizing the difficulty in purchasing such quality items from other than on your site. Uniqueness, price, delivery charge, and refund/return information become more important. If you are selling handcrafted Kachina dolls, then you would be emphasizing their ethnicity and traditions, as well as their authenticity. *In all cases, your site needs to emphasize value and that it's better, faster, or easier to use than other locations.* It is this value that gives even informational sites the ability to charge on a subscription basis for what was first given away for free.

However, as your business or service becomes more regulated or controversial, you'll need to be more legally watchful. For example, if you want to create a lotto or "games of chance," be careful. You might run afoul of varying state and/or country prohibitions on gambling. If you are selling a service for disposing hazardous wastes, then you must be careful about disclosures that might be regulated differently, depending on the applicable city, state, or even federal regulating entity. If you are selling to children, then the Federal Trade Commission's privacy disclosure statements on children are relevant. (See Chapter 6, " 'Junk Dog' Statements and Privacy Concerns.")

Whatever the business you intend to market, call your state's regulatory agencies before you begin your operations. There are numerous important marketing considerations when creating your site, so read books on Internet marketing, talk to others in the Net field, or even hire a Web marketing consultant. *Given the international reach of your site and the growing Net markets in all countries, you'll want to consider bilingual or multilingual access, and perhaps even tailor your marketing approach and legal provisions to countries other than your own.*

Domain Name Registration

Chapter 13, "Domain Names and Conflicts," indicated the complexity of these conflicts and how seriously businesspeople take this issue. You'll want to reread portions of that chapter, especially if you're concerned over your proposed name. Although it helps in marketing and opening your site up, the domain name you select doesn't necessarily have to be the exact name of your Web site. For example, it's likely that William Nike's new Web site of "Nike's Products" wouldn't have a domain name of "nike.com" or even "nikeproducts.com." However, "williamnike.com" might do just fine.

Take your time to secure the right name—and don't take shortcuts. Let's say that you like the name "www.powerone.com" but find out that this name isn't available (it isn't). It's a losing situation to try the "typo" pirate approach and reserve "wwwpowerone.com." Going with close versions such as "powerones.com" or some very slight variation won't be winning solutions either. These days, shortcuts just seem to end up causing more headaches.

Establish Your Site Criteria

At the very beginning, you will need to establish specifically what you want your site to accomplish. Think about what someone who's visiting your Net site for the first time would want. What are your visitors looking for and how does your site meet their needs? The operators of successful commercial sites let their users and customers know that they're "Kings and Queens."

Successful operators: (1) know who their users are; (2) let their visitors know what their site does better than others; (3) give their users what they're interested in; (4) are credible with their visitors by creating good will; (5) target their users with every bit of the site's content; and (6) do this legally without misrepresenting, making "wild" promises, or shaving the truth.

If you're creating a service site, then think about what best shows that you provide great service—and can deliver as promised, even if a user lives outside your normal area. If you're designing a product site, then you need to present what makes your product a unique and desirable item to be purchased. Even if you are building a personal site, ask yourself what your message is and what your personal stamp on this site will be. Above all, check out what's legal and what isn't. For example, can you insert under your state law this statement: "A service fee of 1.5 percent a month will be assessed on each delinquent account until paid in full." If yours is a home improvement site, can you refer business for a fee to your sister-in-law, who's a real estate agent in the same city?

Basically, you need to know and specifically target your niche users, give them what they want, and be credible when you do this. Most importantly, design your marketing niche, strategies, and promotions after you have done thorough market research, talked to those in the business, and perhaps even hired a consultant. As you surf through various sites, see what others do in this regard. For example, do your competitors establish an attractive home page, make it easy for users to travel back and forth between pages, join associations or memberships, and build credibility? Is it easy to browse their site for information, contact the owners, and interface with them? Are their sites comfortable and convenient? What does their "legal jargon" provide for?

Let's say you're creating a site to sell your services as a financial planner. Your criteria should be: (1) be truthful; (2) sell your services; and (3) establish a promotional gimmick (i.e., "First two hours free for Web users"), so that users will contact you. You'll list your experience, name some representative clients, and even add a few testimonials. You'll also want to consider the site's logo, design/color scheme, and overall "look and feel" so that your site projects a professional and trustworthy approach.

Above all, make your site easy and convenient to use. It must be "user friendly" and appear simple. At the same time, don't make easy or slick promises that you can't deliver on.

Design Considerations

Once you've decided what your site specifically is going to accomplish, the next step is to design it in accordance with these basic criteria. The design should include both creative and legal factors. Viewing both competitive and noncompeting sites on the Net is helpful in learning how others do this and in gaining more ideas. For example, how do others arrange their home page and position their logo, images, e-mail boxes, Privacy, and Terms of Use policies? Other questions might be:

- Do they have a "Frequently Asked Questions" page, membership requirements, and/or a "hit" counter?

- Are security safeguards, Better Business Bureau, privacy, or dispute resolution "seals of approval" present?

- Do their statements on Privacy, Terms of Use, and security sound credible and reassuring? Are they understandable with limited "legalese"?

- What type of links to other sites do they provide, and to what extent are these "deep links"? How are these displayed and what credits are given?

- What services should you design into your site, and which inner pages should be more prominently displayed than others?

- If you plan to accept advertising, how should this be woven into your Net content? What's the best way to attract users so that they don't become "turned off" by "glitzy" ads? Where should these ads be best positioned?

- What's the right "look and feel" for your site? For example, if you're designing a travel site, where should you place the pictures of Stonehedge, the Mayan temples, or the Taj Mahal, in relation to your ads? What will be the size and layout of each?

FINDING THE RIGHT "LOOK AND FEEL"

Surf around the world and see what everyone else is doing with sites comparable to yours, but then create your own. Whether you're creating a site that matches farmers and wholesalers or sells steel coils, gain ideas about what others in your field are doing, both design and operations-wise.

Let's say you're going to create a Web site that will sell your services as a Web-site developer. Start by typing competitors' names, professional associations, and larger firms into a search engine, then review the sites that you're directed to. See how others arrange their pitch, information, credits, and biographies. Why do some sites grab your attention and others are simply "ho-hum" places? Look at their arrangements of informational layouts, colors, visual and audio displays, "look and feel," and links—but view them with a mind of creating your own independent "look."

If you own an antique furniture store, then there will be different considerations. What specific markets are other antique stores "pitching": Colonial, French Provincial, or even modern? Do the owners use strictly informational sites, or can customers order from those sites with their credit cards? See what designs, colors, pictures, sizes, ordering information, and background material appeal to you. Note how their text, images, "come-ons," pricing, and other data are positioned and presented.

If you are creating a nonprofit, governmental, or educational site, then what are the services that you want to emphasize? What aspect of your site should be more prominently displayed than others? In this regard, it's helpful to look at any site that's close to how you want yours to be. For example, if you're creating a Web site for a local YMCA, then view not only other YMCA sites, but also sites for YWCAs, for-profit gyms and exercise facilities, and swimming clubs. It is important to get as

It is copyright infringement to take someone else's unique Web site design and present it as yours. Just think what you would do if someone else did that to your site, given the amount of time, effort, and money you've invested in it. Adding your creativity to surround and merge with any ideas so gained can only give your site an even better look for your customers to enjoy. Emphasize "your touch."

many ideas and questions answered at the start as possible, and the only way to create a truly interesting site is to review the possibilities broadly but then be specific when you create your own site.

As you look at other sites, you'll be gaining ideas on what you want or don't want to do with your Web site. Sit down and sketch out how your location should look. It's axiomatic that you don't want to "rip off" any part of the "look and feel" of a competitor's Web site—that only buys you a later trip to an attorney's office.

Also, be careful in how much you "borrow" from other sites as to how they handle returns, refunds, pricing, credit card ordering, and the like. It's not copyright infringement to use the same or similar business policies; competitors do this all the time in our world. However, there is a fine line that you need to be aware of, especially when it comes to operational and technological features. Web sites are patenting their site operations. Amazon.com patented with the U.S. Patent Office its "one click" shopping feature for customers. It has already sued Barnes & Noble over an alleged violation of Amazon's feature. If Amazon.com wins this lawsuit, it's likely that the company will require others (like yourself) to license this feature from them at negotiated rates or be sued. Be sure your Web consultant or programmer knows what can or cannot be done in these operational areas.

Don't Just Take

As we discussed at Chapter 4, "Copying in Cyberspace," you shouldn't indiscriminately copy or rip off someone else's writings, images, or pages to paste on your site. If you really like a famous picture (i.e., an Ansel Adams picture of Yosemite), it makes sense first to obtain permission to use it. Send a requesting e-mail, or use the form in this book. If you really need that great picture of Brad Pitt, then ask for permission. In the case of text, news releases, and poems, don't copy "great gobs," but see if your use could fit into a "fair use" exception (and review Chapter 5, "Posting Pictures, Music, and Videos"). Then, when your site has become an overwhelming success, you won't have to hire an expensive lawyer to defend your use, especially when that loss could mean the dismemberment of a good portion of your site and loss of most of its value.

In any event, be judicious, use common sense, and see whether your actions can qualify as "fair use." In difficult cases to decide, it's better to access those copyrighted works by inserting links instead of copying. For most of us, taking this balanced approach isn't hard to do—it simply gives you control over your Web site and its growth in valuation. To the few out there who don't really care: You will need to find an experienced Net lawyer. Consider your legal options, the likelihood of your being sued, the costs involved, and whether this action is a long-term builder of value.

Follow the Long-Term Rules of the Road

If you aren't sure about what is or isn't appropriate, then talk to other users and operators, or hire a consultant. For example, it doesn't make sense to "deep link" into a Web site, bypassing the home page and its advertising, then "framing" that page as if it was your own. Although we will be treating this further in Chapter 15, "Can You Link Freely?," common sense and "following the rules of the road" dictate this. Think what your reaction would be if someone linked deep into your expensively designed information banks or copied pages from your site. *The Golden Rule, "Do unto others as you would have them do unto you," means just that—you'll go after those who infringe on your rights, just as they'll do with you.*

Whether you produce a site by yourself or hire a site developer to create a more complex one, the key is to be a long-term player and play by the rules. People who take shortcuts usually don't last long or build a site with lasting value. Responsible Web site operators have fewer headaches, threatening letters, and trips to the lawyer's office, but they do go to the bank more often.

Reviewing and Decision Making

CHECK OUT THE CONTRACTS

Be sure you know what your exact rights are with your ISP or Web hosting service. How does it handle downtime and "crashes," and what service levels, guarantees, or assurances does it give? Who owns what, when you create a site, and what happens when there's a dispute? You should read the small-print sections—or at least ask what they mean—so that you don't run into later problems.

For example, the language used by a Web hosting service might indicate that it owns the content to your site. Check that out *before* you sign with this service. This problem has happened before. (See Chapter 9, "Web Site Disclaimers and Protections.") Pay attention to the fees, costs, and hidden expenses. For example, just what are the charges if you accidentally run over the stated storage requirements for your site? For more, see Chapter 16, "Web Site Operating Considerations."

MAKE THE DECISIONS

Before you get too involved in the creative scheme of your Web site, you need to decide what is to be included on it. Let's say you decided to construct a site to sell videos on the proper breeding, raising, and training of show dogs. First you'll decide whether your site will take orders over that location or be an informational "sales" site only. If you plan to take orders, you'll need to make decisions on order information, the appropriate forms to use, credit card and encryption details, returns and refund disclosures, privacy policies, Terms of Use policies, how users can get off your electronic mailing list, among other factors. If you don't want to bother with these considerations, then make your site into a strictly informational site and deal with the sales details at your home office. You can leave all of this to face-to-face chats, telephone calls, or fax—and your site will suddenly become simpler. On the other hand, you might be losing some sales by using this approach.

The need to emphasize and assure your site's credibility surfaces quickly when you decide to be an online selling site. For example, do you want to enroll, pay for, and meet the requirements of the Better Business Bureau's BBBOnLine Reliability Seal Program (bbbonline.com)? Along with its identifying logo, this program is gaining widespread acceptance as a standard because a member promises to respond promptly to customer complaints, agrees to binding arbitration for unresolved disputes, has been in business for at least one year (there are limited exceptions), and has joined a local BBB organization, among other requirements. As discussed before, there are various reliability, privacy, customer complaint, certified merchant guarantee, security lock, and encryption technology seal programs, not to mention various associations that one can join.

Let's say that you're creating a stamp collection sales/trading site. Will surfers be able to post comments, enter into chatrooms, or e-mail comments back and forth? Will you accept advertising in the form of links to stamp sellers, binder stores, stamp associations, or even the U.S. Post Office? What will ads cost and where will they be placed? You'll need to make decisions on the links you plan to either make or permit.

Whether you're selling a product or not, do you plan to have a "clickwrap" agreement in place? Even when you're not selling goods, services, or information over the Net, it's desirable to have all users agree (by clicking an "I agree" icon before visiting chatrooms or accessing files) to your disclaimers of liability, e-mail and chatroom conduct, and other Terms of Use statements, as well as your privacy policies. For example, if you're going to operate a research site on geophysical anomalies, you might want users to agree that they won't extensively use or publish your data unless they first receive your written permission—among other conditions.

If important enough, you could create a registered ID requirement for access, and condition any access to your site on agreeing to certain conditions. This control can be accomplished either by using a "clickwrap" approach (the preferred legal alternative, as described in Chapter 9) or simply creating a Terms of Use page (where just accessing the site creates the agreement), which is easier and less expensive technically. However, as we've seen before, the more that users need to do something affirmatively to indicate their consent, the more likely it is that a court will uphold those provisions.

Final decisions need to be made on how technologically advanced your site will be. What browsers will you accept, and how fast should users be able to download your home page, visual displays, and other pages? Will encryption play any part in your sending or receiving of electronic data? How sophisticated will be the visual displays on your Web site (stationary or interactive)?

You'll also need to pin down the language of your Terms of Use, Privacy, and other disclosures on your site. For example, if you plan to allow e-mailed postings in a chatroom, then you'll need to post the rules and conditions on that use. If you have the technical ability to track users, or if they send you information (whether purchasing products or not), then you need to disclose your privacy policy. In fact, it is recommended that you state a privacy policy, even if all you say is: "We have no ability to track our users, nor do you need to disclose any information about yourself." Terms of Use statements always should be present, regardless of the type of Web site you have created, even if it only states your copyright, trademark, privacy, and user restriction policies.

You need to make the decisions that can affect the design and makeup of your Web site, before you start constructing it. There is nothing worse than changing your mind afterwards, and then having to make the changes throughout. Otherwise, you are incurring unnecessary and higher expenses. Think everything through before you start the actual work. (See Chapter 16, "Web Site Operating Considerations," further.)

When Hiring Someone Else

The time comes, however, when what we want to do is more complicated or would take more time than we are willing to commit. Unless we're using a simple program on another site to create our own home page, the technological considerations, by themselves, can become too much when we're trying to create our own site. Then it's time to talk with and hire a Web site developer. However, be sure that you've considered all of the major areas that we've talked about before.

Take the time to talk to a few developers, before you settle on and hire one. For leads and recommendations on whom to talk with, call your local ISP (presumably, the one who'll host your site), a university's computer department, Internet friends, professional acquaintances, and anyone else who has this exposure.

If you can take the time to meet with each developer personally (rather than relying on e-mail), this time investment will always pay dividends. You need to see how this person relates to you and what "chemistry" exists. It's important to have a frank discussion about the costs and fees in the beginning. If you can't afford the charges, then you should find someone who is more affordable, or scale down your site design and plans. The more developers you talk to, the more ideas you will gain to make your proposed site even better. Be sure to diligently check out all references and recommendations that are supplied.

A number of major areas should be discussed before you hire any particular developer. Be sure to have these in a written, signed agreement; as this is typically provided by the developer, be sure to read it carefully and make changes along the lines discussed below. Or use the provided form with changes for your transaction (and reviewed by a cyberattorney before being signed).

INDEPENDENT CONTRACTOR

Any agreement should state clearly that the developer is working as an independent contractor and not as an employee of the owner, whether it is you or somebody else. This is crucial because if an independent-contractor relationship exists, then the developer is responsible for paying his or her own payroll taxes (i.e., Social Security, Medicare, unemployment, and so on); this responsibility also includes making the required payments of state and federal income tax withholdings. The owner basically needs to make these payments, if the developer was held to be the owner's employee.

If there wasn't an actual independent contractor relationship (the IRS and the courts balance a variety of factors), then the danger is that a later IRS audit could sock the owner with making these payments, including substantial penalties and back interest. If the developer has other clients, sets his own time schedule, provides his own equipment, and the client has no control over how the work is performed, then this is probably an independent contractor relationship. However, this can be a complex assessment. If in doubt as to the status of your developer, then you'll need to consult with a lawyer, given these risks. If the developer is really your employee, however, saying otherwise in your agreement won't make any difference.

There are other advantages to hiring an independent contractor. If any work-related injuries occur (i.e., carpal tunnel syndrome), then the worker's compensation claims and/or medical bills are the responsibility of the developer, not the owner. Further, if an independent contractor is negligent (i.e., crashes into a car while working for the owner), this negligence won't generally be implied to the owner, while it would be if the developer was held to be the owner's employee. *Given that a true independent-contractor relationship is existing, this fact must be documented in the written development contract.*

THE FEE

A major consideration is how expensive a developer is. The fee that's paid is always negotiable, and the best strategy is to negotiate a fixed fee. Unless you've worked with somebody before (still, be careful), it isn't good practice to pay an open-ended hourly rate. Developers do resist agreeing to a fixed fee—but remember, your best strategy is always to work with a well-recommended, experienced person who has a good reputation, when you can't get a fixed fee. As part of this fee discussion, you'll be establishing precisely what services and Web features are to be included for that fee. A general description that the developer is "creating a Web site for Ace for $3,000" is not recommended. The better approach would be to write down and agree:

> The fee for developer's services is $3,000, payable 25 percent down and the remainder payable in monthly installments on the first of each month for the contract period of three months. The developer will create a good working Web site for Ace that will include the following: five pages of text, including seven pictures to be supplied by client; e-mail receipt and sending capability; ability to determine the numbers of "hits" to this site; and further as detailed in the attached written Addendum to this contract.

The more specifics, the better. The contract will include the reimbursement of reasonable expenses incurred by the developer, such as travel expenses, access fees for ISPs, and the like. The better practice is to further state in your contract: "Any expense, prior to reimbursement, must be discussed in advance and receive the prior written approval of the owner." Additionally, the expenses most likely to be so incurred should be agreed to.

PROJECT DEFINITION AND CHANGES

Whether you are on a fixed-fee or hourly-rate contract, it is important that you tie down, as best you can, what the project scope is. If you spend time in the beginning and determine exactly what your site is to do, what features are needed for its success, and what you can afford, then this task is easier. You and the developer should agree not only to the features, as discussed above, but also to the technical specifications, such as how fast pages can be downloaded (discussed later), ease of modifying, and the ability to add more features.

The experience of most developers and operators, however, is that the final Web site design and specifications are usually different from what was initially thought about, and the costs are higher than what they were expected to be. For example, the owner decides later that she wants to add a "clickwrap" feature to the site. Some developers quote a fixed fee for work that's not included in the set contract: "Should owner desire a clickwrap feature to be installed, the contract price shall be increased $2,500," or something to that effect. Most developers quote an hourly rate for changes after the initial contract. It's always advisable to agree on what these "extras" will cost, in the event they are added on later.

You should also agree to a "change order" system, as is done in real estate construction. When additional changes to the work scope and compensation are agreed on, then a formal amendment to that agreement should be written, signed, and attached to the original contract. Not only can parties forget over time what was orally agreed, but also, if they end up in an expensive, serious disagreement, not having their later understandings in writing can escalate into unnecessary court appearances. *The rule: Put everything, including all changes and later modifications, in writing, and signed by all parties.*

OWNERSHIP OF WORK PERFORMED

A critical written provision is that all work performed by the developer is "work for hire," and that all screens, graphics, content, specific software developed, site "look and feel," and all developer creations belong to you, the client owner. If you don't have this provision in your written deal, then the developer will retain the rights to that work, even though well paid for doing it. Without such an agreement, you as an owner will have waived your rights to this ownership, including any paid-for software that was developed, and you will then need to get that developer's consent for any later modifications to your own site. Only if your employee does this work will you, as the employer of a "work for hire," own these rights (but get that in writing, as well).

On the other hand, the developer may want to retain ownership of any proprietary rights to the software that's utilized (or any developments to it)—and this is certainly negotiable. The agreement sometimes states that the developer grants the client/owner the irrevocable, royalty-free license to the use of that software or source code for the life of that Web site, as long as it isn't transferred to nonaffiliated third parties (you then have to get consent). However, the client owner should retain all copyrights and trademarks to everything else that's created.

RESPONSIBILITY FOR SECURING RIGHTS AND LICENSES

The client is typically responsible for securing any necessary copyrights for the material that the developer posts to that Web site (but if the developer secures such material, then this contractor should indemnify the owner against any copyright complaints). The developer is, however, typically responsible for securing the rights and licenses to any software or technology that's required to create a working site. This responsibility includes the payment of all expenses and fees needed to secure those rights. However, some developers want the client to pay for all of these out-of-pocket expenses. Whichever way you go, this area must be discussed and agreed to in writing, including the extent of payment and reimbursement.

TIMETABLE AND BUDGET FOR COMPLETION

The time for completion of the project needs to be discussed and agreed, including the "drop dead" time by when that site needs to be up and running. A budget won't be necessary if you've agreed to a flat fee for the work. However, if you've agreed to an hourly rate, then you had better put in an agreed budget number and continually monitor how actual costs are comparing to that budgeted estimate. Keep in mind that as you push your developer to meet a timetable, usually your costs increase as the expended time goes up. You'll need to be careful here. If you push too hard to meet a deadline, you might make unnecessary mistakes and lose the overall concept. Later repairs might be needed, and there would be arguments over whose cost and fault that was. If the deadline is important enough, see if the developer in the beginning would agree to a fee reduction if it wasn't met (assuming the client was not at fault and had not insisted on additional changes).

THE TECHNICAL FACTORS

The agreement should clearly specify the technological requirements that the site will meet. Some of these areas are: the maximum download time per page, desired speed and bandwidth of the Internet connection, browser compatibility (such as Microsoft, AOL, and Netscape), ease and ability to add more features later, and the number of users that can simultaneously access the site, among other technical areas for discussion. Try to go over all the possible areas by asking your developer what's thought to be important. Listen, talk to others in the field, and then make your decision based on what you can afford.

FIXING "BUGS"

The contractor/developer should agree to a period of joint beta and any other testing during which the client can review and decide whether all of the functions are working as anticipated. The contractor also needs to agree to fix any bugs and links that don't work, and to state the time needed to complete the project. Basically, the developer should stand by its work. As part of this, the contractor should warrant to the client that all work performed is of the highest quality and free of defects; any software used or placed on the site is free of viruses; and the site will meet all functionality requirements. There should be a warranty period within which the developer will fix any problems for free. This will also be a subject of negotiation, as owners typically want longer warranty periods of no-cost "maintenance"; developers, of course, want to stand by their product, but typically for much shorter periods of 30 to 60 days.

CONFIDENTIALITY

The client will want the developer to be obligated to keep all work, client information, trade secrets, and anything learned about the company in a confidential and discrete manner. This requirement is best met by working with someone who is trusted, respected, and has a good reputation in this field. *Working with the best is always the best protection.*

THE IMPORTANT BOILERPLATE

We have seen before that any limitations on liability, damages, warranty disclaimers, applicable law, and where to sue are very important "legalese." Most important, we have seen that these limitations on liability and damages can be one-sided and upheld by the courts between parties of "equal" bargaining power. Later negotiations by you or your attorney will be more difficult if you're trying to argue from this hole. *You always need to pay attention to the boilerplate that's buried in any contract.*

These liability limitations can be that the developer doesn't warrant its work at all, that you accept all work "as is" without any express or implied warranties (except to the extent not allowed by state law), and that you waive any claims of liability for bad work. Additionally, there can be limits on damages to low amounts or, even in more generous cases, to the amounts that you paid for the performed work.

The problem is that your actually incurred damages can be large multiples of these stated contractual damages—due to forever lost customers, forgone revenues, and increasing bad will when your site malfunctions. If you're a particularly large customer, you should be able to work meaningful changes into this boilerplate.

You could try to increase the damages if the developer is at fault, arguing that this is an important consideration to you and that the developer should stand behind the work that's done. See if the developer will agree to a clause that says in the event of its mistake, all repairs are free and it will assume all out-of-pocket costs to correct, including purchasing any needed licenses or copyrights. If the developer won't change the boilerplate, then work for a mutual limitation on liability: if it's good for one party, then it's good for both. Keep in mind that these favorable limitations on liability and damages for the developer, in most standard site-development contracts, are one-sided, unfavorable to the client, and numerous times upheld by the court. ("You did read and sign that contract, didn't you?", as the argument goes.)

Another area to watch includes third-party liability for copyright infringement. If the developer created a site that infringed on somebody else's software, "look and feel," application, or other copyright, then the developer should indemnify you for those problems. You should not assume them. Otherwise, it's possible that you could have no rights against the person who created those problems in the first place.

There are additional discussions on indemnification, warranties, testing, and other areas in the sample forms on the next pages.

A *Creative Development Agreement* and a *Web Site Development Agreement* follow, along with further discussions of the provisions. The Creative Development Agreement is to be used when you are hiring someone to create something for your Web site. This could range from creating the entire "look and feel" or design of your site to writing text, creating a logo, or even formulating ad copy and strategies. The Web Site Development Agreement is to be entered into with your Web site developer, with provisions as discussed throughout this chapter.

Both of these forms (as with all those in this book) are presented for your information and will need to be changed for any specific situation. If you receive the other party's standard contract, pay particular attention to the "small print" and the issues discussed at that form and throughout this book. Regardless of who prepares any contract, be especially watchful with important, complex agreements (and secure appropriate tax and legal advice).

Creative Development Agreement

This Creative Development Agreement is entered on [*Date of Agreement*] between [*Name and Address of Hiring Party*], called the "Client," and [*Name and Address of Party Performing Services*], called the "Contractor." The parties, in consideration of the mutual promises made by each other and other valuable consideration, agree as follows:

1. **Independent Contractor.** Client and Contractor agree that Contractor's services are being performed as an independent contractor and not as a joint venturer, partner, or employee.

2. **Services.** Contractor agrees to complete the following creative development services in a professional and competent manner for Client: [*Describe the Specific Services to be Completed and by When*].

3. **Compensation and Reimbursements.** Client agrees to pay Contractor for these services as follows: [*State the Agreed Compensation, the Installment Payment Provisions (if agreed), When Payable, and Other Terms*]. Client also agrees to reimburse Contractor for the following expenses, if reasonable in amount: [*Describe the Agreed Reimbursable Costs*].

4. **Ownership of Work Product.** As a work for hire, contractor agrees that Client is the sole owner of all work performed under this Agreement (the "Work Product"), except for the following described work, exceptions, or components: [*State Specifically What Contractor and Client Each Owns as to the Work Product*]. Each party agrees to irrevocably assign to the other the rights each is to own by this contract, will execute any later agreements needed to ensure this understanding, and will take all necessary steps to ensure that the other party has the rights and ownership as agreed. To the extent either can't assign the desired rights to the other, then that party grants a license to use the same without cost or expense and as necessary to meet the intent of this Agreement.

5. **Warranties.** Contractor warrants it: (a) has the full power and authority to enter into and perform this Agreement without violating any agreements with other parties; (b) will not subcontract any of its services performed without first receiving Client's written consent; (c) will keep to itself and confidential forever any of Client's confidential information (as reasonably deemed to be confidential by Client) that comes into its possession; (d) will return when not needed all of Client's property, regardless of form or type, that it possesses during the performance of these services; (e) has not breached any third-party rights, trademarks, copyrights, or any other rights in its development and performance of its services under this Agreement; (f) has performed its work in a reasonably satisfactory commercial way; and (g) will keep the performance of these services confidential and work diligently to complete them as agreed. These warranties shall survive this termination or completion of this Agreement.

6. **Indemnification.** Contractor agrees to indemnity, hold harmless, and defend Client, its officers, employees, and representatives, from and against all claims, actions, or demands, including reasonable court costs and legal fees, resulting from any breach of the warranties in Section 5 above. Client shall promptly provide notice to Contractor of any such claim or proceeding, and shall assist Contractor, at Contractor's expense, in defending any such controversy.

7. **Termination.** Should Client fail to make any owing payment after receiving a written [*State Notice in Days*] days notice to pay, then Contractor shall have the right to terminate this Agreement. Either party may cancel this Agreement upon [*State Notice in Days*] days written notice upon the breach of any material provision or representation of this Agreement.

8. **Other.** Any dispute arising in connection with this Agreement shall be first settled by mediation. If that's not successful, then the dispute shall be settled by arbitration to be held in [*Location of Arbitration*] in accordance with the rules of the American Arbitration Association. This agreement to arbitrate shall be specifically enforceable. Any award shall be final and binding on all parties, and a final judgment may be entered in the appropriate court of law. Notwithstanding this, should any litigation ensue between the parties, then the prevailing party shall be entitled to reasonable expenses and attorney fees as set by the Court.

Creative Development Agreement *(Continued)*

This Agreement is the final understanding between the parties on this subject matter, superceding all other previous agreements, and may be amended only by the written consent of all the parties. Should any court or proceeding determine that any provision is illegal or in conflict, then all other remaining provisions shall be held severable, valid, and be given separate legal effect.

Neither party may assign this Agreement without the consent of the other, which consent shall not be unreasonably withheld. This Agreement shall bind all the parties, their successors, and permitted assigns, and its legality and interpretation shall be governed by the laws of the State of [*Name of State Whose Laws Govern*] and of the United States.

This Agreement is accepted, understood, and executed as of the date first above written, by and between:

_____

[*Name and Title of Party Signing for Contractor*]
[*Contractor's Name and Address*]

_____

[*Name and Title of Party Signing for Client*]
[*Client's Name and Address*]

Creative Development Agreement

Discussion of Provisions

1. **Independent Contractor.** Given that a true independent contractor relationship exists, then the contractor is responsible for paying its own applicable payroll taxes, not the client deducting them (or making federal and state income tax deductions) from the paid compensation. As it can be difficult to determine true independent-contractor relationships in Net-land, consult an attorney when there are unclear areas—the penalties can be high and the IRS quite unforgiving.

2. **Services.** It is important to detail specifically when the services are to be completed by and what exactly is to be done—whether it is to write text, create logos, or compose music.

3. **Compensation and Reimbursements.** Any standards that must be met before client's payment should be specifically agreed to, including the time period within which the client is to complete its review. Further, if the contractor must remedy all of client's reasonable "fixes" or suggestions after such a review, and before the payment, then that provision should also be added.

4. **Ownership of Work Product.** Under basic law, the contractor owns all ownership rights to the completed work product, regardless how much the client pays those services—without such a clause or contrary agreement being present. At times, the contractor will want to specifically exempt, or keep for itself, modules of proprietary designs that it owned previously. Both parties should be as specific as possible as to "who owns what" under their written agreement.

5. **Warranties.** Both parties should discuss these warranties in detail to understand them in the context of their specific situation. These may be changed depending on those circumstances. This agreement also does not provide for any limitations of liability or damages on the part of the contractor, whether this is due to a breach of its warranties or negligence. To the extent that this is changed by the parties' negotiation (among other provisions), then this form agreement would be accordingly changed.

6. **Indemnification.** These clauses and provisions, along with the others, can be changed depending on the final agreement of the parties. For example, you could add: "Client, to the extent of its own negligence, shall bear its proportionate share of the costs, expenses, and damages."

7. **Termination.** An important, but neglected area, is what do you do when a contract doesn't work out. These provisions should be discussed with the appropriate wording added to reflect that understanding.

8. **Other.** See the discussions on this section in previously reviewed forms.

Web Site Development Agreement

This Web Site Development Agreement is entered on [*Date of Agreement*] between [*Name of Hiring Party*], called the "Client," and [*Name of Party Performing Services*], called the "Developer." The parties, in consideration of the mutual promises by each other and other valuable consideration, agree as follows:

1. **Independent Contractor.** Client and Developer agree that Developer's services are being performed as an independent contractor and not as a joint venturer, partner, or employee.

2. **Developer Responsibilities.** Developer agrees to use its best efforts to complete in a professional and competent manner the following Web Site development services for Client: [*Describe the Services to be Completed, including the Specifics of What the Web Site Will Be and Can Do*].

    (a) **Software and Tools.** Developer [*"is" or "is not"*] responsible for obtaining and paying for all required licenses for the necessary software and development tools to complete the services identified above. If Developer is not so responsible, then [*State Party Who's Responsible for Third-Party Licenses*] shall be responsible for obtaining this, including the payment of license fees.

    (b) **Design.** The Web Site design shall [*"meet Client's specifications" or "be designed by Developer, subject to Client's approval"*] as to user interface, how users will navigate parts of the Web Site, hyperlinks to be created, overall "look and feel," and other design criteria. This design criteria shall include: [*State Technological Design Criteria, such as User's Ability to Interface, Speed of Access, Volume Capabilities, Etc.*]. Developer shall communicate regularly and as reasonably necessary to keep Client informed as to its progress, problems encountered, and possible solutions.

    (c) **Items Delivered and Timetable.** Developer shall use its best efforts to complete the following items and by the date indicated: [*State What Developer is to Deliver—i.e., E-Mail Capability, Encryption for Credit Card Payment Information, Specific Hyperlinks Established, Etc.—and by When*].

    (d) **Testing and Repair.** Developer shall thoroughly test all items prior to delivery to Client and make all necessary corrections before delivery of same. Client shall have [*State Days Within Which to Test Items*] days within which to test any items delivered to it; if it reasonably determines that further corrections are required, Contractor shall do so within an agreed and reasonable time span. Developer shall have [*State Number of Times, Developer May Attempt to Correct Problems*] attempts to correct the problem. If it doesn't do so after the last attempt, then Client may terminate this contract without penalty, provided it does so in good faith and pays for all work reasonably performed to date by Developer.

    (e) **Changes.** Any changes in the scope of the services to be completed by Developer from what's stated in this Section 2 shall be performed by Developer, provided agreement is reached as to the additional compensation to be paid to it by Client for this additional work. These change orders shall be set down in writing, signed, and attached to this Agreement as amendments.

    (f) **Source Material.** Upon completion of the project, Developer shall deliver to Client all originals and copies—except one retained by Developer for its files and/or maintenance responsibilities under this Agreement—of the Web Site content, source materials (source code and materials developed by Developer under this Agreement to perform the required services), and all Client materials used in the course of Developer's assignment.

    (g) **Warranty Period.** Developer agrees to correct, modify, or repair problems without extra charge or expense for a period of [*State Number of Days for Repair Period*] days after delivery of any particular item and after final turnover of the completed Web Site.

    (h) **Maintenance.** Developer [*"is" or "is not"*] responsible for performing maintenance functions, after expiration of the period(s) referred to in Section 2(g) above, provided it receives the compensation agreed to in Section 3.

Web Site Development Agreement *(Continued)*

3. **Client Responsibilities.**

   (a) **Internet Access.** Client [*"is" or "is not"*] responsible for obtaining Internet access through an Internet Service Provider. If client is not so responsible, then [*State Party Whose Responsible for ISP Access*] shall be responsible.

   (b) **Required Third-Party Consents and Licenses.** Client [*"is" or "is not"*] responsible for obtaining all required third-party consents and necessary licenses for the content and "look and feel" of the Web Site, including the costs of obtaining all licenses for same. If client is not so responsible, then [*State Party Who's Responsible for Third-Party Consents*] shall be responsible.

   (c) **Compensation and Reimbursements.**

      (1) **Compensation.** Client agrees to pay Developer for the services identified in Section 2 above as follows: [*State the Agreed Compensation, How Paid (Installments or By Item Delivered), Review Standards, "Fixes," and Other Terms*].

      (2) **Reimbursements.** Client also agrees to reimburse Developer for the following expenses, if reasonable in amount: [*Describe the Agreed Reimbursement Costs, if Applicable*].

      (3) **Maintenance.** Further, Client agrees to pay Developer the following compensation for its maintenance services: [*Describe the Agreed Payment for Maintenance Services, if Applicable*].

4. **Ownership of Work Product.** As a work for hire, developer agrees that Client is the sole owner of all work performed under this Agreement (the "Work Product"), except for the following described work, exceptions, or components that is the property of Developer: [*State Specifically What Developer and Client Each Owns of the Work Product*]. Each party agrees to irrevocably assign to the other, the rights each is to own by this contract. Each party will execute any later agreements needed to ensure this understanding is fulfilled. To the extent either can't assign the desired rights to the other, then that party grants a license to use same without cost or expense and as necessary to meet the intent of this Agreement.

5. **Developer Warranties.**

   (a) **Warranty Representations.** Developer warrants that all of its work performed will be of high quality and free of defects in material and workmanship in all material respects and will conform to the specifications agreed to in Section 2 above. Developer also agrees to fix any errors at its own expense for the warranty period described in Section 2(g). Except as stated in this Section 5, DEVELOPER DISCLAIMS ALL IMPLIED WARRANTIES, INCLUDING WITHOUT LIMITATION, THE WARRANTIES OF MERCHANTABILITY AND FITNESS FOR A PARTICULAR PURPOSE.

   (b) **Additional Warranties.** Developer warrants that it: (a) has the full power and authority to enter into and perform this Agreement without violating any other agreements; (b) has not breached any third-party rights, trademarks, copyrights, or any other rights in its development and/or maintenance of Client's Web Site; (c) will not subcontract any of its services to be performed without first receiving Client's written consent; (d) will keep confidential any of Client's confidential information that comes into its possession; (e) will return when not needed all of Client's property, that it possesses while performing these services; and (f) will work diligently and use its best efforts to complete its services timely and as agreed. These warranties shall survive the termination or completion of this Agreement.

6. **Indemnification.** Developer agrees to defend, indemnify, and hold harmless Client, its officers, employees, and representatives, from and against all claims, actions, or demands, including court costs and reasonable legal fees, resulting from any breach of its warranties in Section 5 above. Client shall promptly provide notice to Developer of any such claim or proceeding, and shall assist Developer, at Developer's expense, in defending any such controversy.

Web Site Development Agreement *(Continued)*

7. **Termination.**

   (a) Either party may terminate this Agreement without cause upon giving [*State Number of Days Notice to be Given*] days written notice to the other.

   (b) Upon the expiration of [*State Number of Days Notice*] days written notice, Developer may terminate this contract with cause for not receiving from Client any owing payment when due; and Client may terminate this Agreement for cause for Developer not making its best efforts to complete the services required under Section 2 above, the failure to do same within any agreed time frame, or failure to make any reasonable repairs (Section 2(d) and 2(g)) as required on any item.

   (c) Regardless of how terminated, the Developer may keep all prior payments received to date, but must turn over all work that has been or is in the process of being completed. Client is to pay the reasonable accrual of what is owing for the work completed to date when it terminates without cause—however, it does not owe any accrued compensation if termination is made with cause.

8. **Other.** Any dispute arising in connection with this Agreement shall be first settled by mediation. In the event this doesn't work, then the dispute shall be settled by arbitration to be held in [*Location of Arbitration*] in accordance with the rules of the American Arbitration Association. This agreement to arbitrate shall be specifically enforceable. Any award from such arbitration proceeding shall be final and binding on all the parties, and a final judgment may be entered in the appropriate court. Notwithstanding this, should any litigation ensue between the parties, then the prevailing party shall be entitled to reasonable expenses and attorney fees as set by the Court.

This Agreement is the final agreement between the parties on this subject matter, superceding all other previous agreements, and may be amended only by the written consent of all parties. Should any court or proceeding determine that any provision of this Agreement is illegal or in conflict, then all other remaining provisions shall be considered severable, valid, and be given separate legal effect.

Neither party may assign this Agreement without the consent of the other, which consent may not be unreasonably withheld. This Agreement shall bind all the parties, their successors, and permitted assigns. This Agreement shall be governed by the laws of the State of [*Name of State Whose Laws Govern*] and of the United States.

This Agreement is accepted, understood, and executed as of the date first above written, by and between:

_____

[*Name and Title of Party Signing for Developer*]
[*Developer's Name and Address*]

_____

[*Name and Title of Party Signing for Client*]
[*Client's Name and Address*]

Web Site Development Agreement

Discussion of Provisions

1. **Independent Contractor.** Given that a true independent-contractor relationship exists, then the client is not responsible for making payroll and income tax deductions. Further, clients generally speaking are not responsible for the negligence of independent contractors, as they are with their employees. Whether a party is an independent contractor or not can be a complicated area of the law. You should consult a legal specialist when you have questions in this regard, as the penalties for being wrong can be high.

2. **Developer Responsibilities.** It is important to detail specifically what services are to be completed by the developer and by when. Further, both parties need to ascertain what criteria determines the project's acceptability—i.e., that the site meets certain speed, volume of "hits" handled, technological criteria, and/or other standards. This provision allows a "best efforts" attempt, which means that the developer doesn't need to warrant that it will achieve the exact design dimensions—the parties may want to change this provision in other situations.

   Both parties should have an open and honest discussion as to what the client wants and the developer can do, then set this down exactly in their agreement. Writing a 50-page document in legalese isn't as important as covering all of the issues, ranging from the developer's responsibilities and Web site design criteria to critical testing, repair, and change orders. It is important to have an exact understanding as to what the developer specifically is to do—and won't be added as a change order with extra compensation to be paid. Another troublesome area is also how often can (or will) a developer try to repair a problem before the parties throw up their hands.

3. **Client Responsibilities.** The parties need to decide who is responsible for what. The client is usually responsible for obtaining third-party consents in the use of copyrighted material (i.e., videos, photographs, and text quotations) and ISP/Internet access, while the developer must pay for obtaining the software and development tools required to make the Web site operational. However, these issues should be discussed, agreed to, and written down in the contract.

   Any review standards before the client is obligated to make a payment should be specifically listed, including the time period within which the client is to complete its review. If the developer is to remedy all of the client's reasonable "fixes" after such a review, then the specifics by when and how that's done should also be established.

   A prime issue in any contract is how much will be paid for the provided services. As part of these discussions are the issues of whether a fixed fee is agreeable, what expenses are to be reimbursed, and what maintenance charges will be paid.

4. **Ownership of Work Product.** Under basic law, the developer accrues all ownership rights in the work product and creations brought about on the site by the developer, regardless how much a client pays for those services—without such a clause or contrary agreement being present. At times, the developer will want to specifically exempt, or keep for itself, modules of proprietary software or designs that it owned previously. Both parties should be as specific as possible as to "who owns what" afterwards.

5. **Developer Warranties.** The language in 2(g) and 5(a) provides that the developer accepts a responsibility to fix "bugs" during an agreed warranty period to meet the design standards, but operates as a general disclaimer of other implied legal responsibilities. Paying attention to the negotiated specifics of what the developer is responsible for fixing and how long will pay dividends.

   Both parties should discuss the 5(b) warranties in detail to understand them in the context of the specifics of their situation. To the extent that one or another can't be made, then the parties must discuss them and agree otherwise before signing an overall agreement. A typical area for discussion is when the Web site developer has performed work for prior clients, where proprietary work was developed that those clients could possibly lay claim to in the work being completed on this job.

Web Site Development Agreement *(Continued)*

6. **Indemnification.** This clause places the responsibility on the developer to defend the client if one of its warranties doesn't work out. This agreement does not provide for any limitations of liability or damages on the part of the developer, whether it's a breach of its warranties under Section 5 or its negligence. To the extent that this is changed by the parties' negotiation (among other provisions), then this form agreement would be accordingly changed.

7. **Termination.** Among the termination provisions is the distinction made between terminating "without cause" and "with cause." Basically, this means the right to end a contract, depending on whether a party is at fault or not. In this form, the developer does not have the right to receive accrued compensation if the contract end is due to its fault—it receives this accrual for work completed to the date of termination, if there is no fault involved. Please review carefully these termination conditions; these provisions vary widely, depending on the particular size and standing of the developer or owner.

8. **Other.** Please see the discussion on this topic at previously discussed forms.

CHAPTER 15

Can You Link Freely?

The World Wide Web depends on linking for its existence—it's this ability for anyone to instantaneously "surf" around the globe that makes the Internet what it is. With the Net's maturity, however, the previous unconditional freedom to link has evolved, over a short time period, into a framework of commonsense legal and Netiquette rules. The rapid rise of uses and linking has not only fueled the Internet's growth, but also has dictated the limits on this freedom.

Linking

Linking is how one Web site connects with another. Sites provide links to pages within their own location, but often link directly to other sites. It is this "networking" that allows users to "hop, skip, and jump" from one site to another, page to page, and back and forth. Simply put, a "link" is a Web address coded on a Web site [i.e., the highlighted word(s), text, pictures, or logo, including banner advertisements] that permit users to click on that location and call up on their computer the Web site to which the link refers. Every Web page has its own address—the famous "URL" (Uniform Resource Locator). A URL is like a street address or a telephone number, and a Web browser's software is able to pick up the URL in a link to connect the user with that precise site. A link is analogous to a forwarding address on one Web site that directs the user instantaneously to another.

Virtually all the links in place on the Web are created out of a technology entitled HREF. A HREF link basically instructs the Web browser to transport that user to some other point. This type of link allows someone to jump to a different URL and site, or to move around the same site with the same URL. These links are the word links or images that identify what the site is. A hypertext link stands out from ordinary text; its highlighted, light blue print is usually underlined. After the link has been used, the link color changes to its typical highlighted crimson red, letting users know that they've already been to that linked site. This "you've already been there" indicator shows up even after the computer has been shut down and used at different times later.

To Link or Not to Link?

Web owners usually want more visitors; they hope that the links to their sites will increase. The links sought after are from Web locations with similar interests, and whose users would be interested in the same or related content. In the beginning of the Web (this sounds almost biblical), people typically would send an e-mail to request permission to link to another's site. The common practice now is to just link and not worry about it, assuming that everyone wants the extra viewers to be directed that way. That's not always a correct assumption.

IS PERMISSION REQUIRED?

The general rule is that one doesn't need permission to link directly to another site, provided the site doesn't gain commercially or realize some competitive informational advantage by that linkage (which includes nonprofit institutions). It is clear, however, that users should receive permission when they're "deep linking" or "framing" (if not as a courtesy). These situations are discussed later in this chapter.

There are commonsense times when users should ask permission or even refrain from linking—and the courts will uphold this. For example, if a customer has become disgruntled with a purchased product or service, it wouldn't be appropriate to post on the Web: "AceRetails sucks and it lies, oh how it lies all the time. Their products are lemons, a danger to the entire consuming public, and should be destroyed. See the site of AceRetails for yourself." Then, the unhappy person creates a link to AceRetails.

Nor can someone take credit for the work of another, for example, by linking to an entirely different site with the words: "If you'd like another example of my great work, take a look at TigerRetails." Clearly, any stated or implied representation, created by linking, that another's work is yours would be trademark infringement (i.e., using their logo), unfair competition, and libel (i.e., saying something is yours when it's not), or a violation of the covenant of "good faith" that's implied in Netiquette. (See Chapter 3, "The Developing Law of 'Netiquette'" for more on this.)

Another commonsense "no, no" is to copy someone else's logo or trademark into a link without permission. The great majority of noncommercial links use only the blue-colored words to click on, with no identifying trademarks included. For example, there's no reason to highlight IBM's logo in a link to the IBM homepage. However, if permission has been given to link and use a trademarked logo, then typically this is part of an advertising contract. (These agreements are described later in this chapter.)

Linking to illegal content by itself may also be illegal. In a classic case, a Web site was held to be liable for posting copyrighted software for downloading on that site. A court ordered the site to remove the software, which it did, but in the process it posted links to other sites that offered the same pirated software. The court also prohibited this linking.

NETIQUETTE

Whether one should ask permission before linking can be another question that's quite distinct from the law and its requirements. It's helpful to look at this question as if you were the owner of the targeted Web site. You most likely want people to notify you in advance as to what they're planning to do, especially when it can affect you. It's also like a polite introduction when you first meet someone. You could "chat" with them as to what their site's objectives are, or even make cross-links with common interests, and more traffic could flow by using this approach.

Some site operators use common sense in their standard linking policies; they ask for permission when they suspect that there's a conflict of commercial interests, but they normally create links without advance contact. Others feel that they don't have the time for these "introductions" and believe that one of the basic freedoms of the Net is to link "as you like." We've already seen a few of the exceptions—and there are more. If a user's policy is to "link and be damned," then at least that person should know the times when this practice could very well result in expensive trouble.

Numerous Web locations have already established a page disclosing their procedures on what links they'll accept and how others can receive permission to link to their site. These locations can then review the provided information and determine whether the proposed linkage is in accordance with their policies, including whether they would request payment for the right to link under certain commercial circumstances.

There are those who feel strongly that these policies violate a basic "freedom to link." It is also true that the totality of the circumstances will determine whether legally, or even ethically, such a policy overreaches the basic tenets of allowing general Internet access. However, as we've seen, some situations present conditions in which linking shouldn't be tolerated, even with noncommercial sites. For example, let's assume that you've constructed your own personal Web site dealing with ecological issues, and it has received good press. All of a sudden you begin receiving e-mails that basically read: "Now, I see why you don't understand the issue. You're a dummy." It turns out that one of your critics created 15 pages of false, expensively researched arguments as to why your site was nonsensical, and wrote things like "Take a look at these off-the-wall, silly and trite arguments . . ." with links to your site. Or you're a Net retailer and among your products are fine, black-lace nightgowns. You then discover that a pornographic site has linked directly to the pictures of your models.

Legal and Netiquette constraints need to be in place—and these commonsense rules are being developed. Linking to content is important because it is bottom-line law that simply reposting the content of another site is usually an act of copyright infringement. For example, in *Los Angeles Times v. Free Republic,* the court held that the full-text reproduction of newspaper stories on the *Free Republic* Web site did not constitute "fair use" and was infringement. Creating a link is a much-lower risk substitute.

The basic rule is that users do have the legal right to "link, link, link." However, this right is not absolute, as we have seen. It is also polite to ask, and it makes sense for users to introduce themselves first, not only when they have time but also in situations where there could be a potential conflict, whether commercial in nature or not. The Golden Rule is still in effect—and, given the circumstances, the courts are enforcing it.

The Importance of Linking

A late-1999 court case against Amazon.com indicates the importance that today's Web sites place on linking, especially with widely visited places like Amazon. Toby Press, a tiny book publisher with offices in London, England, and New Milford, Connecticut, filed a lawsuit against the Internet giant, demanding that Amazon provide Toby's customers with a link to the Toby Press site (www.tobypress.com). The book publisher alleged that whenever a customer tried to purchase a Toby Press title on Amazon (six titles were then registered with Amazon), a message popped up advising that the title wasn't currently available as the books were "out of stock." Toby argued that it had sufficient stock and asked the court to order Amazon to allow a hyperlink from its site to that of Toby Press for customers who wanted their books. Unfortunately, Toby didn't get its way legally, and the small press's Web site presently sells direct to its customers without relying on Amazon.

On the other hand, if the wrong site links with yours, even more problems can be created. In Chapter 1, "The World's at Your Fingertips," we discussed the widespread popularity of the Hamster Dance site (see "hampsterdance2.com") where 392 animated hamsters dance to the repetitive beat of music (á la Roger Miller's 1973 recording of "Whistle Stop"). This Web location became widely popular, and as people went "hampster" over it, imitation sites quickly popped up. When the owner tried to e-mail those sites into giving up their practice, other "First Amendment" freedom-surfers linked the hamster pages to pay-to-view pornographic sites. Others established a site declaring that "The Hampster Dance should be Free!" Another site was created which showed the hamsters being killed by stepping on mines, splattered by bullets, and other bloody executions. Imitation and parody sites sprang up (put "hampsterdance" in your search engine), as the owner created a new site. Such is the price of fame these days.

Deep Linking

When links bypass homepages, connecting instead to pages deep within those sites, additional considerations become present—for example, when an entity links deep into the *New York Times* or *USA Today*'s Web site, evading all of the advertising, procedures, and trademarked logos along the way, to present the targeted information as its own. These type of links are most likely to be challenged and found illegal.

Lawsuits have been filed and settled in the plaintiff's favor where the plaintiff complained about "deep links" bypassing the advertising on its homepage, decreasing its "hit count" (users following the link went directly past the "count" page), diminishing its site's value, and allowing the defendant to "pass off" that information as its own (as in the Total News case discussed later).

A dispute between Microsoft and Ticketmaster in 1997 brought the issue of deep linking to the forefront. Microsoft maintained a number of city guides on its Microsoft Network, including its Seattle Sidewalk site, which offered a guide to entertainment events and restaurants in the Seattle area. When clicking on an event logo on the Microsoft site, users saw the Ticketmaster URL on their browser and were directed to the specific Ticketmaster page where tickets could be purchased for any particular event. When negotiations to agree on this linkage failed (and Microsoft offered to pay money for this right), Microsoft continued the deep link past Ticketmaster's home page so that its users could purchase tickets for the specific date, time, and event that they wanted.

Ticketmaster promptly filed a lawsuit against Microsoft over this linkage, arguing that Microsoft's action was an unfair business practice because the link bypassed its homepage advertising, violated the terms and conditions of use (that prohibited such commercial usage), prevented it from fulfilling its contractual advertising responsibilities with MasterCard (prominently displayed on Ticketmaster's homepage), and created the false impression of an endorsement or business relationship with Microsoft, among other claims. Microsoft argued that the mere presence of any site on the Internet was an invitation to others to visit or link to it without restraint. Before the lawsuit could go to trial, Microsoft settled the case by agreeing that its sites would only link directly to Ticketmaster's homepage, rather than continuing to link deep inside the site.

At the same time, the U.S. legal community watched closely one international case in particular. The owners of a local newspaper, the *Shetland Times,* in Scotland, brought a lawsuit against the *Shetland News,* a startup news service located in the same town. The *Shetland Times* published a daily online version of its newspaper; the *News* was the first local daily to publish solely on the Web. It linked directly into the *Times* for news, and the *Shetland Times* went to court. The court granted the *Times* a temporary restraining order against the *News* and its linking practice, and the case shortly settled out of court.

The international cases continued on. For example, the online recruiting firm of StepStone in 2001 obtained an injunction in Germany that prevented a competitor from linking to its Web pages. The injunction was issued against OFiR, a Danish media group that owns online recruiting companies in Germany, the United Kingdom, Denmark, and France. OFiR was apparently using the information gained from StepStone in its services to its clients. As a result of the injunction, OFiR removed its hypertext links to StepStone.

At best, deep linking will cost an infringer heavy legal defense costs, not to mention that any business generated from these links may need to be replaced after any negotiated settlements. *Any long-term Web-site development strategy requires that all deep linking be accompanied by written agreements, if at all possible, substantiating that permission has been so received.*

The driving force behind these legal cases isn't just the large Web sites. Let's say you've extensively researched the subject of pet care. You post your location with lots of different pages, all on how to best care for dogs, cats, parakeets, and even snakes. You've labored long and hard to ensure that your advice is the best and is supported by veterinarians. One day, you discover someone else has established a competing pet site, supported by large advertising spots sold based upon their content (or both of you are nonprofit, but the other owner is lazy). Among its links, there's a prominent one to your Web site that ends directly on your advice pages, completely bypassing your homepage. What would you do? Right—hire a lawyer. And your odds of winning would be good, based on unfair competition (typically, the strongest argument), trespass, and trademark infringement or "passing off" arguments. This is the classic example of "deep linking."

Prior to linking with any site, users should check to see whether there are any policies that govern linking. Numbers of commercial and even nonprofit sites prohibit deep links; instead, they require links to be made only to their homepage, and they establish procedures for notification and approval of any such proposed linkage. In this case, Netiquette and legal common sense are good reasons why users should follow those procedures—and ask for permission. The owner of even a nonprofit site may feel that visitors should read its homepage first; perhaps it wants to do internal maintenance work without needing to notify people that their links could become severed in the process.

Framing

Netscape introduced hyperlink "framing" in 1996 as part of its Netscape Navigator 2.0 program. This technique rapidly became accepted and is now a standard HTML (hypertext markup language) feature. "Framing" allows a user to link directly to another site while still remaining in the frame of the first site. In linking, the URL displayed is that of the linked-to Web site, whereas the URL displayed in framing remains as the first or linking site. The content of the material framed in the linked page is presented as if the user had gone directly to that page. Because the framed site is retrieved as a "window" within the linking site, it can eliminate all advertising or identification of the framed site, while the viewing site can retain or superimpose its IDs and advertising—in essence, creating the potential for true "passing off" situations.

One well-publicized framing case was the 1997 lawsuit brought by various media companies against Total News for its framing strategy. Total News had created a hub site that pointed to the big names in the U.S. media. When a user followed a link, the destination news material appeared in the Total News frame, but with only its advertising displayed at the bottom of the frame. Media companies such as CNN, Time Warner, the *Washington Post, USA Today,* and MSNBC then argued in their lawsuit that the use of these frames, whereby Total News showed their news stories with only its advertising displayed, violated their copyright and trademark rights. Total News reached a settlement before trial whereby it agreed not to display any content within a frame; the plaintiff media companies in return entered into a license agreement with Total News. Under this deal, Total News paid to link to their sites, and those links opened in a separate window. Although some of the links changed, Total News (www.totalnews.com) continues these direct linking practices today.

As one would suspect, there is case precedence that framing is less legally acceptable than linking. In *Hard Rock Café v. Morton,* the court found that framing was more objectionable. In this case, a licensing agreement had been entered into between the parties as to the use of certain material. However, this agreement was found by the court not to confer framing rights, and framing the material was held to infringe upon the owner's rights. The court decided that the "seamless presentation" of the material, in which the information appeared as a window within the original linking page, resulted in users not realizing that they had left the Hard Rock Hotel site. Users could be entirely unaware that they had left the framing Web site, because the browser only displayed the framing Web site's URL.

You're Now Linked: Problem or Not?

Most people want to be linked to and aren't that concerned when permission isn't asked. When another site links to yours, the basic question to ask is: Do you really care? If this helps your site's exposure and creates more "hits," you might even send the linking party an e-mail, welcoming that person into the family. Let's say, however, that the link has penetrated deep into your site and is profiting from your information or taking credit for it.

First, you'll send an e-mail or registered letter firmly requesting the removal of that link. If that doesn't work, you'll consult with a cyberlawyer who'll probably send another threatening letter. By this time, some linking parties have complied and others haven't.

If this doesn't work, then you'll need to consider the costs of filing and pursuing a lawsuit versus the "lost opportunity" costs of leaving the link alone. If the legal fees are too high or your site isn't popular, you might change the URL of your image or substitute a nuisance image in place of the original one. If all else fails and the linking site is popular, then you might simply give up the fight and cross-link to the other.

Be sure to put prohibitions in your Terms of Use against the commercial use of your site by any linking method. Also, include that any linking to your site, regardless of its nature, is subject to your consent. Thus, if you do litigate the matter, you will have the added argument that the other site's use was in direct conflict with your policies and the site owners knew about it. This argument will also be helpful in your negotiations with that site.

Meta Tags

Another issue is the practice of placing misleading or trademarked meta tags in Web pages. Basically, meta tags are a type of HTML code that can only be read by computers. (HTML code is the universal computer language that browsers use to view sites or access information on the Web.) A meta tag is one type of hidden HTML that Internet search engines read when searching for sites that users have keyworded. Web designers often use meta-tag keywords to guarantee that their site receives numbers of "hits" from surfers' use of various search engines.

These code tags provide a description of what the Web page is about for a search engine's robotic software to pick up. For example, the operator of a Net site selling expensive old furniture would code the words "antique furniture," "Colonial desks," and "fine interior items," among others, into its pages. Another way would be to include "sex," "playboy," and other misleading or trademarked words—another "no, no."

As we've learned, the fact that a mark is trademarked is not enough to prove trademark infringement. More than one user can use that mark, provided there's no likelihood of confusion in a user's mind (being in entirely different businesses is one part of the test) or of dilution (i.e., bringing it into disrepute). For example, a local merchant named Nike could use the name "Nike's Saws," but not "Nike's Shoes"; a local sexpot striptease bar couldn't call itself "Nike's Ladies of the Night." The "Lexus" mark for the car isn't the same as the "Lexis" name for legal research, and both can coexist by one court decision.

The courts have employed a good faith, "fair use" test in trademark infringement cases. In one leading case, a former *Playboy* model, Terri Welles, found herself hauled into court by Playboy Enterprises for using the words "playboy," "playmate," and "Playboy Playmate of the Year, 1981" as meta tags to promote her Web site with search engines. In fact, Terri Welles had been featured as the "Playmate of the Month" in *Playboy*'s December 1981 issue, as well as being named Playmate of the Year. Among other information, her Web site featured clothed and naked photographs of herself and other women with biographical notes of her Playboy Mansion days. Subscribers to her site paid a monthly fee to access a special photo collection, and the site contained banner ads with links to explicit pornographic sites. Anyone using search engines with these words would be directed to her location, as well as that of *Playboy*.

Playboy sued for trademark infringement over her use of the meta-tag words involving "playboy." The judge dismissed its lawsuit, holding that if it was fair use to use a prominent headline in any advertisements that *Playboy*'s Bunny Welles was a Playmate of the Year, it was equally fair to use that term in any meta tags, including hers.

Playboy has prevailed in several lawsuits against companies with competing Web sites; in those cases, the defendants not only used the terms "playboy" and "playmate" in their meta tags, but at times also used the marks in their domain names. However, these sites had no connection to those words as did Ms. Welles. Pursuing a legal policy to put the word out that it didn't tolerate misleading meta tags or trademarks, *Playboy* prevailed over a California clothing designer's use of the word "playboy" in its meta tags to pull surfers into its designer-label site. Given that the businesses were in different areas, these intentions were certainly questionable.

The company also litigated with Excite over the search engine's use of the word "playboy" in its meta tags. Users rely on search engines, such as Excite, to lead them through the Web maze. Whenever a user typed "playboy" on Excite's engine, that person was directed to a banner ad for certain adult Web sites. To make money, search engines sell banner ads that appear on the screen above the search results, and these ads are often keyed to the words of the phrase. This practice isn't uncommon—or used only by Excite. All of us have used a search engine and found ourselves looking at some address or site that doesn't have the remotest connection with what we're looking for. This case was settled, and inputting "playboy" on Excite now ends up with no banner ad and Playboy.com as the first listing brought up. (Note: At this time, the Federal Trade Commission is investigating a complaint that search engines should disclose when money is paid by a site for preferential search treatment.)

These cases are in line with other decisions that enjoin such use—especially when the meta tags are likely to cause confusion in users, owing to some misrepresentation. For example, in *Brookfield Communications v. West Coast Entertainment Corp.*, the plaintiff owned the trademark "MovieBuff," and the defendant used the term "MovieBuff" as both its domain name and part of the site's meta tags. Although the meta tag wasn't visible to viewers of the Web page, the court held that the use of "MovieBuff" in its domain name and the meta tags was illegal and would create a likelihood of confusion.

When you're developing a Web site, it's always better to avoid words that are misleading or could infringe on the trademarks of others. For example, if you create a Web site for your used-car lot, don't use the descriptive words "General Motors" as a meta tag. However, do come up with descriptive and accurate words that search engines would find attractive.

The Law of Linking

The directions of the law seem to be clear: (1) the general rule is that users don't need permission to link directly to the homepage of another site, provided they don't disparage, misrepresent, or misappropriate; (2) given that these facts aren't present, framing and deep linking (as opposed to linking) will more likely constitute a violation; and (3) deep linking in commercial situations, as opposed to noncommercial ones, are likely to be violations when (a) direct competitors are involved, (b) there is an advantage being taken by that linkage, and (c) there is an element of "unfairness" or bad faith on the part of the linking party. Further, if data is misappropriated, misused, or passed off by another as its own, even nonprofit or noncommercial sites may have valid causes of action.

If a court determines that there was a violation, then the site can either drop that activity or pay for it. It's important to determine this before there's a court battle. Make the decision as to whether that right is important enough to pay upfront for its use, before any anticipated legal expenses and battles can arise. Also, keep in mind that the United States and most countries in the European Union follow these legal "rules of the road." In other countries, however, there presently are no laws that prohibit deep linking. Typically, this is due to those countries not having "unfair competition" laws as in the United States—laws that are quite useful in this regard. If an operator based, let's say, in Thailand deep links to you, then there's the additional real conflicts-of-law question, as we've seen before. Whether or not protective laws are passed overseas, you'll need to be making the tough business decisions when this situation arises.

Paying to Link

An accelerating Net phenomenon has been the rise of linking agreements where a linked site pays for the exposure. These situations occur basically in two ways: (1) the linked site commercially profits or otherwise benefits from the deep link; or (2) the linkage is in reality a referral or advertising contract. In both cases, a written linking agreement is essential.

'BOTS AND SPIDERS

We have seen that deep linking activities for commercial advantage can be prohibited and paying licensing fees for these activities are an end result. Commercially profiting without an agreement, through the use of quite sophisticated software, is another growing legal area. Known as "robots," "'bots," "spiders," or "crawlers," these automated software systems provide an automatic approach to seeing what data lives out there in the Net universe. Rather than "clicking" on links, this software races through the Net, steams past the homepages of Web sites, penetrates deep into their internal pages, gathers the desired information, and transports back to the host site copies of whatever information is desired. In essence, spiders and 'bots create myriad spider webs of links to find data and transport them back. If done frequently enough, the "hits" can create a near simultaneous look at whatever information is out there.

A contentious legal dispute between two auction sites turned on this aspect of "linking." The largest Internet auction service, eBay, filed a lawsuit in late 1999 against Bidders Edge, one of several Internet auction search services. Shoppers at Net locations such as Bidders Edge can search for items at many Web auction sites, rather than having to make numerous separate visits to each one. Many auction houses welcome these sites, believing that they increase their numbers of visitors. eBay, however, apparently didn't want another site to be able to profit on information that's posted on its Web site. The lawsuit accused Bidders Edge of trespass, copyright and trademark infringement, false advertising, and other evils.

Interestingly enough, eBay had previously agreed to licensing agreements with AuctionRover and iTrack, permitting these rival companies to include eBay's listings in a separate area on their sites. Bidder's Edge had turned down eBay's terms for a similar linking/licensing agreement, having found the proposed terms to be unacceptable. eBay clearly brought the lawsuit to enforce its belief that any linking or "roboting" with it, by Bidders Edge, would need to be paid for. This case marked one of the first times that a Web site attempted to exclude itself from listings in search-engine databases, such as those used by these "spiders."

The federal court district judge in the case issued a preliminary injunction against Bidder's Edge, prohibiting the company from using its "'bots" and "spiders" to search eBay's site, gather eBay's data, and store this data in its own database. Although eBay had first consented to having Bidder's Edge post data about its auctions, it objected when Bidder's Edge conducted successive queries of its site during the day. In fact, eBay alleged that Bidder's Edge used its 'bots to access the eBay site up to 125,000 times each day (as much as 1.53% of its total daily hits). eBay argued that this practice would encourage others to do this and created the risk that its computer systems would be adversely affected in their functioning.

The importance of the judge's holding was that he agreed with eBay's contention that Bidder's Edge and its robots were trespassing on eBay's site by using and diminishing the resources of its computer systems without permission. Bidder's Edge quickly appealed the granting of the injunction, but just before the appellate court issued its decision, the two companies agreed to settle the lawsuit in early 2001. eBay reported that the settlement prohibited Bidder's Edge from sifting through its site for information, and that Bidder's Edge had agreed to pay an undisclosed sum of money, as well as dropping its appeal of the preliminary injunction. eBay's auction results are reported separately now on Bidder's Edge.

Two courts considered the trespass holding by the judge in the eBay matter as soon as it was issued, and they reached two different conclusions based on differing facts. The bottom line of these decisions is that deep linking is not a copyright infringement problem, but that trespass will be found where the actions of the Web spiders would adversely affect the functioning of the plaintiff's site. In the eBay case, linking without permission that averaged 1.5 percent of the daily volume was sufficient to find this adverse effect.

REFERRAL AND AD CONTRACTS

Amazon.com has been a leader in paying commissions to more than 500,000 "associate" Web sites for each sale they refer by linking to its various products, and multi-thousands of other Web sites also pay for similar sales referrals. This "affiliate" marketing has sprung up owing to the Web's vast networks of millions and millions of links. As one click of a mouse transports people instantly around different sites, Web operators know that information at one site can be linked easily with products for sale at another. Web sites visited by purchase-oriented users have suddenly become large sales forces for retail sites (whether B2B or B2C), and these linking relationships usually are formally documented. Should you be interested in establishing a referral system, check out the programs at the large online bidding/retailers sites and see how they handle the registration process. This system will require additional technology features with your Web site, but should be looked into when needed.

Linking agreements can also be advertising contracts with moneys paid for the linking right. Sites wanting customers will link with a host site that's visited by that profile of consumers. A logo, promotional device, or slogan usually surrounds the linking connection, and users who click on it are immediately transported to the advertising site. The retail site, or advertiser, pays moneys to the host site for the privilege of this tie-in. Monetary linking agreements are distinct from Internet advertising contracts, which typically involve more text, flashing displays, "hit" counts, and changing ad features with correspondingly different legal provisions.

In ad-linking contracts, the link is made from the host to the advertising site (or the linked site); in this case, the advertising entity pays for the privilege of placing its link on the host site. In a situation such as eBay's, where the auction search house wants information for its users, the link is made from the search house to the linked site (or eBay's). The auction house pays for this privilege of using the deep-linked information.

A written contract is always your best bet against the risks from an important linking relationship, whether commercial interests are present or not. Although it's easy to request permission in an e-mail, special considerations are present in deep linking or framing situations with even noncommercial sites. Check the site's Terms of Use provisions and see what their procedures are to procure its consent. A written agreement protects you from that site suddenly "pulling the plug" on what is an important linkage asset of your site.

This chapter concludes with two form agreements. Both are *Linking Permission Agreements.* One is used when no money needs to be exchanged; the other, when payment is being made for that right.

The first linking (no payment) contract is a simple form that's useful when one party desires to formalize that long-term permission has been granted for that right to link. The second form is useful when a commercial benefit is being gained by this arrangement. Whether it's the eBay situation requiring permission to access another site's information or direct "linked" advertising, this contract is useful when the permission to link is being purchased.

If the other party doesn't want a formal agreement, then e-mail the important concepts of the applicable form, ask for a response, and try to work it out from there. This approach can be used with basically any of the forms in this book.

Linking Permission Agreement
(No Payment)

This Linking Permission Agreement is entered into on [*Date of Agreement*] by [*Name of Party Giving Permission*], called Grantor, and [*Name of Party Requesting Permission*], called Grantee. The parties, in consideration of the mutual promises made by each other and other valuable consideration, agree as follows:

1. **Agreement.** Grantor owns a Web site called [*Name of Grantor's Web Site*] and which is located at http:[*State Grantor's Domain Address*]; Grantee owns a Web site called [*Name of Grantee's Web Site*] and which is located at http:[*State Grantee's Domain Address*]. Grantor by this Agreement grants to Grantee the right to provide a hypertext link from Grantee's Web site to the home page of Grantor's Web site.

2. **Liability.** Neither party shall be liable to the other for the content or links on its own Web site.

3. **Termination.** Either party may terminate this Agreement without cause by giving the other a five-day written notice of termination. In the event that such a notice is given or received, both parties shall take all steps necessary on their end to remove the linkage within 24 hours of its receipt of the notice.

4. **Indemnification.** But for any contrary provisions in this Agreement, each party agrees to fully defend, indemnify, and hold harmless, the other, its officers, directors, employees, and agents, from any and all claims, actions, or controversies, including reasonable attorney fees and court costs, owing to its negligence or fault. Each party shall provide immediate notice to the other of any such claim, action, or controversy, and shall cooperate with that party at the cost of whichever party is at fault.

5. **Other.** Any dispute arising in connection with this Agreement shall be first settled by mediation. If that's not successful, then the dispute shall be settled by arbitration to be held in [*Location of Arbitration*] in accordance with the rules of the American Arbitration Association. This agreement to arbitrate shall be specifically enforceable. Any award shall be final and binding on all parties, and a final judgment may be entered in the appropriate court of law. Notwithstanding this, should any litigation ensue between the parties, then the prevailing party shall be entitled to reasonable expenses and attorney fees as set by the Court.

This Agreement is the final understanding between the parties on this subject matter, superceding all other previous agreements, and may be amended only by the written consent of all the parties. Should any court or proceeding determine that any provision is illegal or in conflict, then all other remaining provisions shall be held severable, valid, and be given separate legal effect.

Neither party may assign this Agreement without the consent of the other, which consent shall not be unreasonably withheld. This Agreement shall bind all the parties, their respective estates, heirs, personal representatives, successors, and permitted assigns; its legality and interpretation shall be governed by the laws of the State of [*Name of State Whose Laws Govern*] and of the United States.

This Agreement is accepted, understood, and executed as of the date first above written, by and between:

_____

[*Name and Title of Party Signing for Grantor*]
[*Grantor's Name and Address*]

_____

[*Name and Title of Party Signing for Grantee*]
[*Grantee's Name and Address*]

Linking Permission Agreement
(No Payment)

Discussion of Provisions

1. **Agreement.** Although most Web sites want other sites to link to them for the exposure and "hits," it is good practice to gain their permission—especially in this day and age of commercialization. You should discuss ahead of time whether a site wants you to pay for this "privilege." Some sites have in place their own approval procedures that should be followed for their linking process. However, most Web sites still don't, and this form can be used when someone asks you for permission (or vice versa) and compensation is not required. In this case, the "Grantee" is the party who wants to link, and the "Grantor" is the one who is approving that link. Additionally, if the link will involve pages other than the home page, then this section would need to be changed to reflect those facts.

2. **Liability.** If there is a concern in this area, then the grantor can require that the linking party maintains certain content or standards as a condition to keeping that link. Section 2 of the Agreement would be changed to reflect that the linking party, or grantee, would be liable to the approving party for any damages owing to such changes.

3. **Termination.** The termination provisions of this form are simple and quick, since no money is being invested in this agreement. When a Web site pays for the linkage, this association becomes an asset and necessitating more contract protections. (See the "Linking Permission Agreement (Payment)" form, which follows, for these important details.)

4. **Indemnification.** It makes sense to add provisions stating that the other party will protect you if its Web site becomes controversial and lawsuits are consequentially filed (which may include your site due simply to that linkage).

5. **Other.** This "boilerplate" stipulates that the alternate dispute resolution techniques of mediation and arbitration are to be used. Should arbitration not be agreeable, then these provisions would have to be accordingly changed to reflect the parties' agreement. Additionally, this form provides that any assignment requires the written approval of the other (which may not be "unreasonably withheld"). If either party desires the ability to assign without this restraint, then the following could be substituted: "Either party may assign its rights and responsibilities under this Agreement as it so chooses." This agreement provides that U.S. law applies, but this could also change if one or both parties aren't U.S. residents.

   If there's no chance that this particular linking could result in any liabilities or damages, and it's not an important asset to you, then sections 4 and 5 of this agreement could be eliminated. In that case, you could simply e-mail your understanding or "meeting of the minds" to one another.

Linking Permission Agreement
(Payment)

This Linking Permission Agreement is entered into on [*Date of Agreement*] by [*Party's Name Granting Permission*], called Licensor, and [*Party's Name Receiving Permission*], called Licensee. In consideration of the mutual promises made by each other and other valuable consideration, the parties agree as follows:

1. **Agreement and Term.** Licensor owns a Web site called [*Name of Licensor's Web Site*], which is located at http:[*State Licensor's Domain Address*]; Licensee owns a Web site called [*Name of Licensee's Web Site*], which is located at http:[*State Licensee's Domain Address*]. Pursuant to this Agreement's terms and conditions, Licensor grants to Licensee the right to [*Describe Link(s) to be Created (i.e., Hyperlink, Graphics, Framed, or Access by Spiders*] from Licensee's Web site to Licensor's Web site.

   Users will be able to [*State Access (i.e., "point and click" on this hyperlink)*] and move from Licensee's site to Licensor's. This link will be a: [*Describe Hyperlink, such as Simple Text, Graphics, or Frame*] hyperlink. The Term of this Agreement shall be for [*State Number of Months*] months, beginning on [*State Beginning Date of Agreement*] and ending on [*State Ending Date of Agreement*].

2. **Fee.** In return for Licensor agreeing to the hyperlink on its Web site, and for other valuable consideration, Licensee agrees to make monthly payment to Licensor of $[*State Monthly Dollar Payment, Revenue-Sharing, or Other Compensation Agreement*], plus any applicable state and local taxes, all payable within [*State Grace Period in Days*] days of [*State Date When Payment Is Initially Due*].

   Should Licensee not pay any invoice within the period set forth above, then a service charge of [*State Percentage Monthly Service Charge*]% is payable each month until that balance, and all other monthly balances, are paid in full.

3. **User Data Sharing.**

   (a). **Licensor.** Licensor [*State "shall" or "shall not"*] collect data and information on users to Licensor's site who use the link. As agreed between the parties, and to the extent possible, the data collected shall include, to the extent possible (including aggregate information), the user's name, address, e-mail address, preferences, purchases, income, occupation, and other personal information. Licensor shall give all required legal notices to users that this information may be collected, transferred, disclosed, and used by others, so that this process will be legally-compliant for those countries the users reside in. Licensor [*State "shall" or "shall not"*] send copies of this data to Licensee for its use only in making internal business decisions.

   (b). **Licensee.** Licensee [*State "shall" or "shall not"*] collect data and information on users to Licensee's site who use the link. As agreed between the parties, and to the extent possible, the data collected shall include, to the extent possible (including aggregate information), the user's name, address, e-mail address, preferences, purchases, income, occupation, and other personal information. Licensee shall give all required legal notices to users that this information may be collected, transferred, disclosed, and used by others, so that this process will be legally-compliant for those countries the users reside in. Licensee [*State "shall" or "shall not"*] send copies of this data to Licensor for its use only in making internal business decisions.

4. **Placement and Design.** Licensor and Licensee agree that Licensee's linkage will be placed on Licensor's Web site as follows: [*State Where Linkage Impacts or is Located on Licensor's Web Site*]. The [*Describe Hyperlink, such as Simple Text, Graphics, or Framed*] link shall be of the following design: [*Describe the Design and "Look" of the Link*]. It will meet the following technical criteria: [*Describe the Technological Criteria to be Met*].

Linking Permission Agreement (Payment) *(Continued)*

5. **Representations and Warranties.** Each party warrants and represents to the other that: (a) its site does not violate the laws, statutes, or regulations of any country, state, or territory; (b) its site does not violate any other party's copyrights, trademarks, intellectual property, or any other ownership rights; (c) it has the right and power to enter into this Agreement and will not violate any other contract or agreement with any other party; (d) its site does not contain any threatening, obscene, defamatory, or other hurtful material; (e) its site is truthful and not misleading; (f) EACH DISCLAIMS ALL IMPLIED WARRANTIES, INCLUDING WITHOUT LIMITATION, THE WARRANTIES OF MERCHANTABILITY AND FITNESS FOR A PARTICULAR PURPOSE; (g) each will use reasonable commercial efforts to keep its site available to users 24 hours each day, 7 days each week; and (h) each will stay reasonably technologically competent so that users can access their sites quickly and comfortably, regardless of the type of Web browser they are using, and that quality standards of access and use are maintained.

6. **Trademarks and Copyrights**

   (a). Each party retains its own copyrights, trademarks, and all ownership rights in their Web site.

   (b). Licensee, during the term of this Agreement, grants to Licensor a nonexclusive, worldwide license to reproduce and display Licensee's image on Licensor's Site. This right expires upon the termination of this Agreement.

7. **Liability and Indemnification**

   (a). **Liability.** Each Party agrees that it [*State "shall" or "shall not"*] be liable to the other for the content or links on its Web site to that of others.

   (b). **Indemnification.** But for the provisions of this Agreement, each party agrees to fully defend, indemnify, and hold harmless, the other, its officers, employees, and agents, from any and all claims, actions, or controversies, including reasonable attorney fees and court costs, owing to its negligence, fault, or breach of a warranty or representation. Each party shall provide immediate notice to the other of any such claim, action, or controversy, and shall cooperate with that party at the cost of whichever party is at fault.

8. **Termination**

   (a). This Agreement shall terminate on its own at the end of a particular Term as indicated in Section 1 above.

   (b). Should any payment not be made when due, then the Licensor may terminate this Agreement without penalty after the expiration of a written [*State Days within which Payment Must be Received*] days notice to pay without payment being so received.

   (c). Either party may terminate this Agreement without penalty, provided the other has committed a material breach of a provision of this Agreement, and such failure continues uncured for 30 days after written notice to that party.

   (d). Either party may terminate this Agreement without penalty in the event that the other party materially changes the "look and feel," content, or structure of its Web site; provided that a 30 day notice to cure such breach must be first given and such failure continues uncured after that period.

9. **Other.** Any dispute arising in connection with this Agreement shall be first settled by mediation. If that's not successful, then the dispute shall be settled by arbitration to be held in [*Location of Arbitration*] in accordance with the rules of the American Arbitration Association. This agreement to arbitrate shall be specifically enforceable. Any award shall be final and binding on all parties, and a final judgment may be entered in the appropriate court of law. Notwithstanding this, should any litigation ensue between the parties, then the prevailing party shall be entitled to reasonable expenses and attorney fees as set by the Court.

Linking Permission Agreement (Payment) *(Continued)*

This Agreement is the final understanding between the parties on this subject matter, superceding all other previous agreements, and may be amended only by the written consent of all the parties. Should any court or proceeding determine that any provision is illegal or in conflict, then all other remaining provisions shall be held severable, valid, and be given separate legal effect.

Neither party may assign this Agreement without the consent of the other, which consent shall not be unreasonably withheld. This Agreement shall bind all the parties, their successors, and permitted assigns, and its legality and interpretation shall be governed by the laws of the State of [*Name of State Whose Laws Govern*] and of the United States.

This Agreement is accepted, understood, and executed as of the date first above written, by and between:

_____

[*Name and Title of Party Signing for Licensor*]
[*Licensor's Name and Address*]

_____

[*Name and Title of Party Signing for Licensee*]
[*Licensee's Name and Address*]

Linking Permission Agreement
(Payment)

Discussion of Provisions

1. **Agreement and Term.** The contract details must change when payment is made for the right to connect to another's Web site, and the agreement must contain more provisions that protect this "asset." This is a licensed right, subject to termination for stated reasons—rather than being ended without any cause. It typically has a stated term with a beginning and ending date. The parties will need to agree on the link location, type of linkage (frame or otherwise), and quality details, as well as other aspects.

   These "hyperlink" agreements can operate as advertising contracts in one sense, but they are basically distinct from these agreements. Although the links can publicize a site (by building the site's presence through the other's access) or create more hits (by moving a user from one site to another), the link itself does not necessarily have the "bells and whistles" of a typical ad. These linking agreements for money also can involve deep linking (avoiding the homepage to access information), framing, or "robotic" links; in this event, the wording needs to be changed to reflect the realities of such linking.

2. **Fee.** The fee paid for the linkage can vary from a cash payment for a stated term to an installment contract, or even to a percentage of sales or revenue-sharing arrangement. The fee is presented here as a monthly payment, which may or may not be the actual case.

   As the fee structure becomes more complicated (i.e., percentage of sales paid by the licensee), other provisions need to be added. For example, the percentage of sales paid can be a straightforward, negotiated percentage; or it can be a pro-rata payment based on the number of "hits" brought to the host site as a percentage of all "hits" or "impressions" (however that is defined). As the revenues at stake become higher, and the provisions more complicated, legal counsel should definitely be employed to draft the agreement from the beginning.

   We don't live in a perfect world, so the penalty for late payments (such as a service charge after an agreed-on grace period) needs to be discussed and in the contract. These provisions would be coordinated with the termination rights for when payments are not received.

3. **User Data Sharing.** This agreement provides for the sharing between the parties of "cookies," purchasing data, and other discovered user "profile" information. The privacy provisions on such sharing become important, given that this is a worldwide market—and that some countries are more restrictive than others as to what must be disclosed to users, as well as what can or cannot be collected. This provision may be changed, depending on what the parties' expectations are and what their respective privacy policies are. This clause only allows for the use of the information for "internal" purposes—and not for reselling, to third parties, data that belong to the other. Additionally, this section would be changed if the linking agreement involved the accessing and sharing of the Licensor's information through deep linking or the use of robots.

4. **Placement and Design.** The parties need to agree on the location, design, and technological details of the linkage. The location is critical because the licensee is paying for this right of linkage and will want the maximum number "hits" due to this linking. Further, the design and technology of the link will be part of the overall discussion and contract.

   The technological aspects can become quite important as to the method, specific quality of downloading, accessibility to various Web navigators, and modifications for the latest technological updates. The contract can even go into the details of defining by pixels how sharp images should be.

Linking Permission Agreement (Payment) *(Continued)*

5. **Representations and Warranties.** Given that the two Web sites are "connecting" to one another with commercial purposes in mind, the warranties that each makes are mutual. A number of these warranties are standard (i.e., the sites are legally compliant, don't violate other copyrights, have the power to enter into this contract, and don't contain defamatory or obscene material, among other provisions). Both warrant that they will use "reasonable commercial efforts" to stay in continuous operation (but don't warrant that this in fact will be the case). There is a disclaimer of implied warranties, owing to the technological vulnerability of Web sites. These warranties may change owing to what, in fact, each can represent.

6. **Trademarks and Copyrights.** In these contracts, both parties are given assurances that they will retain their copyrights, trademarks, and ownership rights in their Web sites—which, in fact, should be the case.

7. **Liability and Indemnification.** A party may desire that the other guarantees that its site with the linkage won't drag the first into a legal controversy. In that case, Section 7(a) would be modified. However, a mutual indemnification provision is present, so that a party "at fault" will contractually protect an innocent one that becomes financially injured owing to that negligence. A party that doesn't live up to its warranties should protect the other from any adverse results.

8. **Termination.** The Agreement can end by its term concluding, by one party or both violating a material provision (such as not meeting a warranty that was made) after a notice period, and by the licensee not making a required payment within the allowed time span. As the "look and feel" of Web sites can change rapidly as they shift to gain other marketing segments, a provision allowing termination in the event of such a drastic change is present. It may very well be that the "material" change of a Web site to attract another audience could mean that users wouldn't be as interested in the now-quite-different site of the other.

9. **Other.** Please see the discussions on this topic at previously reviewed forms.

Web Site Operating Considerations

Whether you're telling customers about your dude ranch, selling heavy equipment, or offering courses under an online undergraduate degree program, you need to consider various operating business and legal areas *before* you activate your site. For example, a medical-supply Web site, which sells kidney-dialysis and heart-monitoring devices, is subject to regulations on advertising that are quite different from those on a used-car site. A location exhibiting paintings has different business and legal considerations than one that sells privately held stock and is subject to heavy state and federal regulations. The government, educational, and nonprofit sectors must do their homework, as well (including posting Terms of Use and Privacy statements), before opening more online doors.

Conduct your legal/business checkup before your users or the regulators do. At the same time, surf other sites in your field and see what issues they're trying to deal with that you aren't. There are common areas also to consider, such as reviewing the regulations surrounding your business operations, protecting your copyrighted content, reviewing insurance and liability considerations, seeing the factors on advertising policy and content, addressing security and rights-of-privacy concerns, among others. This chapter explores these areas.

Have You Met All the Regulations?

We live in a highly regulated world, and, before you flick on the computer switch, you need to be aware of how your online site fits into your specific business world. Many business areas are subject to rules and regulations by federal *and* state agencies, as well as those of other countries, when sales or ads reach into their jurisdictions. For example, the U.S. Federal Trade Commission (see www.ftc.gov, as well as Chapter 7, " 'Great Deals,' 'Easy Money,' and Other Ads") regulates the sale of franchises, business opportunities, online and offline advertising, and other areas. The Food and Drug Administration (FDA) regulates numbers of products, ranging from the most common food ingredients to complex medical and surgical devices, life-saving drugs, and radiation-emitting consumer and medical products. It administers rules on vitamin supplements, baby food, microwaves, cell phones, and others, including the advertising and disclosures needed to be made. At Chapter 7, we discussed the responsibilities of the U.S. Securities and Exchange Commission (SEC).

Any federal or state agency that regulates the offline world can stretch its regulatory powers into the virtual world. (See also Chapter 17, "The Internet Faces More Legal Shape-Shifting Ahead.") The question is: To what extent do these agencies—including those in different countries—have regulations and powers that could affect your specific Web site? This should be looked into at the very beginning.

On a local basis, states regulate from real estate brokers, insurance salespeople, and doctors to lawyers, hair salons, and CPAs—and the rules can vary in different states and countries. Every activity, from selling wine to filling prescriptions online, is either regulated or prohibited in numerous worldwide jurisdictions. Whatever your particular business or service, you will want to check the applicable regulations with the responsible regulatory agencies before you go ahead. *Once your site is under way, there's nothing worse than having to change your Web site and its operations because you've neglected to discover the rules and regulations that apply specifically to your business.*

Because the Internet has no boundaries, your customers can be scattered around the globe and protected by varying rules and regulations. Enacting fair and reasonable return and refund policies, complaint procedures, Terms of Use, Privacy, and other procedures is not only good business, it also meets numbers of these legal regulations. If you are uncertain about specific countries; you can (1) list just those that you will sell and deliver to; (2) state those specific states or countries where it's illegal for citizens to purchase from your site (i.e., if you're selling wine, war memorabilia, religious artifacts, and so on); or (3) establish specific country and language sites—it depends on your reach and budget. But do consider this area.

The Internet's broad exposure also affects geographical contractual restrictions, especially if the governing agreements were entered into before the dawning of this new age. If you're creating a Web site as part of your present business operations, then be sure to look closely at all of your preexisting contracts. For example, distribution, franchise, and other marketing agreements can be unintentionally violated if sales now, through your virtual presence, will be made outside your permitted area. Let's say that your company was granted the rights to sell and service appliances in a three-state area. Before you market your new Web presence, it might be a good idea to talk with your franchiser or client and find out what its position is—especially as you could be receiving orders not only from outside your territorial limits, but from distant countries.

Web Site Copyright Protection

How do you keep others from "taking" or copying images and text from your site without your permission? The first step is to file the appropriate copyright registrations to protect your site and its creations. Next, place conspicuous copyright notices on your Web pages. And there are other ways.

Under U.S. and international copyright law (see also Chapter 4, "Copying in Cyberspace"), an original work is protected by a copyright when it's first created from an idea (the legal jargon is "fixed in a tangible medium"). Thus, as soon as words are typed, colors are painted, or pictures are taken (even before they're posted on a site), the copyright protections accrue, regardless of whether a registration is filed or a © copyright notice is affixed.

When you register your original work in the United States, U.S. law gives certain advantages to a registration: a presumption that the person owns that slogan, picture, or Web site's "look and feel"; if you sue, you can receive statutory damages, in addition to being granted an injunction and being reimbursed for your legal fees. If you choose not to register your copyright at this time, but wait until you decide to sue, then be aware that you can lose the ability to receive statutory damages for those acts occuring prior to the registration. Statutory damages are quite helpful in cases where you can't prove what your damages were (i.e., just what portion of your lost sales was due to that infringing competitor's Web site?). The statutory damages can be from $750 to $30,000 per infringement (up to $150,000 if willful) under this law.

It costs only $30 to register your copyrights (and about eight months or so to receive the copyright registration certificate), so head to www.loc.gov/copyright, the site of the U.S. Copyright Office. You can download the requisite forms, review the "Frequently Asked Questions" (FAQ) for assistance, fill in the forms, and submit the registrations today. It's even possible to submit a CD of your work, rather than bulky physical copies. Given the low cost and these advantages, businesses and individuals alike should register copyrights on an ongoing basis—and often. Other countries also provide for advantages in registering a copyright. Check out those that are or could become part of your revenue stream. If you can't find this information on the Web, then you'll need to secure the services of an attorney and decide whether the costs are worth the additional advantages. For copyrights created in the United States, you'll typically need a U.S. copyright registration certificate to file in those selected foreign countries (and vice versa).

More importantly, registering a copyright tells the world that you own this creation and establishes the specific facts and time of your ownership. Otherwise, you're reduced to arguing relatively difficult to prove facts, such as why, how, when, and where you created this work. This can be troublesome when another Web site argues that you don't own those ownership rights—typically, after the site has ripped you off. Registration sets down these facts and dates of creation, so potential challenges can be met by your simple statement: "Look, I've already registered it," and fax the challenger a copy.

Type the key words of your slogan, text, or image into a search engine, and see what turns up. Surf sites similar to yours, seeing the extent to which those sites match your "look and feel." It's also relatively easy to check on who's claiming copyrights that are within your business area. Anyone can search federally registered copyrights for free, and the same address is used (check out www.loc.gov/copyright). Keep in mind that only those who registered their works with this federal agency will be located; it's quite possible that similar works have been created by people who haven't registered those works, or only did so with a state agency. They may even live in another country. Think about how much time, energy, and money you want to invest in maintaining your copyrighted creations. Then, decide.

Web site owners do place © copyright notices, even though legally they don't need to, for notification reasons and because users may take them seriously. It also allows them to argue that the infringer knew that those images were protected. The notice to be posted lists the copyright notice, the year of first publication, and then the copyright owner (i.e., your name)—for example, © 2001-2 AceRetails.

This is also your chance to state what you consider to be a "fair use" of your Web site and its copyrighted contents. For example, you might post, at the bottom of each Web page, "Copyright, 2001-2, Dana Jones. All Rights Reserved. You may copy for your personal home use only." Or post, "© 2001-2, Dana Jones. All rights reserved. You may copy only as our Terms of Use allow, and any other use is strictly prohibited."

In a copyright dispute, keep in mind that you can utilize the provisions of the Digital Millennium Copyright Act. If an infringer doesn't follow your polite e-mail or your more threatening letter, your next step can be to send a demand letter to the offending Web site's ISP and demand that it pulls the plug on the infringing material. Some people have complained to ISPs in countries that haven't yet enacted these provisions—and have had success in doing this. ISPs are wary of the potential third-party liability for harboring defamatory, illegally copyrighted, or other offensive material, especially when they don't yet enjoy the "safe harbor" protections of U.S. law.

The easiest way to keep people from taking content from your site is to control their access through the use of passwords and paid subscriptions. You can even program controls on your site as to which addresses are allowed. However, these approaches are complicated, can be expensive, and most of us want lots of visitors. If you feel that your site has particularly valuable copyrighted or trademarked materials, then consult an experienced intellectual property attorney for the best ways and places to register them, display notices, and even use search robots to keep tabs on what the competition is doing.

Trademark Protection

As we've seen previously, protecting your domain and brand names (e.g., "AceRetails.com" and AceRetails) by trademark law is different from protecting the advertising and informational content on your site by copyright. Although there are some exceptions, they don't apply to most of us. Free trademark or patent searches may be made at the U.S. Patent and Trademark Office (PTO) Web site (uspto.gov). You can also conduct online searches, as well as make online trademark and service-mark registrations, at this site. *As when you're searching for copyrights, remember that numbers of people haven't registered their trademarks or service marks with the appropriate federal or state agency, including other countries' equivalents. More sophisticated (and expensive) searches can be made to look for these.*

Surf the sites you pick up on search engines with the words "trademark search"—then make your decision. (Consult Chapter 13, "Domain Names and Conflicts," for more information.) Remember, if you own a trademark, service mark, or domain name that is a mark, then be sure you use it on your stationery, business cards, and advertisements. Otherwise, you can lose it if another business runs with it all over the globe. Be sure that you register any mark in use with the PTO and appropriate state agency.

As with copyright registrations, the failure to register a trademark or service mark does not invalidate that right. However, an appropriate registration makes it much easier to prove your rights because you have the data set down in a date-stamped record. Moreover, this information is now accessible by others. When they're searching to see if a certain mark has already been registered, they'll pick up your registration. As we have seen, the same process is used to see whether a mark is available (and can be registered) or to determine whether anyone is using your now-registered mark elsewhere.

Whether you've registered your marks or not, be sure to place the symbol ™ on your trademarks. Anyone who claims a right in a mark may use a ™ (or the ˢᴹ service mark equivalent) at the end, and it's not necessary to possess a valid registration, or even have a pending application in place. However, you cannot place ® on a trademark or service mark until you've received the federal registration approval for that mark. These symbols can be helpful if you must argue with others that they knew the mark belonged to somebody else when they took it. However, because anyone can affix a ™ or ˢᴹ to a mark without penalty, no extra rights should be implied to their presence. *As with the previous copyright discussion, watching trademarks means not only protecting your own, but also not infringing on the rights of others.*

Additionally, if you're doing or foresee doing business in other countries, then pay attention to protecting your trademarks, servicemarks, and domain names in those countries, just as you do with your copyrights. You'll need to register this intellectual property under their laws. (Note: Use your search engine; however, if a foreign site is not in English or is not available, you'll need to hire foreign counsel for those registrations.) You also should consider registering all your domain names in those countries, given a country-code designation (i.e., "*.uk*" if you conduct business in England).

Insurance

The subject of insurance and risk management is another important area to review, then make your decision as to what's important. Let's say that you've decided to create a Web site on Early American antiques that swaps information on collectibles. If this was strictly a hobby site, then you would have limited liability problems. Although you always want to give out accurate information, noncommercial sites typically don't have the liabilities of those that sell products, services, or information for a fee. People take offense more quickly if they've paid money for something.

Thus, if you create a site that sells collectibles, there is a different story. These are expensive items, and delivering them in excellent condition is important. You should arrange to have fire and damage insurance coverage that equals the value of your collectibles, both in your warehouse (or home) and while in transit to your customer's place. Although not as risky as if you were selling deep-sea diving helmets (a defective product here creates a multimillion-dollar liability), you would want to check with your insurance agent as to what insurance is required to cover your potential liabilities. For example, if someone sits on one of your chairs and it collapses, you'll want to have insurance coverage to cover any resulting liability.

Liability insurance becomes even more necessary if the products being sold are more likely to cause injury when there's a defect. For example, if you sell mountaineering equipment, then there's a real risk of a wrongful death lawsuit. For example, if a climbing pin fractures and a climber consequently falls to his death, you had better have significant liability insurance in place.

If you establish a travel site, then what happens if your information is wrong and someone gets hurt? Let's say that you recommend a hotel on your Web site as being "safe and secure with old-time friendly service," not thinking about the legal consequences. If a user relies on this information and is beaten up by the doorman, will your insurance company defend you in any litigation? Will your policy cover all of the possible damages that could be assessed against you?

The insurance industry has been determining what levels of Internet activities are covered by its standard comprehensive general liability (CGL) policies that already apply to offline commercial activities. These CGL standard business policies are a good start. For example, if you sell homemade preserves at your Web site, the fact that a customer buys bad jam from you over the Net doesn't necessarily mean that your insurer won't defend and indemnify you per a policy's terms. If you are an accountant, the fact that you find clients from a Web site presence doesn't mean that your malpractice liability coverage won't cover your errors. Although it seems to the experts that the insurance industry has been narrowing the CGL coverage,

As a general rule, coverage under traditional CGL policies is not excluded simply because you sell online, especially if you created your Web site to complement your normal offline commercial activities. However, do check with your insurance agent for all of the details as to your situation—there may be exclusions.

insurance companies also have been developing specialized policies for their clients' Net activities. *However, you'll want to check out all policies and verify precisely what coverage exists and in what amounts.*

New liabilities occur these days from the Net: programming errors, advertising injury (i.e., copyright infringement, product disparagement, and so on), Net-related defamation and invasion of privacy, losses to numerous users when bad information is provided, spread of computer viruses, security breaches, and theft of online credit card information, to name several. Many insurance companies have beefed up their traditional commercial liability coverage with online policies that guard against specific risks, such as loss of revenue if Web sites crash, loss of reputation (i.e., computer outages cause important data to be lost), stolen trade secrets and business data, e-publishing liabilities (i.e., defamation and copyright infringement lawsuits), and others.

Discuss all of your site's potential Internet liabilities in a "what could go wrong" call with your insurance consultant. You will want to learn the costs, exceptions, and availability of insurance policies that could cover your business's Net activities, both now and in the future. At the same time, check out whether you have adequate insurance coverage for all of your business property, including your expensive computers, systems, and networks. Then, make your decisions.

Although the topic is beyond the scope of this book, you should review closely with your attorney whether your online and offline enterprise should be incorporated, limited liability corporation or partnership, or be protected by other limited-liability concepts. Whether problems are related to financial losses, giving out bad information, or product liability lawsuits, any business can run into unanticipated liabilities, and it's best to consider these issues—before there's a problem. *If you have good net worth built up in your home or other outside assets, you will need to discuss with a business attorney the best ways to protect those assets, should something unanticipated go wrong with your operations.*

Terms of Use Policies

Whether yours is a for-profit business or not, you'll need to decide on the appropriate disclosures and Terms of Use provisions for your operations and Web site. (See Chapter 9, "Web Site Disclaimers and Protections.") What's amazing is many sites still don't have these provisions—even in this modern age—and that is a big mistake. Regardless of whether your users read the provisions or not, these policies give you legal protections, as we've discussed before. Some lawyers argue that you must protect yourself against any and all problems with the most comprehensive and detailed language possible. On the other hand, you risk alienating your users by providing too much legalese with nonunderstandable, long-winded, and boring discussions. *These days, reasonable (not overreaching), understandable, and easy-to-find provisions are in order,* whether you sell products, provide services, or post information.

Some portals and retail-oriented sites have made a conscious trade-off. They place their "condensed" disclaimers in pages accessible from the homepage, but usually the link is found at the very bottom of the page. They condition its effectiveness on simply a user's visit to their site. As we have seen, this approach can run into legal problems if a court holds that a user must do some affirmative act (i.e., "click" on an "I agree" icon) before the requisite consent to those conditions is obtained. *The more your customers and users have to do to affirmatively indicate their approval, the stronger your legal position will be, should you someday find yourself in court.*

Also, place these policies where users can easily see them. *Don't put them in "hard-to-read" or tiny script, as the courts generally will not enforce these. And don't bury them at the bottom of a page, where palmcorder and handheld wireless devices won't show them at all.* You really want your users to see and understand what your rules are.

Other sites provide a much shorter but legally effective version of their Terms of Use and privacy policies—for example, check out the policies of Amazon.com in this regard. Keep in mind a site that simply provides a place to swap stamps doesn't have the same needs as one that sells high-speed racing bikes. After reviewing the concepts of Chapters 8 ("Purchasing on the Net") and 9 ("Web Site Disclaimers and Protections"), take a close look at competitive and other sites, then adapt what you find into your own words. *It's advisable to retain a cyberlawyer to review your drafted policies before you post them—and this approach saves money over hiring a lawyer to draft everything from scratch.*

SPECIFIC AREAS

The following specific disclaimers and provisions should be considered from an owner's or operator's perspective. Note that this is quite different from a user's or consumer's viewpoint (see Chapter 9).

- Keep in mind how global your reach is, especially with sales being derived from other countries. Although there are conflict-of-laws and where-to-sue questions in these cases, it's obviously not possible for you to be in compliance with all possible interpretations of your Terms of Use policies in all countries. *Although you can't meet all of the possible worldwide interpretations, enacting reasonable ones is your safest alternative and best approach.* Consider bilingual access, even if you are marketing now only in the United States or in a one-language region.

Alternately, if your operations become large enough, consider establishing separate pages on your site for access and use by residents of other countries with approaches that are quite different from your standard provisions. These policies, more in keeping with those countries' requirements, will be applicable only to those residents—and in their native language. Further, the largest companies operate different Web sites hosted in the countries in which they have the greatest sales penetration. To get an idea of what this looks like, check out the largest sites and their global coverage (i.e., Yahoo!, Lycos, IBM, Amazon, and so on).

- Put in a disclaimer of liability: the user takes everything "as is"; you disclaim all implied warranties to the extent permitted by law, and, basically, you aren't responsible for any mistakes or negligence.

- As part of this disclaimer, indicate that you're not responsible for any downtime, disconnects, or problems caused by your Internet Service Provider. State you'll check your Web site for postings by others and for hyperlinks, but that you will give no warranty, nor assume any responsibility for them. You don't want to warrant what another sites' policies are or how they follow them, whether their collection of data, accuracy of provided information, or service reliability is at issue.

- Decide what damages a user would incur if you make a mistake, whether you're providing information, services, software downloads, or selling products. Insert a limitation on damages (limit to replacing the purchased product or some dollar amount—but avoid the infamous limit of $1, if you can). You might consider even more reasonable provisions, trading off customer goodwill versus what you truly can afford and should do in the event of a loss.

- Determine the limits on any use of your posted material and information. Ask yourself: To what extent do you really care if everything is duplicated and spread over other sites?

  —As part of this determination, include your statements on copyright ownership and limitations on use. For example, "Any use is limited to one download for personal, noncommercial uses only" or "No derivative uses or modifications are to be made to that download").

  —Insert the © copyright symbol where appropriate. Include proper ℠ and ® trade/service mark identifications.

  —If you don't own all copyrights or trademarks, then identify those that you don't. For example, if you refer to Apple Computer or Microsoft products or hardware, indicate who owns which registered trademarks or copyrights. You can use the language that those companies place on their products.

- If you operate a chatroom, be sure to post your guidelines. These policies can be part of your defense in a defamation lawsuit.

- Prohibit any commercial use of your site through any linking method, and state that any linking to your site, regardless of its nature, is subject to your consent.

- Insert favorable choice of law and venue (the location of the lawsuit) provisions. Although it's unclear as to how these will be legally enforced, they allow room for further negotiation in a high-damage lawsuit.

- Apply the ADRs of mediation and/or arbitration in your policies. (See Chapter 12, "Cyberlaw Dispute Resolution.") The low expense and Net-friendliness of ADRs do pay dividends, and you can always follow the courtroom track if mediation fails.

- State that your terms are subject to change without notice. However, when you do change terms, make the changes conspicuous and highlight them. For example, insert a button that reads "Please see our latest policy revisions."

- For others, check Chapter 9 and other Terms of Use policies, then adapt or modify them accordingly.

Rights of Privacy

From the Web operator's view, the issue of privacy rights is much more than a legal issue. It is a matter of creditability. You need to assure people who don't know you one bit to spend time on your Web site, part with their valued personal information, and then buy what you sell (or accept your information). This also becomes the challenge of balancing the legal requirements and long-winded language we discussed in Chapter 9, "Web Site Disclaimers and Protections," against what your users will tolerate. Whether yours is a for-profit, profit, governmental, or educational site, you should use plain language, think about what your users would worry about, and honestly assure them as to what your true intentions are. Review the policies of other sites in your field, then draft your own, keeping them simple but fair; again, you might retain an experienced lawyer to review that document before you post it.

Be sensitive to the rights of privacy and the confidentiality concerns of others—it's good business. For example, if you will be e-mailing people on "lists," then use this method judiciously. Place the following statement in your e-mail text: "If this type of message is not of interest to you, please reply with the word 'Remove' in the subject line, send it back to us, and you won't hear from us again." *And follow this up by not contacting those people again. Not respecting their wish loses customer good will—and all of us can attest to this.* Be sure that you have a correct address for that reply. There is absolutely nothing more maddening for users and potential customers than to send such a "remove" e-mail, then have it delivered back with an "address unknown" tag. Potential customers and users will remember your site and its logo because of its courtesy (or lack of).

Industry groups also are establishing their own voluntary privacy codes of conduct for members to follow. *The Online Privacy Alliance is an excellent source for privacy information, policies, industry developments, and news on what other companies are doing in this area; check out http://www.privacyalliance.org.* The FTC (ftc.gov) has been active, as well, with its regulations on the Children's Online Privacy Protection Act (COPPA). Should you market to children under the age of 13, you will have more obligations, such as needing to gain the written consent of parents before you can collect information on this age group; and the penalties are high for noncompliance—up to $11,000 *per violation,* depending upon the circumstances.

Your site is subject to COPPA's provisions if it is "directed" toward kids under 13. This depends on the Web site's subject matter, whether the ads center on kids, the age of the models, whether a site uses animated characters or other child-oriented features, and other weighed factors. If so, then you must (1) post clear privacy policies that describe your data practices; (2) provide notice to their parents of this collection; (3) not collect personal info on any children, unless you've obtained "verifiable parental consent" as well; and (4) provide parents with access to their kids' personal data, for review and/or deletion of that information, among other provisions.

Even the FTC advises that the easiest way to comply with COPPA is not to collect personal information from kids under 13. If young children really aren't your target market, then add a provision to your Terms of Use section discouraging kids from using your site (i.e., you will sell only to those 13 and over) or so limiting those who should register with you.

You could use their clicking on the "I Agree" button of your Terms of Use section to verify this, or you could even add a box asking users to certify that they aren't under 13. Even foreign-run Web sites must comply with COPPA if they advertise in the offline U.S. media or on U.S. Web sites. If you do earmark your virtual operations to kids, then you'll have to carefully review COPPA's provisions. See www.ftc.gov at "Kidz Provisions" for more.

SPECIFIC SITE PRIVACY GUIDELINES

The following guidelines will be helpful to you when setting up your privacy policy.

- Users expect that Web sites will have a privacy policy, even if many sites don't yet have them. The FTC is pushing privacy policies, as well as pending federal and state legislation; additionally, litigators are lining up class-action lawsuits to enforce privacy policies and judicially require what one should or shouldn't be doing under them (in addition to large damages). If you show your customers and clients that you place importance on privacy, then your operations can only benefit and you'll gain a competitive edge.

- Be careful of individual privacy areas that concern your operations and are regulated by federal or state statutes. For example, credit collectors, health-care providers and medical record disclosures, insurance companies, and financial institutions (the Gramm-Leach Act requires privacy policy disclosures and protection of personal data, among other areas).

- Look closely at the "opt-in" versus "opt-out" issue. If you must gain a customer's consent before you can collect his or her private data, then that's an opt-in decision (users must click "in" to agree to this before you can collect the information). If you decide on opt-out, then that customer must affirmatively take the steps to stop collection activities (you can collect as much as you want up until that point). Most Web sites now don't make this decision; they only disclose generally what they collect and then do with the data. *Over time, industry standards will rise, and opt-in will become the required choice (although it's expected that the first federal legislation to pass will be opt-out for most sites, with opt-in reserved for those collecting health and financial information). Over time, a pure opt-in regulation will be enacted eventually to apply to all sites.*

- Keep in mind the internationalism of your Net operations—for example, the policies of the European Union (EU) that restrict the import of privacy data. It is expected that the EU initiative will apply over time to many more U.S. firms than as at present. Generally, you may need to obtain a user's consent when you take any private information. Although you can't meet all of the global requirements that could be enacted, adhering to reasonable policies is your safest alternative—and, again, makes good business sense.

- Make your provisions understandable and easy to read. Cover the private information you basically collect and what you do with it. (See Chapter 9, "Web Site Disclaimers and Protections," for the factors to be disclosed.)

- Make the privacy disclosures conspicuous, so that your users can get to this easily. Keep in mind that small handheld wireless devices and palm devices can cut off your policies, especially when placed at the bottom of a page.

- Have a "Frequently Asked Questions" section, to make it easier to answer specific users' concerns. Create an e-mail address for e-mailed questions. This also will allow you to gain borderline customers.

- Watch what advertisers do with any data collected from your site. For example, what would happen if it were disclosed that your Net marketing firm sells your customers' data—with or without your consent?

- Obtain a privacy seal, such as Truste (truste.com), WebTrust (webtrust.org), or BBBOnLine (bbbonline.com). *Truste also has an excellent "build your own" privacy policy at its site.* Given that you can afford one of these programs, then you can use that privacy seal as part of your advertising and further allay users' concerns. Regardless of where your site resides in, pay particular attention to this.

- Follow your privacy policy precisely and always, once you've posted it. Nothing will damage your goodwill faster than the news that you don't follow your posted policies.

- If you change your provisions, then highlight those changes and insert a button reading, "Please See Our New Policies."

When Selling Products or Services

If you plan to sell products over your site, then the issues of sales policies, delivery charges, returns and refunds, online purchase and product registration forms, credit card security, encryption safeguards, and internal security present themselves. On the one hand, users need assurances that their private information and credit card numbers won't be intercepted in cyberspace or misappropriated; on the other hand, you need protection against bogus credit cards. You will need to review security and encryption software and devices (see the next section), and to talk with your bank about designing safeguards against bad credit.

When a Web site accepts online credit-card payments, the risk of fraud increases somewhat, even for well-known merchants. It's not possible to check out the holder and the credit card visually, with signature comparisons, so the risk that an online operator will become victimized by fraud does increase. There are systems that can minimize this risk (enter "credit-card fraud" or a comparable term in your search engine) by ranking potential fraud facts. For example, the telephone area code doesn't match the zip code; a customer uses a free e-mail address (i.e., Yahoo! or hotmail) rather than one to a local provider; large purchases have been charged on that card within a few hours; the shipping address is different from the billing address. By themselves, these events do not necessarily indicate a problem; legitimate purchasers exhibit any number of these factors—but these are high-risk indicators, especially when some or all occur together. *Talk to your bank for software leads, credit systems, or referrals to a credit security expert.*

When you are considering the appropriate policies for returns, refunds, and other policies, check out your competitors. We discussed the major purchasing considerations, from the viewpoint of users, in Chapter 8, "Purchasing on the Net." As we view them now from the sellers' perspective, keep those factors in mind, as well as the requirements of states (e.g., California) that have passed laws regulating refunds and mandating certain disclosures with online retail activities.

Typically, selling services over the Web is less complex than selling products. Because services are more personal, these sites typically are more informational in nature, and less product, sales marketing, or order related. Service providers such as attorneys, dentists, consultants, real estate brokers, insurance agents, and engineers typically don't rely on their Web site as their prime way to attract and secure new clients. However, entities selling information—such as software downloading sites, newspapers and other publications, and even cybermediation locations—do and need to address credit card payment, encryption, and other security concerns.

SECURITY CONSIDERATIONS

It makes sense to talk to your programmer about adding what is called the "Secure Socket Layer" (SSL) technology to encrypt credit card and other sensitive information. This is the "golden padlock" security logo that is seen on sites. If you decide to use such encryption assurance, you can add the following to your homepage:

> At AceHotels, we want you to feel safe and secure when booking your hotel accommodations online with us. For this reason, we use Secure Socket Layer (SSL) technology to encrypt your credit card and other sensitive information when you make reservations for our services. This process of encryption prevents unauthorized individuals from viewing your information as it is securely transmitted over the Internet. Once we've received this, your credit card information is not transmitted again over the Web.

However, your Web site's security doesn't begin or end with the encryption of credit card information. You should conduct a security audit, both inside and out. This means that you review more than how you protect transmitted customer orders, credit card numbers, and other sensitive data with your site. A security audit also looks at how well protected this information is when it's in the hands of your employees.

The studies have indicated the greatest risk to a Web site is from insider access by disgruntled employees, inside fraud and theft, and other internal risks. Keep this in mind when you think about security for your business. You should put adequate safeguards in place, including whether you or another officer independently reviews the orders received, proper crediting of payments, and status of placed orders. A dual-signature requirement should be in effect on any disbursements greater than a set amount—let's say, $500—and stay vigilant for any security "loopholes."

You will want to determine how vulnerable your site is to hackers, software viruses, or its systems being overwhelmed. If needed, ask a software consultant about the best ways to utilize backup data centers, in case your system crashes or a hacker sneaks in. Talk with your ISP representative to see what you can do if its service crashes or has bouts of irregularity.

Put in place rules such as not double-clicking to open unknown or "strange" e-mail and attachments (which avoids receiving certain software viruses). Think about dual-ID requirements. Rather than relying just on a password for entry to sensitive data, add a second requirement—one's Social Security number or a PIN number—especially for entry to sensitive areas or data.

You might hire a security consultant to assist you in these deliberations. *Whether caused from the inside or out, the risk of security breaches is not only financial and intellectual property loss, but also potential civil litigation and damage to your business reputation.* An emphasis on security for your customers and users can also equate into positive assurances, such as, "We at AceHotels take pride in the following procedures for your security . . . ," and then list them.

TAXING THE NET

As we discussed in Chapter 8, "Purchasing on the Net," various U.S. states are already taxing sales made over the Internet, due to preexisting tax laws in effect prior to the enactment of the U.S. federal three-year Internet tax moratorium (which then expired on October 21, 2001). Under well-established tax law, online retailers can charge sales taxes on online sales whenever they have a physical presence in the state where the customer resides.

At the time when this Act expired, 45 states (including the District of Columbia) already were charging some form of a sales tax on tangible products purchased online, if the seller had some form of a physical presence or "nexus" (i.e., a warehouse, retail store, office, or some physical location) in that state. Additionally, 19 states charged an "Internet Access Charge" (allowable under the original three-year moratorium), and 11 states assessed a sales tax on online downloads of software (grandfathered under the provisions of the Act). Two-thirds of the states exempted a pure online sale of software, even when there was a nexus—which meant that one-third of all states already taxed them.

Governmental entities through the Internet Access Charge already are taxing Net access through ISP providers (i.e., your local ISP, CompuServe, or AOL, for example) in lieu of assessing sales taxes, and all when that "moratorium" was in effect. You'll need to check your state (or foreign country, if applicable) sales, use, and other tax structures to see if you have to collect any taxes for the goods and services that you sell over the Web. If so, you'll need to establish a vendor account, meet the deadlines for filing returns, and enclose the appropriate amount due, among other compliance responsibilities. While you're contacting these taxing authorities, you should ask what possibilities exist for additional taxes to be assessed on your Web site in the future—just in case. For example, a few states already are taxing the services of professionals, such as attorneys and accountants.

The U.S. and World Trade Organization (WTO) currently are trying to keep a lid on Internet taxation, but various nations have been taxing goods sold on the

Internet in selected ways. Although the states and nations of the world are chomping at the bit, it is believed that the U.S. approach will be continued in some modified way. Congress is and will continue to look at additional proposals, some favorable to states and others to online sellers. Whatever is enacted will be subject to amendment and continued court challenges. The WTO is expected to follow reluctantly, but as the European Union already taxes certain online sales of goods (such as books and CDs), there are pressures in this regard. The experts wouldn't be surprised at an eventual entirely different result, as every governmental entity looks at the Net as an excellent source of more needed revenues.

As the Internet further erodes the base of revenues that governments receive from traditional "brick-and-mortar" stores and their sales, there are additional pressures to tax Internet sales, at least to this extent—especially when online retail sales are in their growing stage. The great majority of local and state governments back this concept. When it comes to taxing the Internet more in the future, you'll be making an unfortunately good bet that this will happen. The only question is how and when. You'll need to check from time to time to see which ones your site is to assess and collect.

The Technical Considerations

Test your site at length before you open your doors to the virtual public. It's always better if you work out the bugs before your customers find them. You'll want to be sure your e-mail capabilities, chatrooms, encryption on credit card data, links, download time, number of users handled, and other technical aspects are working well. Be sure that your site has the ability to accurately track the "hits" it receives, for both internal use and any advertising contract requirements. Your meta tags and site "labeling" should accurately describe your operations, so that you get the hits you want from interested visitors. If your site is more complicated than most, your use of "cookies" and ways of securing data from your users should be appropriate and reasonable. It makes sense to work up your "corrections" list with your software programmer as soon as possible, and get the repairs made before a user brings them to your attention.

Once you're hooked up, pay particular attention to the sites that are linking to you—or those you've linked with—to ensure that they are the types of sites you want to be affiliated with. As part of this, you will want to gain permissions to link, especially when you plan to deep link or frame.

Advertising Content and Policy

Whether you're selling plants and flowers, financial consulting, or nonprofit services, any discussion of advertising strategy takes two directions. The first is the content of your advertising and whether it is effective but not misleading. The second is the ad content that you accept from others.

There's no question that if you want to be in business for the long term, you need to advertise your business well and deliver to your customers as good as you promise. Goods, services, or information that don't live up to their promises just mean heavier returns, angry e-mail, and complaints to some consumer agency. For example, if you're selling health foods, don't make wild claims. Providing misleading or fraudulent information, of course, isn't a good business strategy—nor is it legal.

> Be careful with what you represent that a product or service can do—these representations will be viewed as an express warranty. If you advertise that "this combination screwdriver will last for years," then it had better do just that. Otherwise, during the next years, you'll be dealing with more returns than sales.

You should be familiar with the FTC's rules on your business (see ftc.gov), if regulated by it. Pay particular attention, moreover, as to how you make your necessary product disclosures. Although making these disclosures in an advertisement is easier in the offline world, it becomes a problem when you're using banner advertisements within more limited space. Wherever you put a disclaimer or warning (i.e., "May not be suitable for outdoor use"), be sure that it is easily readable and accessible when ordering. *Whether you're using a link to a disclaimer site or indicating where a purchaser should scroll to, be sure that getting there is easily understood and prominently displayed.*

If you're accepting the ads of others, take the time to see that these advertisements aren't misleading. Be sure you feel comfortable that any ad content is compatible with your site. Given this, a Web site also needs to accept any advertisements in the context of its overall business strategy. Although the impulse is to accept all ads that come your way, for cash-flow reasons, the better strategy is to take your time and check out the site and people. Try to assess that they will be in business that year (otherwise, you'll be stiffed down the road), and that their Web site looks professional and successful. A form Digital Advertising Agreement is discussed at the end of this chapter for further information.

Online and Offline Marketing

> One of the most important areas—and the subject of numerous books written about the Internet—is online and offline marketing. Marketing campaigns that don't integrate both are doomed to failure. Finding customers for your site is not just a function of having good meta tags in your pages, advertising, and an updating program with search engines, but also that your site has a strong offline marketing program that fits in, as well.

Relying simply on search engines finding your site is not going to give you the assurances of success you want, whether your site sells greeting cards or provides astrology services. Borrow a success secret from the big players: Notice how the large portals and Web sites, like Yahoo! and Amazon.com, advertise directly to the public with expensive TV ads. They know the need to build up brand or Web loyalty, and they understand well that "hits" from search engines aren't enough.

A small site will need a combination of mailing campaigns, old-fashioned "hand shaking" with everyone that's met, always handing out business cards, promotions, local ads, PR releases, and more. Although much of this depends on your budget, the message is clear: *For the success of any site, you can't rely solely on the Web. You have to get the message out in non-Net ways.*

This applies whether you have a profit interest or not. If you have a personal Web site, then print the domain address on your stationery and get the word out. If you're operating a hobby site, advertise it in that hobby's publications. The more visitors you have, the more information and fun contacts you'll enjoy, so work at your advertising, marketing, and public relations to bring about a more successful site.

New Features and Routine Checks

To keep your contacts and visitors coming, you'll need to vary your content and adjust your "look and feel" from time to time. You'll want to post new features and change the approach, to "keep 'em coming." The experts recommend that you design a consistent strategy to develop and post these new features. For example, promise that you will add, each Tuesday, a new saying, or link, or helpful tip. Clean house, every six months or so, by adding different colors or a new category of products or information.

It's also important to regularly check your links and the Web sites that have linked to you. Look at your site from the view of your visitors and customers. They like to freely surf on the links you've created, so be sure that these connections are operable to sites that are still compatible with yours. For example, when one site operator checked his links, he discovered that two linked sites had changed: one was out of business and the other had now posted obscene pictures.

Site owners should check any e-mail postings made on their site in a regular, consistent way. Whether due to software failure, hackers, or even viruses, Web sites are subject to crashing, and operators also need to continuously save their files and Web contents in a separate location. Any changes made to a site should be dated, so that everyone knows when it was last revised.

In the fast world of the Internet, change is the name of the game—and you need to be aware of what others are doing. You will want to use search engines with your site's keywords, slogans, and approach, to find out if any copycat sites have surfaced. If they have, then you'll want to investigate further and see whether a polite request solves the problem. Otherwise, you'll be talking with a lawyer, especially when the situation is important enough.

The experts recommend typing in slight variations on your domain name to see if a copycat has ripped off your trademarks or names. For example, if your domain name is "AceInformation.com," then try "Ace1Information.com." It would be really upsetting to type in "bluemtn.net" (instead of your "bluemtn.com") and discover that a site completely identical to yours is in operation—except for the name and address to contact for further information. However, at least you would know and could make an informed decision on what to do next. (See Chapter 13, "Domain Names and Conflicts" on this.)

Check Out Your Contracts and Due Dates

Before you sign any of your tech contracts, you or your cyberlawyer should closely check out their provisions. We previously discussed Web site development contracts in Chapter 14, "Creating Your Own Web Site." You'll want to be sure you negotiated, as best as possible: (1) who owns the created intellectual property (if you paid for it, you had better own it); (2) to what extent the standard limitations of liability exist (if there is a problem, you don't want to be entitled to $1); (3) the exclusions of liability to third parties (i.e., if the developer infringed on somebody's copyrights in its work, the developer—and not you—should be liable for that infringement); (4) what happens if the developer goes over budget, misses time deadlines, or the site doesn't meet specifications, among other areas discussed.

As important, you should negotiate and thoroughly understand your ISP (Internet Service Provider)/Web site Hosting and/or ASP (Application Service Provider) agreements prior to signing. The ISP and/or Web site host contracts are what open your site to the Internet; they can provide also services such as e-mail delivery and response (among others). ASP contracts provide technical application services such as order processing, encryption, credit card and other security, interactive features, and the like.

It is important in all these contracts that you (and/or your lawyer) define the required service levels, guarantees of service (24/7, 365 days), and the operational warranties that are in place. These business contract provisions should be specific and should detail precisely their obligations, scope of responsibilities, performance standards, how secure your transactions will be, numbers of simultaneous users handled, and commitment to perform what they say they will. Areas need to be addressed, such as, whose responsibility is it to repost data if there's a site crash, or to handle updates; if it is yours, then you'll need to know how to access your site past security codes, and whether there is a cost involved. Be specific as to what functions your site will have, how often, and who is responsible for repairs and maintenance.

As important, watch the one-sided, legal boilerplates of limited liability, no special or indirect damages, services provided "as is," no warranties, and that their law and place controls in these agreements. Judges are inclined to uphold these limiting provisions between sophisticated businessowners, even if the actual damages, due to negligence in systems crashing or not performing, are high. For example, if your ASP or ISP crashed and you lost a long-awaited Valentine's Day or Thanksgiving sales holiday, you had better change the limitations on liability and damages, if you can. Otherwise, all you'll get will be: "We'll try our best to get you up and running again . . . and, by the way, here's one dollar for your damages, per our contract." At least, negotiate ahead of time and don't just settle for what the small print says.

You'll want to see if their response time provisions are satisfactory to you: "We'll get to your problem within 24 hours of receipt of your complaint" won't be a great help. Try to get a faster response time, as well as an estimate of what costs, if any, will be assessed. Who is the "crisis-point person" for your provider, and who will handle your problems in the event that he or she isn't available or can't handle them? *If you can't get relief from the "standard provisions for all," at least be satisfied that you chose the best provider around, tried your best to chisel out legally what you could, arranged backup services in case of an emergency, and understood completely what you did agree to.*

You'll also need to set up a date file as to what needs to be done and by when. Put in this file any equipment leases and the dates by when monthly and final payments are due. The lease on your office should be tagged for when you need to formally extend an option. Advertising contract deadlines and time periods should be detailed. Also, you will want to know when you must renew your domain name and any trademarks.

Keep in mind what the quite large and prestigious, multibillion-dollar banking conglomerate of J.P. Morgan & Company discovered. All of its operations were disconnected from its Web site until it paid a $35 annual renewal fee on its domain name. It was lucky: no one else grabbed that name during the suspension. At one time, even Microsoft forgot to renew the registration of a domain name critical to its Hotmail e-mail service. You don't want to do this.

Train Your Employees, Well

Should you have employees, continually training your workers is an important managerial function—especially when part or all of your operations involve the Internet. In addition to training people on how best to perform their tasks, conflict resolution, teamwork, and the like, you need to train employees on the proper use of the Net. As we observed at Chapter 4, "Copying in Cyberspace," copyright owners own their creations whether or not they're posted on the Internet, don't have a copyright notice affixed, or lack whatever common fable exists as to their ownership. It is too easy for part-time and full-time workers to get a company into trouble by injudiciously copying posted material, sending defamatory e-mails, or treating the Internet as a fun place to surf while on company business (i.e., "researching" adult Web sites while in the presence of others).

Your Web site and its operations are your business. Put in place a reasonable Internet Use Policy, train your employees on how best to follow this policy, and explain why it is important for them to adhere to it. Simply having your employees sign such a policy might not be enough; the more employees you add over time, the less ability you have to monitor what they are doing on their "breaks." Filtering software, which prevents workers from viewing certain types of sites, is available; however, before buying any particular filter, check out how effective it is. It's also possible to monitor when and where your employees visit the Net while using company equipment. However, the question always is: How much monitoring should you do, given that you've hired first-rank, trustworthy employees in the first place?

Two final forms follow here: a *Digital Advertising Agreement* and an *Internet Use Policy.* The ad agreement can be used whether you're the advertiser or the ad-selling Web site. The Internet Use Policy sets down the allowable terms and use by your employees, whether regular or part-time, on your computer facilities and software. Regardless of how extensive or formal your Internet Use policy is, you should have one in place. For those important policies and agreements, consult also your cyber-lawyer over your questions—to avoid later, expensive legal disputes.

Digital Advertising Agreement

This Digital Advertising Agreement is entered on [*Date of Agreement*] between [*Name of Site Hosting Ad*], called the "Provider," and [*Name of Customer*], called the "Customer." The parties, in consideration of the mutual promises made by each other and other valuable consideration, agree as follows:

1. **Agreement and Term.** The Provider operates a host site known as [*Common Name or Domain Name of Web Site*] and which is located at http:[*Specify Web Address*]. Provider sells advertising where the graphics of advertisers are shown on its site and host-site users can "point and click" on such a hyperlink and move to the customer's advertised Web site. Under the terms of this Agreement, Provider agrees to provide advertising services for Customer in return for Customer's agreement to pay for this right. The Term of this Agreement shall be for [*State Number of Months*] months, beginning on [*State Beginning Date of Agreement*] and ending on [*State Ending Date of Agreement*].

2. **Service Provided and Fee.** Provider offers advertising programs on its Web site at different costs. Provider and Customer agree for the Provider to provide the following advertising service: [*Describe the Advertising Program Details*]. In return for providing this service, Customer agrees to make a monthly payment of $[*State Monthly Payment*], plus any applicable sales tax, all payable within [*State Grace Period in Days*] days of receipt of billing.

   Should Customer not pay any invoice within the period set above, then a service charge of [*State Percentage Monthly Service Charge*]% is payable each month until that balance, and all other monthly balances, are paid in full.

3. **Advertising Layout and Location.** Customer shall submit its digitized graphics and advertisements at least [*State Days Lead-Time for Graphics Submittal*] days ahead of when that ad is scheduled to run. All advertisements must meet Provider's specifications attached at the end of this Agreement, and Provider has full discretion over whether to accept the ads or not, regardless of their meeting the specifications or not. The advertising shall be placed at the following location: [*State Specific Location of Advertising Graphics or Logo*].

4. **Continual Operation and Provider Warranties.**

   (a) **Continual Operation.** Provider shall make all commercially reasonable efforts to cause its host site to be fully functional and operational, twenty-four hours a day, seven days a week. It warrants to Customer that it will make all reasonable efforts to perform its services under this Agreement in a competent manner. Provider will also institute a commercially reasonable method of collecting and analyzing data related to its advertisements, Customer's ad, the traffic, number of "hits" and impressions, and other information so that Customer can make reasonable decisions regarding the efficiency of Provider and its advertisement.

   (b) **No Warranty on Continuous Operation.** Customer understands that unforeseen technological problems and "glitches" can occur. Provider does not warrant that operations will be continuous, nor that they will be error-free. Accordingly, it can not warrant that Customer always will receive uninterrupted availability of its host site to all potential users, nor that users will always be directed to Customer's Web site.

   (c) **Minimum Monthly Impressions.** Provider does warrant that Customer will receive a minimum of [*State Number of Minimum Monthly Impressions per Month*] minimum monthly impressions, defined as follows: [*Define Minimum Monthly Impressions per Month*]. Should customer in any month not receive the agreed minimum monthly impressions per month, regardless of the reason, then Customer shall receive additional time on its advertisement at no charge until that ad receives the additional number of impressions necessary to make up that deficit.

   (d) **Disclaimer of Implied Warranties.** Provider makes no warranty regarding any third party provided features or services. But for any contrary provisions in this Agreement, PROVIDER DISCLAIMS ALL IMPLIED WARRANTIES, INCLUDING BUT NOT LIMITED TO, THE WARRANTIES OF MERCHANTABILITY AND FITNESS FOR A PARTICULAR PURPOSE.

Digital Advertising Agreement *(Continued)*

5. **Copyrights, Reports, and Provider Liabilities.**

   (a) **Copyrights.** Each party retains its ownership rights and copyrights in their respective Web Sites; provided, however, Customer grants Provider a no-cost, nonexclusive license to set up and display Customer's advertisement (including its trademarks and copyrights) during the term of this Agreement— which license shall end at the termination of this contract.

   (b) **Reports.** Provider will provide Customer with monthly reports within *[Days within which Reports Are to be Provided]* days after the end of each month. These reports will report the ad traffic, number of "hits" and impressions, and other data, as normally reported by Provider's information systems.

   (c) **Provider Liabilities.** Provider shall not be responsible to Customer for "downtime" or errors owing to acts of God, electrical shortages, brown-outs, riot, strikes, or any other reason beyond its reasonable control; provided, however, that should this interruption continue for more than *[State Number of Days Interruption before Customer Can Cancel]* days, then Customer at its option may cancel this Agreement without penalty.

   In the event that any failure to display Customer's advertisement is owing to Customer's fault, then Customer shall not be entitled to any reduction in the advertising fee. If the failure to display this advertising is owing to Provider's fault, act, or omission, then Customer, at its option, shall be entitled to a pro-rata refund of its advertising payments to the extent of such downtime or being credited with free time until the minimum monthly impressions set forth at Section 4(c) has been achieved.

   Provided, however, PROVIDER SHALL NOT BE RESPONSIBLE, OR LIABLE, FOR ANY INDIRECT OR CONSEQUENTIAL DAMAGES (i.e., LOST DATA OR REVENUES) SUFFERED BY CUSTOMER, OWING TO PROVIDER'S FAULT AND REGARDLESS OF NATURE.

6. **Customer's Warranties.** Customer warrants that its advertisement (a) does not violate any copyright, trademark, or other right owned by any other party; (b) does not contain any threatening, obscene, defamatory, or other hurtful material; (c) does not violate any foreign, federal, state, local, or other law or regulation; and (d) is truthful and not misleading.

7. **Indemnification.** But for the provisions of this Agreement, each party agrees to fully defend, indemnify, and hold harmless, the other, its officers, employees, and agents, from any and all claims, actions, or controversies, including reasonable attorney fees and court costs, owing to its negligence, fault, or breach of any warranty or representation. Each party shall provide immediate notice to the other of any such claim, action, or controversy, and shall cooperate with that party at the cost of whichever party is at fault.

8. **Termination.**

   (a) This Agreement shall terminate by itself at the end of a specific term as indicated in Section 1 above.

   (b) Should any payment not be made by Customer when due, then the Provider may terminate this Agreement without penalty after the expiration of a written *[State Days within which Payment Must be Received]* days notice to pay and payment has not been so received.

   (c) Either party may terminate this Agreement without penalty, provided the other party has committed a material breach of a provision of this Agreement, and such failure continues uncured after a 30-day notice period to that party to correct that breach.

   (d) Either party may terminate this Agreement without penalty in the event that the other party materially changes the "look and feel," content, or structure of its Web site; provided that a 30-day notice to cure such breach has been given and such failure continues uncured after that period.

   (e) Customer may terminate this Agreement without penalty in the event that Provider, for whatever reasons, does not maintain continuous operations for *[State Number of Days Interruption before Customer Can Cancel]* days. This right is in addition to any time credits or pro-rata refund of advertising paid for as permitted by this Agreement.

Digital Advertising Agreement *(Continued)*

9. **Other.** Any dispute arising in connection with this Agreement shall be first settled by mediation. If that's not successful, then the dispute shall be settled by arbitration to be held in [*Location of Arbitration*] in accordance with the rules of the American Arbitration Association. This agreement to arbitrate shall be specifically enforceable. Any award shall be final and binding on all parties, and a final judgment may be entered in the appropriate court of law. Notwithstanding this, should any litigation ensue between the parties, then the prevailing party shall be entitled to reasonable expenses and attorney fees as set by the Court.

   This Agreement is the final understanding between the parties on this subject matter, superceding all other previous agreements, and may be amended only by the written consent of all the parties. Should any court or proceeding determine that any provision is illegal or in conflict, then all other remaining provisions shall be held severable, valid, and be given separate legal effect.

   Neither party may assign this Agreement without the consent of the other, which consent shall not be unreasonably withheld. This Agreement shall bind all the parties, their respective estates, successors, and permitted assigns; its legality and interpretation shall be governed by the laws of the State of [*Name of State Whose Laws Govern*] and of the United States.

   This Agreement is accepted, understood, and executed as of the date first above written, by and between:

_____

[*Name and Title of Party Signing for Provider*]
[*Provider's Name and Address*]

_____

[*Name and Title of Party Signing for Customer*]
[*Customer's Name and Address*]

[*Attach Provider's Advertising Specifications as a Separate Exhibit*]

Digital Advertising Agreement

Discussion of Provisions

1. **Agreement and Term.** An Internet or digital advertisement is where a hypertext link exists between the advertising Web site and the advertised site. A customer clicks on the graphics at the host or provider's site and is immediately moved to the advertised site that is paying for that advertisement. This contract is different from a linking contract (with payment) by the emphasis placed on the ad use, advertising contents and counts, graphics, location, and host provider provisions. There is typically a stated term with a beginning and ending date.

2. **Service Provided and Fee.** Advertising providers can provide any number of programs, ranging from stationary or static displays (where the ad is displayed without movement or rotation on the Host Web Pages) to rotating displays (where the ad moves on different pages, whether the pages have been assigned or not). Customers need to select among these differing programs and costs. Because people don't always pay their obligations, a penalty for late payment (i.e., a service charge after an agreed grace period) is provided in this form contract, along with termination provisions.

3. **Advertising Layout and Location.** All advertisements should meet prior agreed-on specifications and design criteria. This contract allows for the provider's specifications to be attached at the end of the contract. The agreement also needs to provide where the advertisement is to be located, down to the page and precise area. Some contracts attach a Web page layout indicating the precise location of an ad, including the points to where it will move over time.

4. **Continual Operation and Provider Warranties.** This contract sets forth that the host advertising site (or provider) will collect data on the users of the advertisement, so that the advertiser knows how effective the ad is. If the provider hasn't agreed to such data collection, then this language would be deleted.

   As good money is being paid for the ad placement, advertisers want to have the site and their ads shown on a continuous basis. This contract states that the provider "shall make all commercially reasonable efforts" to cause its site to be continually operated—but no warranty is given in this regard. Although providers shy away from giving strong warranties of continuous operations, with penalties for violations (they have limited control over their ISP's connections, among other variables), one way to give an advertiser the necessary assurances is to allow a free-time credit to regain any "hits" that were missed when the site went down.

   One approach to achieve this is to set a minimum number of guaranteed impressions each month, whereby free time is given so that the advertiser can receive those minimum hits. This Agreement uses this approach in return for a disclaimer of implied warranties. If other approaches are utilized, then this language would accordingly need to be changed.

5. **Copyright, Reports, and Provider Liabilities.** Each party retains its copyrights, of course, in its respective Web site. If the provider has agreed to collect data, this section reflects that it will supply the customer with the necessary reports; the time within which these reports are to be supplied will need to be determined.

   The question of downtime is also addressed. If this is due to an "act of God," then the customer's sole right is to terminate this agreement after a set number of days. If this downtime is within the provider's control, then the customer has the right to a pro-rata refund. Given an adjustment or refund of the advertising payments based on the provider's fault, this form contract does not hold the provider responsible for consequential damages—which is typical of the standard contracts that Web hosts provide. This, as well as all other provisions, can be negotiated to reach different understandings from what's presented in this form.

6. **Customer's Warranties.** The customer warrants basically that its advertisements will not cause the provider to be sued over their content. Although the host has the ability to screen the ads, it is usual for the advertiser to be held responsible for its content—especially given the worldwide markets that are exposed by Internet advertising.

Digital Advertising Agreement *(Continued)*

7. **Indemnification.** A mutual indemnification provision is present so that whichever party is "at fault" will contractually protect the innocent one that's financially injured by that negligence. Further, any party that doesn't live up to its warranties and representations must protect the other from those results. There is no continuous-operation warranty by the provider in this form, as the customer has the rights of termination and offset of advertising payments, along with the provider's assurances of making "all commercially reasonable efforts" to cause the site to be continuously operational.

8. **Termination.** The Agreement can end by its term concluding without renewal; by the customer not making a required payment after a notice period; one or both parties violating a material provision of the contract (i.e., a warranty is violated), after a notice period to cure; and by the provider not being in continuous operations for an agreed number of days. Further, there is a right of termination in the event that either Web site changes materially from what it first was. It may very well be that the "material" change of a Web site to attract a different type of audience could turn off users, to the detriment of either site.

9. **Other.** See the discussion at this section for previously discussed forms.

Internet Use Policy

This Internet Use Policy of [*State Name of Company*] sets forth our policies regarding the appropriate use of our computers, e-mail, networking, software, telecommunication, and other Company equipment, systems, and facilities.

1. **Company Ownership.** We, as employer, own all of the computer equipment, software, networking, e-mail, telecommunication systems, and all other facilities. Our employees are allowed access to this equipment, these facilities, and the Internet solely to allow them to perform their job responsibilities better and further the objectives of [*State Name of Company*]. All of our facilities are to be used strictly for business purposes, unless an area has been designated as available to be used for personal purposes. For example, smoking areas have been designated outside for the use of employees, and coffee rooms may be used for short personal discussions.

2. **Business Purposes and E-Mail Usage.** All employees should use the Company's computers, e-mail and telecommunication systems, and all other systems or facilities for business and not personal purposes. Further, all employees should exercise caution in their usage of e-mail for communications. E-mail messages last more than a lifetime, so all workers should avoid making derogatory statements about other employees, the Company, competitive products, and others.

3. **Monitoring E-Mail and Ownership.** [*State Name of Company*] has the right and obligation to monitor all aspects of its computer, communication, e-mail, telecommunication, and other systems. This includes, but is not limited to, monitoring Web sites visited by employees, reviewing e-mail sent and received by employees, and other inspections. All employees, having previously read and signed our statements on this and other Company policies, understand that e-mail messages received or sent on Company computers are business communications that are the property of [*State Name of Company*], not personal or confidential information that belongs to employee.

4. **Respecting Copyrights and Trademarks.** All employees should respect and avoid infringing on the copyrights, trademarks, and intellectual property rights of others when using the Internet. The Company strictly prohibits the use of our facilities to conduct any illegal activities, including the violation of the intellectual property rights of others. For example, care should be taken when copying material on the Internet to avoid creating copyright infringement complaints that could come back against the Company.

5. **Internet Access and Use.** Employees may access the Internet only through our Internet system and protecting devices. Any other access is prohibited unless the accessing computer is connected to our computer network. All material downloaded from computers, files, or the Internet from outside the Company should be screened for viruses before being placed on Company computers or files. Each employee should use all due care in any transmission of sensitive company information, trade secrets, and the like.

6. **Prohibited Activities and Use.** Employees may not use our facilities for any non-Company purposes, including, but not limited to, any personal, illegal, sexual harassing, obscene, discriminatory, or other offensive/non-Company actions. Further, employees may not use our equipment or facilities for non-Company purposes, such as personal business activities, illegal endeavors, or any other activities that don't further our business goals and objectives.

7. **Passwords.** All employees should advise [*State Name of Company*] of all passwords and access codes to their computers and programs. This is in case of illness, emergency, and for security purposes. Under no circumstances, should any employee use unauthorized passwords to access any files or programs of the Company. Further, no employee should access the computers, files, or programs of any other employee or representative without their express consent.

Internet Use Policy *(Continued)*

The undersigned employee has read, understands, and agrees to abide by this Internet Use Policy, as indicated by his or her signature. Employee further understands that a violation of this policy and its provisions may be grounds for discipline pursuant to the Company's policies, including termination, among other remedies.

_____   _____
[Employee's Name and Title]   *[Date of Signature]*

_____   _____
[Owner's or Manager's   *[Date of Signature]*
Name and Title]

Internet Use Policy

Discussion of Provisions

1. **Company Ownership.** The basic premise of an Internet Use Policy is that since the company owns the computers, e-mail, telecommunications, and other equipment and facilities, it can impose reasonable business constraints on their use. This written policy serves to establish this ownership, as well as the "code of conduct" for its employees. Establishing such a written policy—and following it—can also reduce a firm's legal exposure when an employee acts inappropriately.

2. **Business Purposes and E-Mail Usage.** This provision establishes that the company has the right to expect its employees will only use this equipment and facilities for business purposes. Also, that each employee needs to be especially watchful on e-mail communications, given their distribution and long-term viewing potential.

3. **Monitoring E-Mail and Ownership.** Although monitoring employee communications is an especially controversial provision and practice, the courts have generally upheld this policy, given the firm's ownership of that equipment (including e-mail applications) and a reasonable business purpose. As this area of employer monitoring is especially regulated, both federally and state-wide, you should consult legal counsel before implementing such a practice.

4. **Respecting Copyrights and Trademarks.** Another potential area for company liability is in the area of employee violation of another's intellectual property rights. It is too easy for employees to surf and copy on the Net, as they may do at home; these provisions need to set the limits at work.

5. **Internet Access and Use.** Regulating Internet access to the company's equipment can reduce the danger of viruses and security breaches occurring.

6. **Prohibited Activities and Use.** An essential ingredient of any Internet Use Policy is what the firm considers to be prohibited conduct. This section can be broadened, depending on your firm's business and how widely its software applications may reach.

7. **Passwords.** In case of an emergency or illness, the owner or manager should be able to access work files when the employee is absent.

Given your specific work circumstances, additional provisions may and should be added (i.e., handling of customer private data, transferring credit-card information, and others).

17

The Internet Faces More Legal Shape-Shifting Ahead

Hold onto your hats, the Internet hurricane of change is still howling—but inside your office or study. Every day, after you've turned on your computer, it seems that something new has surfaced or something "old" has changed. The pace of technological change continues unabated, as we all know.

Three areas of change stand out: the continued growth of selective B2C (business-to-consumer) markets in areas such as banking, financial transactions, and general consumer goods; an acceleration in B2B (business-to-business) activities, where businesses are dealing directly with suppliers through Internet networks; and last, but not least, the connection of wireless phones and other devices with the Net.

The growth in B2B activities will deliver even more significant gains in productivity and lower costs, as companies continue to set up private marketplaces with their suppliers. Purchasing today is being done more and more by bid, auction, and competitive pricing from virtual worlds of suppliers. From Boeing and General Motors to the smallest of companies and entrepreneurs, businesses are opening up their channels of distribution to go direct to their customers, along with dealing direct with all of their suppliers and distributors—to obtain the best price and delivery time for inventory, supplies, equipment, and raw material requirements.

Once wireless technology is connected cheaply with voice recognition, the impact will be even greater. People will be able to do from a phone many of the things that they now do over a personal computer, from e-commerce and multibidding on purchases to checking inventory and stock valuations. Soon, when you call a customer center for technical support, the service representative will help you by transmitting multimedia content to your computer, or via your cellular phone, to visually show you what to do.

Small businesses around the world are seeing the advantages of the Net, from making online applications for needed equipment leasing and loans (see Sierra-Cities at www.sierracities.com) to broadening their customer bases—just like their larger corporate counterparts. Small retail shops and service companies can extend their marketing coverage past once-confining, geographical locations. Service professionals, from plumbers to doctors, are similarly motivated.

These trends are impacting the basic fabric of all institutions around the world, including the legal world. Federal and state courts are opening up virtual offices, as well as sponsoring seminars across the country to educate attorneys on just when and how virtual e-documents can be filed in their districts. Already effective, the U.S. District Court for Oregon requires attorneys to register to receive e-mail verification of orders, opinions, and findings, as part of a new requirement for electronic filing; only "good cause indicating a lack of computer technology to access the Internet" allows a lawyer to not so register (and see www.ord.uscourts.gov further). State courts are heading in the same direction—check out the Federal and state court in your area as to what they're doing virtually.

Virtual legal-document delivery services are also developing. For example, JusticeLink.com is fine-tuning its e-filing service. A lawyer can serve or deliver documents from his or her computer to the Web site; JusticeLink then notifies the court and other parties that a document has been filed. From there, the document is available for viewing, downloading, and printing by the judge, clerks, and all of the parties. The speed, availability, and ability to cut down on lost documents are prime advantages, not to mention the convenience and substantial cost savings.

Cyberbanking is already a reality; virtual banks advertise for deposits in newspapers and on TV. They pay higher interest owing to their low overhead (i.e., no expensive brick-and-mortar branches or personnel to worry about). Regardless of your bank, making deposits and payments electronically is accessible to all. Customers in an area where loan rates are high can e-mail applications to lending Web sites for loans that are offered nationally at lower interest rates. An independent escrow office in the borrower's locality closes the loans, and these financial institutions weren't even imagined a few years ago. Cyberbanks have completely changed banking to where you can get a loan or make a deposit without leaving your office or home.

Stock markets have instituted "after-hours" Net trading and are moving to virtual trading, discarding the "old" way of stockbrokers yelling at each other over a brokerage floor to put trades together. For example, the brick-and-mortar Pacific Stock Exchange (pacificex.com) joined with Archipelago (tradearca.com) to develop a totally open, electronic stock market as a new national exchange. Archipelago is one of the original four electronic communications networks (ECNs) approved by the U.S. Securities and Exchange Commission (SEC) in 1997 to establish electronic trading and exchanges. The exchange adopted proposed rules for a new, fully electronic trading system for equity options—and all exchanges are moving in this virtual direction. Individual customers can create personalized investment Web pages and make all of their stock, bond, and money market transactions over the Internet.

Politicians have discovered a better weapon to raise money than the strong handshake and jolly slap on the back. Today, credit cards and the click of a mouse are replacing this traditional way of doing "business." From Bill Bradley and John McCain to George Bush and Al Gore for the year 2000 Presidential elections, today's political candidates raise millions of dollars through Internet campaign Web sites. Their sites attract tens of thousands of volunteers ordinarily not available, all discovering one easy location in which to match interests.

Moreover, the First Amendment has been doing just fine, so far, in cyberspace. As discussed before, the courts have upheld the rights of complaint "suck.coms" to parody and skewer numbers of companies and celebrities—and with more freedom than traditional media outlets are willing to assume. In Quebec, organizers put together an online boycott against high gasoline prices (see abacom.com/essence), and a similar site (gasbusters.net) allows visitors to compare gasoline prices throughout Canada. No medium ever invented has had such an ability to zip across geographical boundaries, centralize information, and communicate with such large populations of people.

Cutting Out the Middleman

So far, the consumer has been gaining the benefit from the ability to comparison-shop and to use online auction sites for even the most inexpensive items. The cost efficiencies of selling direct to customers (and needing to meet competing Web sites head-on) has forced manufacturers to modify their existing wholesale and retail distribution relationships. From vehicles and earthmoving equipment to perfume and clothing, manufacturers have established Web sites to sell their products or give information that is in direct competition with their distributors. There is no stopping this trend, as B2B and B2C consumers go direct to save money, and all businesses recognize these advantages in turn.

Traditional retailers have fought back, both in the courts and by creating their own Net presence—and winning the war, in many cases. For example, traditional bookstores sued virtual stores on false-advertising grounds, to try and preserve their competitive edge. Representing over 3,000 stores and textbook retailers, the National Association of College Stores sued VarsityBooks.com over its advertised discounts. In 1997, Barnes & Noble similarly sued the then upstart Amazon.com for false advertising, in part over Amazon.com's use of the words "the world's largest bookstores" in its advertising. The lawsuit was settled six months later, and Barnes & Noble, six months after that, started up its own Internet site. These battles will continue until the online and offline industries have adjusted to each other's competitive presence. Over time, the only question will be what companies provide these services—not whether these virtual services will be provided at all.

Franchisers (e.g., McDonald's, 7–11, or Subway) as a whole didn't anticipate the rise of the Net in the beginning. Their standard franchise agreements didn't prohibit their individual stores from using this form of "advertising," so their franchisees created their own Web sites—all in competition with their franchisers, or the people that licensed them to do business in the first place. The attorneys and sometimes the courts have had to sort out these differences.

While the competition heated up over which entity would have the dominant Net presence, the traditional "middleman" function was either changed or dented. For example, the travel industry and the airlines battered the poor travel agents with their Web sites, and airlines relied more and more on the direct sale of tickets through these sites. New travel-oriented Web sites, like Travelocity, Expedia, and Priceline.com (with its "name your own price" approach), rose and grew in this climate. Destination sites created their own Web presence, whether they were hotels, amusement parks, or museums.

Railroads and transportation companies also saw the advantages and challenges of the Internet. One of the largest railroads in North America, Union Pacific (UP), has offered its customers the Net to trace their shipments across the United States, dating back to 1995. Via its Web site, customers can locate reduced rates on shipments where UP has empty cars to fill. Burlington Northern Santa Fe experimented with establishing an Internet marketplace for buyers and sellers of freight transportation. Numbers of railroads use the Internet for tracking, and, through the North American Freight Rail Industry, have established "Steelroads" (www.steelroads.com) where customers can bid on shipments and access information on every major freight rail carrier in the United States.

After watching the rapid growth of the Net, and how e-mail and e-commerce have eaten into its core business of delivering first-class mail, the U.S. Postal Service is joining e-commerce rather than fighting it. It's offering a fee-based, online service that allows the secure transfer of sensitive documents, such as medical records and birth certificates. Called NetPost™ Certified, this service is an electronic version of certified mail. The Social Security Administration is testing this program. (For more, see the U.S. Postal Service site at usps.gov.) The Postal Service is also developing numbers of other e-commerce activities, ranging from electronic payment systems to online mailing and virtual stamp purchasing. Offsetting a portion of the first-class mail declines, parcel shipments are increasing, owing to the increasing online sales of products.

As businesses cope with the challenges of the Net, they are also reaping cost benefits because of the Internet's great efficiencies. From American Airlines to Italy's Alitalia, airlines across the globe have created systems on the Internet for public flight information, bookings, and e-tickets, as well as private sites to reduce their paperwork burden when dealing with suppliers. Instead of sending paper invoices and data back and forth, they use the Internet for paperless transactions. From airport operations and airplane maintenance to cost control and sales, airlines are using the Net to streamline their businesses—just like every other industry. These developments are as important as the cost-efficient ways companies have discovered to sell over the Internet. And as traditional companies clash over how to best preserve their ways of doing business, the legal disputes and battles escalate.

Selling Wine, Lawyers, and Doctors

The ability of the Internet to destroy geographical borders runs into direct conflict with local and state laws. For example, there were only 100 wineries in the United States 30 years ago; today, there are over 2,000. During this time period, the numbers of wholesale wine distributors consolidated from 5,000 dealers to fewer than 250, leaving small wineries in a lurch to sell their products. The Internet then changed all of that. With their excellent premium wines, small wineries can now sell direct without undue worry over the problem of limited wholesale distribution. A Sonoma or Napa Valley winery in California can sell its wine now over the Internet to customers from Washington State to Connecticut, right? Sorry, it's not.

The direct sale of wine across state lines is regulated by all 50 states, of which about half make this act illegal. In some states, even the interstate transportation of wine (which includes online sales) is a felony. The wine wholesalers, of course, generally support these laws and their enforcement.

In the pro-Internet corner are the small wineries, brewers, and distillers that rely on the Internet for their sales. In the other corner are the wholesalers, legislators, and regulators who worry about the loss of tax revenues for their local producers, not to mention the difficulty in policing online purchases by underage kids. These concerns and disputes spilled into the courts and legislators' hands.

A Missouri state appeals court held that a North Carolina microbrewery couldn't sell to Missouri residents over the Internet, unless the company complied with its consumer protection laws (which meant Missourians had to go somewhere else). Congress keeps getting close to enacting legislation that would allow state authorities to prosecute violations of state alcohol laws in federal courts. Regardless of what laws are enacted, it's only a matter of time before lawsuits are filed to challenge whatever's passed legislatively. In various areas, the Internet is rapidly becoming a litigating attorney's best dream.

At the same time, lawyers have created Web sites hawking their services to a global public. Whereas only a few years ago, state bar associations jealously guarded the jewels of in-state legal work from attorneys not licensed by their state, lawyers from Florida to California can now beam into the living rooms of all other states. The ability to charge comparatively smaller fees to advise virtual clients on matters ranging from adopting a child to drawing up a will is sending shivers down this profession's spine.

Rushing in to fill this market niche, Web sites signed on celebrities to pitch their "cyberability" to meet the needs of nearly every legal consumer, no matter where located. Harvard law professor Arthur Miller joined AmeriCounsel, and former New York mayor Ed Koch signed up with TheLaw. These and other sites opened up a business and personal national consumers' market for lawyers, right inside the heart of the varying state laws and regulations on this subject.

The legal issue is which state laws regulate when a businessperson—let's say, with operations in Colorado—e-mails questions over a portal hosted in New York to an attorney's Web site in Florida. Among these conflicting jurisdictions, which states have the regulatory authority over the lawyer and this transaction? As with many other professions (i.e., from doctors and pharmacists to accountants and civil engineers), the legal profession is tightly governed by rules, including those of 50 individual state bar associations. The American Bar Association is trying to address these concerns, but this issue will take years to sort out.

Meanwhile, the medical field is not lagging behind; it's beset with similar opportunities and challenges. Former U.S. Surgeon General C. Everett Koop and Dr. Andrew Weil similarly offer medical advice and other services, at present, over the Net. Check out Dr.Koop.com (drkoop.com) and Ask Dr. Weil (drweil.com). It's only a matter of time before medical portals offer referrals to medical practitioners in your locality, complete with background information, office hours, and even typical fees.

All professional associations these days are facing Web sites that give information out to potential patients, clients, and customers, and state licensing boards are taking issue with this "practice without a required state license." This area will be well litigated over time.

Selling Prescriptions Online

Another conflict between the Web's global ability to sell products and the prohibition of local laws is seen in the filling of online prescriptions, given that the online pharmacy business has rocketed upward over the past few years. The problem is that where local pharmacies are subject to the close scrutiny of state regulators, the sale of online prescriptions at this time isn't. While customers flock to the Net due to the cost savings, the regulators are pointing an accusing finger at pharmacists unlicensed in their states who are okaying, from distant places, the prescription drugs to be sold online to their residents.

The Attorneys General of Kansas and Missouri (among other states) filed lawsuits against several online pharmacies and physicians, charging that this was the unauthorized practice of medicine and pharmacy, and won temporary restraining orders. In one notable Missouri case, the online site was ordered to pay back Missouri residents who bought prescriptions from the site, pay a $15,000 fine, and post that it could not sell prescriptions to Missouri residents via the Internet.

The National Association of Boards of Pharmacy (NABP, at nabp.net) established a seal program in 1999, entitled Verified Internet Pharmacy Practice Sites (VIPPS). To be VIPPS and seal certified, an Internet site must comply with all licensing and inspection requirements of their state *and each state they deliver pharmaceuticals to.* Several of the largest retail drug chains and some online pharmacies have met the certification standards of this voluntary program. Congress, meanwhile, is currently debating legislation on this issue. Again, there's no question that laws eventually will be passed regulating these online sales, just as there's no doubt that online prescription drug sales are here to stay.

The same drug companies that want to regulate online prescription sales are also concerned over whether the Food and Drug Administration (FDA), or its equivalent in other countries, will enforce their rules on international Web sites. The problem is that these global sites, with their drugs and information, may be legal in one country but illegal in another. It will take an international treaty to sort out these details.

Bypassing State Authorities

The same issue of products and services bypassing the regulators and entering a state is seen in many other situations. State Attorneys General have been busy issuing interpretive decisions stating that their laws control certain Net activities when it comes to their residents, but the jurisdictional and conflict-of-laws questions keep arising.

Internet gambling is another fascinating, but legally troubling development to regulators. Located in the Bahamas or other countries where gambling is allowed, offshore gambling sites with 24-hour, credit-card-only virtual casinos have sprung up. What happens when those Internet operations, available to the citizens of the world, run afoul of contrary local laws?

One New York case held in 1999 that the operators of a Net gambling casino based in Antigua violated New York State and federal U.S. anti-gambling laws. This was the first case to hold that no matter where an online gambling site was located, if it created a virtual casino in a local resident's computer, then this operation was subject to the jurisdiction of local law. The court held that the gambling site could only avoid New York's, and any other locality's jurisdiction, by making a good-faith effort to screen out unauthorized users in states or places where the law prohibited those activities.

In an ironic twist, the casinos and banks began complaining about a tactic that their customers began using. For example, when one gambler couldn't pay her massive MasterCard and Visa gambling debts (which amounted to $115,000 in total) on 12 credit cards, the gambler's attorney argued that these debts were unenforceable. As a general rule, courts won't enforce illegal contracts and will "leave the parties where it finds them" in these types of cases. A gambling debt is such an illegal contract, and that's exactly what happened in this case. Congress is currently debating laws that would prohibit all or some forms of gambling over the Internet—and other countries are debating the same issue.

At the same time, police are scrambling to keep up with cybercrimes. In 2000, New York City authorities charged one Las Vegas man with peddling the date-rape drug "Special K" from his Web page. The accused posted a message in a newsgroup about the drug's availability through his site. Although they signed a disclaimer that this drug's sale into their home state didn't violate any laws, NYC investigators ordered the banned substance. When the undercover cops received the delivered drug, they promptly served an arrest warrant. The court fights in this case are still going on. More and more, we'll be reading stories about local authorities arresting people for their Net operations, and the courts will be forced to set down the applicable First Amendment standards.

An Alarming Trend

There's no question that the megasites and huge portals (such as AOL and Yahoo!) dominate the Internet. In fact, most studies show that over one-third of all the time spent on the Internet is spent on the 50 most popular sites—and this use is rising.

Sites such as AltaVista, Lycos, Excite, and Yahoo! offer one-stop informational malls for nearly everything, ranging from news, search engines, and entertainment to on-line shopping and business tools.

Additionally, Net giants and brick-and-mortar superchains are teaming up in powerful combinations, whereby they mutually offer each other's services in their stores or sites. For example, Wal-Mart and Sears have teamed up individually with America Online (which is also venturing with Circuit City). Best Buy and Microsoft established an online partnership with BestBuy.com being advertised on MSN's service, and MSN's Internet access being sold in Best Buy's stores. Kmart and Yahoo! have joined in an online venture that stands alongside other ventures between the giants in the online and offline world.

Meanwhile, America Online's acquisition of gigantic Time Warner, Inc. triggered public concern over the deal's potential to limit Internet access. The issue forced the two companies to grant rival Internet ISPs "open access" to their high-speed cable-TV lines. AOL had to open up its Instant Messaging service, and other agreements were made with federal regulatory agencies to gain approval for this merger. Yahoo! and eBay at one time looked at combining their powerful Net presence. In late 2000, the Federal Trade Commission did not block (but deferred further review to the future) the Covisint proposed cyber joint-venture. This virtual venture organized the world's six largest car manufacturers and their suppliers, so that efficiencies could be reached in combined design, supply chain management, and centralizing procurement functions.

As this trend toward greater concentrations of power continues, we'll be seeing more mergers and acquisitions. Does this mean that we'll eventual see antitrust actions and Justice Department inquiries into these super offline and online combinations? The answer is "Yes."

This practice isn't limited, of course, to the United States. The media continues to announce mergers and investments by Net companies around the world—from European Union countries to the Asia-Pacific rim. For example, Singapore companies are snapping up Internet companies in their part of the world, imitating their U.S. counterparts. Keppel T&T bought a stake in Anew Corporation, just so that it would have access to a Thai corporate and dial-up customer base, as well as a platform from which to deliver e-commerce applications.

Internationalism

Amazon.co.uk, the English Web site of Amazon.com, concluded a deal in July 2001, with Waterstone's, Great Britain's largest specialist bookseller, to take over the operations of its Web site—Amazon.com United Kingdom's operations were some 15-times larger than the e-book sales of Waterstone's. This agreement followed a similar one that Amazon.com cut with Borders, a bookstore chain in the United States, whereby it would run the online business of that competitor. Basically, Amazon agreed to run Waterstone's Web site with all deliveries coming from its warehouse, in Amazon packaging, and with the right to "encourage" customers already registered online with Waterstone's to reregister with Amazon. The giant had swallowed up another e-commerce competitor.

All businesses are going international, consuming or acquiring the online sites of less-competitive ones. Every Global 500 company based in Europe has an e-commerce presence now—the majority of those companies expecting more than one-quarter of their sales to be conducted over the Internet in five years. At the same time, the experts believe that massive consolidations will take place throughout the world, just as illustrated in the Amazon.com example.

This is an international phenomenon—a premise that we started off with in Chapter 1, "The World's at Your Fingertips." The world is growing by geographical areas in cyberspace, starting first with North America. The European Union now is growing towards its expectations, to be followed in turn over time by Asia, Latin America, and then Eastern Europe, Africa, and the Middle East. Their businesses, in turn, will reach out to establish Web operations in other regions and acquire others—no different than the offline conduct of companies. As these regions prosper in cyberspace, the inevitable conflicts and fine-tuning required will result in extensive cyberlaw and conflicts-of-law developments, just as seen in the United States and other developed countries.

Cyberlaw in the New Millennium

The existing framework of laws has created a growing body of cyberlaw with reasonable certainty and applicability. We've seen how the existing law in the fields of fraudulent advertising, e-commerce contracts, returns and refunds, trademark infringement, copyright law, linking, and more, have proven flexible enough to handle the demands of the Internet and its conflicts.

Lawyers eagerly await the new decisions that are to be handed down in these and other areas. Although it's true that new legislation will be enacted in various specifics and varying court decisions will be handed down, it is also certain that the basic cyberlaw concepts discussed so far will continue to provide a fundamental and guiding legal foundation. And Web site operators and their users will continue to be able to rely on them.

As we have seen, legislatures around the world have not been idly standing by as just observers of this opportunity; they are busily legislating away at all levels. From establishing new Internet taxes, regulating e-commerce and user privacy, and restricting various Internet sales (i.e., gambling, alcohol, and online prescriptions), to encryption safeguards, regulation of professions locally, and false advertising, to name just a few—all in a global world—new laws, among laws, are a virtual reality.

The European Union has enacted or is discussing a variety of cyber-initiatives. Among these are: the Electronic Signatures Directive, which legally recognizes electronic signatures; the E-Commerce Directive, which centers basically on which country's laws would govern in the online sale of goods and services; the Distance Selling Directive, which is a consumer protection law for online purchasers; the Data Protection Directive, which seeks to strengthen protection in users' privacy; and others.

When a German court in 2001 ruled under 1932–1933 laws that Letsbuyit.com's (a European-wide virtual retailer) selling practices were illegal, the German legislature began reviewing the extent to which old laws should be changed in the New

Millennium's time of e-commerce. Then, we can add in the virtual laws of countries from the Philippines to Pakistan, knowing that these laws will give clarity as well as conflict at the same time.

The legislatures, the courts, and most users on the Internet have been guided basically by principles of good faith and "fair play" when making their decisions as to what's right or wrong. For example, it makes sense that a *Playboy* Bunny could use the word "Playboy" and "Playmate of the Year" in her meta-tagged Web pages, as she had been doing. It makes sense that a computer company by the name of "Clue Computing" could keep its domain name of "clue.com" over Hasbro's game of "Clue," because they were in different businesses and the computer company used good faith. And it made just as much sense that someone who grabbed the name of "wwwpainewebber.com"—where the "dot" was missing—shouldn't be allowed to retain that name over the rights of the true company. Misleading advertising and statements should and will continue to be punished, both civilly and criminally.

We've also seen that there are great differences in how the conflicting laws of the various countries play out over the Net. Each country has a reason to enforce its own local laws, just as each state has an interest in its statutes. Although a series of reasonable rules has developed as to when a consumer's state can take control, assert jurisdiction, and apply its own laws, the law becomes unclear when we add in a site's standard terms and conditions—and finding certainty becomes quite expensive when we consider the distances involved and the fights over just what law is to be applied. You can expect legislation and treaties eventually in this area, as well.

Only the largest companies have the ability to sustain these massive courtroom and legal battles so it makes more sense that the ADR techniques we discussed in Chapter 12, "Cyberlaw Dispute Resolution," will continue to accelerate in their acceptance. The likelihood is high that virtual mediation (and even "cyberarbitration") will find their way into becoming a common method to settle Internet disputes.

Regardless of the new Internet business opportunities and legal controversies that will develop further in the New Millennium, three realities exist: (1) the legal concepts already in place have proved to be quite adaptable to these challenges; (2) the concepts of "fair play," common sense, and "Netiquette" are filling in the gaps; and (3) ADRs on the Net will continue to grow over time, given the high expense and inappropriateness of litigation to "solve" the cyberdisputes among the citizens of the world.

The Internet has enhanced our lives and challenged our laws. The legal system has met the challenge, but the world will never again be the same.

Selected Bibliography

Accola, John. "Web-Name Firm Loses Round." *Denver Rocky Mountain News,* February 16, 2000, 4B.

"Adobe Cracks under Hacker Pressure." *Financial Times Information, Global News Wire, Newswire (VNU),* July 24, 2001.

Arthur, Charles. "First Film Released for Rental over the Internet." *The Independent (London),* January 23, 2001, 7.

Atkins, Ralph. "German E-Commerce." *Financial Times (London),* October 31, 2000, 18.

Balint, Kathryn. "Credit-Card Cons Leaving Online Shoppers Wary." *The San Diego Union-Tribune,* March 24, 2000, A-1.

Barrett, Rick. "Woman Charged with Online Fraud." *Milwaukee Journal Sentinel,* January 24, 2001, 1B.

Booth, Michael. "'Spam' Labeling Required by Bill." *The Denver Post,* February 18, 2000, C-1.

Brett, Barry J. and Gilbert C. Hoover IV. "Exploring the Brave New World of Internet Litigation." *New York Law Journal,* August 29, 2000, 1.

Brinson, J. Dianne and Mark F. Radcliffe. *Internet Legal Forms for Business.* California: Ladera Press, 1997.

Brown, Joel. "The Web Browser; Hollywood Head for the Net." *The Boston Herald,* January 28, 2001, A11.

Burnett, Thane. "Spite Sites Revenge Sweetens as Dirty Little Secrets Appear Online." *The Toronto Sun,* May 14, 2000, 32.

"Buy.com Targets small Businesses." *Sunday Telegraph (London),* January 21, 2001, 9.

"Buy Online at your Own Risk." *Gannett Companies, USA Today,* December 20, 2000, 12A.

Cairncross, Frances. "The Internet Promises Governments Huge Scope to Improve Services." *The Financial Times (London),* April 25, 2001, 19.

Carlinksy, Michael B. and Jeffrey A. Conciatori. "Cybersurfers Beware: No Trespassing on the Internet." *Mealey's Cyber Tech Litigation Report,* February 2001, vol. 2. no. 12.

Carson, Larry. "Maryland Politics Is Getting Wired." *The Baltimore Sun,* March 13, 2000, 1B.

Carter, Rochelle. "Online: Click on your Favorite Organizations." *The Atlanta Journal and Constitution,* February 3, 2000, 1JD.

Cha, Ariana Eunjung. "Your PC Is Watching." *The Washington Post,* July 14, 2000, A01.

"Charges Laid in EBay Fake Painting Case." *CNN.com,* March 9, 2001.

"Claiming a Name: Even Online It's about Location." *The Seattle Times,* November 26, 2000, B5.

Clarida, Robert. "EBay Case Recognizes New IP Theory." *The Intellectual Property Strategist,* June 2000, vol. 6, 9(7).

Clark, Eugene. "Use the Web to Resolve Disputes Cheaply." *The Federal Capital Press of Australia, Ltd., The Canberra Times,* March 19, 2001, A14.

Clausing, Jeri. "In New Forum for Domain Name Disputes, Trademark Holders Dominate." *The New York Times,* May 19, 2000.

"Clearer Domain Name Rules Needed." *The Yomiuri Shimbun,* December 8, 2000, 6.

Cohen, Benjamin. "The Law Could Silence Napster." *American Lawyer Media, Fulton County Daily Report,* September 29, 2000.

Colden, Anne. "Sending a Message: Companies Go to Court to Stop 'Cyber- smearers.'" *The Denver Post,* January 15, 2001, E-1.

Collier, Rebecca. "Professor's Correspondence E-Censored by Courts." *The Indiana lawyer,* May 24, 2000, 13.

"Commerce in the Digital Age." *Continuing Legal Education of the State Bar of Oregon,* November 17, 2000.

"Computer Law Update: Critical Issues for Business Attorneys, Litigators, and Computer Lawyers." *Continuing Legal Education of the State Bar of Oregon,* February 4, 2000.

"Copyrights and MP3." *The Boston Globe,* May 12, 2000, A26.

Crane, David. "Much of the Internet's Impact Yet to Come." *The Toronto Star,* January 29, 2001.

Cruz, Humberto. "Fraud One of Many Dangers Facing Internet Investors." *Milwaukee Journal Sentinel,* September 17, 2000, 3D.

Cushman, John H., Jr. "Post Office Is Full of Ideas to Survive an E-Future." *The New York Times,* December 18, 2000, C12.

Davidson, Paul. "Marketing Gurus Clash on Internet Privacy Rules." *Gannett Company, USA Today,* April 27, 2001, 1B.

Davies, Jennifer. "S.D. Judge Kills Suit over EBay Fake Items." *The San Diego Union- Tribune,* January 19, 2001, C-1.

Dixon, Pam. "Cyber Artists' Toy War Is Not Child's Play." *The San Diego Union- Tribune,* March 5, 2000, E-5.

Dolan, William F. and Marc D. Levi. "Striking a Balance between Linking and Infringing." *The National Law Journal,* October 16, 2000, C6.

Dorsey, Kristy. "Putting a Stop to the Name Drain." *Scottish Media Newspapers, The Herald (Glasgow),* January 28, 2000, 26.

"DoubleClick Suits Allowed to Proceed." *The Chronicle Publishing Co., The San Francisco Chronicle,* June 15, 2001, B3.

Dougherty, Sarah. "Virtual Court in Session." *Southam, The Gazette (Montreal),* June 23, 2000, C3.

Doward, Jamie. "Why ICANN Can't Cope." *The Observer (London),* November 5, 2000, 11.

"Dr. Wins $675K Internet Libel Case." *Associated Press, Schwab-news.excite.com,* December 9, 2000.

Druckenmiller, John and Betty Parham. "Living Online: Several Sites Share Napster's Old Glory." *The Atlanta Constitution,* July 24, 2001, 2C.

Eaglesham, Jean. "Safeguards against Cybersquatters." *The Financial Times (London),* February 2, 2000, 12.

_____. "Publisher Sues over Web Link Internet." *The Financial Times (London),* January 10, 2001, 3.

_____. "How Far Does Copyright Extend in Cyberspace?" *The Financial Times (London),* January 15, 2001, 18.

_____. "Online Recruiter Wins Ban on Rival's Web Links." *The Financial Times (London),* January 17, 2001, 4.

"EBay, Bidder's Edge Settle Suits on Web Access." *Bloomberg News, Los Angeles Times,* March 2, 2001, C2.

"E-Business Vital to Future." *The Irish Times,* April 10, 2000, 8.

Eckberg, John. "Internet 'Speech' Center of Dispute." *Phoenix Newspapers, The Arizona Republic,* January 7, 2001, J1.

Eckstein, Ron. "Strange Bedfellows Back Betting Ban on the Net." *American Lawyer Media, Fulton County Daily Report,* March 15, 2000.

Emling, Shelley. "Online Arbitration Offers Faster, Cheaper Way to Settle Disputes." *The Atlanta Journal and Constitution,* April 29, 2001, 1P.

Evangelista, Benny. "Napster's Success Hits Sour Note." *The San Francisco Chronicle,* March 3, 2000, A7.

_____. "EBay Immune from Suits over Pirated Music." *The San Francisco Chronicle,* November 9, 2000, B2.

_____. "Yahoo Joins Net Music Bandwagon." *The San Francisco Chronicle,* April 6, 2001, B1.

Evans, Robert. "World Watchdog Wants Pact against Cyber-Squatting." *Pacific Press, Ltd., The Vancouver Sun,* February 22, 2001, E4.

Ferra, Gerald R., Stephen D. Lichtenstein, Margo E. Reder, Ray August, and William T. Schiano. *Cyberlaw: Text and Cases, 1st Edition.* Ohio: South-Western College Publishing, 2000.

Fisher, Matthew. "Cybersleuths Needed to Patrol the Web." *The Toronto Sun,* May 21, 2000, C5.

Flavelle, Dana. "Montreal Web-Caster Pushes Legal Limits." *The Toronto Star,* May 14, 2001.

Fletcher, Richard. "'Dot Biz' Tag Sparks New Internet Gold Rush." *Southam, The Ottawa Citizen,* May 20, 2001, A1.

Flint, David. "It's Checkmate in the Chess Site Domain Name Dispute." *The Scotsman Publications, Ltd., The Scotsman,* March 9, 2001, 5.

Flynn, Laurie J. "Whose Name Is It Any Way?" *The New York Times,* September 4, 2000, C3.

"Foes of Ahmanson Ranch Warned to Close Web Site." *Los Angeles Times,* June 24, 2000, B4.

Fowler, Tom. "New SierraCities Buyer Is American Express." *The Houston Chronicle,* February 15, 2000, 3.

Fried, Joseph P. "Internet Complaints Are Climbing." *The New York Times,* November 2, 2000, B8.

Frietas, Ian De. "Worldwide Web of Laws Threatens the Internet." *The Times (London),* January 9, 2001.

"FTC Details Internet Scams, Vows Crackdown on 'Dot-Cons.'" *The Denver Post,* November 1, 2000, C-01.

"FTC Opens Antifraud Site to Consumers." *The New York Times,* January 30, 2001, C6.

Furman, Phyllis. "FCC Signs Off on Time Warner & AOL." *Daily News (New York),* January 12, 2001, 40.

Gallagher, David F. "Tough fight ahead for Operator of Sports Betting Site." *The New York Times,* March 10, 2000.

Gallivan, Joseph. "Cambridge Don Corners Market in Authors' Domains." *Newspaper Publishing PLC, The Independent (London),* March 14, 2000, 5.

"Gateway Settles FTC Charges Over Free Internet Service." *Bloomberg News, Los Angeles Times,* May 16, 2001, C3.

Geewax, Marilyn. "Anti-Spam Legislation under Fire." *The Atlanta Journal and Constitution,* May 11, 2001, 5C.

"Get Your Act Together, Net Firms Are Warned." *The Toronto Star,* February 24, 2000.

"Global Alliance Targets Online Fraud." *Financial Times, Ltd., Global News Wire (VNU),* April 27, 2001.

Goldberg, Laura. "All Aboard the E-Train." *The Houston Chronicle,* October 1, 2000, 1.

"Government to Regulate Electronic Signatures." *Gazeta Mercantil S/A,* July 2, 2001.

Granahan, William L. "Using Risk Retention Groups to Insure Cyberliability Exposures." *Insurance Communications, The Risk Retention Reporter,* April 2000, vol. 14(4).

Grande, Carlos. "Waterstone's Online Operations Goes to Amazon." *The Financial Times, Ltd., Financial Times (London),* July 26, 2001.

Grant, Fleming. "Mediators may Use Internet." *The Evening Post (Wellington, England),* November 15, 2000, 19.

Greenbaum, Perry J. "Growing the E-Forest." *Southam, The Gazette (Montreal),* January 27, 2001, S3.

Grossman, Mark. "Accepting Credit Card Payments Online." *The Miami Herald,* Techlaw, July 25, 2000.

———. "Staying Out of Trouble Online." *The Miami Herald,* Techlaw, October 30, 2000.

———. "Website Hosting Agreements." *The Miami Herald,* Techlaw, December 18, 2000.

———. "Legal Tips for Website Owners." *The Miami Herald,* Techlaw, February 12, 2001.

———. "Computer Users Beware! Electronic Evidence never Dies." *The Miami Herald,* Techlaw, April 23, 2001.

Guernsey, Lisa. "Ban on Nazi Items Upsets Collectors." *The New York Times,* May 10, 2001, G11.

Hann, Steven A. "Commission on E-Commerce Reports to Congress." *American Lawyer Media, The Legal Intelligencer,* May 30, 2000, 7.

Hansel, Saul. "Reaching for Less than the Sky." *The New York Times,* December 13, 2000, H1.

Hargreaves, Deborah. "Microsoft to Adopt EU's Data Privacy Rules." *The Financial Times (London),* May 16, 2001, 12.

_____ and Michael Peel. "London warns EU against Internet Tax." *The Financial Times* (London), May 17, 2001, 10.

Harris, Mikal. "Area Municipalities Are Riding Wave of the Future." *St. Louis Post-Dispatch,* February 7, 2000, 1.

Harris, Ron. "Court Says Napster Must Stop." *Associated Press,* February 12, 2001.

_____. "Test Drive: File-Sharing Software." *Orlando Sentinel,* July 27, 2001.

Harris, Sheryl. "Internet Fraud: Let the Bidder Beware." *The Plain Dealer (Cleveland),* August 17, 2000, 1B.

Hasib, H.J. Azarainy. "Brunei: Consumers Body to go on the Net." *Global News Wire, Borneo Bulletin,* June 1, 2001.

Henley, Jon. "Yahoo! Agrees to Ban Auction of Nazi Memorabilia." *The Guardian (London),* January 4, 2001, 13.

Hirst, Clayton. "Internet Providers Press for Protection from Libel." *Newspaper Publishing, PLC, The Independent (London),* January 28, 2001, 2.

Hornbeck, Mark. "State Plugs Students into Virtual High School." *The Detroit News,* June 1, 2000, 1.

Huber, Nick. "Europe on Track for E-Business Boom." *Reed Business Information, Ltd., Computer Weekly,* June 28, 2001.

Huffstutter, P.J. "Napster Buys Some Time as Judges Consider Appeal." *Los Angeles Times,* October 3, 2000, C1.

_____. "MP3.Com Digital Copyright Infringement." *Los Angeles Times,* December 20, 2000, C8

Hunter, Ewan. "Law of Internet Jungle Where 'Original' Ideas Risk Being Aped." *The Scotsman,* March 2, 2000, 26.

Ihnatko, Andy. "Signing off on PGP for E-signatures." *Chicago Sun-Times,* October 10, 2000, 58.

"India: Growing Internet Penetration in Asia, Latin America." *FT Asia Intelligence Wire, The Hindu,* August 15, 2000.

"Internet Body Approves Plans for 2 Suffixes." *Reuters, Los Angeles Times,* May 16, 2001, 3(6).

"Internet Domain Arbitration Body to Debut." *Hankook Iibo, Korea Times,* July 3, 2001.

"It's Art for Art's Sake, E-Comm for God's Sake." *The Irish Times,* November 21, 2000.

Iwata, Edward. "E-Commerce Losses Drive Dot-Com Insurance." *Gannett Company, USA Today,* February 11, 2000, 13A.

James, Michael. "Another Deal Draws Napster Closer to Truce." *The Baltimore Sun,* January 8, 2001, 1C.

"JAMS to Take Dispute Mediation to the Net." *Los Angeles Times,* October 17, 2000, C4.

Jesdanun, Anick. "Domains in Discord: Cybercolonies Clash with the Internet Establishment." *The San Diego Union-Tribune,* January 16, 2001, C-1.

Johnson, Alan. "Taft Signs Bill Making Renewals for License Tags Available Online." *The Columbus Dispatch,* June 15, 2000, 11C.

Johnson, David R. "Online Solutions Needed for Online Problems." *The San Francisco Chronicle,* September 17, 2000, 6.

Johnson, Greg. "The Costly Game for Net Names." *Los Angeles Times,* April 10, 2000, A1.

Jordan, Steve. "Campaign Aims to Discourage Business Scams." *Omaha World-Herald,* March 8, 2000, 20.

Joshi, Pradnya. "Amazon, Borders Form Partnership." *Mail Tribune,* April 12, 2001, 1C.

Kanth, D. Ravi. "U.N. Body to Expand Scope of Arbitration to Disputes in the ASP Industry." *Business Times (Singapore),* May 4, 2000, 19.

Kaplan, Carl. "Judge Says a Spider is Trespassing on EBay." *The New York Times,* May 26, 2000.

_____. "Cyber Law Journal: Cool Sites for 2001." *The New York Times,* May 25, 2001.

Katz, Frances. "High Court: No E-Mail Liability for ISPs." *The Atlanta Journal and Constitution,* May 2, 2000, 3C.

Kehoe, Louise. "Counting the Cost of Being Free." *The Financial Times (London),* January 26, 2000, 18.

_____. "Trespass Ruling Adds Tangles to the Web." *The Financial Times (London),* May 31, 2000, 17.

"Keppel T&T Buys 20% of Thai Internet, E-Commerce Firm." *Business Times (Singapore),* March 15, 2000, 4.

Kerber, Ross. "Suit Called Test of Online Right to Free Speech." *The Boston Globe,* May 12, 2000, A1.

Kirby, Carrie. "Web Surfers Not always Aware that Site Guarantees Don't Keep User Information Private." *The San Francisco Chronicle,* April 6, 2000, B1.

Knight, Jerry. "Penny-Stock Scam Keeps Replenishing Rogues' Gallery." *The Washington Post,* February 12, 2001, E01.

Krupa, Gregg. "Legal Counsel Just a Click Away." *The Boston Globe,* February 25, 2000, E1.

Labate, John. "Privacy Suit over Online Ad Company's Database." *Financial Times (London),* January 29, 2000, 5.

Landon, Laura. "Freer System to Spark Cyber Battles." *The Ottawa Citizen,* May 23, 2000, C1.

"Lawmakers Pass 1st Reading of Electronic Signatures Act." *Global News Wire, Taiwan Economic News,* May 24, 2001.

Lerner, Dan. "Congress to Consider Web Tax Proposal." *The Financial Times (London),* April 10, 2000, 3.

Macero, Cosmo, Jr. "Meehan Camp Battles Cyber-Squatters." *The Boston Herald,* January 21, 2000, 1.

Mackintosh, James. "Germans Push Signature Cards." *The Financial Times (London),* May 15, 2001, 17.

MacPherson, Robert. "Euro MPs Pass EU Copyright Directive." *Agence France Presse,* February 14, 2001.

"Man to Pay for Internet Slur." *Newspaper Publishing, PLC, The Independent (London),* May 12, 2001, 5.

Mann, Michael. "International Economy: European Parliament Halts Song Swaps." *The Financial Times, Ltd., Financial Times (London),* February 15, 2001, 12.

Martinson, Jane. "E-Finance: MP3.com Seeks Broader Review." *The Guardian (London),* January 9, 2001, 27.

Marzulli, John. "NYPD Busts Man in Net Drug Sting." *Daily News (New York),* February 25, 2000, 40.

"Masters of their Domain Name: Magazine's Joke Turns into a Web-Address Windfall." *Southam, The Gazette (Montreal),* June 21, 2000, D3.

Mathews, Anna Wilde. "Copyright and the Web: The once-obscure U.S. Copyright Office Is busy Sorting out the Law in a Digital Age." *Star Tribune* (Minneapolis, MN), June 15, 2000, 1D.

McGeehan, Patrick. "For Want of $35, J. P. Morgan Loses its Web Site and E- Mail." *The New York Times,* June 14, 2000, C17.

McLester, Susan. "Family Tech: Learning the Rules of Cyberspace." *Los Angeles Times,* November 2, 2000, T6.

Meyer, Josh. "1 Held, 1 Sought in Internet Fraud Case." *Los Angeles Times,* December 27, 2000, B1.

Middleton, James. "E-business; EC Law Ratifies Digital Signatures." *VNU, Computing,* July 26, 2001, 11.

Millar, John. "Trustmark Can Cut Risk of E-Buying." *Sun Media Corp., London Free Press,* April 27, 2001, D3.

Monseau, Susanna. "Balancing Trademark Rights on the Internet: The Case of Domain Name Disputes." *Journal of Legal Studies in Business,* Winter 2000, 91–110.

Mulvihill, Maggie. "Web Site Can Help mediate." *The Boston Herald,* October 17, 2000, 36.

"Napster Users Can Pay for Music off the Net." *Milwaukee Journal Sentinel,* January 12, 20001, 1D.

Nemeroff, Michael A. and Matthew P. Pasulka. "'No Trespassing': Internet Spin on an old Doctrine." *The National Law Journal,* November 13, 2000, B17.

Nesbitt, Jim. "Keeping it Confidential; Taking Charge of Internet Privacy." *The San Diego Union-Tribune,* May 30, 2000, 6.

"New Online Arbitration Service Has 90 Domain Name Cases Filed." *The Irish Times,* February 25, 2000, 60.

Ng, Eric. "Legal Awareness Required for On-Line Business Transactions." *South China Morning Post,* April 10, 2000, 2.

Nimmo, Elise. "Deep Links that Could Just Connect to Trouble." *The Scotsman,* November 30, 2000, 7.

Nissman, Cara. "Get a Clue: Netiquette Lessons." *The Boston Herald,* November 8, 2000, 64.

O'Harrow, Robert Jr. "Music Industry Will Offer Songs Online." *The Washington Post,* July 25, 2001, E01.

"Online Card Fraud Is an Exaggerated Problem." *The San Diego Union-Tribune,* January 23, 2001, 10.

"Online Education." *FT Asia Intelligence Wire (Bangkok Post),* May 21, 2001.

Peterson, Kim. "Universal Records Sued for Copyright Violations." *The San Diego Union-Tribune,* December 8, 2000, C-1.

_____. "A Musical Free-For-All Firms that Zapped Napster May Face Worse Threat." *The San Diego Union-Tribune,* August 17, 2001, C-1.

Pham, Alex. "Domains Don't Net as many Buyers." *Los Angeles Times,* December 29, 2000, C1.

"Pharmaceuticals: Suing Online Druggists." *Associated Press, New York Times,* April 9, 2000, 14NJ (p. 9).

Phelps, David. "Eminent Domains." *Star Tribune (Minneapolis, MN),* January 3, 2000, 1D.

"Philippines: Yahoo! Wins Dispute vs. Local Company over Domain Names." *FT Asia Intelligence Wire, Computer World (Philippines),* April 30, 2001.

Pledger, Marcia. "Online Buying." *The Plain Dealer (Cleveland),* November 19, 2000, 1H.

"Postal Office Offers Secure Online Service to Government." *The New York Times,* January 22, 2001, C12.

"Postal Service to Sell Rare Items on EBay." *The Washington Post,* June 15, 2000, A7.

"Privacy: E-Firms just Don't Get It." *Los Angeles Times,* May 29, 2000, B6.

"Protocol for Handling E-Commerce Discord to be Released Today." *The New York Times,* January 4, 2001, B4.

Rahman, A. Shukor. "New Internet Law Not Necessary." *New Straits Times (Malaysia),* May 21, 2001, 17.

Randall, Julian and Bridget Treacy. "Digital Buccaneers Caught in a Legal Web." *The Financial Times (London),* May 30, 2000, 6.

Rashiwala, Kalpana. "Developers Plan Direct Sourcing Via Net." *Business Times (Singapore),* May 4, 2000, 36.

"RealNetworks Launches New Audio Technology." *The Toronto Star,* October 24, 2000.

"Representing High-Tech and Emerging Businesses." *Continuing Legal Education of the State Bar of Oregon,* 2001.

Ruth, Robert. "Cyberpiracy Suit is being Settled." *The Columbus Dispatch,* August 16, 2000, 1F.

———. "Stanley Steemer Wins Cyberpiracy Suit." *The Columbus Dispatch,* August 9, 2000, 5B.

Said, Carolyn. "Net Services Referee Disputes Between Online Sellers, Buyers." *The San Francisco Chronicle,* June 12, 2000, C1.

Sandburg, Brenda. "Does a Web Site Link Infringe?" *The National Law Journal,* July 3, 2000, B9.

Sanders, Edmund. "Web Privacy Programs Are Scrutinized." *Los Angeles Times,* December 11, 2000, C1.

———. "Politicians, Industry Gear up for Public Battle over Privacy." *Los Angeles Times,* January 22, 2001, C1.

Saunders, James. "ISPs Face Fresh Challenge after Defamation Case Legal Issues." *The Scotsman,* May 4, 2000, 24.

Schroeder, Michael. "Teenage Trader Runs Afoul of the SEC." *The New York Times,* September 21, 2000, C1.

Schwartz, John. "E-Signatures Become Valid for Business." *The New York Times,* October 2, 2000, C1.

Scott, Jeffry. "Web Vengeance: Angry Consumers Taking Crusades to Internet." *The Atlanta Journal and Constitution,* March 9, 2000, 1A.

"SEC Fights Alleged Net Stock Fraud." *The Associated Press, via ClariNet,* March 1, 2001.

Segal, David. "Napster and Former Foe Plan Online Song Sales; Bertelsmann to Quit Industry Lawsuit." *The Washington Post,* November 1, 2000, A1.

"Settlement Reached in Stock Fraud." *Bloomberg News, Los Angeles Times,* January 24, 2001, C2.

Seymour, Jim. "AOL is a Big Winner in the Regulatory Wars." *TheStreet.com,* January 12, 2001.

Shepardson, David. "AOL Spam Battle Moves to Michigan." *The Detroit News,* April 10, 2000, 1.

Sheron, Don. "Small Businesses Develop New Customer Base Using Web." *The Houston Chronicle,* January 28, 2001, 5.

Shiver, Jube. "Internet Firms Gain Foothold in Washington." *Los Angeles Times,* March 12, 2000, A1.

Siegel, Andrea F. "Doll is Model in Net Case." *The Baltimore Sun,* June 5, 2000, 1B.

Singh, Andrea. "Governors: Tax E-Commerce." *Newsday,* August 16, 2001, A48.

"Sites Risk Breaking the Law." *FT Asia Intelligence Wire (Bangkok Post),* March 19, 2001.

"Sometimes a Sucks.Com Site Is the Best Revenge." *The Toronto Star,* December 4, 2000.

"Sony and MP3.com Make Sweet Music Together." *The National Law Journal,* September 11, 2000, B9.

"State Sues over Alleged Fraud in Online Auction." *St. Louis Post-Dispatch,* March 13, 2001, D2.

Stevason, John C. "Copyrights and Copywrongs. *Lane, Powell, Spears, and Lubersky,* presentation materials, 2001.

Stellin, Susan. "New Contract Covering Internet Domain Registry." *The New York Times,* May 21, 2001, C4.

"Stock Charges at a Tender Age." *The New York Times,* January 2, 2001, C2.

Stoughton, Stephanie. "Looks like a Tough Year on the Net." *The Boston Globe,* January 8, 2001, C2.

Streitfeld, David. "Making Bad Names for Themselves; Firms Preempt Critics with Nasty Domains." *The Washington Post,* September 8, 2000, A1.

Swartz, Jon. "Profiteers Get Squat for Web Names; Cybersquatters Lose IP Rulings." *Gannett Company, USA Today,* August 25, 2000, 1B.

Tamaki, Julie. "Riverside County Official Is Selling Tax-Delinquent Time Shares Online." *Los Angeles Times,* February 7, 2000, A3.

Tedeschi, Bob. "E-Commerce Reports; DoubleClick." *The New York Times,* January 29, 2001, C9.

Thompson, Clive. "President Bush Tries to Dodge the E-Tax Tax Bullet." *Newsday,* May 20, 2001, B15.

"Three Men Charged in Online Scam to Offer Beanie Babies." *The Seattle Times,* March 3, 2000, C3.

"To Save the Sales Tax." *Omaha World-Herald,* December 23, 2000, 42.

"Toysmart Debacle Put to Rest." *The Toronto Star,* January 18, 2001.

Vuong, Andy. "Company Pays High Price for Site." *The Denver Post,* January 29, 2001, C-1.

———. "'Dot-coms' Have Company New Domain Names." *The Denver Post,* January 29, 2001, C-1.

Wallace, Bill. "Companies Battle bill that would Protect Privacy." *The San Francisco Chronicle,* May 20, 2001, A6.

Waters, Richard. "VeriSign Keeps Domain Control." *Financial Times (London),* May 19, 2001, 8.

Waldmeir, Patti. "Credit Card Arbitrators Fill Cross-Border Legal Vacuum." *The Financial Times (London),* March 9, 2000, 10.

Westermeier, J.T. "Crawlers & Spiders & Bots, OH MY." *The Recorder,* November 27, 2000, 14.

Whitestone, Randy. "Dot-Coms Shutting Down at Faster Pace." *Chicago Sun- Times,* November 17, 2000, 63.

"Will Musical Mayhem Lead to a 'Free' Net?" *FT Asia Intelligence Wire, The Hindu (India),* May 18, 2000.

Williams, Frances. "WIPO Cyber-Arbitration Kicks off to Flying Start." *The Financial Times (London)*, February 23, 2000, 12.

Williams, Fred O. "Guard your Password." *The Buffalo news*, February 15, 2000, 8D.

Wolf, Barnet D. "Add Ricart to List of Companies Suing over Cybersquatting." *The Columbus Dispatch*, January 30, 2000, 1H.

Wong, Karen. "Judiciary Launches Online Mediation." *The Straits Times (Singapore)*, September 17, 2000 (1).

"Your Browser Is Selling You Out." *PC Computing*. March 2000, 91–93.

Yu, Tonny. "Modify Privacy Law for Internet." *Gannett Company, USA Today*, January 16, 2001, 15A.

Selected Virtual Bibliography

Alternb v. Halladay (wired.com/news/politics/0,1283,18274,00.html)

Anti-Abortion Site Wins Appeal/Nuremburg (wired.com/news/politics/0,1283,42708,00.html)

Arts Group Wins Domain Name Battle With eToys (adlawbyrequest.com/inthecourts/toybattle.shtml)

Bensusan Restaurant Corp. v. King (jmls.edu/cyber/cases/blue2.html)

California Tax Policy and the Internet (lao.ca.gov/013100_inet_tax/013100_internet_tax.html)

Canada Online (contractscanada.gc.ca)

Charles Huttoe (sec.gov/litigation/litreleases/lr16632a.htm)

CNN—The Star Trek Copyright Battle—October 29, 1997 (http://www.cnn.com/TECH/9710/29/star.trek.sites/index.html)

Dear Star Trek fan, from Paramount (paramount.com/openletter/)

Dell Computer Corporation Settles FTC Charges (microsmarts.com/fraudalert/dell.htm)

eCitizen—Singapore (ecitizen.gov.pg)

Emory Doctor (ama-assn.org/sci-pubs/amnews/pick_01/prbf0115.htm)

EToys Drops Domain Name Suit (internetnews.com/bus-news/article/0..3_295511,00.html)

Felix Somm- Compuserve (www.cnn.com/TECH/computing/9805/28/germany.internet/)

France Online (minefi.gouv.fr)

FTC: AOL/Prodigy/Compuserve (ftc.gov/opal/1997/9705/online.htm)

FTC Hits Dell (consumeraffairs.com/news/ftc_hits_dell.htm)

Harvard Files Lawsuit To Protect Name (news.harvard.edu/gazette/1999/12.09/lawsuit.html)

Harvard/Michael Rhys Lawsuit (http://chronicle.com/free/v46/i48/48a04102.htm)

IBM—Select a Country (ibm.com/planetwide/select/)

iCrave Loses (internetnews.com/streaming-news/article/0,,8161_745341,00.html)

IPC Synopsis Paper on Trademark Cyberpiracy Prevention Act (ipc.songbird.com/cyberpiracy_paper.html)

J.P. Morgan Site Goes Down (info-sec.com/denial/00/denial_061400a_i.shtml)

Missouri Press Release—Online Drugs (http://www.ago.state.mo.us/7899.htm)

Missouri Won (http://www.wired.com/news/business/0,1367,32137-1,00.html)

MPAA | ICRAVE Press Releases (mpaa.org/Press/iCrave_settlement.htm)

Nevada Department of Information Technology (psp.state.nv.us/IEM_POL_5.7.htm)

Nevada Journal: Spam Be Dammed (nj.npri.org/nj98/07/spam.htm)

NFL Files Trademark Suit against Gambling Site (news.cnet.com/news/0-1005-200-1488783.html)

"No Electronic Theft (NET)" Act (usdoj.gov/criminal/cybercrime/netsum.htm)

The Nuremberg Files (christiangallery.com/atrocity/aborts.html)

Onsale Settles Suit over 'At Cost' Ads with DA (12/28/1999) (http://www.mercurycenter.com/srtech/news/indepth/docs/onsale122999.htm)

Ontario Canada Courts (ontariocourts.on.cal/english.htm)

Oregon Live: 1-3-99 Decision (oregonlive.com/news/99/02/ed020301.html)

Prince Lawsuit (the smokinggun.com/archive/theartist1.shtml)

Real Networks & Online Drugs (http://mishpat.net/cyberlaw/archive/informer33.shtml)

Software Industry Issues: Digital Signatures (softwareindustry.org/issues/1digsig.html)

Star Trek: First Contact—Lawyer Mail (bradley.edu/campusorg/psiphi/mov/FC-letter1.html)

STARTREK.COM:Terms of Use (startrek.com)

UK Online (ukonline.com)

UNC: Trademark Infringement, Copyright, and Censorship on Web Sites (http://www.unc.edu/courses/jomc191/mirrors/)

Uptown—Lawsuits (uptown.se/lawsuits)

Utah Division of Corporations & Commercial Code of Digital Signatures (commerce.state.ut.us/corporat/dsmain.htm)

Woodside Site (http://members.tripod.com/~cyberstalked/)

Note: Given how fast site/page addresses can change these days, there are no assurances that all addresses will open to the identified information. The information at these locations, and others, were reviewed with newspaper, magazine, and other articles to form part of the factual basis in this book. The opinions, of course, in all of these articles—both online and offline—are those of the respective authors.

Index